Naturalism and Protectionism in the Study of Religions

Scientific Studies of Religion: Inquiry and Explanation

Series editors: Luther H. Martin, Donald Wiebe, William W. McCorkle Jr., D. Jason Slone and Radek Kundt

Scientific Studies of Religion: Inquiry and Explanation publishes cutting-edge research in the new and growing field of scientific studies in religion. Its aim is to publish empirical, experimental, historical, and ethnographic research on religious thought, behaviour, and institutional structures. The series works with a broad notion of scientific that includes innovative work on understanding religion(s), both past and present. With an emphasis on the cognitive science of religion, the series includes complementary approaches to the study of religion, such as psychology and computer modelling of religious data. Titles seek to provide explanatory accounts for the religious behaviours under review, both past and present.

The Attraction of Religion, edited by D. Jason Slone and James A. Van Slyke
The Cognitive Science of Religion, edited by D. Jason Slone and William W. McCorkle Jr.
Contemporary Evolutionary Theories of Culture and the Study of Religion, Radek Kundt
Death Anxiety and Religious Belief, Jonathan Jong and Jamin Halberstadt
The Impact of Ritual on Child Cognition, Veronika Rybanska
Language, Cognition, and Biblical Exegesis, edited by Ronit Nikolsky, Istvan Czachesz, Frederick S. Tappenden and Tamas Biro
The Learned Practice of Religion in the Modern University, Donald Wiebe
The Mind of Mithraists, Luther H. Martin
New Patterns for Comparative Religion, William E. Paden
Philosophical Foundations of the Cognitive Science of Religion, Robert N. McCauley with E. Thomas Lawson
Religion Explained?, edited by Luther H. Martin and Donald Wiebe
Religion in Science Fiction, Steven Hrotic
Religious Evolution and the Axial Age, Stephen K. Sanderson
The Roman Mithras Cult, Olympia Panagiotidou with Roger Beck
Solving the Evolutionary Puzzle of Human Cooperation, Glenn Barenthin

Naturalism and Protectionism in the Study of Religions

Juraj Franek

BLOOMSBURY ACADEMIC
LONDON • NEW YORK • OXFORD • NEW DELHI • SYDNEY

BLOOMSBURY ACADEMIC
Bloomsbury Publishing Plc
50 Bedford Square, London, WC1B 3DP, UK
1385 Broadway, New York, NY 10018, USA
29 Earlsfort Terrace, Dublin 2, Ireland

BLOOMSBURY, BLOOMSBURY ACADEMIC and the Diana logo
are trademarks of Bloomsbury Publishing Plc

First published in Great Britain 2020
Paperback edition first published 2021

Copyright © Juraj Franek, 2020

Juraj Franek has asserted his right under the Copyright,
Designs and Patents Act, 1988, to be identified as Author of this work.

For legal purposes the Acknowledgements on p. vi constitute an
extension of this copyright page.

Cover image © Shutterstock

All rights reserved. No part of this publication may be reproduced or
transmitted in any form or by any means, electronic or mechanical,
including photocopying, recording, or any information storage or retrieval
system, without prior permission in writing from the publishers.

Bloomsbury Publishing Plc does not have any control over, or responsibility for,
any third-party websites referred to or in this book. All internet addresses given
in this book were correct at the time of going to press. The author and publisher
regret any inconvenience caused if addresses have changed or sites have
ceased to exist, but can accept no responsibility for any such changes.

A catalogue record for this book is available from the British Library.

A catalog record for this book is available from the Library of Congress.

ISBN: HB: 978-1-3500-8237-3
PB: 978-1-3502-7785-4
ePDF: 978-1-3500-8238-0
eBook: 978-1-3500-8239-7

Series: Scientific Studies of Religion: Inquiry and Explanation

Typeset by RefineCatch Limited, Bungay, Suffolk

To find out more about our authors and books visit
www.bloomsbury.com and sign up for our newsletters.

Contents

Acknowledgements		vi
List of Abbreviations		vii
1	Introduction: Methodological schism in the study of religions	1
2	Naturalistic paradigm: Critical reflexion of religion in Presocratic philosophy	9
3	Protectionist paradigm: Early Christian literature between faith and reason	31
4	Naturalism and protectionism in the study of religions (1): The beginnings	51
5	Naturalism and protectionism in the study of religions (2): The rise and fall of phenomenology	75
6	Cognitive science of religion (1): Methodology	99
7	Cognitive science of religion (2): Terminology	117
8	Cognitive science of religion (3): Practical application	131
9	Conclusion: A return of the prodigal son?	145
Notes		153
Editions		223
References		229
Index		259

Acknowledgements

The present book is a slightly reworked and revised English translation of the Czech *editio princeps*, published by Masaryk University in 2017 in the series *Opera Facultatis philosophicae Universitatis Masarykianae*. I would like to thank Jana Horáková and Katarina Petrovićová for their kind assistance with copyright transfers to Bloomsbury. Several chapters of the book are based on materials previously published in English elsewhere. I am very grateful to Brill, Cambridge University Press, Czech Association for the Study of Religions and Masaryk University for a kind permission to reprint the following texts (all rewritten to greater or lesser extent):

Franek, J. (2018). Invocations of the Muse in Homer and Hesiod: A Cognitive Approach. *Antichthon* 52: 1–22.
Franek, J. (2016). Methodological Consilience of Evolutionary Ethics and Cognitive Science of Religion. *Journal of Cognition and Culture* 16 (1–2): 144–70.
Franek, J. (2016). Beyond Faith and Reason: Epistemic Justification in Earliest Christianity. *Graeco-Latina Brunensia* 21 (2): 125–56.
Franek, J. (2014). Has the Cognitive Science of Religion (Re)defined 'Religion'? *Religio* 22 (1): 3–27.
Franek, J. (2013). Presocratic Philosophy and the Origins of Religion. *Graeco-Latina Brunensia* 18 (1): 57–74.

The author would like to express his gratitude to numerous friends and colleagues for their helpful assistance, editorial care, useful suggestions, sharp criticisms, words of encouragement and countless other benefits bestowed upon his person. Thank you Mirela Ahmetovic, Leonardo Ambasciano, Vladimír Bahna, Han Baltussen, Radim Brázda, Lucy Carroll, Aleš Chalupa, Radek Chlup, Rosanna Di Pinto, Tomáš Glomb, Břetislav Horyna, Petr Kitzler, Markéta Kulhánková, Radek Kundt, Eva Kundtová Klocová, Tom Lawson, Luther Martin, Michaela Ondrašinová, Matúš Porubjak, Irena Radová, Nickolas Roubekas, Konrad Talmont-Kaminski, Stelios Virvidakis, Don Wiebe, Daniela Urbanová and David Zbíral. The rights to reproduce Raphael's *Transfiguration* have been generously granted by the Vatican Museums. The final stages of the preparation of the book have been kindly supported by the Grant Agency of Masaryk University (MUNI/E/0523/2019). The book would never have seen the light of day without the constant loving support of my family.

Abbreviations

A&A	*Antike und Abendland*
ABG	*Archiv für Begriffsgeschichte*
Abull	*Art Bulletin*
AC	*L'Antiquité classique*
Acme	*Acme, Annali della Facoltà di Lettere e Filosofia dell'Università degli Studi di Milano*
Aevum	*Aevum, rassegna di scienze storiche, linguistiche e filologiche*
AHIg	*Anuario de historia de la Iglesia*
AJPh	*American Journal of Philology*
AJS	*American Journal of Sociology*
Annales (ESC)	*Annales: Économies, Sociétés, Civilisations*
Annu Rev Ecol Evol Syst	*Annual Review of Ecology, Evolution, and Systematics*
APB	*Acta Patristica et Byzantina*
ARG	*Archiv für Religionsgeschichte*
AS	*Actes Semiotiques*
ASR	*American Sociological Review*
AT	Adam and Tannery, *Oeuvres de Descartes*
Atl Mon	*Atlantic Monthly*
BAC	*Biblioteca de Autores Cristianos*
BAGB	*Bulletin de l'Association Guillaume Budé*
BCPE	*Bollettino del Centro Internazionale per lo Studio dei Papyri Ercolanesi (Cron. Erc.)*
Behav Brain Sci	*Behavorial and Brain Sciences*
BICS	*Bulletin of the Institute of Classical Studies*
BM	*Burlington Magazine*
BP	*Biblioteca Patristica*
BR	*Biblical Research, Journal of the Chicago Society of Biblical Research*
Br J Sociol	*British Journal of Sociology*
Brit J Med Psychol	*British Journal of Medical Psychology*
ByzNH	*Byzantion: Nea hellás*
CCCM	*Corpus Christianorum, Continuatio Medievalis*
CCSL	*Corpus Christianorum, Series Latina*
ChHist	*Church History*
CJ	*Classical Journal*
CPh	*Classical Philology*
Cognitive Sci	*Cognitive Science*
Cogn Syst Res	*Cognitive Systems Research*

CQ	*Classical Quarterly*
CW	*Classical World*
DK	Diels and Kranz, *Die Fragmente der Vorsokratiker*
DRCH	*Nederlands Archief voor Kerkgeschiedenis / Dutch Review of Church History*
ECS	*Eighteenth-Century Studies*
EEcl	*Estudios Eclesiásticos*
Emerita	*Emerita, revista de lingüística y filología clásica*
EThL	*Ephemerides theologicae Lovanienses*
EQ	*Evangelical Quarterly*
FAT	*Forschungen zum Alten Testament*
FC	*Fontes Christiani*
FRLANT	*Forschungen zur Religion und Literatur des Alten und Neuen Testaments*
GLB	*Graeco-Latina Brunensia*
GRBS	*Greek, Roman and Byzantine Studies*
HA	Goethe, *Hamburger Ausgabe*
Harv Hum Rts J	*Harvard Human Rights Journal*
HR	*History of Religions*
HSCPh	*Harvard Studies in Classical Philology*
H&T	*History and Theory: Studies in Philosophy of History*
HThR	*Harvard Theological Review*
ICS	*Illinois Classical Studies*
IJPR	*International Journal for Philosophy of Religion*
J Am Acad Relig	*Journal of the American Academy of Religion*
JAF	*The Journal of American Folkore*
JBerlM	*Jahrbuch der Berliner Museen*
JECS	*Journal of Early Christian Studies (Second Century)*
Jew Q Rev	*The Jewish Quarterly Review, New Series*
JHI	*Journal of the History of Ideas*
JHS	*Journal of Hellenic Studies*
JOCC	*Journal of Cognition and Culture*
JR	*Journal of Religion*
JRAI	*Journal of the Royal Anthropological Institute of Great Britain and Ireland*
JSOT	*Journal for the Study of the Old Testament*
JSRNC	*Journal for the Study of Religion, Nature and Culture*
JSSR	*Journal for the Scientific Study of Religion*
JThS	*The Journal of Theological Studies*
JWI	*Journal of the Warburg and Courtauld Institutes*
KSA	Nietzsche, *Kritische Studienausgabe*
LCL	*Loeb Classical Library*
LwJb	*Literaturwissenschaftliches Jahrbuch*
MD	*Materiali e discussioni per l'analisi dei testi classici*
ME	Marx and Engels, *Werke*

MGH	*Monumenta Germaniae Historica*
MH	*Museum Helveticum*
MKNAW	*Mededeelingen der Koninklijke Nederlandsche Akademie van Wetenschappen*
MTSR	*Method & Theory in the Study of Religion*
Myrtia	*Myrtia, Revista de Filología Clásica de la Universidad de Murcia*
NatHist	*Natural History*
Nat Rev Neurosci	*Nature Reviews – Neuroscience*
NRTh	*Nouvelle revue théologique*
NT	Nestle and Aland, *Novum Testamentum Graecae*
NZSTh	*Neue Zeitschrift für systematische Theologie und Religionsphilosophie*
OECT	*Oxford Early Christian Texts*
PCPhS	*Proceedings of the Cambridge Philological Society*
PEGS	*Publications of the English Goethe Society*
Perspect Psychol Sci	*Perspectives on Psychological Science*
PhilosQ	*The Philosophical Quarterly*
PhR	*The Philosophical Review*
Phronesis	*Phronesis: A Journal for Ancient Philosophy*
Physik Z	*Physikalische Zeitschrift*
Proc R Soc B	*Proceedings of the Royal Society, Biological Sciences*
Psychol Bull	*Psychological Bulletin*
Psychol Rev	*Psychogical Review*
PTS	*Patristische Texte und Studien*
RAL	*Rendiconti della Classe di Scienze morali, storiche e filologiche dell'Accad. dei Lincei*
RBB	*Religion, Brain & Behavior*
RBen	*Revue Bénédictine*
REAug	*Revue des Études Augustiniennes*
REByz	*Revue des études byzantines*
RecSR	*Recherches de Science Religieuse*
REG	*Revue des études grecques*
RenQ	*Renaissance Quarterly*
Restor Q	*Restoration Quarterly*
RET	*Revista Española de Teología*
Rev Univ Brux	*Revue de l'Université de Bruxelles*
RFIC	*Rivista di filologia e di istruzione classica*
RHE	*Revue d'histoire écclesiastique*
RhM	*Rheinisches Museum für Philologie*
RHPhR	*Revue d'histoire et de philosophie religieuses*
RHR	*Revue de l'histoire des religions*
RM	*Die Religionen der Menschheit*
RPhA	*Revue de philosophie ancienne*
RPhilos	*Revue philosophique de la France et de l'étranger*

RPhL	*Revue philosophique de Louvain*
R+R	*Religion and Reason*
Relig Stud	*Religious Studies*
RSPh	*Revue des sciences philosophiques et théologiques*
RSR	*Revue des sciences religieuses*
SC	*Sources Chrétiennes*
SG	*Sammlung Göschen*
SIFC	*Studi italiani di filologia classica*
SMSR	*Studi e materiali di storia delle religioni*
SNTSMS	*Society for New Testament Studies Monograph Series*
SRC	*Science, Religion and Culture*
STh	*Studia Theologica: Scandinavian Journal of Theology*
StudPhil	*Studia philosophica: Annuaire de la Société suisse de philosophie*
Stud Renaissance	*Studies in the Renaissance*
SVF	Von Arnim, *Stoicorum veterum fragmenta*
TAPhA	*Transactions (and Proceedings) of the American Philological Association*
Th&Ph	*Theologie und Philosophie*
Trends Cogn Sci	*Trends in Cognitive Sciences*
TrGF	Nauck/Kannicht, *Tragicorum Graecorum Fragmenta*
T&V	*Teología y vida*
VChr	*Vigiliae Christianae*
WdF	*Wege der Forschung*
WS	*Wiener Studien*
ZA	Schopenhauer, *Zürcher Ausgabe*
ZPE	*Zeitschrift für Papyrologie und Epigraphik*
ZfK	*Zeitschrift für Kunstgeschichte*

Raphael, Transfiguration, 1518-1520
Pinacoteca Vaticana
Photo credits: (c) Vatican Museums, reprinted with permission

1

Introduction: Methodological schism in the study of religions

I am really no friend of images. The more recent literature has made them exceedingly repulsive for me, so much so, that the moment I chance upon an image, I am seized by an involuntary fear that the true purpose of the image is to hide the obscurity of thinking.

Sören Kierkegaard[1]

In the preface to the first edition of his *opus magnum* that bears the ominous title *The World as Will and Representation*, Arthur Schopenhauer has been kind enough to inform his reader that although he intended to communicate one single idea, he found no shorter way to do so than to write a hefty monograph which is to be read twice, since the perfect understanding of the earlier chapters presupposes the information contained in the later ones.[2] In the third book of this work, Schopenhauer argued that a work of art is capable of revealing the representation independent of the principle of sufficient reason – that is to say, as an adequate objectification of the thing-in-itself (i.e., will) on a certain degree.[3] It is to be said that the requirement to read the book twice may rather represent the objectification of Schopenhauer's arrogance, the magnitude of which has been inversly proportional to the interest learned and unlearned contemporaries showed for his thought – and therefore always extraordinarily high; the latter proposition may amount to an intellectual violation of Kant fuelled by Schopenhauer's desire to present himself not only as a deep philosophical mind, but also as a connoisseur of fine arts. Be that as it may, the primary objective of my work being the development and the defence of a single idea – namely that the study of religions was, is and most likely will remain splintered into two competing and mutually incommensurable paradigms – and since I surely want to abstain from asking kind readers to work double shifts, I will try to illustrate the central thesis of this work via a particular work of art.[4]

Raphael's last oeuvre, *Transfiguration*, was commissioned in 1516 by cardinal Giulio de' Medici (future pope Clement VII) as an altarpiece for his metropolitan cathedral in Narbonne.[5] The works began in 1518 and scholars are unanimous in considering the painting unfinished.[6] Some thought it was completed by one of Raphael's students (Giulio Romano being the most likely candidate),[7] but the results of a large-scale restoration from the years 1972–76 indicate that the work is, indeed, the great master's autograph.[8] Giorgio Vasari noted that 'according to the *communis opinio* of the artists, it is the most famous, the most beautiful and the most divine of all of his works';[9] but for modern scholars, it has become an enigma on both formal and iconographical fronts. This oil on wood of considerable proportions (405 × 278 cm), housed today in the Vatican picture gallery, represents two otherwise discrete scenes related by synoptic gospels.[10]

The upper half of the painting shows the transfiguration of Christ on the mount Tabor, which he mounted together with the Apostles Peter, James and John. In the centre of the ring composition, Jesus is levitating above the ground, vested in white robes, eyes looking upwards, hands outstretched as a symbol of his redeeming power. On his sides, Moses and Elias, in conversation; at his feet, the Apostles in awe, protecting by hands their eyes from the supernatural radiance with which their master bathes the entire upper half of the painting. On the left side, two assistant figures are portrayed, whose presence is not warranted by canonical texts. Art scholars often identified them with martyrs and saints. Felicissimus and Agapitus have been proposed,[11] as well as Stephen and Lawrence,[12] but they are most likely Justus and Pastor, since their feast is celebrated on 6 August, which, ever since 1457, happens to also be the Feast of the Transfiguration, and both are titular saints of the cathedral of Narbonne, the original final destination of the altarpiece.[13]

The lower half of Raphael's masterpiece transports us under the mount Tabor. In Christ's absence, the remaining Apostles are trying their best to heal a boy possessed by an evil spirit, their efforts continually frustrated. From a compositional standpoint, the scene is cut in half by a *figura serpentinata* of a beautiful young woman, identified variously as Mary Magdalene,[14] Erythraean Sibyl,[15] even 'the divine manifestation of the radiant Christ'.[16] Nine Apostles on the left side are flanked by nine family members of the possessed boy (including himself), whose wobbly posture, distant look and the tension of every muscle and tendon set in physical and emotional movement all the figures.

It has been repeatedly pointed out that the painting as a whole is built on a series of antitheses:[17] the upper half is overflowing with light, the lower half features almost Baroque *chiaroscuro*; calm and majestic figure of Jesus, accompanied by Moses and Elias, contrasts with the earthly chaos of agitated gestures that is taking place under the mount; the triumphant transformation of Christ as the ultimate confirmation of faith stands in counterpoint to the failure of his disciples, whose faith has not been strong enough. The depiction of two independent episodes runs counter to the classical unities of action, time and place, formulated for ancient Greek drama by Aristotle,[18] and through analogy between painting and theatre very much in vigour in the Renaissance.[19] In spite of Vasari's high praises, this disunity led to less than enthusiastic appreciations of the *Transfiguration* in later times and ages.

Jonathan Richardson, in the second half of the eighteenth century, reproached Raphael for the violation of classical unities in a grotesquely deferential form;[20] several years later, Goethe informed us from Rome that the *Transfiguration* is far from being considered the master's most beloved work by the fellow citizens of the Eternal City;[21] both verdicts appropriated by otherwise very responsive French art circles at the beginning of the nineteenth century, when the painting was 'liberated' from Rome and moved to Paris.[22] Even the Nestor of modern Renaissance studies, Jakob Burckhardt, considered the *Transfiguration* 'a daring work'[23] and his good friend, Friedrich Nietzsche, did not shy from using it as an illustration for the main differences between the Apollonian and Dionysian principles in his first book, *The Birth of Tragedy*.[24]

It comes as no surprise, then, that the striking dichotomy, cleaving the painting into two apparently disconnected episodes, brought forth a multitude of different interpretations. Some preparatory drawings and a *modello* by one of Raphael's students (likely Giulio Romano) seem to indicate that the Renaissance master intended to depict only the episode of the transfiguration, fully in line with traditional iconographic conventions we find in the paintings of the same subject by Botticelli or Bellini. It is possible that the inclusion of the scene portraying the unsuccessful attempt of the Apostles to heal a possessed boy has been incorporated due to the rivalry between Raphael and Michelangelo's *protégé* Sebastiano del Piombo, who also happened to win a contract for an altarpiece – a contract sponsored by the very same Giulio de' Medici and for the very same altarpiece of the Narbonne cathedral. Sebastiano produced the dramatic *Resurrection of Lazarus*, which may have prompted Raphael to rework his project *ex post* and to introduce no less dramatic motif of the cleansing of the possessed boy.[25] Other interpretations identified in the painting are a symbolic reference to the 1456 Siege of Belgrade and the resulting victory of Christian armies over Ottoman forces, a victory closely connected with the Crusades against Muslims fomented by the popes Callixtus III and Leo X.[26] For others still, Raphael's *Transfiguration* is a visual representation of the *primatus Petri* ('you are Peter, and on this rock I will build my Church, and the gates of Hades will not prevail against it').[27] Peter is, after all, one of the Apostles accompanying Jesus on the mount Tabor and it has been suggested that it was his absence that frustrated the efforts of other Apostles to work miracles and heal the possessed boy – a visual representation of Peter's singular authority has been viewed as a counter-reaction to the emerging Protestant movements.[28]

Some scholars contextualized the painting on the background of the liturgy of Ember days: In Mark, Jesus says to his disciples that the evil spirit possessing the boy 'can come out only through prayer [and fasting]';[29] moreover, the professional curriculum of the contractor might have played a role as well – Giulio de' Medici had been elected cardinal on Ash Wednesday and his titular Roman church of Santa Maria in Domnica had been the station church for the second Sunday of Lent.[30] Raphael's *Transfiguration* has also been connected to Sebastiano del Piombo's frescoes in the Borgerini chapel of San Pietro in Montorio, the church that was the first to house Raphael's last painting, which Giulio eventually donated to the Vatican several years later.[31] However, the frescoes depicting the transfiguration of Christ in the upper lunette above the scene of the flagellation of Christ in the central space may rather be read in the context of Joachim de Fiore's apocalyptic visions, expanded by João de Menezes da Silva (Amadeus of Portugal) in his *Apocalypsis nova* (whose copy, as it happens, has been found in San Pietro in Montorio), i.e. as a call for the *renovatio Ecclesiae* in the expectation of the Second Coming of Christ, who will institute to Church an angelic Pope that will cleanse it of all the sins of depravity and corruption. The cardinal Bernardino Lopéz de Carvajal, who supported these views during the 1511 Pisa council, has been promptly excommunicated, together with likeminded apostates.

Notwithstanding the number of learned and ingenuous interpretations presented above, I do believe that we may choose to read Raphael's *Transfiguration* in a different way, especially if we follow closely the textual basis provided by the synoptic gospels. Firstly, it must be said that the text of the gospels nullifies the possibility of mutual interaction between the upper and the lower half, since Jesus explicitly prohibits the three Apostles that accompanied him on the mount Tabor to speak about the events that transpired there, at the very least until the time of his resurrection.[32] Even more important for the overall interpretation of the painting is Jesus' indignation at the inability of the Apostles to drive out the evil spirit from the possessed boy: 'You faithless and perverse generation, how much longer must I be with you? How much longer must I put up with you?'[33] When Jesus finally casts out the evil spirit and the Apostles ask him about their failure to do so themselves, their master identifies the reason for their impotence in no unequivocal manner. It was their 'little faith' (διὰ τὴν ὀλιγοπιστίαν ὑμῶν); however, should the Apostles 'have faith the size of a mustard seed, you will say to this mountain, "Move from here to there," and it will move; and nothing will be impossible for you.'[34] In Mark, Jesus says to the father of the possessed boy that '[a]ll things can be done for the one who believes' (πάντα δυνατὰ τῷ πιστεύοντι); the father only has to proclaim his faith (πιστεύω· βοήθει μου τῇ ἀπιστίᾳ) and the boy is miraculously healed.[35]

The semantic field of the canonical texts relating the episode of Jesus' transfiguration and the failure of his Disciples to cleanse the evil spirit teems with 'faith'-compounds (ἄπιστος, ὀλιγοπιστία, πιστεύω, ἀπιστία) and allows us to read Raphael's *Transfiguration* as a symbolic epitome of Christian faith.[36] Faith as a cardinal theological virtue, emanating from Jesus and spreading through the upper half of the pictorial plane, stands in sharp contrast to the human, all-too-human wisdom and its ultimate failure depicted in the lower half, especially through the Apostle holding a large book in the lower left corner, identified at times with Matthew.[37] According to Christian Kleinbub, '[h]e has consulted texts but has found nothing there to address the current situation', since '[his] error has been to seek in a work of merely human wisdom the answer to a larger, spiritual problem';[38] for Jodi Cranston, 'the foreshortened books suggest the deceptions of logic and reason found in books and in the foundations and practice of perspective, and their irrelevance to matters of faith'.[39]

Raphael's genius is far removed from providing liturgical marginalia or symbolic depictions of recent historical occurrences. Rather, his last painting illustrated one of the central dogmas of Christianity, that of faith as a virtue, a virtue to which the Classical Antiquity has been blissfully oblivious. It is revealing that when Xenophon in *Memorabilia* defended his philosophical hero against the charges of impiety, he argued, firstly and most importantly (πρῶτον μὲν οὖν), that Socrates always fulfilled all civic obligations dictated by the public cults;[40] and even the νομίζειν of the charges pressed against him has very little to do with Christian 'belief' or 'faith'.[41] The piety of ancient Greeks resides in greater measures in its outward displays and Christian martyrs of the first few centuries were not condemned because of their lack of inner belief in Jupiter or other Olympians, but because of their refusal to take part in the public religious activities, such as an oath to the Caesar or an expiatory sacrifice to his genius.[42]

With the triumph of Christianity, 'faith' became not only the central soteriological concept, but also the basis of those theories of knowledge with which Christianity for centuries moulded the self-understanding of the Latin West, as well as the first blueprints for the modern study of religions in the nineteenth and twentieth century. In its purest, most distilled form, it assumed – quite like Raphael's *Transfiguration* – a clear separation of the religious experience from all other modalities of human perception, emotion and knowledge. When the proper object of the study of religions was the living God, faith, religious experience or the sacred, these items were established as being *sui generis* and constructed as autonomous, ahistorical, irreducible facts unamendable to standard scientific methods used in other disciplines, especially those of a 'naturalist' pedigree. Religious experience, ultimately unassailable by our feeble human minds, was to be hermeneutically courted and gradually unveiled, not explained and explained away. Every and any attempt for explanation necessarily resulted in failure, a failure not unlike the failure of the Apostles trying to cast out the evil spirit from the possessed boy. In opposition to this protectionist methodology stood those approaches who may well fully accept the primacy of faith in the lives of individual believers, in theology, confessional apologetics, or even in art, but refused to consider it a guiding light in the academic study of religions that wishes to be consilient with other domains of human knowledge. Methodological naturalism holds close to Terence's *immo aliis si licet, tibi non licet* ('it may well be allowed to others, but not to you')[43] – if religious studies wants to be taken seriously as scientific enterprise, it must play according to certain rules that happen to rule out *a priori* methodological protectionism.

In the first part of this book, I will first try to excavate the historical origins of the leading two methodological approaches in the study of religions, and subsequently outline their development in the nineteenth and twentieth centuries. Chapter 2 profiles the proto-naturalistic approach to religion in Presocratic philosophy. Despite their importance as first theorists of religion *simpliciter*, Presocratics are, on one hand, often completely overlooked in the context of explanatory theories of the origins of religion put forward by scholars in religious studies;[44] on the other, their interpretations by classicists often direly lack a background in the history of the modern studies of religion.[45] By the end of this chapter, I also introduce somewhat simplified concept of 'epistemic justification', which I then apply to the Presocratic discourse on the origins of religion.

Chapter 3 pivots on the main competitor of naturalism, namely protectionism, a view that considers religion (and, in this particular case, Christianity) to be an autonomous domain that is not liable to naturalistic explanation. I intentionally omit some very interesting modern theological and philosophical interpretations;[46] my focus lies with the varieties of protectionism formulated in the earliest Christian literature, since these are, as is the case with Presocratics, very rarely discussed in contemporary theorizing about religion. I also replace the traditional dichotomy of 'faith' and 'reason' with the concept of epistemic justification, introduced in the preceding chapter.

Chapters 4 and 5 map the naturalist and protectionist methodologies in the modern, nineteenth- and twentieth-century study of religions. While the first four chapters, comprising the first part of the monograph, focus on the historical development of mutually competing theories, the second part switches gears and assumes a more systematic perspective. It details the cognitive approach to religion and its application on selected problems of the study of religions, since its introduction in the nineties marks a return of naturalist approach, following decades of domination of various phenomenological strategies. To support this thesis, I chose three topics connected with the cognitive science of religion, the first one assuming interdisciplinary perspective, the second one operating on a theoretical level and the third one of putting these theoretical concepts to work in an attempt at a practical application.

In Chapter 6, I show how two distinct scientific disciplines, namely cognitive science of religion and evolutionary ethics, are methodologically consilient. Chapter 7 deals with the problem of defining religion and the role cognitive science of religion played in the naturalization of the term. Chapter 8 is dedicated to the practical application of theoretical concepts and offers a cognitive interpretation of a much-discussed problem of classical scholarship, namely the character and function of invocations of the Muse in earliest Greek epic poetry. Given the rather 'theoretical' nature of the previous two chapters, I found it convenient to show that it is possible to apply concepts established in the cognitive science of religion in various (and at times methodologically quite conservative) domains, such as Classics.[47] Finally, Chapter 9 summarizes the results and briefly discusses the role of the cognitive approach in the context of the naturalistic paradigm.

As this very brief overview makes clear, the scope of the book is considerable, both chronologically (spanning from the beginnings of Western literature and philosophy to the present times) and systematically (in attempting to put together the results of various disciplines, such as classical philology, philosophy, religious studies or cognitive science). I am aware of the risks this approach brings about and I can only hope that all the necessary simplifications and errors will be outweighed by the benefits of a wider, interdisciplinary perspective. In writing, I kept Heraclitus's πολυμαθίη νόον ἔχειν οὐ διδάσκει ('erudition does not teach common sense') in mind.[48] Despite this undoubtedly wise counsel, I still wished to escape the fate of a diligent expert on the brains of the leeches, once trodden down in a swamp by Nietzsche's Zarathustra – a fitting metaphor for the over-specialization that casts a large shadow over the landscape of much of modern academia:

> Rather know nothing, than know much half way! Rather be a fool in one's own right than a wise man according to strangers. I – go to the ground of things: – what does it matter whether it is big or small? Whether it is called swamp or sky? A hand's breadth of ground is enough for me, if only it is real ground and bottom! – a hand's breadth of ground: on that one can stand. In proper science and conscience there is nothing great and nothing small.
>
> 'So perhaps you are the expert on the leech?' asked Zarathustra. 'And you pursue the leech down to its ultimate grounds, you conscientious one?'
>
> 'Oh Zarathustra,' answered the stepped on man. 'That would be a monstrous undertaking, how could I presume to such a thing! What I am master and expert of, however, is the leech's brain – that is my world! And it is a world too! But forgive

me that my pride speaks up here, for in this matter I have no equal. That is why I said "here I am at home." How long already have I pursued this one thing, the brain of the leech, so that the slippery truth no longer slips away from me here? Here is my realm! – this is why I threw away everything else, this is why all else is the same to me; and right next to my knowledge my black ignorance lurks. My conscience of spirit wants of me that I know one thing and do not know everything else; I am nauseated by all halfness of spirit, all hazy, soaring, rapturous people.'[49]

2

Naturalistic paradigm: Critical reflexion of religion in Presocratic philosophy

> *A Greek it was who first opposing dared*
> *Raise mortal eyes that terror to withstand,*
> *Whom nor the fame of Gods nor lightning's stroke*
> *Nor threatening thunder of the ominous sky*
> *Abashed; but rather chafed to angry zest*
> *His dauntless heart to be the first to rend*
> *The crossbars at the gates of Nature old.*
>
> Lucretius[1]

In the following two chapters, I will identify and discuss historical roots of the two central paradigms of the modern study of religions, which may be provisionally termed 'naturalism' and 'protectionism'. The naturalist approach presupposes that it is possible to *explain* religious phenomena by reducing them to some more fundamental, non-religious realities, while the protectionist approach considers religious phenomena to be in principle irreducible and the scholars of religion can do no more and no less than to try to *understand* them. It will be shown that these two approaches to the religious experience originated in the world of the Antiquity and their influence in the context of Western 'histories of mentalities' delineates the main discursive fields of the study of religions up to the present day.[2] Another reason to focus more closely on the Presocratic thinkers in this chapter is their surprising absence in most of the modern handbooks dealing with the history of the discipline, which not only omit Presocratics, but often the entire period of the Antiquity.[3] By way of example, Preus' *Explaining Religion* starts with Jean Bodin (born 1530),[4] Waardenburg's already classical compendium *Classical Approaches to the Study of Religion* with Johann Bachhofen (born 1815)[5] and Strenski's *Thinking About Religion*, despite the inclusion of an entire chapter entitled *The Prehistory of the Study of Religion*, with the Renaissance thinkers.[6] Yet Presocratic philosophers surely tried to explain religion, their approaches are (quite literally) 'classical' and their theories, crude and simplistic as they might seem to us, stand at the very beginning of Western thought and as such qualify at the very least as 'prehistoric'.

Naturalistic approach to religion in the Greek Archaic and early Classical age was, of course, far from being common. Rather, it was a deviation of a few inquisitive minds, since the affiliation to a particular religion or a religious tradition was not a matter of free choice, as it is in the more developed parts of the world today, but rather a factual sociocultural situation that most people do not critically reflect upon, but, rather, are born into and unreflectively accept it because of the lack of any critical forms of knowledge that could shake the *Weltanschauung* shared by their family and peers.[7] The much discussed Greek transition 'from myth to *logos*'[8] has been a dynamic process lasting several centuries and the epic poetry, whose importance for Greek culture and its educational system cannot be overemphasized,[9] stood (at least declaratively) on a purely receptive premises: the songs of the poets are not described in terms of individual, subjective communication of the rhapsodes towards the audience, but these rather present themselves as mouthpieces of the divinity that talks through them.

In the opening lines of the *Iliad*, 'Homer' asks the goddess to sing about the wrath of Achilles;[10] at the beginning of the *Odyssey*, Muse is invoked to chant praises of the eponymous hero;[11] in the second book of the *Iliad*, prefacing the *Catalogue of Ships*, the poet again turns to the Muses for help, since only they are present everywhere and know everything (θεαί ἐστε πάρεστέ τε ἴστέ τε πάντα), while we mortals are, in comparison, epistemically deficient (κλέος οἶον ἀκούομεν οὐδέ τι ἴδμεν).[12] We find echoes of these invocations in Hesiod, who in the *prooimion* of his *Theogony* claims that Muses were the ones to teach him the beautiful song while he was herding sheep on Helicon.[13] A shift from absolute knowledge to a subjective one, from the antithesis of memory and oblivion to the antithesis of truth and falsehood,[14] from the 'half-sleep of the mind' to its awakening,[15] is all but required to establish a naturalistic approach to religion. These transformations did not magically emerge *ex nihilo* during the Axial Age, but its seeds may be identified in earlier stages. Already in the Homeric epics, Zeus complained that mortals unjustly blame gods for evils they themselves cause,[16] which is to say that mortals' representations of gods may be mistaken or otherwise deficient. Hesiod's Muses are seemingly capable of lying and proclaiming falsehoods wrapped in a veil of truth (ἴδμεν ψεύδεα πολλὰ λέγειν ἐτύμοισιν ὁμοῖα).[17] Pherecydes of Syros pointed out that gods are not born, but their existence is eternal (Ζὰς μὲν καὶ Χρόνος ἦς<αν> ἀεὶ καὶ Χθονίη)[18] and Pindaros pioneeringly used the metonymy Μοῖσα φιλοκερδής ('gain-desiring Muse') to denote poets and their works rather than a divine authority that was believed to be the true spring and origin of their efforts.[19] However, for a full-fledged naturalism in the reflection of the traditional Greek religious notions and ideas we have to turn to the Presocratic philosophy.[20]

2.1 Xenophanes

At the very beginning of the naturalistic approach to religion in Greek philosophy, there is a handful of painfully truncated fragments preserved almost exclusively by Sextus Empiricus and Clement of Alexandria – all that is left from the work of Xenophanes of Colophon. Xenophanes was likely one of the very first thinkers of the West who not only critically reflected on the nature of religion and gods, but also attempted to explain the origins of our religious representations and ideas. He formulated his opinions in an explicit confrontation with the traditional Greek notions of gods and the uncompromising critique of the Olympians found in the fragments was grounded in a dramatic *dénouement* of the internal inconsistencies between the common perception of divinities as keepers of some basic forms of morality and their not-exactly-moral actions. Some scholars claimed that Xenophanes' interpretation cannot be taken too seriously,[21] yet such claims should be rejected as unfounded.[22] Xenophanes explained away traditional ancient Greek divinities as mere by-products of religious anthropomorphism, which may be here provisionally defined as a largely unconscious psychological tendency to attribute to gods physical and mental properties of mortals. This critical analysis of ancient Greek god-concepts in turn paved the way for Xenophanes' strongly 'reformed' theology, which we will touch upon only in passing.

2.1.1 Fragments

Sextus Empiricus, *Adversus mathematicos* 9.193 = DK 21 B 11
πάντα θεοῖσ' ἀνέθηκαν Ὅμηρός θ' Ἡσίοδός τε, | ὅσσα παρ' ἀνθρώποισιν ὀνείδεα καὶ ψόγος ἐστίν, | κλέπτειν μοιχεύειν τε καὶ ἀλλήλους ἀπατεύειν.
Homer and Hesiod have attributed to the gods all sorts of things which are matters of reproach and censure among men: theft, adultery, and mutual deceit.[23]

Sextus Empiricus, *Adversus mathematicos* 1.289 = DK 21 B 12
Ὅμηρος δὲ καὶ Ἡσίοδος κατὰ τὸν Κολοφώνιον Ξενοφάνη ὡς πλεῖστ(α) ἐφθέγξαντο θεῶν ἀθεμίστια ἔργα, κλέπτειν μοιχεύειν τε καὶ ἀλλήλους ἀπατεύειν.
According to Xenophanes of Colophon, Homer and Hesiod sang of numerous illicit divine deeds: theft, adultery, and mutual deceit.

Clemens Alexandrinus, *Stromata* 5.109 = DK 21 B 14
ἀλλ' οἱ βροτοὶ δοκέουσι γεννᾶσθαι θεούς, | τὴν σφετέρην δ' ἐσθῆτα ἔχειν φωνήν τε δέμας τε.
But mortals suppose that gods are born, wear their own clothes and have a voice and body.

Clemens Alexandrinus, *Stromata* 5.110 = DK 21 B 15
ἀλλ' εἰ χεῖρας ἔχον βόες <ἵπποι τ'> ἠὲ λέοντες | ἢ γράψαι χείρεσσι καὶ ἔργα τελεῖν ἅπερ ἄνδρες, | ἵπποι μέν θ' ἵπποισι βόες δέ τε βουσὶν ὁμοίας | καί <κε> θεῶν ἰδέας ἔγραφον καὶ σώματ' ἐποίουν | τοιαῦθ' οἷόν περ καὐτοὶ δέμας εἶχον <ἕκαστοι>.
But if horses or oxen or lions had hands or could draw with their hands and accomplish such works as men, horses would draw the figures of the gods as similar to horses, and the oxen as similar to oxen, and they would make the bodies of the sort which each of them had.

Clemens Alexandrinus, *Stromata* 8.22 = DK 21 B 16
Αἰθίοπές τε <θεοὺς σφετέρους> σιμοὺς μέλανάς τε | Θρῇκές τε γλαυκοὺς καὶ πυρρούς <φασι πέλεσθαι>.
Ethiopians say that their gods are snub-nosed and black; Thracians that theirs are blue-eyed and red-haired.

Clemens Alexandrinus, *Stromata* 5.109 = DK 21 B 23
εἷς θεός, ἔν τε θεοῖσι καὶ ἀνθρώποισι μέγιστος, | οὔτι δέμας θνητοῖσιν ὁμοίιος οὐδὲ νόημα.
One god is greatest among gods and men, not at all like mortals in body or in thought.

Sextus Empiricus, *Adversus Mathematicos* 9.144 = DK 21 B 24
οὖλος ὁρᾶι, οὖλος δὲ νοεῖ, οὖλος δέ τ' ... whole he sees, whole he thinks, and
ἀκούει. whole he hears.

Simplicius, *Physica* 23.19 = DK 21 B 25
ἀλλ' ἀπάνευθε πόνοιο νόου φρενὶ πάντα ... but completely without toil he shakes
κραδαίνει. all things by the thought of his mind.

Simplicius, *Physica* 23.10 = DK 21 B 26
αἰεὶ δ' ἐν ταὐτῶι μίμνει κινούμενος ... always he abides in the same place, not
οὐδέν | οὐδὲ μετέρχεσθαί μιν ἐπιπρέπει moving at all, nor is it seemly for him to
ἄλλοτε ἄλληι. travel to different places at different times.

Philo Alexandrinus, *De aeternitate mundi* 39 (so-called 'Lebedev-fragment')
οὐδὲ γυνὴ τοσσόνδε νόου ἐπιδεύεται Not even a woman is so weak of mind as
ἐσθλοῦ, | ὥστε χερείον' ἑλέσθαι to choose the worse whenever there is
ἀμεινοτέρων <παρεόντων>. [something] better available.

2.1.2 Commentary

Notwithstanding occasional attempts to deny the authenticity of Xenophanes' fragments preserved by Clement of Alexandria,[24] we may organize these into three groups. The first group (comprising fragments B 11 and B 12) outlines explicit critique of Homer and Hesiod that is based on the inconsistency between the actions of the members of Homeric pantheon and the rather high expectations Xenophanes harbours with respect to their moral profiles. While it is true that Greek gods were hardly portrayed as paragons of morality, it would be hard to deny that they did play a regulatory role as moral guarantors of selected social interactions.[25] The asymmetry between these functions and their behaviour then informs Xenophanes' critique.[26] Gods often commit shameful deeds (ὀνείδεα καὶ ψόγος)[27] and *in lieu* of keeping with the divine obligations (θέμις) they act contrary to them and delight in unlawful actions (ἀθεμίστια ἔργα).[28] Xenophanes did not limit himself to a simple confrontation of presumed normativity and its failure to materialize in gods' own lives, but he set out to explain this incongruity via empirical observation of other, non-Greek cultures, which is connected with a peculiar thought-experiment.

To see how Xenophanes tried to explain, in a naturalistic fashion, Greek religious ideas of the Archaic age, we have to turn to what has been termed his 'criminal anthropology',[29] contained in the second group of Xenophanes' fragments (B 14; B 15; B 16) and describing the origin of the god-representations in humankind. The first fragment (B 14) contains only a simple factual description that highlights the high degree of symmetry between human and divine attributes and characteristics. People believe that gods are born, wear the same clothes, speak the same voice and have the same form as they themselves do (ἀλλ' οἱ βροτοὶ δοκέουσι γεννᾶσθαι θεούς, | τὴν σφετέρην δ' ἐσθῆτα ἔχειν φωνήν τε δέμας τε).[30] An interesting observation, but clearly nothing that would in itself provide any meaningful explanation of the origin of religious ideas and god-concepts. In the second fragment (B 15), Xenophanes already moves from a simple description to a type of argumentation that will, in the centuries and millennia to come, become a staple of the philosophical discourse, namely a thought-experiment. Xenophanes invites us to imagine cows, horses and lions as endowed with the ability to express their own religious ideas. He does not credit them with the capacity of emitting voice (to his own credit, one might add, since his later colleague will be adamant in arguing that 'if a lion could talk, we could not understand him'),[31] but he does grant his imaginary animal companions the ability to paint. Should cows, horses and lions have this ability, so Xenophanes, they would paint their animal gods in the shapes of cows, horses and lions, respectively (καί <κε> θεῶν ἰδέας ἔγραφον καὶ σώματ' ἐποίουν | τοιαῦθ' οἷόν περ καὐτοὶ δέμας εἶχον <ἕκαστοι>).[32]

The third and final fragment of the second group (B 16) points to another facet of anthropomorphism of religious representations. Xenophanes notes that the inhabitants of Northern Africa ('Ethiopians') portray their gods as snub-nosed and black, while Thracians picture them as blue-eyed and red-haired. By drawing our attention to this empirical observation, our philosopher seems to argue that, speaking anachronistically, religious representations are to a large extent influenced not only by the biology of the species – that is to say, humans construct humanlike gods and lions lionlike gods – but also by the cultural specifics of the nations, since we may well presuppose that the gods of 'Ethiopians', Greeks and Thracians are not differentiated only by the colour of their eyes, but also by a score of other specific attributes. Anthropomorphism, i.e. largely unconscious inclination of human beings to attribute humanlike characteristics to non-human entities, is then, according to Xenophanes, instrumental in the explanation of the traditional religious ideas of his Greek compatriots.[33]

The last group of fragments (B 23; B 24; B 25; B 26; so-called 'Lebedev fragment'), is comprised of bits and pieces of information pertaining to Xenophanes' 'reformed' theology. With the possible exception of the Lebedev fragment, these are not directly relevant to the themes and topics pursued in this chapter. Let it be only briefly said that a *communis opinio* in the vividly debated issues pertaining to Xenophanes' positive theology is virtually non-existent and the range of possible interpretations may be conveyed by comparing the esteemed opinions of two preeminent scholars of ancient Greek philosophy: according to John Burnet, Xenophanes 'would have smiled if he had known that one day he was to be regarded as a theologian';[34] according to Werner Jaeger, he can only be understood as being one.[35] Xenophanes has been also considered by many to be one of the first monotheists or henotheists in the Western tradition,[36] but some scholars emphatically deny this characterization,[37] especially because of our philosopher's common use of the plural οἱ θεοί, not only in his sympotic elegiac poems (e.g., θεῶν <δὲ> προμηθείην αἰὲν ἔχειν ἀγαθόν),[38] but also in philosophically relevant fragments (e.g., εἷς θεός, ἕν τε θεοῖσι καὶ ἀνθρώποισι μέγιστος).[39] Many solutions have been offered to alleviate this apparent incongruity, with some classical philologists understanding the plural as meaning 'gods of the traditional religion',[40] others interpreting it as denoting multiple parts of the same one god.[41] I am inclined to agree with those who consider abovementioned instances to be a poetic *façon de parler*.[42] It is important to keep in mind that Xenophanes is a philosopher-poet who expressed his thought in verse[43] and polar expressions or merisms are a standard feature of poetic language.⁴⁴ With respect to another traditional characteristic of Xenophanes' philosophy, namely his presumed pantheism, similar interpretational chaos reigns.⁴⁵

An important piece of evidence attesting Xenophanes' methodical attempt to recreate and reconstruct the god-concept in such a way as to make it internally coherent is the fragment preserved in Philo Alexandrinus' work *On the Eternity of the World* (*De aeternitate mundi*), identified and attributed to Xenophanes only in 2000 by a Russian scholar Andrei Lebedev.⁴⁶ The fragment comprises two verses in dactylic hexameter and likely contains a part of a more general argument that runs as follows: If a god changes the world in any way, he makes it better, the same, or worse. If he is making the world worse, he is more foolish than a woman, since even she is not so foolish as to choose the worse if something better is available. If god is making the world the same, he behaves no better than children do, building castles of sand only to destroy them and then build them anew. If the change effectuated by god is making the world better, god does not deserve to be called μέγιστος ('greatest'), since he could have created a better world than he actually did. Therefore, god does not change the world (or himself, should we, under the pantheistic interpretation, equate him with the world). Assuming the correctness of the attribution of this fragment to Xenophanes, it shows that Xenophanes did not formulate his theses dogmatically, but on the basis of rational criteria and logical reasoning, which is something many of his modern interpreters stubbornly deny.⁴⁷

To summarize, Xenophanes is one of the first thinkers to explain naturalistically the origin of religious ideas and representations. A token of this *modus operandi* may also be found in his explanation of meteorological phenomena, which were traditionally connected with gods or understood to be manifestations of their will and power. For instance, on the identification of rainbow and the goddess Iris, he says: 'And she whom they call Iris, this too is by nature a cloud, | purple, red and greenish-yellow to behold.'⁴⁸ Simply put, god-concepts originated from the psychological inclination of living beings (humans and – in his thought experiment, also other animals) that we would call today 'anthropomorphism' (or 'zoomorphism' in the latter case). His arguments are constructed on a thoroughly rational basis and it is symptomatic that his positive theology failed to win any public support among his contemporaries. John Burnet noted that they would, in fact, most likely consider Xenophanes an atheist *tout court*.⁴⁹ This is hardly surprising, since our poet-philosopher, as far as we know, did not connect his original religious innovations with a public cult and worship (which is true of Presocratic philosophers in general)⁵⁰ and his god seems to lack any meaningful relation to humans.⁵¹ These two features may explain why Xenophanes' critical philosophy of religion did not find a larger audience, notwithstanding the important exception of a few elite Athenian intellectuals a century later.⁵²

2.2 Democritus

Democritus' atomistic theory and his attempt at a naturalistic explanation of religion has been hailed as 'the first truly godless world view in the Greek philosophical tradition'.⁵³ This conclusion, however, is not free from a degree of simplification of Democritus' thought, since some fragments of his works do contain traces of positive theology, albeit their importance is sometimes overestimated.⁵⁴ Preserved fragments of and commentaries on Democritus' philosophy do not offer one, but two hypotheses on the origin of god-concepts. The first one takes on the form of an anthropological speculation of sorts and argues that the ideas and representations of gods emerged because of humankind's inability to explain meteorological phenomena mechanically or naturalistically. Religion is born from the deeply rooted desire to 'make sense' out of phenomena in those obscure domains of potential human knowledge which are impenetrable by the light of rational explanation. The second hypothesis is firmly grounded in Democritus' atomistic ontology and presupposes that thin atomic emanations, called εἴδωλα, hit human organs of sense and create the images of gods. *Prima facie*, the mutual coherence of the two hypotheses seems to be somewhat problematic and scholars usually omit the former in favour of the latter.⁵⁵ In what follows, I will discuss both and try to integrate them into one coherent whole.

2.2.1 Fragments

Cicero, *De natura deorum* 1.12.29 + 1.43.120 = DK 68 A 74

[Democritus] *qui tum imagines eorumque circumitus in deorum numero refert, tum illam naturam quae imagines fundat ac mittat, tum sententiam intellegentiamque nostram, nonne in maximo errore versatur? cum idem omnino, quid nihil semper suo statu maneat, negat esse quicquam sempiternum, nonne deum omnino ita tollit, ut nullam opinionem eius reliquam faciat?* [...] *mihi quidem etiam Democritus, vir magnus in primis cuius fontibus Epicurus hortulos suos inrigavit, nutare videtur in natura deorum. tum enim censet imagines divinitate praeditas inesse in universitate rerum, tum principia mentis, quae sunt in eodem universo, deos esse dicit, tum animantes imagines, quae vel prodesse nobis solent vel nocere, tum ingentis quasdam imagines tantasque, ut universum mundum conplectantur extrinsecus: quae quidem omnia sunt patria Democriti quam Democrito digniora.*	What about Democritus? Does he not go completely astray in counting among the gods images and their wanderings, as well as that nature which grounds and emits the images and our thought and intelligence? Since he denies that anything at all is eternal, on the ground that nothing remains in the same state for ever, surely he eliminates the divine so completely as to leave no room for any belief in it. [...] In my opinion even Democritus, a man of the first rank from whose springs Epicurus watered his garden, vacillates about the nature of the gods. For he says that the universe contains images endowed with divinity, and also that the gods are the basic principles of mind in that universe, that they are living images which are beneficial or harmful to us, and again that they are images of such an enormous size as to enfold the entire world. All of this is worthier of Democritus' native city than of Democritus.⁵⁶

Sextus Empiricus, *Adversus Mathematicos* 9.19 = DK 68 B 166

Δ. δὲ εἴδωλά τινά φησιν ἐμπελάζειν τοῖς ἀνθρώποις καὶ τούτων τὰ μὲν εἶναι ἀγαθοποιὰ τὰ δὲ κακοποιά· ἔνθεν καὶ εὔχετο εὐλόγχων τυχεῖν εἰδώλων. εἶναι δὲ ταῦτα μεγάλα τε καὶ ὑπερφυῆ καὶ δύσφθαρτα μέν, οὐκ ἄφθαρτα δέ, προσημαίνειν τε τὰ μέλλοντα τοῖς ἀνθρώποις θεωρούμενα καὶ φωνὰς ἀφιέντα. ὅθεν τούτων αὐτῶν φαντασίαν λαβόντες οἱ παλαιοὶ ὑπενόησαν εἶναι θεόν, μηδενὸς ἄλλου παρὰ ταῦτα ὄντος θεοῦ [τοῦ] ἄφθαρτον φύσιν ἔχοντος.

Democritus says that some *eidōla* encounter people, and of these some are beneficial and some harmful; hence he prayed to find propitious *eidōla*. These are huge and gigantic and difficult to destroy, but not indestructible, and they foretell future events to people by appearing to them and speaking. It was from the appearance of these very things that the ancients came to believe in the existence of gods, though apart from these there is no god possessing an immortal nature.

Sextus Empiricus, *Adversus Mathematicos* 9.24 = DK 68 A 75

εἰσὶ δὲ οἱ ἀπὸ τῶν γιγνομένων κατὰ τὸν κόσμον παραδόξων ὑπονοήσαντες εἰς ἔννοιαν ἡμᾶς ἐληλυθέναι θεῶν, ἀφ' ἧς φαίνεται εἶναι δόξης καὶ ὁ Δ.· ὁρῶντες γάρ, φησί, τὰ ἐν τοῖς μετεώροις παθήματα οἱ παλαιοὶ τῶν ἀνθρώπων καθάπερ βροντὰς καὶ ἀστραπὰς κεραυνούς τε καὶ ἄστρων συνόδους ἡλίου τε καὶ σελήνης ἐκλείψεις ἐδειματοῦντο θεοὺς οἰόμενοι τούτων αἰτίους εἶναι.

Some people think that we arrived at the idea of gods from the remarkable things that happen in the world. Democritus seems to me to be of that opinion; he says that the people of ancient times were frightened by happenings in the heavens such as thunder, lightning, thunderbolts, conjunctions of stars, and eclipses of the sun and moon, and thought that they were caused by gods.

Philodemus, *De pietate* 5a, p. 69 Gomperz = DK 68 A 75

θέρος <ἐν τῆι γῆι καὶ> χειμὼν καὶ ἔ<αρ καὶ> μεθόπωρον καὶ πάντα ταῦτα ἄνωθεν διειπετῆ γείνεται· διὸ δὴ καὶ τὸ ἐξεργαζόμενον γνόντας σέβεσθαι. οὐ φαίνεται δ' ἐμοὶ Δ. ὥσπερ ἔνιοι τὸν [...]

Thence summer and winter and spring and autumn and all these things are sent from above by the gods, and so they recognize and venerate their author. Democritus does not seem to me, like some...

Hermippus, *De astrologia* 1.16.122, p. 26, 13 Kroll-Viereck = DK 68 A 78

τὸ μέντοι τοῦ Δημοκρίτου <οὐ> καλῶς ἂν ἔχοι παραλιπεῖν, ὃς εἴδωλα αὐτοὺς [τοὺς δαίμονας] ὀνομάζων μεστόν τε εἶναι τὸν ἀέρα τούτων φησί.

It would be unfitting to make no mention of Democritus, who calls deities *eidōla* and claims that the air is full of them.

Clemens Alexandrinus, *Stromata* 5.88 = DK 68 A 79

καθόλου γοῦν τὴν περὶ τοῦ θείου ἔννοιαν Ξενοκράτης ὁ Καλχηδόνιος οὐκ ἀπελπίζει καὶ ἐν τοῖς ἀλόγοις, Δ. δέ, κἂν μὴ θέληι, ὁμολογήσει διὰ τὴν

In fine, then, Xenocrates the Chalcedonian was not quite without hope that the notion of the Divinity existed even in the irrational creatures.

ἀκολουθίαν τῶν δογμάτων· τὰ γὰρ αὐτὰ πεποίηκεν εἴδωλα τοῖς ἀνθρώποις προσπίπτοντα καὶ τοῖς ἀλόγοις ζώιοις ἀπὸ τῆς θείας οὐσίας.

And Democritus, though against his will, will make this avowal by the consequences of his dogmas; for he represents the same images as issuing, from the divine essence, on men and on the irrational animals.

Lucretius, *De rerum natura* 5.1186–1194 = DK 68 A 75
ergo perfugium sibi habebant omnia divis | tradere et illorum nutu facere omnia flecti. | in caeloque deum sedes et templa locarunt, | per caelum volvi quia sol et luna videtur, | luna dies et nox et noctis signa severa, | noctivagaeque faces caeli, flammaeque volantes, | nubila ros imbres nix venti fulmina grando | et rapidi fremitus et murmura magna minarum.

Therefore they took refuge in ascribing everything to the gods and in supposing that everything happens in obedience to their will. And they located the habitations and sacred quarters of the gods in the sky, because it is through the sky that night and the revolving moon are seen to pass, yes the moon, day and night, and night's austere constellations, and the night-roving torches and flying flames of heaven, clouds, sunlight, rains, snow, winds, lightning, hail, and the rapid roars and mighty menacing rumbles of thunder.

Plinius, *Naturalis historia* 2.5.14 = DK 68 A 76
innumeros quidem credere atque etiam ex vitiis hominum, ut Pudicitiam, Concordiam, Mentem, Spem, Honorem, Clementiam, Fidem, aut, ut Democrito placuit, duos omnino, Poenam et Beneficium, maiorem ad socordiam accedit.

To believe in innumerable gods, and to model them on human failings, for instance Modesty, Concord, Mind, Hope, Honour, Clemency, Honesty, or, as Democritus did, to believe in just two, Punishment and Reward, is to reach a greater height of folly [*sc.* than to attribute human form to the gods].

2.2.2 Commentary

The fragments of Democritus' hypotheses concerning the origin of religion are best preserved by Sextus Empiricus. On the one hand, Sextus claimed, and quite unequivocally so, that according to Democritus, the origin of religion was to be found in the attempts to explain meteorological phenomena and in the fear caused by the absence of such an explanation. When our ancestors observed heavenly phenomena, such as thunder, lightning or the eclipses of sun and moon, they were gripped by fear and attributed them to gods (ὁρῶντες γάρ, φησί, τὰ ἐν τοῖς μετεώροις παθήματα οἱ παλαιοὶ τῶν ἀνθρώπων καθάπερ βροντὰς καὶ ἀστραπὰς κεραυνούς τε καὶ ἄστρων συνόδους ἡλίου τε καὶ σελήνης ἐκλείψεις ἐδειματοῦντο θεοὺς οἰόμενοι τούτων αἰτίους εἶναι).[57] This reconstruction seems to operate with an unspoken assumption of almost Frazerian pedigree, namely that the fear of humankind is alleviated because the will of the gods (unlike nature) may be swayed in our favour by worship and sacrifice. Thus, the formerly uncontrollable and threatening aspects of nature may in fact be reined in via interactions with gods. Philodemus, in his work *On piety* (*De pietate*), also seemed to associate Democritus with this line of thought: θέρος <ἐν τῆι γῆι καὶ> χειμὼν καὶ ἔ<αρ καὶ> μεθόπωρον καὶ πάντα ταῦτα ἄνωθεν διειπετῆ γείνεται· διὸ δὴ καὶ τὸ ἐξεργαζόμενον γνόντας σέβεσθαι.[58]

On the other hand, Sextus also claimed that, according to Democritus, there is another way of looking for the origins of religious representations, namely through the effects of 'emanations', 'effusions' or 'images' (Gk. εἴδωλα, Lat. *imagines*). Atomistic epistemology postulates that these are thin films of atoms that are 'peeled off' from objects (i.e. large and more or less stable clusters of atoms) and thereby make sensory perception possible: εἴδωλά τινά φησιν ἐμπελάζειν τοῖς ἀνθρώποις [...] ὅθεν τούτων αὐτῶν φαντασίαν λαβόντες οἱ παλαιοὶ ὑπενόησαν εἶναι θεόν.[59] What exactly are these εἴδωλα or 'images', terms used in various contexts and with equivocal meanings, when already Cicero complained about their obscurity (*tum imagines eorumque circumitus in deorum numero refert, tum illam naturam quae imagines fundat ac mittat, tum sententiam intelligentiamque nostram*)?[60]

One option would be to understand this term as being synonymous to other atomistic terms denoting 'effusions' or 'emanations' that make perception possible, such as δείκελον or ἀπόρροια,[61] Ciceronian *imagines*. Sextus himself pointed to this direction by saying that these 'images' (εἴδωλα) produce in humans 'representations' (φαντασίαν) that, however, have no corresponding object in the cases of god-concepts (μηδενὸς ἄλλου παρὰ ταῦτα ὄντος θεοῦ).[62] Under this interpretation, the mental representation of a divinity is a result of a delusion, noise in the usually reliable signal of atomic films peeling off objects and affecting our organs of sense. Alternatively, the term εἴδωλα could denote 'effusions' or 'emanations' (just as it did previously), but in this case the extension of the term would be the divinity that corresponds to the 'effusion' and brings it forth. The term has been understood in this way by Clement of Alexandria, who argued that, according to Democritus, εἴδωλα emanate towards human beings 'from a divine essence' (ἀπὸ τῆς θείας οὐσίας).[63] Both of these interpretations then take εἴδωλα to denote 'atomic effusions', but they differ in the answer to the question of whether there is any correlate that corresponds to them as their source. Last option available is to understand gods themselves as the extensions of the term εἴδωλα, i.e. those extraordinarily stable atomic structures that cause these 'effusions' or 'emanations'. This much seems to have been suggested by Hermippus, according to whom Democritus used the term εἴδωλα to denote gods and divinities (εἴδωλα αὐτοὺς [τοὺς δαίμονας] ὀνομάζων).[64]

Scholars battling with this terminological issue rarely commit to one view or the other.[65] In my view, Jonathan Barnes offered one of the more comprehensive interpretations.[66] He showed that all fragments related to the possible meaning of the term εἴδωλα are most likely based on Sextus' account (B 166),[67] in which it is emphatically denied, however, that the 'effusions' or 'emanations' could find their correlates in independently existing atomic structures. Barnes then understands εἴδωλα to be a sort of 'dream images', that is to say, thin atomic films that are (randomly?) generated without necessarily being 'peeled off' off some more stable structures.[68] It has been already mentioned that the anthropological speculation (which explains the origin of religion through misguided attempts of our ancestors to explain some puzzling meteorological phenomena) and the atomic hypothesis (according to which god-concepts are caused by 'noise' in the regular signals of thin films of atoms emanating from any more complex atomic clusters) are usually contrasted one against the other and considered mutually incompatible. Barnes considered them to be mutually congruent and argued that, according to Democritus, religion and the representations of gods emerged first as a reaction to potentially threatening meteorological or natural phenomena and secondarily as a reaction to the emerging contents of sleeping human mind, while the term εἴδωλα is best understood as denoting precisely these 'dream images'.[69]

I largely agree with Barnes, but I believe it is more meaningful to consider these 'dream images' to be the foundational (and not secondary) source of the god-concepts, while their use to explain some features of the natural world would be a secondary development or a by-product, once the 'dream images' are a cultural *Gemeingut*. I would therefore propose to accept Barnes' interpretation with inverted diachrony. No matter which variant we choose to prefer, it remains clear that Democritus approached religion in a naturalistic fashion. Both hypotheses he put forward explain the origin of religious ideas and representations by human emotional and intellectual reactions to unknown and potentially threatening forces or by treating them as visual or auditive 'noise' in the context of the atomistic theory of sensory perception. Both are tokens of the same type, namely of a reductive naturalistic explanation that demasks religion as 'illusion' through its reduction to non-religious phenomena.[70]

2.3 Sisyphus-fragment

Critias, unscrupulous Athenian politician, sophist and author of dramas and elegies, Plato's uncle, one of the participants of the mutilation of *hermai* in 415 BCE, one of the leaders of the tyranny of the thirty in 404/403 BCE or, put simply by Philostratus, 'the most abominable of all humans' (κάκιστος ἀνθρώπων ἔμοιγε φαίνεται ξυμπάντων),[71] has been traditionally considered to be the author of forty-two preserved verses from an otherwise unknown drama, most likely a satyr play entitled *Sisyphus*.[72] The speaker in this 'Sisyphus-fragment' presents the gradual constitution and subsequent refinement of human society, in which the 'invention' of religion plays a crucial role. As I have already shown, Democritus analysed the origin of religion in terms of recurring 'dream images' that were used to explain meteorological and other puzzling natural phenomena. Religion therefore played for him a primarily explicative role and gods were constructed as causes of those phenomena for which humans did not have any alternative explanation. In contradistinction to this intellectualistic approach, the author of the Sisyphus-fragment laid much stronger emphasis on the social effects of the belief in a divinity.

The fragment, considered by Charles Kahn to be 'the best-preserved example of fifth-century accounts of the origin of religion' and 'the most outspoken example of fifth-century atheism',[73] has been preserved by Sextus Empiricus, who quoted it with the explicit purpose of demonstrating Critias' atheistic views.[74] The analysis of form and subject matter (see, e.g., the diminutive χωρίωι, which some scholars considered unsuitable for the high language register of classical Athenian tragedy) makes it probable (but by no means certain) that the fragment comes from a satyr play.[75] The speaker, likely Sisyphus himself, describes in it the cultural evolution of humanity from its pre-civilizational 'natural state' to the creation of society, codification of laws and introduction of religion. The choice of a formal vehicle of a satyr play to expose radical new ideas about the origin of religion in Athens of fifth century BCE was probably intentional, since an open and personal endorsement of the contents of this fragment could, under the legal force of Diopeithes' Decree, mean running a risk of being prosecuted for impiety, under pain of death.

2.3.1 Fragments

Sextus Empiricus, *Adversus mathematicos* 9.54 = DK 88 B 25

ἦν χρόνος, ὅτ᾽ ἦν ἄτακτος ἀνθρώπων βίος | καὶ θηριώδης ἰσχύος θ᾽ ὑπηρέτης, | ὅτ᾽ οὐδὲν ἆθλον οὔτε τοῖς ἐσθλοῖσιν ἦν | οὔτ᾽ (20) αὖ κόλασμα τοῖς κακοῖς ἐγίγνετο. | κἄπειτά μοι δοκοῦσιν ἄνθρωποι νόμους | θέσθαι κολαστάς, ἵνα δίκη τύραννος ἦι | <ὁμῶς ἁπάντων> τήν θ᾽ ὕβριν δούλην ἔχηι | ἐζημιοῦτο δ᾽ (25) εἴ τις ἐξαμαρτάνοι. | ἔπειτ᾽ ἐπειδὴ τἀμφανῆ μὲν οἱ νόμοι | ἀπεῖργον αὐτοὺς ἔργα μὴ πράσσειν βίαι, | λάθραι δ᾽ ἔπρασσον, τηνικαῦτά μοι δοκεῖ | <πρῶτον> πυκνός τις καὶ (30) σοφὸς γνώμην ἀνήρ <θεῶν>[76] | δέος θνητοῖσιν ἐξευρεῖν, ὅπως | εἴη τι δεῖμα τοῖς κακοῖσι, κἂν λάθραι | πράσσωσιν ἢ λέγωσιν ἢ φρονῶσί <τι>. | ἐντεῦθεν οὖν τὸ θεῖον (35) εἰσηγήσατο, | ὡς ἔστι δαίμων ἀφθίτωι θάλλων βίωι, | νόωι τ᾽ ἀκούων καὶ βλέπων, φρονῶν τ᾽ ἄγαν | προσέχων τὰ πάντα,[77] καὶ φύσιν θείαν φορῶν, | ὃς πᾶν τὸ (40) λεχθὲν ἐν βροτοῖς ἀκούσεται, | <τὸ> δρώμενον δὲ πᾶν ἰδεῖν δυνήσεται. | ἐὰν δὲ σὺν σιγῆι τι βουλεύηις κακόν, | τοῦτ᾽ οὐχὶ λήσει τοὺς θεούς· | τὸ γὰρ φρονοῦν |	There was a time when the life of human beings was disordered and beastly, and life was ruled by force, when there was no reward for the virtuous nor any punishment for the wicked. And then I think that humans decided to establish laws to punish [wrongdoers] so that justice might rule and be master over crime and violence. And they punished anyone who did wrong. Then, since the laws held public deeds in check and prevented men from open acts of violence, but they acted secretly, then it was, I believe, that a shrewd and clever-minded man invented for mortals a fear from the gods, so that there might be a detergent for the wicked, even if they act or say or think anything in secret. Hence from this source the divine was introduced [with the claim] that there is a deity who enjoys imperishable life, hearing and seeing with his mind, his thought and attention on all things, his nature so divine that he will hear whatever is said among mortals and be able to see whatever is done. If ever you plot some evil deed in silence, even this will not escape the gods. For they

(45) <ἄγαν> ἔνεστι. τούσδε τοὺς λόγους λέγων | διδαγμάτων ἥδιστον⁷⁸ εἰσηγήσατο | ψευδεῖ καλύψας τὴν ἀλήθειαν λόγωι. | ναίειν δ' ἔφασκε τοὺς θεοὺς ἐνταῦθ', ἵνα | μάλιστ' ἂν (50) ἐξέπληξεν ἀνθρώπους λέγων, | ὅθεν περ ἔγνω τοὺς φόβους ὄντας βροτοῖς | καὶ τὰς ὀνήσεις τῶι ταλαιπώρωι βίωι, | ἐκ τῆς ὕπερθε περιφορᾶς, ἵν' ἀστραπάς | κατεῖδεν (55) οὔσας, δεινὰ δὲ κτυπήματα | βροντῆς, τό τ' ἀστερωπὸν οὐρανοῦ δέμας, | Χρόνου καλὸν ποίκιλμα τέκτονος σοφοῦ, | ὅθεν τε λαμπρὸς ἀστέρος στείχει μύδρος | ὅ θ' ὑγρὸς (60) εἰς γῆν ὄμβρος ἐκπορεύεται. | τοίους δὲ περιέστησεν ἀνθρώποις φόβους,⁷⁹ | δι' οὓς καλῶς τε τῶι λόγωι κατώικισεν | τὸν δαίμον(α) οὗ<τος> κἀν πρέποντι χωρίωι, | τὴν (65) ἀνομίαν τε τοῖς νόμοις κατέσβεσεν.	have knowledge. It was such stories that he told when he introduced this most delightful teaching and hid the truth with a false tale. He said the gods dwell there and placed them where they might make the greatest impression upon human beings, there where he knew that fears come to mortals and benefits also [to relieve] the miseries of life, from the vault on high, where they beheld the shafts of lightning and the fearful blows of thunder and star-filled gleam of heaven, the beautiful design of Time the clever builder, parade-ground for the brilliant mass of the sun and source of rainfall moistening the earth below. Such were the fears with which he surrounded humans and by which this clever man established the deity in the proper place, with a handsome story, and extinguished lawlessness by means of laws.⁸⁰

2.3.2 Commentary

Before discussing the contents of the fragment, I want to touch briefly on the problem of authorship, since, in the past few decades, an intensive polemic put Critias' authorship in doubt.⁸¹ The standard edition of Presocratic fragments attribute the fragment to Critias, but already in the ancient doxographical tradition we find it attributed also to Euripides, the famous Athenian dramatist.⁸² Among modern scholars, Albrecht Dihle has been forcefully advocating his authorship, citing the peculiarity of Sextus' attribution and the incoherence of the whole section discussing atheism in his work (according to Dihle, it is nothing more than a compilation from other doxographical sources) or sparsity with which Sextus quoted authors of tragedies. Dihle considered it improbable for Sextus to have had Critias' play at his disposal; Sextus' other quotations, however, make it clear that he did possess the texts of (at least some of) Euripides' plays.⁸³ Moreover, in order to proclaim Critias an atheist, ancient authors probably would not need to go further than to his participation at the mutilation of the *hermai* or his political activities in and around 404/403 BCE.

Critical reactions to Dihle's attribution of the Sisyphus-fragment to Euripides appeared immediately afterwards and Marek Winiarczyk, in his paper 'Once again on the satyr play "Sisyphus"' revindicated Critias' authorship.⁸⁴ Alongside metrical and stylistic elements speaking against Euripides Winiarczyk explicitly denied Dihle's claim that Euripides has been generally considered an atheist in the Antiquity, contrasting a single appearance of Euripides in the atheist-lists (in Aetius) against four such appearances of Critias (in the atheist-lists of Epicurus, Cicero, Sextus and Theophilus). Nonetheless, Winiarczyk's argumentation has been in turn rejected only a year later by Harvey Yunis, who came to a conclusion that '[r]egarding our understanding of the doxographical tradition and the sources of the Sisyphus fragment, the situation stands as Dihle left it in 1977'.[85] Yunis himself attempted to identify the verse couplet cited in *Vita Euripidi* by Satyros as a part of the Sisyphus-fragment, which would strengthen the case for Euripides' authorship.[86]

Since the discussion of the authorship is ongoing and no general consensus is in sight,[87] I will limit myself to the two following considerations. Firstly, given the availability of primary sources (or rather, the lack thereof), it seems doubtful to me that the question of authorship could be solved in one way or the other. One part of the doxographical tradition attributes the fragment to Critias, the other to Euripides. Some elements of subject-matter or stylistic criteria speak for Critias, others for Euripides. Secondly, even if it were possible to prove beyond reasonable doubt that Critias has been the author of the fragment, it would still be impossible to prove that the opinions put forward by one of the personae in the play coincide with the opinions of its creator.[88] If Critias let Sisyphus (of all people, a character with a rather dubious moral fibre) present the theory that touches on the creation of first human society, and he did so in a satyr play (where almost anything goes, quite like in the ancient Greek comedy), then anyone claiming that this 'Sisyphus' must have represented Critias' own ideas on the origin of religion would be hard pressed to produce any relevant evidence for it. Indeed, Dana Sutton argued that 'the chances that our fragment expresses Critias' own philosophy appear minimal'[89] and Malcolm Davies even considered this view to be a *communis opinio*.[90] The same caveat would apply to Euripides, who in his plays often pondered whether in a world replete with injustice there could exist any divine beings that would function as paragons of morality.[91]

In the Sisyphus-fragment itself, we find numerous elements of previously discussed hypotheses: the author mentions in connection with the origin of religion 'fear' and 'awe' (δέος, l. 28; δεῖμα, l. 29; φόβους, ll. 44, 52) as well as those meteorological phenomena that according to the tradition belonged firmly and squarely in Zeus' domain (ἀστραπάς, l. 46; κτυπήματα βροντῆς, ll. 47–48; ὄμβρος, l. 51). The theory of the origin of religion is formulated in the wider context of the evolution of human society and civilization and presented as a sort of a primitive socio-cultural anthropology. In contrast to Democritus' hypotheses, an important change of perspective is established through the analysis of the social dimension of religious ideas and representations, which is in turn used to explain the origin of religion itself.

'Sisyphus' first describes a 'natural state' of humankind, which has been 'disordered, beastly, and ruled by force' (ἄτακτος ἀνθρώπων βίος | καὶ θηριώδης ἰσχύος θ' ὑπηρέτης, ll. 16–17) or, as Hobbes will later put it, 'solitary, poore, nasty, brutish, and short'.[92] In a prophylactic reaction to this miserable existence, humans introduced laws that were supposed to regulate and limit violent or otherwise damaging actions of individuals, thus creating the first society. The original problem has not been solved, however, since the laws were effective only insofar as they were enforced. Since the permanent control of all individuals in society was (and, at least in the short term, hopefully still is) an impossibility, laws were being broken in those circumstances in which there was no significant threat of a sanction. The origin of religion is then intimately linked with the enforcement of laws.

At this critical juncture, with laws already in place but with little means to enforce them, an anonymous 'shrewd and clever-minded man' (πυκνός τις καὶ σοφὸς γνώμην ἀνήρ, l. 27) introduced into the society a notion of a deity not dissimilar to the Orwellian Big Brother – this is a god that hears every little piece of gossip (ὃς πᾶν τὸ λεχθὲν ἐν βροτοῖς ἀκούσεται, l. 35) and sees all mortal deeds (<τὸ> δρώμενον δὲ πᾶν ἰδεῖν δυνήσεται, v. 36). The deity is introduced in order to enforce better moral behaviour, since laws alone – as has been pointed out previously – are deficient in this respect: people simply ignore them the moment they feel they have a good chance of getting away with their misdemeanors. In the context of the Sisyphus-fragment, the origin of religion is then understood as sprouting from the attempts to integrate society and the religion itself is the best 'political invention to ensure good behaviour'.[93] It is notable that the speaker in the fragment explicitly pronounced the belief in the deity to be a 'lie' (ψευδεῖ καλύψας τὴν ἀλήθειαν λόγωι, l. 41),[94] albeit a lie that is, from the social standpoint, most necessary and useful (διδαγμάτων ἥδιστον, l. 40). This distinction between *truth* and *social utility* of religion, appreciated by the author of the Sisyphus-fragment already in the fifth century BCE, remains very often obfuscated in the study of religion, which caused some interpretative entanglements in the case of the fragment.[95] Needless to say, the enigmatic author of this radical hypothesis clearly belongs to the naturalistic paradigm, since he attempts to explain religion reductively as a human invention introduced to enforce laws and establish more effective social control.

2.4 Prodicus

Prodicus, famous Athenian sophist of the fifth century BCE, hailed as 'one of the earliest anthropologists, with a theory about a purely human origin of belief in gods which would not have disgraced the nineteenth century',[96] developed a hypothesis that tried to explain the existence of god-concepts by deification of all people (and things) that benefit our earthly existence. Just like in the case of the Sisyphus-fragment, also for Prodicus the gods seemed to exist only as mental representations inhabiting human minds.[97] This view stands somewhat in contrast to Xenophanes' thoughts, since for the latter the anthropomorphic representations of gods, a trademark of 'Homeric' religion, were erroneous, but Xenophanes (unlike the author of the Sisyphus-fragment and Prodicus) did not deny the existence of deities *simpliciter* (as his reformed theology shows) – he only denies that the deity could possess those attributes and properties that were traditionally ascribed to it. Remnants of Prodicus' hypotheses of the origin of religion are collected under the B 5 entry in the Diels–Kranz edition, to which we took the liberty to add a fragment found in the Herculaneum papyri and one mention from Minucius Felix (both absent in DK).

2.4.1 Fragments

Philodemus, *De pietate* c. 9, 7, p. 75 Gomperz = DK 84 B 5[98]

Περσα[ῖος δὲ] δῆλός ἐστιν [ἀναιρῶν] ὄντω[ς κ]α[ὶ] ἀφανί]ζων τὸ δαιμόνιον ἢ μηθὲν ὑπὲρ αὐτοῦ γινώσκων, ὅταν ἐν τῶι Περὶ θεῶν μὴ [ἀπ]ίθανα λέγηι φαίνεσθαι τὰ περὶ <τοῦ> τὰ τρέφοντα καὶ ὠφελοῦντα θεοὺς νενομίσθαι καὶ τετειμῆσθ[αι] πρῶτον ὑπὸ [Προ]δίκου γεγραμμένα, μετὰ δὲ ταῦτα τοὺ[ς εὑρ] όντας ἢ τροφὰς ἢ [σ]κέπας ἢ τὰς ἄλλας τέχνας ὡς Δήμητρα καὶ Δι[όνυσον] καὶ τοὺ[ς Διοσκούρ]ους...	It is clear that Persaeus is really abolishing and removing the divine or recognizing nothing about it, when in his *On Gods* he says that it does not appear to be unconvincing what was written by Prodicus about the nourishing and useful first having been considered and honoured as gods, and after these those who discovered food or shelter or other skills as Demeter and Dionysus and the Dioscuri...

Cicero, *De natura deorum* 1.42.118 + 1.15.38 = DK 84 B 5

quid? Prodicus Cius, qui ea quae prodessent hominum vitae deorum in numero habita esse dixit, quam tandem religionem reliquit? [...] Persaeus [...] eos esse habitos deos, a quibus aliqua magna utilitas ad vitae cultum esset inventa, ipsasque res utiles et salutares deorum esse vocabulis nuncupatas.	Or Prodicus of Cos, who said that the gods were personifications of things beneficial to the life of man – pray what religion was left by his theory? [...] Persaeus [...] says that men have deified those persons who have made some discovery of special utility for civilization, and that useful and health-giving things have themselves been called by divine names.

Sextus Empiricus, *Adversus mathematicos* 9.18 + 9.51 + 9.52 = DK 84 B 5

Πρόδικος δὲ ὁ Κεῖος 'ἥλιον, φησί, καὶ σελήνην καὶ ποταμοὺς καὶ κρήνας καὶ καθόλου πάντα τὰ ὠφελοῦντα τὸν βίον ἡμῶν οἱ παλαιοὶ θεοὺς ἐνόμισαν διὰ τὴν ἀπ' αὐτῶν ὠφέλειαν, καθάπερ Αἰγύπτιοι τὸν Νεῖλον', καὶ διὰ τοῦτο τὸν μὲν ἄρτον Δήμητραν νομισθῆναι, τὸν δὲ οἶνον Διόνυσον, τὸ δὲ ὕδωρ Ποσειδῶνα, τὸ δὲ πῦρ Ἥφαιστον καὶ ἤδη τῶν εὐχρηστούντων ἕκαστον. [...] μὴ εἶναι δὲ [sc. θεόν] οἱ ἐπικληθέντες ἄθεοι, καθάπερ Εὐήμερος [...] καὶ Διαγόρας ὁ Μήλιος καὶ Πρόδικος ὁ Κεῖος καὶ Θεόδωρος [...] Πρόδικος δὲ τὸ ὠφελοῦν τὸν βίον ὑπειλῆφθαι θεόν, ὡς ἥλιον καὶ σελήνην καὶ ποταμοὺς καὶ λίμνας καὶ λειμῶνας καὶ καρποὺς καὶ πᾶν τὸ τοιουτῶδες.	And Prodicus of Ceos says: 'Sun and moon and rivers and springs and generally everything that benefits our life the ancients considered gods because of the benefit from them, just as the Egyptians considered the Nile.' And because of this bread is considered Demeter, and wine Dionysus, and water Poseidon, and fire Hephaestus, and so on for each of the things that are useful. [...] ... those called 'atheists' say that he [sc. god] does not exist, just like Euhemerus ... and Diagoras of Melos and Prodicus of Ceos ... [...] Prodicus said that what benefited life had been supposed to be god, thus sun and moon and river and lakes and pastures and crops and everything of this sort.

Minucius Felix, *Octavius* 21.2
Prodicus adsumptos in deos loquitur, qui errando inventis novis frugibus utilitati hominum profuerunt. in eandem sententiam et Persaeus philosophus et adnectit inventas fruges et frugum ipsarum repertores isdem nominibus, ut comicus sermo est 'Venerem sine Libero et Cerere frigere'.

Prodicus says that those who in their wandering were beneficial to the interests of humans with newly discovered crops were raised up among the gods. Persaeus philosophizes to the same opinion, and he connects the crops that have been discovered and the discoverers of these very crops by the same names, as the lines of the comedy go: 'Without Liber and Ceres Venus grows cold.'

Philodemus, *De pietate* 2 = *PHerc* 1428 *frg*. 19[99]
...ὑ]πὸ [τ]ῶν ἀνθρώπων νομιζομένους θεοὺς οὔτ' εἶναί φησιν οὔτ' εἰδέναι, τοὺς δὲ καρποὺς καὶ πανθ' ὅλως τὰ χρήσιμα πρ[ὸς τ]ὸν βίον τοὺς ἀρ[χαίο]υς ἀγα[σθέντας]...

...considered gods by humans he [i.e., Prodicus] says neither exist nor know, but the crops and virtually everything that is useful with a view to life the ancients, having admired...[100]

Themistius, *Oratio* 30, p. 422 Dindorf = DK 84 B 5
...πλησιάζομεν ἤδη ταῖς τελεταῖς καὶ τὴν Προδίκου σοφίαν τοῖς λόγοις ἐγκαταμίξομεν, ὃς ἱερουργίαν πᾶσαν ἀνθρώπου καὶ μυστήρια καὶ τελετὰς τῶν γεωργίας καλῶν ἐξάπτει, νομίζων καὶ θεῶν ἔννοιαν ἐντεῦθεν εἰς ἀνθρώπους ἐλθεῖν καὶ πᾶσαν εὐσέβειαν ἐγγυώμενος.[101]

...and then we'll already be approaching the initiations and we'll mix into our words the wisdom of Prodicus, who connects all sacred rites of humans and mysteries and festivals and initiations to the goods of farming, thinking that even the conception of gods came to humans from here and so securing all piety.

2.4.2 Commentary

As these fragments make abundantly clear, the original hypothesis of Prodicus explaining the origin of religion has been connected by ancient authorities with another author, namely Persaeus, Stoic philosopher active in the third century BCE, a favourite student of the founder of the school, Zeno of Citium. For instance, the Philodemus fragment speaks about Persaeus but emphasizes that the hypothesis was originally formulated by Prodicus (πρῶτον ὑπὸ Προδίκου γεγραμμένα); both philosophers are also mentioned in a single breath by Cicero and Minucius Felix. We are therefore faced with the problem of drawing the line between the two authors and isolating the original hypothesis of Prodicus from possible later modifications introduced by Persaeus. What can be stated with certainty is that both philosophers explained the origins of religion in the context of the deification of things (and/or people) beneficial to humankind. This essentially utilitarian interpretation is safely documented in all extant fragments: (τρέφοντα καὶ ὠφελοῦντα in Philodemus; *ea quae prodessent hominum vitae* in Cicero; πάντα τὰ ὠφελοῦντα τὸν βίον in Sextus; *inventis novis frugibus utilitati hominum profuerunt* in Minucius Felix; πανθ' ὅλως τὰ χρήσιμα πρὸς τὸν βίον in the Herculaneum papyrus).

Together with the previously discussed Sisyphus-fragment, this way of approaching religious phenomena may be viewed as a practical application of the trademark sophistic distinction of everything that exists 'naturally' (φύσει) and is, therefore, unchangeable and 'objective', from what exists only 'by law' (νόμῳ), conventionally and 'subjectively'.[102] Already Plato had applied the φύσει vs. νόμῳ dichotomy to religious matters in the last book of his *Laws*: Θεούς, ὦ μακάριε, εἶναι πρῶτόν φασιν οὗτοι τέχνῃ, οὐ φύσει ἀλλά τισιν νόμοις, καὶ τούτους ἄλλους ἄλλῃ, ὅπῃ ἕκαστοι ἑαυτοῖσι συνωμολόγησαν νομοθετούμενοι.[103] Gods exist only in human minds as concepts that are either policemen regulating social integration or memorials of greatest contributors to human well-being.

A closer look at the fragments could, in my opinion, warrant a distinction between two philosophers, although scholars usually tend to accept both approaches as Prodicus' own, albeit without any compelling argument.[104] The remarks by Philodemus, Cicero and Minucius would seem to suggest that Prodicus argued for the deification of beneficial *things* (inventions) as the proper explanation of the origin of religion, while Persaeus later expanded this theory with the deification of beneficial *people* (inventors) as well. Philodemus, for instance, used a neuter plural (τὰ τρέφοντα καὶ ὠφελοῦντα) when crediting Prodicus with the authorship of this hypothesis and then continued with the expression μετὰ δὲ ταῦτα (which might be interpreted as a temporal 'after that', or a content-related 'on the top of that'), demarcating thus the new addition to the original hypothesis that Persaeus brought forward. According to the Stoic philosopher, then, not only beneficial things, but also beneficial people were deified by our ancestors (τοὺς εὑρόντας ἢ τροφὰς ἢ σκέπας ἢ τὰς ἄλλας τέχνας).[105] This seems to be supported by Cicero, who also used a neuter plural when speaking about Prodicus (*ea quae prodessent*) and a masculine plural when speaking about Persaeus (*eos esse habitos deos*). Minucius Felix explicitly stated that the deification of people has been Persaeus' innovation (*adnectit*). All attempts to differentiate between Prodicus and Persaeus are further complicated by the fact that Greeks often made no distinction between 'inventors' and their 'inventions' and as such remain on the verge of speculation.[106]

For our purposes, it should suffice to say that Prodicus applies a symbolical or allegorical approach to religion and the origin of human representations of gods.[107] Whenever mortals use terms that denote individual deities, their extensions are not 'real' gods, but rather people or things that our ancestors celebrated for their supreme usefulness for humankind. This approach again stands in opposition to Xenophanes, for whom the extension of the term 'god' is a divinity that exists also outside human minds, even though we humans often conceive it in inappropriate, anthropomorphic ways. It therefore comes as no surprise that Prodicus has been (quite like Critias) considered an atheist, i.e. a person that denied the existence of gods *simpliciter* (and not only the pantheon of traditional Greek or 'Homeric' religion, as Xenophanes did). Prodicus' atheism is attested both by his inclusion in the ancient 'catalogues' of unbelievers (such as the one elaborated by Sextus),[108] but also in the Herculaneum papyrus, which clearly argued that Prodicus did not believe in gods and emphatically denied that these gods could have the cognitive capabilities that are generally attributed to them (θεοὺς οὔτ' εἶναί φησιν οὔτ' εἰδέναι).[109] For ancient doxographers, then, an aetiological explanation of the origin of gods, a trademark of the naturalistic paradigm, was closely connected with atheism. Prodicus' and Persaeus' explanation of religion is, in a sense, quite evocative of Nietzsche's 'first' religion, conceived as an expression of thankfulness and the life-affirming celebration of the human condition:

> A people that still believes in itself still has its own God too. In him it reveres the conditions through which it has come out on top, his virtues – it projects its delight in itself, its feeling of power, into a being one can give thanks to. He who is rich wants to deliver up; a proud people needs a God, in order to *offer up* ... Religion, within such presuppositions, is a form of thankfulness. One is thankful for oneself: for that one needs a God.[110]

2.5 Conclusion: Main characteristics of the naturalistic paradigm

The discussion of the Presocratic views on the origin of religion in this chapter hardly exhausted the topic, but it is hoped that it did present a representative sample of historically first formulations of the naturalistic paradigm in European cultural and philosophical tradition. All four philosophers I considered attempted to explain religion in a reductionistic manner, despite their approaches, methods and solutions being idiosyncratic and variegated. For Xenophanes, religious ideas and representations are shaped by human psychological inclination to construct concepts that share with their creators significant physiological or mental attributes and properties, while his views were informed primarily by empirical observation and thought-experiments. Democritus contextualized religious representations within a conceptual frame of his atomistic theory and attempted to explain the origin of religion via human propensity to search for causes of puzzling and potentially dangerous meteorological phenomena and other enigmatic features of the natural world. The author of the Sisyphus-fragment argued that the origin of religion lies in the gradual construction of human society and its need to enforce laws while Prodicus focused on the utilitarian and functional aspects of the religious ideas and his argumentation has been likely influenced by pragmatics of the terms denoting divinities in Ancient Greek.

Another important feature all discussed Presocratics share is an implicit commitment to a specific manner of argumentation. For my purposes, it is not necessary or expedient to delve deep into the philosophical concept of epistemic justification and I will limit myself to adopt Richard Fumerton's adequately vague definition of it as 'that which makes probable the truth of a proposition'.[111] I further differentiate two distinct types of epistemic justification: Epistemic justification *per rem* is defined as an argumentative procedure in which the truth value of the propositions is established via a process that is indifferent to special abilities or properties of the individuum that is asserting said proposition. Simply put, epistemic justification *per rem* does not contain any argumentation *ad hominem* or *ex auctoritate*, whether of positive (Peter is a reliable person, therefore he is right) or negative (Peter often lies, therefore he is wrong) modality. Epistemic justification *per rem* presupposes that the truth values are properties of the propositions themselves while holding it impossible for the truth values to change whenever there is a change in the individual asserting them. This is to say that truth values are invariant with respect to the speaker. To use anachronistic terminology, it could be argued that Presocratic (and classical) philosophy on a general level subscribed to one or another variant of the correspondence theory of truth,[112] in which the truth-maker of any proposition is the factual state of the world (Wittgenstein's *Gesamtheit der Tatsachen*), and not some special property of the speaker that is asserting the proposition.

I have already mentioned the peculiar relationship between the Muse and the bard in earliest epic poetry. If Homer would have wanted to corroborate the truthfulness of his poems by pointing to the aid of the goddess who boasts perfect access to knowledge, it would have been a good example of a type of epistemic justification that lies beyond the boundaries of epistemic justification *per rem*. Homer would be substantiating the truth value of the propositions he is asserting via a divine inspiration, i.e. *ex auctoritate*, while the authority in this case is the Muse as an omniscient superhuman entity. In stark contrast to this narrative framing, the epistemic justification *per rem* is the staple of Presocratic discussion of the origins of religion and of ancient philosophy in general.

One could argue against this conclusion by pointing to Parmenides, for instance, who presented his philosophical opinions on a literary level as stemming from an immortal goddess (that is, quite like Homer),[113] but his *prooimion* seems to be a topical libation to epic poetry (the fragment is, after all, in dactylic hexameter) rather than a serious attempt to justify his own philosophical theses via divine inspiration.[114] His follower, Zeno, did not use the figure of Parmenides as an authority with special access to the divine wisdom and knowledge, but constructed a series of thought-experiments to further corroborate his teacher's attack on the reliability of the senses. Empedocles, a self-proclaimed 'immortal god',[115] also invoked the Muse,[116] but this eccentric behaviour reaped laughter, as attested by a charming story preserved by Diogenes Laertius, in which aging Empedocles hurled himself into the Etna volcano in order to do away with his mortal remains. By doing this, he reportedly wanted to make people believe that he ascended to heavens after disposing of his mortal shell (as is befitting of an 'immortal god'), but this philosophical apotheosis has been frustrated by the volcano that spat out one of his sandals.[117]

In Plato's *Crito*, Socrates is adamant in saying that he will never be persuaded by anything except for rational argumentation, and Cicero could be considered as a speaker for the entire ancient philosophical tradition when he claims that 'in discussion it is not so much weight of authority as force of argument that should be demanded' (*non enim tam in auctoritatis in disputando quam rationis momenta quaerenda sunt*).[118] In the lines that follow, he turns against the Pythagorean style of *ipse dixit* argumentation and it is only symptomatic that Pythagorean school has been in this regard considered a 'religious sect rather than a philosophical school'.[119] Jonathan Barnes observed quite rightly that there is most probably no ancient Greek philosophical or scientific text that would in any seriousness tried to prove propositions *ex auctoritate*,[120] and René Braun considered the concept of 'revelation' to be 'an anti-Hellenic term par excellence'.[121] Epistemic justification *per rem* might seem, especially in modern academia, an obvious triviality; but it is precisely in the domain of religion and its study in which a very different model of epistemic justification reigned supreme, as I will demonstrate in the chapters that follow.

3

Protectionist paradigm: Early Christian literature between faith and reason

O Blessed glorious Trinity,
Bones to Philosophy, but milke to faith.

John Donne[1]

In the context of the Presocratic theories of the origins of religion, I argued that the Greek philosophers have used epistemic justification *per rem* to defend their propositions, and quite consistently so. This mode of argumentation presupposed that the truth values of the propositions are independent of the specific attributes and properties of the person that is asserting them. However different the early approaches to religion exposed in the previous chapter may be, they do share a commitment to a reductionist naturalistic explanation that deconstructs religious experience into non-religious elements, as well as to the epistemic justification *per rem*, which is not particular only of the interpretations of religion proposed by Xenophanes, Democritus or Prodicus, but constitutes the standard of philosophical discourse in the Antiquity. I will now turn to the reflexion of religion in earliest Christian authors, focusing especially on the works dated to the first two centuries of the Common Era, irrespective of their canonical status. Excerpted are texts that make up New Testament (esp. gospels and Paul's epistles), the oldest apocryphal writings, so-called Apostolic literature and Greek and Latin apologetic literature, esp. Justin Martyr, Irenaeus and Tertullian. On occasion, I also make use of Clement of Alexandria and Origen.

The main argument in this chapter proceeds in several steps. First, I find it important to have a closer look at the traditional categories used to analyse early Christian literature, namely the dichotomy between 'faith' and 'reason' or 'religion' and 'philosophy'. Due to their extreme polysemy, these concepts are not very helpful in our trying to understand the earliest Christian thought. I therefore replace them with the concept of epistemic justification, introduced in brief in the previous chapter. My focus then lies with expounding the main argumentative strategies used by the earliest Christian writers to defend their central beliefs. I will conclude by arguing that the dominance of the epistemic justification *per rem* (or, *impersonal* epistemic justification), established in Greek philosophy, is replaced in early Christian literature by epistemic justification *per hominem* (or, *personal* epistemic justification).

3.1 Faith and reason

Even a brief glimpse of the bibliographical list of references to this chapter makes clear that framing epistemological problems of the earliest Christian authors in terms of 'faith' vs. 'reason' or 'philosophy' is a scholarly commonplace.[2] Venerable as this tradition is, echoing Paul's introduction of the dichotomy in 1 Corinthians, to be discussed below, its value as a heuristic tool is doubtful, mainly due to extreme polysemy of all central notions involved, and its uncritical use often leads to contradictory assessments of the main protagonists of early Christian literature. To wit, there are modern scholars who argued that 'Paul initiated a negative response to philosophy, especially to the rigour of rational thought';[3] for others, he 'works precariously on the treacherous edges of the realm of logicality, and the spirituality required in the recipient of the Pauline message is not a decoding agent that simply bypasses the hazards which lie in the way of reason' (whatever this obscure phrase might mean).[4] There are those who claim that introductory chapters of Justin Martyr's *Dialogue with Trypho* betray 'anti-philosophical character';[5] others suggest that, in Justin's work in general, 'every nerve is strained to demonstrate that, on assumptions every educated person would share, Christianity is reasonable and wholly tenable by the philosophically minded'.[6] On the basis of those famous and often misquoted lines of Tertullian's *On the Flesh of Christ* ('it is certain, because it is impossible'),[7] Latin apologist is proclaimed to be 'thoroughly rationalistic'; his paradox considered a 'manifesto on behalf of reason in religious faith',[8] even an 'exigency of reason'.[9] For other scholars, Tertullian's notion of faith display 'totalitarian requirements' and constitutes a 'pure position' which entails decisive rejection of any unrevealed wisdom;[10] his paradoxes a testimony to the fact that 'Christian revelation offended common sense and conventional philosophy'.[11]

I suspect that the irreconcilable interpretations of the central protagonists of the early Christianity are in part due to ambiguous use of complex general notions such as 'faith', 'reason' and 'philosophy', which leads me to propose an alternative methodological approach. I will analyse early Christian discourse related to the defence of faith using the concept of epistemic justification. In the previous chapter, epistemic justification was defined very generously as 'that which makes probable the truth of a proposition'.[12] We are engaging in an act of epistemic justification whenever we attempt to render our beliefs more plausible to others, and it is important to highlight the fact that the definition used here does not make any claims as to the nature of the methods used, or their eventual soundness. Given this interpretative framework, early Christian authors are undoubtedly engaging in an act of epistemic justification. At the very low end of the socio-political pecking order, struggling to establish an identity, first against the venerable antiquity of Jewish law and Greek wisdom, later against splintering groups later to be proclaimed heresies, the unlikely message of a Messiah nailed to the cross surely needed all epistemic justification it could muster. Incidentally, the earliest apologists were acutely aware of this. By means of an example, Justin Martyr introduced one of the possible warrants of Christian faith in the following manner:

> Though we could bring forward many other prophecies, we forbear, judging these sufficient for the persuasion of those who have ears to hear and understand; and

considering also that those persons are able to see that we do not make mere assertions without being able to produce proof, like those fables that are told of the so-called sons of Jupiter. For with what reason should we believe of a crucified man that He is the first-born of the unbegotten God, and Himself will pass judgment on the whole human race, unless we had found testimonies concerning Him published before He came and was born as man, and unless we saw that things had happened accordingly [...]?[13]

Indeed, even Tertullian, uncontroversially considered to be grossly inimical to philosophy and ratiocination, claimed that the Christian truth may be argued for by using the rule of faith, the antiquity of the Scripture and the testimony of spiritual powers.[14] Yet there is something rather specific in the methodology early Christian writers used to persuade their readers and listeners. In order to identify this specificity, I propose to differentiate between two basic modes of epistemic justification.

First, as introduced in the previous chapter, I term epistemic justification *per rem* or *impersonal* if and only if *the truth value of a proposition is being determined by a process which precludes any reference to special properties of the person asserting the proposition*. If the truth-maker of a proposition cannot be any special property of the person asserting the proposition, it means that arguments *ex auctoritate* are not to be admitted in discussion. Second, I term epistemic justification *per hominem* or *personal* if and only if *the truth value of a proposition is being determined by a process which is based on the reference to special properties of the person asserting the proposition*. If the truth-maker of a proposition is a special property of the person asserting the proposition, this means that arguments *ex auctoritate* are not only admitted in discussion, but they are actively employed to do heavy lifting in the process of persuading others of one's truth. In what follows, I will demonstrate that the personal mode of epistemic justification is highly characteristic of the early Christian discourse. To do so, I will use a slightly modified list 'warrants of Christian faith', introduced by Anthony Guerra in his discussion of Tertullian.[15]

3.2 Warrants of faith (1): Miracles

The functions that earliest Christian writers attributed to miracles are by no means uniform, but there can be little doubt that miracles play a decisive role in the process of epistemic justification of Christian belief. With respect to the miracles worked by Jesus, Hendrik van der Loos in his already classical work on the subject identified their four main functions, of which no less than three may be seen as directly connected with the process of epistemic justification: (1) *proof of identity*; (2) display of mercy; (3) *means of arousing faith*; (4) *sign*.[16] Notwithstanding some striking differences between the synoptics and John,[17] miracles performed by Jesus were clearly supposed to prove his real identity as the Messiah to the *reader* and consequently to validate the propositional content of anything he had to say. As it is not possible to discuss the miracles of Jesus systematically and exhaustively, several paradigmatic instances will have to suffice.[18]

In Matthew, we read that 'Jesus went throughout Galilee [...] curing every disease and every sickness among the people. So his fame spread throughout all Syria, and they brought to him all the sick, those who were afflicted with various diseases and pains, demoniacs, epileptics, and paralytics, and he cured them.'[19] Once the miracle-healer career of Jesus is thus summarized, the author of Matthew continues with the 'Sermon of the mount', establishing the moral substance of the 'good news', and 'the crows were astounded at his teaching, for he taught them as one having authority (ὡς ἐξουσίαν ἔχων), and not as their scribes'.[20] Should one inquire about the source of this authority, miracles clearly play a major role. Various groups of Jews with whom Jesus had to compete for followers were hardly lacking moral precepts – what they did lack was the ability to legitimize them by, for example, curing normally incurable medical conditions.[21]

Another section from Matthew makes the function of miracles in an act of epistemic justification even clearer. Jesus here reproaches the cities where 'most of his deeds of power (αἱ πλεῖσται δυνάμεις αὐτοῦ) had been done, because they did not repent (ὅτι οὐ μετενόησαν)'.[22] It stands to reason that in order to repent, the inhabitants of those cities would have to recognize Jesus as the Messiah first (thereby accepting what he says to be true, which would give them proximate cause to repent). The reproach only makes sense if we presuppose, as Jesus here certainly did, that the epistemic justification is being achieved by 'deeds of power' (i.e. miracles).[23]

As has been mentioned before, the miracles performed by Jesus in John are somewhat different from those worked in synoptics. They are less numerous, but far more spectacular and the author of the gospel explicitly presents them as acts of epistemic justification. To use but a single example: 'Jesus did this, the first of his signs, in Cana of Galilee, and revealed his glory; and his disciples believed in him.'[24] The miracle first serves as a proof of identity (ἐφανέρωσεν τὴν δόξαν αὐτοῦ), which inevitably leads to successful epistemic justification (ἐπίστευσαν εἰς αὐτὸν οἱ μαθηταὶ αὐτοῦ). In his authentic epistles, Paul used the very same argumentative strategy to establish his authority as an apostle and justify his words and actions.[25] Rebuking Jewish Christians in the church of Galatia for their desire to rigidly uphold the Law, he asked:[26]

> Did you experience so much for nothing? – if it really was for nothing. Well then, does God supply you with the Spirit and work miracles among you (ἐνεργῶν δυνάμεις ἐν ὑμῖν) by your doing the works of the law, or by your believing what you heard?[27]

In 1 Corinthians, Paul notes that his speech and proclamation 'were not with plausible words of wisdom, but with a demonstration of the Spirit and of power (ἐν ἀποδείξει πνεύματος καὶ δυνάμεως), so that your faith might rest not on human wisdom but on the power of God (ἐν δυνάμει θεοῦ)';[28] indeed, '[f]or the kingdom of God depends not on talk but on power (ἐν δυνάμει)'.[29] In the 'fool's speech' of 2 Corinthians, the apostle to the Gentiles again attempts to establish his authority by highlighting his power of producing miracles: 'The signs of a true apostle were performed among you with utmost patience, signs and wonders and mighty works (ἐν [...] σημείοις τε καὶ τέρασιν καὶ δυνάμεσιν)';[30] in the same vein, in Romans we read that Paul converted Gentiles 'by word and deed, by the power of signs and wonders (ἐν δυνάμει σημείων καὶ τεράτων), by the power of the Spirit of God'.[31]

Apocryphal literature of the first three centuries made even heavier use of miracles as means of epistemic justification than writings later awarded canonical status.[32] Many clear examples are provided by the Infancy Gospel of Thomas, in which the reaction of the crowds to the miracles performed by Jesus is explicitly described as that of 'awe' (ἐξεπλάγησαν; ὁ ὄχλος ἐθαύμασεν), promptly followed by conversion and recognition of Jesus' heavenly provenience (ἐδόξασαν τὸν Θεὸν ἐπὶ τῷ γεγονότι σημείῳ, καὶ προσεκύνησαν τῷ Ἰησοῦ; τὸ παιδίον οὐράνιόν ἐστιν).[33] In the Gospel of Nicodemus, titular character defends Jesus in front of Pilate precisely on the basis of his miraculous deeds: Jesus is able to work many astounding miracles (πολλὰ θαύματα ποιεῖ οἷα ἄνθρωπός ποτε οὐκ ἐποίησεν οὐδὲ μὴ ποιήσει), *therefore* let him go (Ἄφετε οὖν αὐτόν)![34]

Apocryphal acts in particular display an overabundance of the miracles worked by apostles and the function of the miracle as means of epistemic justification of Christian belief and means of conversion is often explicitly stated.[35] In its most radical form, miracles worked by apostles are framed in a sort of contest (ἀγών) between the apostle of Christianity and a follower of a pagan god (or Satan). A typical example of this narrative structure is an episode from the Acts of John: While visiting the Temple of Artemis in Ephesus, apostle John harshly reproached the local population (just like Jesus reproached Chorazin, Bethsaida and Capharnaum in Matthew, see above) for not converting and accepting the Christian faith in spite of many miracles performed by the apostle (πόσα εἴδετε δι᾽ ἐμοῦ τεράστια, ἰάσεις νόσων; καὶ ἔτι πεπήρωσθε τὰς καρδίας καὶ οὐ δύνασθε ἀναβλέψαι).[36] John then proposed a dramatic standoff that consisted in Ephesians praying to Artemis and John to praying to his God in order to find out who is mightier (and who, *therefore*, is a true God). The results of this ἀγών are quite remarkable, as John, with the help of his God, achieves a crushing victory, quite literally, in fact, since he destroys a good part of the temple and the altar of the pagan goddess while killing her priest in order to resurrect him after a short while. The outcome of this showdown is unsurprising. Ephesians are converted in crowds because they had seen the miracles of the apostle (νῦν ἐπεστρέψαμεν ὁρῶντές σου τὰ θαυμάσια).[37] A very similar episode is found in the famous *agon fidei* between Peter and Simon the Mage in the Acts of Peter, with identical results.[38]

Although the competence to work miracles in early Christian literature is usually limited to Jesus and his Apostles, we occasionally find testimonies for ordinary members of the Christian communities performing miracles in Jesus' name as well.[39] Justin Martyr knew about 'many of our people exorcising the possessed in the name of Jesus Christ';[40] Theophilus of Antioch writes that even 'up to the present day those who are possessed by demons are sometimes exorcized in the name of the real God' (οἱ δαιμονῶντες ἐνίοτε καὶ μέχρι τοῦ δεῦρο ἐξορκίζονται κατὰ τοῦ ὀνόματος τοῦ ὄντως θεοῦ),[41] and in one of his vitriolic attacks against philosophers, Tertullian contemptuously notes that philosophers (contrary to Christians) do not have the power to exorcize demons.[42] A valuable summary of the role of miracles in the epistemic justification of Christian faith is provided by Origenes:

The law and the prophets are filled with accounts as miraculous as that recorded of Jesus at the baptism about the dove and the voice from heaven. But I think that the miracles performed by Jesus are evidence that the Holy Spirit was seen then in the form of a dove, although Celsus attacks them by saying that he learnt how to do them among the Egyptians. And I will not mention these only, but also, as is reasonable, those which were done by Jesus' apostles. For without miracles and wonders they would not have persuaded those who heard new doctrines and new teachings to leave their traditional religion and to accept the apostles' teachings at the risk of their lives. Traces of that Holy Spirit who appeared in the form of a dove are still preserved among Christians. They charm daemons away and perform many cures and perceive certain things about the future according to the will of the Logos.[43]

Notwithstanding the necessarily limited selection of source material, it seems to me uncontroversial to conclude that one of the most important (albeit surely not singular) functions of miracles worked by Jesus, his apostles and (to a lesser extent) other members of the Christian community in the ante-Nicene Christianity is the epistemic justification of their beliefs. The power of miracles bestows an aura of authority on whoever is able to work them and miracle-stories are without a doubt valuable assets for the missionary work.[44] If we now attempt to identify the underlying logical form of the epistemic justification by miracles, it may be, modestly simplified, reconstructed in the following manner:

($p1$) If an individual x possesses a property P, with P being the ability to work true miracles, then the truth value of a proposition asserted by x is 'true'.

($p2$) Jesus, the apostles, and some of their followers demonstrated the possession of P (the ability to work true miracles).

(c) Propositions asserted by Jesus, the Apostles and some of their followers are true.

By linking the specific properties and abilities of an individual with the truth value of the propositions they might be entertaining, the admission of the conditional of the first premise ($p1$) clearly amounts to personal mode of epistemic justification. ($p1$) is, of course, not always explicitly stated (early Christian literature does not consist of a series of logical treatises), yet it has to be tacitly presupposed for the conclusion (c) to hold. Furthermore, the second premise ($p2$) is not without complications. How do we know, for instance, that Jesus really rose from the dead? Paul provides a tentative answer: We know it because he 'appeared to Cephas, then to the twelve. Then he appeared to more than five hundred brothers and sisters at one time, most of whom are still alive, though some have died. Then he appeared to James, then to all the apostles. Last of all, as to one untimely born, he appeared also to me.'[45] In other words, we know it because it has been reported to us by others. For an effective use of miracles as means of epistemic justification, the concept of a reliable witness is central.[46] This brings us to a second warrant of Christian belief.

3.3 Warrants of faith (2): Moral superiority

'If with merely human hopes I fought with wild animals at Ephesus, what would I have gained by it?'[47] In his struggle to establish the authority of an apostle, Paul made numerous appeals to his own superior moral character,[48] of which the most genuine example is provided by a powerful apophatic argumentation in his 'fool's speech',[49] where moral superiority is rhetorically connected with profound humility. A witness is a good witness only if he or she can be trusted and an epistemic justification of Christian faith by superior moral behaviour of Jesus and his followers eventually became a commonplace in the works of early Christian authors and in their attempts to justify their beliefs.

Ignatius of Antioch, drawing undoubtedly on Paul, argues thus against docetic views of Jesus: 'But if, as some atheists (that is, unbelievers) say, he suffered in appearance only (while they exist in appearance only!), why am I in chains? And why do I want to fight with wild beasts? If that is the case, I die for no reason; what is more, I am telling lies about the Lord.'[50] Of course, Ignatius does not die for no reason; *therefore*, he is not telling lies about the Lord. As he notes elsewhere, 'I am God's wheat, and I am being ground by teeth of the wild beasts, so that I may prove to be pure bread.'[51] In another letter, Ignatius complains that 'certain people' (τινες) are stubbornly denying Jesus and '[n]either the prophecies nor the law of Moses have persuaded them, nor, thus far, the gospel nor our own individual suffering (τὰ ἡμέτερα τῶν κατ' ἄνδρα παθήματα).'[52] For both Paul and Ignatius, the preparedness of Christians (including, of course, themselves) to undergo suffering, even death, is explicitly put forward as an act of epistemic justification, as a means of persuasion.[53]

The prototypical use of the epistemic justification by superior moral behaviour may be found especially in the phenomenon of martyrdom,[54] which came to exercise profound influence on the subsequent development of Christianity, both literal and historical – influence so great, in fact, that the very thought of martyrdom being used as means of epistemic justification still had the power to enrage Nietzsche in the late nineteenth century, writing that '[t]he idea that martyrs prove anything about the truth of a matter is so far from being true that I would like to deny that martyrs have ever had anything to do with the truth'.[55]

To use only one representative example, we may refer to the *Martyrdom of Polycarp*, combining both warrant by miracles and warrant by superior moral behaviour. After receiving a vision that foretold his martyrdom, Polycarp is led to the trial, refuses to abandon his belief, and receives the penalty of death in the form of being burned alive. Unshaken by his impending doom, Polycarp achieves the pinnacle of moral perfection, which is complemented by a miracle:

> And as a mighty flame blazed up, we saw a miracle (we, that is, to whom it was given to see), and we have been preserved in order that we may tell the rest what happened. For the fire, taking the shape of an arch, like the sail of a ship filled by the wind, completely surrounded the body of the martyr; and it was there in the middle, not like flesh burning but like bread baking or like gold and silver being

refined in a furnace. For we also perceived a very fragrant aroma, as if it were the scent of incense or some other precious spice.[56]

Eventually, a sword accomplished what the fire could not, but not without the last miracle – a dove broke out of his wound and the blood of the martyr extinguished the fires of the pyre. The moral of the story? 'This man was certainly one of the elect, the most remarkable Polycarp, who proved to be an apostolic and prophetic teacher in our own time, bishop of the catholic church in Smyrna.'[57] Polycarp is proved to be innocent, Christian belief is proved to be true, and, as Tertullian remarked, '[t]he oftener we are mown down by you, the more in number we grow; the blood of Christians is seed'.[58] *Pace* Nietzsche, martyrdom in early Christianity is, without any doubt, 'the greatest proof of faith' (*probatio maxima fidei*),[59] a proof that extends far beyond the first few centuries. As Candida Moss summarizes, 'for much of the Christian era, martyrdom was viewed [...] as an indication of Christianity's unique possession of religious truth. If Christians alone were prepared to die for their beliefs, it was thought, then there must be something special about Christianity'.[60]

However, not every instance of epistemic justification by superior moral behaviour had to be connected with violent suffering and martyrdom. In *Didache*, for instance, we find the following criterion for differentiating between true and false apostles:

> Now concerning the apostles and prophets, deal with them as follows in accordance with the rule of the gospel. Let every apostle who comes to you be welcomed as if he were the Lord. But he is not to stay for more than one day, unless there is need, in which case he may stay another. But if he stays three days, he is a false prophet. And when the apostle leaves, he is to take nothing except bread until he finds his next night's lodging. But if he asks for money, he is a false prophet.[61]

Once again, the truth or falsehood of a proposition is effectively determined as a function of a perceived moral profile of the individual entertaining that proposition. Humble apostles are true apostles; if there is a reason to doubt the moral character of an individual (occasioned by staying for multiple days or asking for money, thereby falling under the suspicion of greed), there is a reason to distrust what the individual has to say. Moreover, this model of argumentation is not alien even to well-educated proponents of early Christianity. For instance, as Fritz-Peter Hager observed,[62] two main reasons why Tertullian criticizes philosophers are the following: (1) there is a manifest discrepancy between their theories and the way they live their lives; and (2) philosophers stole their teachings from the prophets and disfigured it. Needless to say, both reasons are clear instances of what could be called an inverse of the warrant by superior moral behaviour – just as virtue is thought to engender truth, twisted morality is thought of as producing falsehoods.

This line of thought is further extended to reach the heights of Graeco-Roman pantheon. Early Christian apologists (just like Xenophanes many centuries before them) are quick to point out the moral shortcomings of the Olympians, thereby arguing for their non-existence. Aristides of Athens laments the fact that pagans took their gods for role-models and committed all sorts of criminal and impious acts, polluting both Heavens and Earth by their evil deeds.[63] When Athenagoras speaks about the 'absurdity' of Greek theology (τὸ ἀπίθανον [...] τῆς θεολογίας),[64] he points out the anthropomorphic character of Greco-Roman deities and their domination by passions in particular. He has only rhetorical questions for the Greeks:

> What nobility or value is there in such an account for us to believe that Cronus, Zeus, Core, and the rest are gods? [...] Do they not reject this mass of impious nonsense concerning the gods? Heaven is castrated; Cronus is bound and cast down into Tartarus; the Titans revolt; the Styx dies in battle (already this shows that they regard them as mortals); they fall in love with each other; they fall in love with human beings...[65]

Following a *tour de force* of cataloguing all sorts of perceived moral blemishes of the Greek gods, Clement of Alexandria ironically adds:

> Let such gods as these be worshipped by your wives, and let them pray that their husbands be such as these – so temperate; that, emulating them in the same practices, they may be like the gods. Such gods let your boys be trained to worship, that they may grow up to be men with the accursed likeness of fornication on them received from the gods.[66]

I do not believe it necessary to present the full list of early Christian authors who criticized pagan polytheistic religion and drew ontological conclusions about existence or non-existence of Greco-Roman deities on the basis of their moral profiles.[67] I only found it important to emphasize the connection between immorality and non-existence (falsehood) on one side and superior morality and existence (truth) on the other.[68] To summarize the epistemic justification by superior moral behaviour in a simplified logical form used above:

(p1) If an individual x possesses a property P, with P being superior moral behaviour, especially in face of a great cost to their well-being, then the truth value of a proposition asserted by x is 'true'.

(p2) Jesus, the Apostles, and early Christian martyrs demonstrated the possession of P (superior moral behaviour).

(c) Propositions asserted by Jesus, the Apostles and early Christian martyrs are true.

Inverted argument would, of course, apply to pagan philosophers and the deities they worship: The martyrs are proving the truth of the belief they are offering their life for and, on the contrary, immoral conduct of philosophers demasks their teachings as falsehoods and the immoral conduct of the pagan gods unveils them as non-existent false idols.

3.4 Warrants of faith (3): divine inspiration

If the gospels and the acts of the apostles, both canonical and apocryphal, relied heavily on the warrants by miracles and superior moral behaviour, another important early

Christian literary genre, namely apocalypses, seeks to establish the authority by means of epistemic justification by spiritual testimony and divine inspiration, by which I understand any appeal to supernatural source of the knowledge that is being communicated. In the only canonical writing belonging to this genre, the introduction explicitly states that the revelation is that of 'Jesus Christ, which God gave him (ἣν ἔδωκεν αὐτῷ ὁ θεός) to show his servants what must soon take place; he made it known by sending his angel to his servant John (ἐσήμανεν ἀποστείλας διὰ τοῦ ἀγγέλου αὐτοῦ τῷ δούλῳ αὐτοῦ Ἰωάννῃ)'.[69] The contents of the apocalypse are epistemically justified by means of providing a link from the person 'publishing' the contents ('John') to the ultimate, unerring source of knowledge (God) *via* trustworthy mediators (angel, Jesus).[70]

Warrant by spiritual testimony is obviously not limited to apocalypses (canonical or otherwise), but features heavily in Paul's epistles, which is not surprising, especially if we assume, with David Aune, that Paul is a 'functional equivalent' of an Old Testament prophet, although he never uses the term to describe himself.[71] The apostle is 'sent neither by human commission nor from human authorities, but through Jesus Christ and God the Father, who raised him from the dead (οὐκ ἀπ' ἀνθρώπων οὐδὲ δι' ἀνθρώπου ἀλλὰ διὰ Ἰησοῦ Χριστοῦ καὶ θεοῦ πατρὸς τοῦ ἐγείραντος αὐτὸν ἐκ νεκρῶν)',[72] with Paul further clarifying that 'the gospel that was proclaimed by me is not of human origin; for I did not receive it from a human source, nor was I taught it, but I received it through a revelation of Jesus Christ' (τὸ εὐαγγέλιον τὸ εὐαγγελισθὲν ὑπ' ἐμοῦ ὅτι οὐκ ἔστιν κατὰ ἄνθρωπον· οὐδὲ γὰρ ἐγὼ παρὰ ἀνθρώπου παρέλαβον αὐτό, οὔτε ἐδιδάχθην, ἀλλὰ δι' ἀποκαλύψεως Ἰησοῦ Χριστοῦ).[73]

Elsewhere, Paul notes that 'these things God has revealed to us through the spirit' (ἡμῖν δὲ ἀπεκάλυψεν ὁ θεὸς διὰ τοῦ πνεύματος)[74] and he argues that the beneficiaries of this special kind of knowledge (that is, knowledge provided 'directly' by God) are exempt from any further obligations to produce additional proofs, because '[t]hose who are spiritual discern all things, and they are themselves subject to no one else's scrutiny' (πνευματικὸς ἀνακρίνει [τὰ] πάντα, αὐτὸς δὲ ὑπ' οὐδενὸς ἀνακρίνεται).[75] Finally, the role of the Spirit is clearly spelled out in 2 Corinthians, where Paul, just like Homer almost a thousand years before him, claims to know nothing. For Homer, all knowledge comes from a Muse, the warden of memory;[76] for Paul, from Spirit and, ultimately, God: 'Not that we are competent of ourselves to claim anything as coming from us; our competence is from God (ἡ ἱκανότης ἡμῶν ἐκ τοῦ θεοῦ), who has made us competent to be ministers of a new covenant, not of letter but of spirit; for the letter kills, but the Spirit gives life'.[77]

For later Christian authors, spiritual testimony as a means of authentication usually complements apostle's immediate relationship with Jesus;[78] for Justin Martyr, gifts of the Spirit consist in spiritual wisdom, prophecy and power to perform miracles;[79] and Irenaeus of Lyons assures his readers that 'after our Lord rose from the dead, [the apostles] were invested with power from on high when the Holy Spirit came down [upon them], were filled from all [His gifts], and had perfect knowledge'.[80] As Denis Farkasfalvy explains,[81] the apostles in Irenaeus' treatise *Against Heresies* 'are presented as entirely depending on Christ, having no other task but to channel to mankind the revelations of the Incarnate Word', but the bishop of Lyons also 'declares that it is through the actual and active presence of the Spirit that that the apostles carry out their preaching'.

Notwithstanding minor differences (notably the validity of extra-apostolic appeals to spiritual testimony in Montanism, embraced at one point by Tertullian), the basic mechanism of the warrant by spiritual testimony is similar to the epistemic justifications of faith by miracles and superior moral behaviour introduced above. Summarized in a simplified logical format:

> (p1) If an individual x possesses a property P, with P being special access to the ultimate source of knowledge (God), directly or by means of reliable mediation (Angel, Spirit, etc.), then the truth value of a proposition asserted by x is 'true'.

> (p2) Jesus and the Apostles demonstrated the possession of P (special access to the ultimate source of knowledge).

> (c) Propositions asserted by Jesus and the Apostles and early Christian martyrs are true.

Epistemic justification by spiritual testimony, too, constitutes an instance of personal epistemic justification, since the truth value of a proposition is dependent on the unique personal access to the ultimate source of knowledge and independent on any external verification.

3.5 Warrants of faith (4): Prophecy

Prima facie, one could question the inclusion of the argument from the Scripture under the heading of personal epistemic justification, because it bears superficial resemblance to well-accepted and entirely impersonal type of epistemic justification, namely the evaluation of hypotheses by the success or failure of the predictions they make. Seen from this vantage point, it seems as if the prophets of the Old Testament were making predictions about the coming of the Messiah which are in turn corroborated (that is to say, epistemically justified) by the appearance of Jesus in Galilee and Jerusalem. Undoubtedly, this is how early Christian authors understood the issue.

The core of the argument Justin Martyr makes in favour of a plausibility of Christian belief is constituted by the fulfilment of the prophecies,[82] an argument, incidentally, that played a key role in his personal conversion.[83] Of course, it is not only Jesus' redemptive death that has been prophetically announced. To use another example, Tertullian makes the same argument about the persecution of Christians:

> All that is taking place around you was fore-announced; all that you now see with your eye was previously heard by the ear. [...] While we suffer the calamities, we read of them in the Scriptures; as we examine, they are proved. Well, the truth of a prophecy, I think, is the demonstration of its being from above.[84]

Tertullian, in other words, is operating with a concept scholars termed 'historical correspondence theory'[85] or 'historical rationality' consisting in the 'perfect correspondence between what was foretold in the Old and fulfilled in the New Testaments'.[86] Scripture, legitimized by the fulfilment of the prophecies it contains, is considered to be divinely inspired; also for Irenaeus, 'the Scriptures are indeed perfect, since they were spoken by the Word of God and His Spirit'.[87]

From what has been just said, the inclusion of the warrant by Scripture under the personal mode of epistemic justification does not seem to make much sense. Granted, some authors, like Irenaeus, consider the prophets to be divinely inspired, which would point us to the direction of a warrant by spiritual testimony discussed above, but eventually, the argument from the prophecies is established as a perfect correspondence between a set of predictions and their fulfilment in the coming of Christ. As Bernard Sesboüé notes in discussion of this type of argument in Irenaeus, 'not only is the prophecy a proof of the event [*sc.* of Christ's coming], but the event becomes in its turn the proof of the prophecy: Word Incarnated is sent just as it has been announced'.[88]

Notwithstanding the obvious issue with circularity, the reason why the warrant by Scriptures belongs firmly to the personal mode of epistemic justification lies elsewhere. In order for a warrant from the scripture to hold, it has to be established first that Jesus was Christ, the Messiah foretold by Jewish prophets. After all, Jesus could have well been an impostor, only claiming to be a Messiah, not being one – in fact, this is precisely what many of his contemporaries thought and Jesus was by no means the only one to claim the title.[89] Only if Jesus really is the Messiah, it makes sense to argue from the fulfilment of Scriptures; if Jesus is no Messiah, prophecies cannot be considered to be fulfilled in him and the argument is void. In other words, an additional extra-scriptural proof that Jesus is Messiah is a *sine qua non* for the warrant by Scripture. This simply means that any argument from the fulfilment of the prophecies requires a premise in which it is assumed that Jesus is the Messiah.

Can this be accomplished? Certainly, but only by using other types of personal epistemic justification, such as warrants by miracles, superior moral behaviour or spiritual testimony. Robert Grant reaches similar conclusions, despite not working with the concept of epistemic justification at all, when he states that '[t]he underlying axiom which made prophecy credible was the omnipotence of God. No matter how stable the present world might seem, no matter how apparently unbreakable the chain of cause and effect, God would act and nothing could resist his power. Thus the miracle stories at the same time reflect this belief and are used to confirm it.'[90] Warrant by Scripture (or fulfilment of prophecies) therefore requires an instance of a personal epistemic justification for its conclusions to be valid.

3.6 Warrants of faith (5): Tradition

Lastly, another warrant of the truth of the Christian belief may be found in tradition. For most of the early Christian authors, the power of tradition consists in an unbroken lineage beginning from God as the ultimate source of knowledge and spreading through reliable channels up to their present day. This line of thought has been important for the self-definition of early Christian communities as keepers and guardians of the 'new covenant' preached by Jesus and his apostles. In the First Letter of Clement, we read that '[t]he apostles received the gospel for us from the Lord Jesus Christ; Jesus the Christ was sent forth from God. [. . .] So, preaching both in the country and in the towns, they appointed their first fruits, when they had tested them by the Spirit, to be bishops and deacons for the future believers'.[91]

Irenaeus adds prophets to the equation, when he speaks about the 'preaching of the Church, which the prophets proclaimed (as I have already demonstrated), but which Christ brought to perfection, and the apostles have handed down',[92] thus establishing the truth that has been 'announced by the prophets, taught by the Lord, delivered by the apostles, kept alive and passed on by the church specifically by means of its presbyterial succession'.[93] A lengthier section from Tertullian is well worth citing in full, since it clearly explains the role of the tradition in context of other warrants introduced earlier and brings them together into a coherent, persuasive whole:

> Christ Jesus [...] did, while He lived on earth, Himself declare what He was, what He had been, what the Father's will was which He was administering, what the duty of man was which He was prescribing; (and this declaration He made,) either openly to the people, or privately to His disciples, of whom He had chosen the twelve chief ones to be at His side, and whom He destined to be the teachers of the nations. Accordingly, after one of these had been struck off, He commanded the eleven others, on His departure to the Father, to go and teach all nations, who were to be baptized into the Father, and into the Son, and into the Holy Ghost. [...] they obtained the promised power of the Holy Ghost for the gift of miracles and of utterance; and after first bearing witness to the faith in Jesus Christ throughout Judaea, and founding churches (there), they next went forth into the world and preached the same doctrine of the same faith to the nations. They then in like manner founded churches in every city, from which all the other churches, one after another, derived the tradition of the faith, and the seeds of doctrine, and are every day deriving them, that they may become churches. Indeed, it is on this account only that they will be able to deem themselves apostolic, as being the offspring of apostolic churches.[94]

Again, it is not difficult to see why the warrant by tradition belongs firmly to the personal mode of epistemic justification; or rather, as has been the case with warrant by fulfilment of prophecies, requires personal epistemic justification as a *sine qua non*. This argument further does not concern exclusively the Church, but could be seen as recursive extension of the warrant by spiritual testimony: The trajectory of truth leads from God to Jesus, Jesus as Christ lends authority to both prophets (by fulfilment of prophecies) and apostles (by endowing them with Holy Spirit), and the teaching of both, as it has been written down in parts of the Old and the New Testament, is further disseminated by growing Christian communities, eventually coming together as one Church.

3.7 Athens and Jerusalem

Following this sketchy overview of the basic types of personal epistemic justification in early Christian writings, I will show that (1) the endorsement of the personal mode of epistemic justification does *not* preclude the use of the impersonal mode; yet (2) the impersonal mode is of limited applicability and in case of an apparent conflict between the two modes of epistemic justification, personal mode takes preference. The relationship between personal and impersonal mode is thus hierarchical, not mutually exclusive. The attitude of early Christian writers towards the impersonal mode of epistemic justification can be conveniently gauged by their reception of Greek philosophy, because, notwithstanding the variety of Hellenistic philosophical schools, impersonal epistemic justification provides a common foundation for most, if not all of them. It is important to emphasize again that none of the early Christian authors reject impersonal epistemic justification *a priori*. Recent studies established this conclusion with respect to Paul[95] and it is trivial to show that this thesis holds for later authors as well.

Justin Martyr develops an original approach based on the concept of the 'Spermatic Word', which provides rudimentary knowledge even to the outsiders: 'For each man spoke well in proportion to the share he had of the spermatic word, seeing what was related to it.'[96] Likewise, when Irenaeus is discussing the question of whether the angels could have been ignorant of the Supreme God, he claims that the truth of monotheism can be established without an appeal to revelation on purely rational grounds, because 'although no one knows the Father, except the Son, nor the Son except the Father, and those to whom the Son will reveal Him, yet all [beings] do know this one fact at least, because reason, implanted in their minds, moves them, and reveals to them [the truth] that there is one God, the Lord of all.'[97] Even Tertullian, who, as will be shown below, has not been very accommodative of pagan philosophy, claims that 'the great majority of the human race, though ignorant even of Moses' name, not to mention his written works, do for all that know Moses' God',[98] since '[t]he knowledge inherent in the soul since the beginning is God's endowment',[99] or, as he puts it in another treatise with respect to the immortality of the soul, 'some things are known even by nature'.[100] However, impersonal epistemic justification in things divine, which eventually will be known as 'natural theology', brings about two major problems.

Firstly, although reason unaided by revelation can, according to early Christian writers, establish some truths (e.g. 'God exists'; 'God is one'; 'soul is immortal'), it is hopelessly deficient in establishing others, often even more important truths (e.g. 'God sent Jesus as the Messiah to redeem humanity of its sins by dying on the cross'). Secondly, whenever there is an apparent conflict between revealed truth warranted by personal epistemic justification and any other type of knowledge (warranted by impersonal epistemic justification), revealed truth is always accorded preferential status. Therefore, impersonal epistemic justification in early Christianity stands subordinated to the personal epistemic justification.

Suppose we establish a 'minimal version' of Christianity by using the Pauline formula of faith from 1 Corinthians, which contains the following propositions: (1) Jesus died on the cross; (2) Jesus has been bodily raised from the dead; (3) his death and resurrection took place in order to redeem humanity.[101] This 'minimal version' is by no means chosen arbitrarily, as Chapter 15 of 1 Corinthians is the most cited section of the Pauline corpus in Christian writings of the second century[102] and Paul himself makes the importance of these propositions abundantly clear, since 'if Christ has not been raised, then our proclamation has been in vain and your faith has been in vain' (εἰ δὲ Χριστὸς οὐκ ἐγήγερται, κενὸν ἄρα [καὶ] τὸ κήρυγμα ἡμῶν, κενὴ καὶ ἡ πίστις ὑμῶν).[103]

To establish their truth, one may use the argumentative strategy of personal epistemic justification, as it has been presented above, but is there any conceivable way to warrant their truth by means of impersonal epistemic justification? The answer is an unqualified 'no',[104] or even worse. Here, both basic methodological approaches clash and Paul is well aware of that. This is how, famously, the apostle of the Gentiles solves the conflict at the beginning of the letter:

> For the message about the cross is foolishness (μωρία) to those who are perishing, but to us who are being saved it is the power of God. For it is written, 'I will destroy the wisdom of the wise, and the discernment of the discerning I will thwart.' Where is the one who is wise (σοφός)? Where is the scribe? Where is the debater of this age (συζητητὴς τοῦ αἰῶνος τούτου)? Has not God made foolish (ἐμώρανεν) the wisdom of the world? For since, in the wisdom of God, the world did not know God through wisdom, God decided, through the foolishness of our proclamation (διὰ τῆς μωρίας τοῦ κηρύγματος), to save those who believe. For Jews demand signs (σημεῖα) and Greeks desire wisdom (σοφίαν), but we proclaim Christ crucified, a stumbling block (σκάνδαλον) to Jews and foolishness (μωρίαν) to Gentiles, but to those who are the called, both Jews and Greeks, Christ the power of God and the wisdom of God. For God's foolishness is wiser than human wisdom (τὸ μωρὸν τοῦ θεοῦ σοφώτερον τῶν ἀνθρώπων ἐστίν), and God's weakness is stronger than human strength.[105]

Whenever the impersonal epistemic justification stands in the way of revelation, it is simply discarded. Indeed, 'Paul leaves not the slightest doubt that God has rejected all that rests on merely human wisdom';[106] 'the cross stands in absolute, uncompromising contradiction to human wisdom';[107] '[t]he cross makes hash of all secular and religious attempts based on human wisdom to make sense of God and the world'.[108] However damning these interpretations are for the human faculty of reasoning, almost echoing Luther's critique of 'that beautiful whore' Reason,[109] David Garland is right in adding that '[w]e should not jump to the conclusion that Paul denigrates the human faculty of reason or thinks that faith and reason are irreconcilable'.[110] Using the terms introduced in this chapter, personal and impersonal modes of epistemic justification are not irreconcilable in general, but in this particular instance they unfortunately are, and 'reason' has to make way. Paul's solution, the very first Christian one recorded in writing, served as a blueprint for virtually all early Christian authors, even those who did not shudder from expressing a degree of admiration for Greek philosophy.[111]

Justin readily grants Greek philosophers some access to the truth through the participation on the 'spermatic word' (he even considers all those who lived μετὰ λόγου Christians, including the likes of Socrates and Heraclitus),[112] yet this access is severely limited. First, the provenience of the very term λόγος σπερματικός does not lie with Greek philosophical tradition (notably Middle Platonism; some argue for Stoic origin),[113] but in the expression 'Word of God', prevalent in the Septuagint.[114] More importantly, Justin very openly asserts that revealed Christian doctrine seems to be 'greater than all human teaching' (μεγαλειότερα μὲν οὖν πάσης ἀνθρωπείου διδασκαλίας)[115] and 'loftier than all human philosophy' (πάσης μὲν φιλοσοφίας ἀνθρωπείου ὑπέρτερα);[116] moreover, the use of philosophy in the exegesis of the Scripture is more than limited, as their proper interpretation always requires an element of divine grace to be present.[117]

As Winrich Löhr summarizes, for Justin, '[t]he poets and philosophers had access to divine truth because they read scripture and derived their wisdom from it. But their insight was partial at best; it is only with the incarnation that the fullness of divine truth became accessible'.[118] This 'imperialistic view of history',[119] typical not only for Justin, but for the early Christian discourse in general, considers the knowledge arrived at by means of impersonal epistemic justification to be subordinate to the revelation. It can be hardly denied that '[u]ltimately, Justin establishes a Christological criterion of truth' or that the 'the controlling factor is the truth as it is in Christ which for Justin constitutes an exclusive and exhaustive touchstone'.[120] The subordination of philosophical method to revelation becomes even clearer if one compares the appeals to reason in a Greek philosophical text and a Christian one – Cyrille Crépey, who did just that by juxtaposing Marcus Aurelius' *Meditations* with Justin's *oeuvre*, concluded that for the Roman emperor there is no other authority outside of the reason itself, for Justin, 'human wisdom can attain but a part of the truth, not the whole truth that is revealed only by Christ himself, Reason in the flesh'.[121]

Unlike Justin, Irenaeus is not too preoccupied with the opinions of philosophers and this fact alone probably speaks for itself. There is only one single instance of a positive valuation of a Greek philosopher, with the bishop of Lyons noting that 'Plato is proved to be more religious than these men [*sc*. Marcion and his followers], for he allowed that the same God was both just and good, having power over all things, and Himself executing judgment, expressing himself thus'[122] – however, as William Schoedel remarked, 'one is left wondering whether a somewhat grudging comparison of Plato with Marcion speaks highly of the former'.[123] More to the point, in another section of his work, Irenaeus even sets up an interesting argument in favour of the irreducibility of the revelation to 'natural theology':

> But I will merely say, in opposition to these men [*sc*. philosophers] – Did all those who have been mentioned, with whom you have been proved to coincide in expression, know, or not know, the truth? If they knew it, then the descent of the Saviour into this world was superfluous. For why [in that case] did He descend? Was it that He might bring that truth which was [already] known to the knowledge of those who knew it?[124]

The relationship between 'faith' and human capacity of unaided ratiocination in the writings of Clement of Alexandria is extremely complicated and a detailed analysis would require much more space than what may be allotted to this problem here. His notions of 'truth' and especially 'faith' are highly polysemic[125] and his free, syncretic use of various epistemological systems does not help clarity,[126] yet I find it uncontroversial to conclude that for Clement, just like for Justin and Irenaeus, the impersonal mode of epistemic justification is subordinated to the personal mode and highest authority is accorded to the Scripture, which is 'not a mere book that has authority in the religious community' but 'the voice of God'.[127] His concept of the 'perfect gnosis' described in the *Stromata* is only a superstructure for well-educated Christians and, as has been noted, the difference between illiterate Christian of the Faith and the well-educated Christian of the Gnosis is that of degree, not of kind (unlike the difference between Christians and pagans, which is, of course, qualitative).[128] By all standards, philosophy is a secondary occupation, mere 'propedeutics that is to be surpassed'[129] and – as Clement never tires to point out – everything worthwhile in Greek philosophical writings is stolen from the ancient Jewish wisdom anyway.[130]

As we have seen earlier, Tertullian allows for some knowledge obtained by an impersonal type of epistemic justification to be valid (this much is largely agreed upon),[131] yet this allowance abruptly ends the moment 'reason' starts objecting against the revealed truth warranted by impersonal mode of epistemic justification. When people say that Jesus is not raised, because 'what is dead is dead', Tertullian 'shall remember that the heart of the multitude is reckoned by God as ashes, and that the very wisdom of the world is declared foolishness'.[132]

Elsewhere, he notes that if philosophers happen to be right, it is only by 'some happy chance' (*prospero errore*) or 'through blind luck alone' (*caeca feliciate*);[133] if impersonal epistemic justification fails to vindicate itself in the face of the power of the baptism to save,[134] or vis-à-vis the resurrection of Christ, so much worse for impersonal epistemic justification: 'The Son of God was crucified: I am not ashamed – because it is shameful. The Son of God died: it is immediately credible – because it is silly. He was buried and rose again: it is certain – because it is impossible.'[135]

While there is a standing tradition of scholarship that understands these sections as being merely topical and influenced by Aristotelian rhetoric,[136] the argument remains unconvincing. In what has been aptly called a 'dialectic of the opposites',[137] Tertullian asks: 'What indeed has Athens to do with Jerusalem? What concord is there between the Academy and the Church? What between heretics and Christians?';[138] and further: 'So, then, where is there any likeness between the Christian and the philosopher? Between the disciple of Greece and of heaven? Between the man whose object is fame, and whose object is life? Between the talker and the doer? Between the man who builds up and the man who pulls down? Between the friend and the foe of error? Between one who corrupts the truth, and one who restores and teaches it? Between its chief and its custodier?'[139] The very linguistic and stylistic features of these sections mirror those segments of the New Testament writings in which two irreconcilable opposites are being compared.[140]

The powerful rhetoric of these lines led some scholars to view Tertullian as a champion of 'faith' against 'reason',[141] yet this interpretation does not seem to make justice to someone hailed by modern scholarship as 'first theologian of the West'.[142] Neither can Tertullian be seen as a proponent of essentially modern rationality.[143] Rather, as Justo González noted,[144] Tertullian '*is* saying that the criterion of natural reason, usually valid, is not always ultimately valid, for that reason itself shows that God, who is the ultimate deciding factor, does not have to subject himself to it. He *is* also saying that in such cases the criterion of truth is not some inner logic which one can discover by purely rational investigation, but rather whether God did or did not will the event in question – in this case the incarnation and its sequel – to happen.' In other words, the procedure of impersonal epistemic justification is valid if and only if it does not threaten revealed wisdom established by means of personal epistemic justification. The use of impersonal epistemic justification is thus limited in scope as well as subordinated with respect to its value.

Established primacy of personal epistemic justification is then vital if when used to defend what Irenaeus calls 'the rule of truth'[145] (*regula veritatis*) and Tertullian 'rule of faith' (*regula fidei*).[146] While there have been attempts to connect the development of this concept with anti-heretical polemics,[147] I am rather inclined to accept the views of Bengt Hägglund, for whom the rule is emphatically not 'summary of the doctrine invented or formulated in the fight against heresies', but 'the faith itself, the truth itself'.[148] Its role is to preserve the purity of Christian faith and defend it against any intrusions by impersonal mode of epistemic justification (and heterodox interpretations thereof) – indeed, 'when the biblical message seems to go against reason, rule of faith has something to say about it'.[149]

3.8 Protectionist paradigm and epistemic justification

In confrontation with Christianity, Greek philosophical tradition, and thereby the mode of impersonal epistemic justification, initially played an important, but clearly subservient role, which only withered and waned as the centuries went on.[150] As André Beckaert pithily observed, 'philosophy did not absorb Christianity, but it got absorbed by it'.[151] Religion (in this case, Christianity) cannot and will not be subordinated to 'secular' wisdom, whether in the form of philosophy (as was the case, by and large, in the Antiquity) or in the shape of science (as it is today). Quite to the contrary, the truth of one's religious convictions may be epistemically justified only via the *personal* or *per hominem* argumentative strategies. In fact, this much has been canonically observed by Aurelius Augustinus in the rather famous section of his treatise *On Christian Doctrine* (*De doctrina Christiana*).

On the one hand, Augustine argued that Christians should not hold pagan philosophy in unmitigated contempt.[152] He finds a suitable analogy in the exodus of the Israelites from Egypt: Just like the chosen people made good use of the Egyptian vessels made of gold and silver and of the garments that pertained to the idolatrous enemies and oppressors, Christians may distil some good out of 'liberal arts' (*liberales disciplinae*), despite their pagan origins.[153] Even relatively indulgent Augustine, however, hastens to add that the revealed truth of Christianity cannot be the subject of secular sciences and returns to his analogy: Just like the gold, silver and garments of Egypt cannot be compared with the riches that Jerusalem boasted under the king Solomon, all pagan science and philosophy (*cuncta scientia collecta de libris Gentium*) cannot withstand comparison with the 'science' of the Divine Scriptures (*scientia divinarum Scripturarum*).[154]

Thomas Aquinas argued in the same way, albeit on a more general level. In the *Summa theologica*, he differentiates between philosophy and revealed knowledge thusly: He first defines philosophical disciplines as those that explore the world and our place in it, and this exploration is effectuated by human reason (*philosophicas disciplinas, quae ratione humana investigantur*). Then he does contrast this rational exploration of the world with another kind of doctrine, namely the one that has the power to secure our salvation and is based not on human reason, but on the revelation (*doctrinam quaedam secundum relevationem divinam*).[155] He further specifies that the 'science' that thematizes revealed knowledge is both speculative and practical at the same time, but at any rate vastly surpasses all other speculative and practical sciences (*omnes alias transcendit tam speculativas quam practicas*).[156] Our *doctor angelicus* then evaluates this science from the standpoint of reliability (*secundum certitudinem*) and from the standpoint of its importance for our human life (*secundum dignitatem*). With respect to reliability, Thomas argues that while all other sciences are corroborated only by limited and imperfect human reason (*ex naturali lumine rationis humanae*), the 'science' of revelation is based on unerring and perfect divine reason (*ex lumine divinae scientiae*). With respect to importance, all other sciences are dealing with that which is subordinated to human reason (*quae rationi subduntur*), but the science of revelation makes its subject that which surpasses human reason (*quae sua altitudine rationem transcendunt*).

Virtually until the publication of Pomponazzi's ground-breaking *De incantationibus* (1556, written at the beginning of the sixteenth century and kept on a shelf for decades out of a fear of inquisitorial persecution), that already contained some elements of the return of the naturalistic paradigm,[157] the relationship between 'faith' and 'reason' during the entire *interregnum* of Christianity in the Latin West may be summarized by the words of Petrus Damiani, who, as is well known, claimed that philosophy is useful only as a handmaid to theology.[158] Uncontrolled, unbridled philosophical investigation is an exercise in futility at best and a dangerous distraction at worst. Quite like the apostles in the lower half of Raphael's *Transfiguration*, unable to heal the possessed boy without Jesus' aid, unaided human reason is, in the context of the protectionist paradigm, unable to reach the true knowledge of the sacred.

We have seen in the previous chapter that the naturalistic paradigm aimed to explain the religious experience by reducing it to non-religious elements. Protectionist paradigm not only emphatically denies that such a reductive explanation is possible, but it also subordinates all rational knowledge to the exigencies of faith – or, to use terms introduced in these two chapters, it subordinates epistemic justification *per rem* to epistemic justification *per hominem*.

4

Naturalism and protectionism in the study of religions (1): The beginnings

I do not say that the Science of Religion is all gain. No, it entails losses, and losses of many things which we hold dear. But this I will say, that, as far as my humble judgment goes, it does not entail the loss of anything that is essential to true religion, and that if we strike the balance honestly, the gain is immeasurably greater than the loss.

Max Müller[1]

In the previous two chapters, I have shown that the roots of the two opposing paradigms used to conceptualize human religious experience were constituted already in the ancient philosophical and religious discourse. Presocratic philosophers, using epistemic justification *per rem*, formulated hypotheses of the origins of religion in the form of reductionistic strategies that explained the existence of religion by identifying its constitutive elements which, in themselves, lack any religious dimension. By this, I simply mean that a reductionist explanation used in the naturalist paradigm always intends to provide such an interpretation of the origin of religious beliefs and experiences as to make the 'objective existence' of deities redundant, and therefore (as dictated by the principle of parsimony) unlikely. On the other hand, in the early Christian literature, I have identified ample use of epistemic justification *per hominem* and an approach to religion which *a priori* rejected reductionism and placed religious experience beyond and above every philosophical or scientific effort to explain such an experience. By this, I simply mean that the non-reductive approaches employed in the protectionist paradigm intend to provide such an interpretation of the origins of religious beliefs and experience as to make the 'objective existence' of deities necessary.

In the following two chapters, I will analyse the central works of the most important modern scholars of the study of religions from the second half of the nineteenth century and the twentieth century with respect to their methodological inclination to either naturalism or protectionism. The analysis is necessarily selective and does not, in any case, aim to present an exhaustive account of the history of the modern study of religions in the past two centuries.[2] I will concern myself primarily with authors who – explicitly or implicitly – subscribed themselves to either naturalist or protectionist paradigm, and on those authors who directly criticized one of these positions without necessarily endorsing its counterpart. I apply the term 'paradigm' in accordance with the common use in the philosophy of science for designating a 'big' theory of religion,[3] i.e. a theory that is formulating clear methodological principles and standards of research and, at the same time, attempting to answer fundamental questions related to the origins of religious beliefs and ideas. I use the categories 'naturalism' and 'protectionism' as 'ideal types' (Weber) or blanket terms that loosely share certain 'family resemblances' (Wittgenstein).

The basic differences between naturalism and protectionism can be illustrated as follows:

1. Naturalism assumes that it is possible to explain the origins of religious beliefs and ideas completely by reducing these beliefs and ideas to other, non-religious, constitutive elements. Conversely, protectionism assumes that religious experience is irreducible in principle.
2. Supporters of the naturalistic paradigm generally argue that religion is in a certain sense always an illusion and that its central concepts (especially deities) exist only as shared mental concepts, not as 'objective realities'. Supporters of the protectionist paradigm claim that religion reflects an authentic human religious experience that is ultimately caused by God or some 'sacred' reality.
3. Naturalism denies that a researcher in the field of study of religions would require a personal religious experience or conviction to do his or her job well. Conversely, protectionism claims that a personal religious experience or conviction is a *sine qua non* for any meaningful work in the field of the study of religions.
4. Naturalism denies that the scientific interpretation of religious experience should be limited only to 'understanding' and denies that the ultimate criterion for the truth value of our propositions concerning any religion should be supplied by active practitioners of that religion. To the contrary, supporters of the protectionist paradigm often claim that the final verdict on the interpretation of religious experience may be pronounced only by those who took part in such a religious experience.
5. Naturalism denies that the study of religions as a scientific or academic discipline is a domain *sui generis* and calls for consilience with other scientific disciplines. Protectionism, on the other hand, claims that religion is *sui generis* with respect to human knowledge and experience and that the study of religions must likewise use distinctive theoretical-methodological approaches in order to describe adequately this supposedly unique domain of human existence.

It is clear from what has been just said that I do not consider naturalism and protectionism to be mutually compatible approaches. The acceptance of one of these paradigms implies the refusal of the other. However, I certainly do not claim that all scholars of the study of religions have adopted or should necessarily adopt either naturalistic or protectionist position. An anthropologist describing rituals of a specific African tribe or a classical philologist focusing on the Orphic theology do not need to subscribe to any particular 'big theory of religion'. Their efforts are of a much narrower scope, they do not need to make a choice between naturalism and protectionism as they do not attempt to address the question of the origin of religious ideas in general, either because the particulars of their work do not prompt them to even pose this question or because they might well believe that the question is misguided.[4]

4.1 Naturalistic paradigm in the study of religions until 1945

Naturalistic paradigm, whose prime ambition is the explanation of religious experience by reducing such experience to its original constitutive elements which are not of a religious nature in themselves, may be divided into two main subsets, however it would be hard to establish a clear demarcation line between them. The first subset, psychological theories, aim to explain religion away as an individual psychological reaction at the level of individuals; the second subset, sociological theories, rather emphasize social dimension of religion and aim to explain it away at the level of society.[5] This distinction could be also applied to the explanatory theories discussed in the second chapter: Xenophanes, Democritus and Prodicus tried to identify the origins of religions (in their case, god-concepts) in human psychological mechanisms, while the author of the Sisyphus-fragment offered the first social-functionalist interpretation of the origins of religion.

4.1.1 Psychological theories (1): Comte, Tylor, Frazer

The most significant features of the psychological explanatory theories of the nineteenth and the early twentieth century may be identified already in the work of the French philosopher and sociologist Auguste Comte.[6] In the introduction to the six volumes of his *The Course in Positive Philosophy* (*Cours de philosophie positive*, first edition published in 1830) Comte differentiated three discrete stages of human knowledge and, following the ideological heritage of the Enlightenment, incorporated them into a positivist evolutionary framework.[7] The diachronic sequence starts with 'theological' or 'fictitious' stage (*l'état théologique, ou fictif*), continues with the 'metaphysical' or 'abstract' stage (*l'état métaphysique, ou abstrait*) and concludes with the 'scientific' or 'positive' stage (*l'état scientifique, ou positif*). For my present purposes, Comte's characterization of the 'theological' stage is of particular importance:

> In the theological stage, the human mind, seeking the essential nature of beings, the first and final causes of all effects – in short, absolute knowledge – supposes all phenomena to be produced by direct and continuous action of more or less numerous supernatural beings, whose arbitrary intervention explains all the apparent anomalies in the universe.[8]

According to Comte, then, the origins of religion lie in the natural human desires to explain and understand the world. Because our ancestors living in this first historical stage have not yet reached a proper, far-reaching and all-encompassing scientific understanding of the phenomena, they were forced to explain the 'anomalies' (i.e. phenomena which apparently were subject to no known natural law) by means of the direct intervention of supernatural beings. However, such interventions are entirely 'coincidental' (*arbitraire*) and ultimately, as Comte himself emphasized, 'fictitious'. However, the true nature of these supposed interventions has been revealed as such only *ex post* after humankind entered the final, 'positive' and scientific stage of its existence. It is only then and there that science can explain those observations originally considered 'anomalies' without having to refer to supernatural beings.

Despite his positivist outlook, Comte did not reject religion completely – rather (quite like Xenophanes), he attempted to reform it and establish the 'Religion of Humanity',[9] but it is doubtful whether his own messianic inclinations may be *bona fide* considered religion, since Comte effectively tried to introduce the atheistic analogy to the revolutionary cult of the Supreme Being, whose 'dogmatic' should consist in the knowledge that is obtained by scientifically sound procedures. The significance of Comte's approach lies in the fact that it established three fundamental principles for the further development of psychological theories within the naturalistic paradigm: (1) religion (or, some of its central concepts and propositions) are factually false ('fictitious'); (2) intellectual-psychological mechanisms of human beings, especially their unquenchable desire to satisfactorily explain the world surrounding them and their place in it, is the single most important factor in the origin of religion; (3) religion belongs to a specific historical stage of human evolution and is (or, respectively, should be) overcome and replaced by a 'positive', scientific stage. All three propositions put forward here were, in one way or another, adopted by the two main representatives of the psychological version of the naturalistic paradigm in the study of religions, Edward B. Tylor and James G. Frazer.

Edward B. Tylor, one of the founders of British anthropology, published his groundbreaking work entitled *Primitive Culture* in 1871. Tylor attempted to explain the origins of religion using the theory of animism.[10] He assumed that behind the concept of supernatural beings there is the concept of the soul surviving the physical death of the individual – the souls of the most important members of a tribe or any other community are venerated, which sets the foundation for ancestor worship, which subsequently developed into polytheism, which, finally, transformed into monotheism in the last developmental stage of the evolution of religion. Tylor, similarly as Comte, maintained the evolutionary outlook and was also convinced that the desire to explain the surrounding world, especially those facets of it that are puzzling and resistant to any obvious explanation, play a major role in the emergence of religion.[11]

However, Tylor differed significantly from Comte in an answer to the question of why religion persisted even their own day and age, if they both believed that the humankind is at the threshold of the scientific era. Tylor solved (or, has believed to have solved) this issue using the theory of the so-called 'survivals'. Survivals are those phenomena that originated in an older stage of human culture and the force of habit conserved them in subsequent stages, even though they eventually lost their original purpose. As Tylor noted, '[w]hen a custom, an art, or an opinion is fairly started in the world, disturbing influences may long affect it so slightly that it may keep its course from generation to generation, as a stream once settled in its bed will flow on for ages. This is mere permanence of culture; and the special wonder about it is that the change and revolution of human affairs should have left so many of its feeblest rivulets to run so long.'[12] In the words of one of Tylor's modern commentators, a 'survival' is simply a 'useless fossil washed up on the shores of the present'.[13]

Tylor introduced a long list of various survivals,[14] from children's games to proverbs and puzzles, to what the esteemed author called 'sneezing superstition',[15] which may be used to illustrate what exactly had Tylor in mind when he spoke about 'survivals'. Although the British anthropologist used even more ancient examples, even today, when sneezing, an Englishman wishes '[God] bless you!', a Bavarian 'Helf Gott!', Spaniard '¡Jesús!' or '¡Dios te bendiga!' and an elderly Czech might say 'Pozdrav Pánbůh!'. According to Tylor, the causal connection between the act of sneezing and supernatural being invoked is a 'survival' of those ancient times in which this connection was perceived as meaningful; or, as Tylor put it, '[t]he lingering survivals of the quaint old formulas in modern Europe seem an unconscious record of the time when the explanation of sneezing had not yet been given over to physiology, but was still in the "theological stage"'.[16] With respect to the concept of the soul, a similar conclusion is reached. Despite some rather insignificant differences, this survival is 'continuous from the philosophy of the savage thinker to that of the modern professor of theology', 'the shadow of a shade', a thing that once will be the matter for 'the metaphysics of religion', ultimately to be replaced with psychology based on sound scientific knowledge and biology.[17]

Tylor's detailed description of animism leaves no doubt that religion is for him nothing more than another survival that will be made obsolete by technical and scientific advances.[18] Quite like Comte, Tylor advocated the thesis that not only is religion far from being factually true, but it must and eventually will be overcome by scientific knowledge.[19] Modern scholarship on Tylor highlighted his 'hostility to religion', and rightly so.[20] One only has to go back to the closing sections of the second volume of *Primitive Culture* to witness the grand vision of replacing religion, especially institutionalized religion, with scientific knowledge:

> On the one hand the Anglican blends gradually into the Roman scheme, a system so interesting to the ethnologist for its maintenance of rites more naturally belonging to barbaric culture; a system so hateful to the man of science for its suppression of knowledge, and for that usurpation of intellectual authority by a sacerdotal caste which has at last reached its climax, now that an aged bishop can judge, by infallible inspiration, the results of researches whose evidence and methods are alike beyond his knowledge and his mental grasp. On the other hand, intellect, here trampled under the foot of dogma, takes full revenge elsewhere, even within the domain of religion, in those theological districts where reason takes more and more command over hereditary belief, like a mayor of the palace superseding a nominal king.[21]

Tylor's fundamental assumptions were also shared by Herbert Spencer,[22] but the most important follower of Tylor was undoubtedly James G. Frazer, 'the embodiment of evolutionism in the field of comparative study of religions',[23] in the words of an influential phenomenologist of religion, Geo Widengren. Frazer's monumental compendium of the comparative study of religions, *The Golden Bough* (first edition

1890), has been met with success far beyond the limits of anthropology, emerging study of religions, or academia in general.[24] In his basic methodological orientation, Frazer almost did not differ from Tylor and followed most of Comte's assumptions.[25] He formulated his own theory of three stages of human culture using a triad consisting of magic, religion and scientific knowledge; on the political and social level, there is a corresponding triad of magician, priest and king.[26] First, Frazer argued for an analogy between magic and science and claimed that their basic aims are identical – both approaches, magic and scientific, share the goal of bringing nature under the control of human agents to satisfy their own needs and ambitions.[27] The difference, for Frazer, lies in the fact that magic used ineffective and science (as is revealed later) effective means to pursue this goal. Religion, standing in between magic and science as the intermediate stage, has been defined by Frazer as 'propitiation or conciliation of powers superior to man which are believed to direct and control the course of nature and of human life'.[28] In contrast to magic and science, people living in the religious stage presupposed that the nature is not necessarily uniform and bound by unchangeable laws and that its order cannot be influenced directly, but only by means of turning ourselves to the supernatural beings who are able to alter the course of nature at will.

Following this basic outline, Frazer presented a diachronic evolutionist reconstruction of the three stages discussed above, with the Age of Magic standing at the beginning of the sequence. Because of its ineffectiveness,[29] magic became obsolete and humankind passed from the Age of Magic into the Age of Religion, inspired by the following consideration: If magic failed to deliver the desired results and showed itself to be impotent to control the nature, maybe it is because the nature is already controlled by someone else, namely by supernatural beings who are its creators. Given his academic position at the turn of the nineteenth and twentieth century, Frazer could not or was not willing to criticize religion openly; however, in the preface to the second edition of *The Golden Bough* he did conjure the triumphant vision of the Age of Religion coming to an end and being replaced by the Age of Science, using oblique language imbued with colourful poetics:

> It is indeed a melancholy and, in some respects, thankless task to strike at the foundations of beliefs in which, as in a strong tower, the hopes and aspirations of humanity through long ages have sought a refuge from the storm and stress of life. Yet sooner or later it is inevitable that the battery of the comparative method should breach these venerable walls, mantled over with ivy and mosses and wild flowers of a thousand tender and sacred associations. At present we are only dragging the guns into position: they have hardly yet begun to speak. The task of building up into fairer and more enduring forms the old structures so rudely shattered is reserved for other hands, perhaps for other and happier ages. We cannot foresee, we can hardly even guess, the new forms into which thought and society will run in the future. Yet this uncertainty ought not induce us, from any consideration of expediency or regard for antiquity, to spare the ancient moulds, however beautiful, when these are proved to be out-worn. Whatever comes of it, wherever it leads us, we must follow truth alone. It is our only guiding star: *hoc signo vinces*.[30]

Frazer's cautious attitude to his own project, in which many of the central Christian traditions and notions begged to be compared with its 'pagan' analogues (e.g. Attis, Adonis, Osiris or Dionysus as models for death and rebirth of God; the image of the goddess Cybele as the paradigmatic 'Mother of God' etc.), is understandable. In 1889, he wrote to his publisher George Macmillan: 'The resemblance of many of the savage customs and ideas to the fundamental doctrines of Christianity is striking. But I make no reference to this parallelism, leaving my readers to draw their own conclusions, one way or the other.'[31] Frazer himself, indeed, drew his own conclusions, and the *communis opinio* of modern scholarship rightfully considers him as someone for whom religion represented an unsuccessful attempt of humanity dominating nature.[32]

In conclusion, Comte, Tylor and Frazer are to be considered among the founders of the modern naturalistic paradigm of psychological provenience in the emerging systematic and institutionalized study of religions. All three authors described main stages of the evolution of the human culture and society in a diachronic perspective and jointly argued that the religious stage will ultimately be overcome by the stage of science and technology. According to them, at the core of religion there lies the belief in supernatural beings, and all three attempted to explain this belief away as the result of basic psychological inclinations of humankind: Comte as a result of the intellectual impulse of humanity to explain puzzling observed phenomena rationally; Tylor as a reaction to the existence of dream images and the concept of the soul; Frazer as the consequence of the failure of magic to control nature directly.

4.1.2 Psychological theories (2): Freud, Malinowski, Radin

Sigmund Freud pursued the origins of religion mainly in two of his works: in *Totem and Taboo* (*Totem und Tabu*, 1913), he described applied psychoanalytic theory to totemism, and in his later work *The Future of an Illusion* (*Die Zukunft einer Illusion*, 1927), he focused on more general reflections on the function of religion for individuals and society. Freud's analysis of totemism was based primarily on the anthropological works of his contemporaries. Like Frazer (and unlike Tylor, who spent at least half a year in Mexico studying the local tribe of *Anahuac*), Freud never worked in the field and was therefore relying on secondary reports of adventurers and missionaries. In *Totem and Taboo*, he attempted to explain the two main prohibitions that were staples of any definition of totemism in the late nineteenth and early twentieth century, i.e. the prohibition of killing a totem (usually an animal or a plant) and the prohibition of sexual intercourse among the members of the same tribe (exogamy).[33] Following some of Darwin's ideas, Freud reconstructed the primordial state of the tribal society in the following way.[34] The primal tribe was originally ruled by a despotic and jealous father, who exercised his authority to forbid his sons to approach the females of the tribe sexually. Subsequently, the sons revolted against their father and their revenge signalled the beginning of 'totemism', and thus of religion *simpliciter*, because it was a common belief at the time that totemism is to be seen as the primal form of religion (*Urreligion*), from which all other religions have eventually emerged. Freud described this historical revolt in the following narrative:

One day the brothers who had been driven out came together, killed and devoured their father and so made an end of the patriarchal horde. United, they had the courage to do and succeeded in doing what would have been impossible for them individually. (Some cultural advance, perhaps, command over some new weapon, had given them a sense of superior strength.) Cannibal savages as they were, it goes without saying that they devoured their victim as well as killing him. The violent primal father had doubtless been the feared and envied model of each one of the company of brothers: and in the act of devouring him they accomplished their identification with him, and each one of them acquired a portion of his strength. The totem meal, which is perhaps mankind's earliest festival, would thus be a repetition and a commemoration of this memorable and criminal deed, which was the beginning of so many things—of social organization, of moral restrictions and of religion.[35]

Once the drastic deed has been done, the sons failed to satisfy the one desire that gave them impulse to commit the crime in the first place (namely the sexual access to women), because they became troubled by ambivalent emotions with respect to their action. Although they got rid of the tyrant who kept them from fulfilling their desires, once the father was gone, the sons realized they also had a positive emotional bond with him, perceiving him as a bulwark against the harsh conditions of nature and its denizens. Ultimately, according to Freud, the sons were overwhelmed by remorse and, as a result, they reinstated the father symbolically as a totem of the tribe and his regulations (namely the prohibition of patricide and exogamy) were established as law: 'They revoked their deed by forbidding the killing of the totem, the substitute for their father; and they renounced its fruits by resigning their claim to the women who had now been set free. They thus created out of their filial sense of guilt the two fundamental taboos of totemism, which for that very reason inevitably corresponded to the two repressed wishes of the Oedipus complex.'[36] Freud characterized the gradual transformation of totemism into monotheism as 'a development ... which must be described as a slow "return of the repressed".'[37] It has to be said at this point that the actual content of Freud's theory will undoubtedly strike present-day readers as fanciful, fantastical and only slightly fashionable nonsense.[38] For our purposes, however, it is important to highlight its general focus on the reductionistic explanation of religious experience. Freud shared this perspective with Tylor and Frazer and may be classified as another prototypical figure of the naturalistic paradigm in the study of religions – indeed, it has been rightly concluded that the fundamental programme of Freud's interpretation of religion is the thesis that 'religion – religious experience – is to be *explained* in terms of mental conditions that are themselves *not* religious'.[39]

In addition to the idiosyncratic theory of the emergence of religion in *Totem and Taboo*, Freud returned to the topic with a more general view on religion also in *New Introductory Lectures on Psychoanalysis* (*Neue Folge der Vorlesungen zur Einführung in die Psychoanalyse*, 1933). In these lectures, Freud's resolute denial of any autonomy of religious experience came to the fore. At times, it almost seems as if Freud were preparing the way for E. O. Wilson's modern concept of 'consilience' between scientific disciplines and he clearly did demand the abandonment of the *a priori* methodological limits which prohibit the application of standard scientific procedures (especially those that form part and parcel of the natural sciences) on human religious experience.[40] Freud first described how the progress in scientific knowledge challenged the belief in miracles or mythological cosmogony; then he proceeded to deliver a *coup de grace* to the claims of religion's divine origins using his own psychoanalytic method, as '[t]he last contribution to the criticism of the religious *Weltanschauung* was effected by psycho-analysis, by showing how religion originated from the helplessness of children and by tracing its contents to the survival into maturity of the wishes and needs of childhood. This did not precisely mean a contradiction of religion, but it was nevertheless a necessary rounding-off of our knowledge about it, and in one respect at least it was a contradiction, for religion itself lays claim to a divine origin.'[41]

According to the founder of the psychoanalytic method, religion has no divine, but human, all-too-human origins. His fundamental thesis has been aptly summarized by Jacques Waardenburg, who concluded that '[t]o Freud, religion is basically a projection of infantile dependencies, and the history of religion is to be seen as the history of a collective neurosis'.[42] Freud anticipated two possible objections against the attempts to explain religion naturalistically (the epistemological one and the axiological one) and dealt with them in the following manner. The epistemological objection would argue that religion is beyond the reach of scientific knowledge; Freud dismissed it as *petitio principii*. The inability to study religion scientifically is only *a priori* postulated instead of being proved in any meaningful way. The axiological objection would argue that religion is so valuable and irreplaceable for the humankind that it is inappropriate to subject it to scientific scrutiny and thus expose it to the dangers of falsification. Freud countered this objection in a way which clearly demonstrated his rejection of protectionism on the one hand and the acceptance of the naturalistic paradigm on the other one: 'Whatever may be the value and importance of religion, it has no right in any way to restrict thought – no right, therefore, to exclude itself from having thought applied to it.'[43]

Freud also continued to reflect on religion in the context of the psychoanalytic theory of culture also in the already mentioned work, *The Future of an Illusion*.[44] Here, he argued that culture is indispensable for the humankind because it has the ability to suppress primal human impulses and desires, such as aggression or sexuality; however, by doing so, culture makes people ultimately unhappy because it prevents them from fulfilling their innermost wishes. Even though people learn the laws of nature by scientific means, they are not able to defend themselves against it effectively. Their reflection of this situation on a psychological level is a wish for some sort of protection which is modelled on the paternal protection experienced during their childhood. According to Freud, the gods then have triple function: They alleviate the fear from the nature; they let people come to terms with their fate; and they compensate them for their physical or mental suffering.[45] Just like Tylor or Frazer, Freud did not always criticize religion directly or explicitly. When he called religion an 'illusion', he argued that the term itself (*Illusion*) has a different connotation than the term 'error' (*Irrtum*).[46] It is the general consensus of Freud's modern interpreters, however, that his interpretation of religion is absolutely unacceptable for the believers and ultimately destructive for religion itself.[47] Indeed, Freud himself did, on occasion, conclude as much in his own works:

To assess the truth-value of religious doctrines does not lie within the scope of the present enquiry. It is enough for us that we have recognized them as being, in their psychological nature, illusions. But we do not have to conceal the fact that this discovery also strongly influences our attitude to the question which must appear to many to be the most important of all. We know approximately at what periods and by what kind of men religious doctrines were created. If in addition we discover the motives which led to this, our attitude to the problem of religion will undergo a marked displacement. We shall tell ourselves that it would be very nice if there were a God who created the world and was a benevolent Providence, and if there were a moral order in the universe and an after-life; but it is a very striking fact that all this is exactly as we are bound to wish it to be. And it would be more remarkable still if our wretched, ignorant and downtrodden ancestors had succeeded in solving all these difficult riddles of the universe.[48]

Freud followed Tylor and Frazer in arguing, like they both did, that religion is supposed to be abandoned and replaced by scientific knowledge.[49] In his view, science and religion are two opposing and mutually exclusive approaches to reality. Freud, just as Frazer, was convinced that religion is a regressive element in the evolution of the individual and society.[50] By contrast to Frazer's concept of religion as a tool for controlling the nature and to Tylor's theory of 'survivals', which was hardly convincing even for his contemporaries, Freud attempted to explain not only the origins of religion but also its stubborn presence in the day and age overflowing with the ideas of scientific progress. Religion is resistant and nigh ineradicable because it functions as a control mechanism for aggressive and sexual instincts.[51]

Tylor's and Frazer's anthropological speculations together with Freud's psychoanalytic theories were loosely followed by British anthropologist of Polish extraction, Bronislaw Kaspar Malinowski. Contrary to the authors that have already been discussed, Malinowski accentuated more the social aspect of religion and emphasized the importance of fieldwork. It is clear from the title of his collected essays *Magic, Science, and Religion* (1948, published only after his death) that Malinowski, similarly as Frazer, worked with the triad of magic, religion and the scientific knowledge. However, his approach was not based on diachronic progressive evolutionism, which may be found in Frazer's work, but rather on the synchronic rendering of different aspects of the mentioned triad.

Malinowski argued that there is nothing more important in the primitive society than tradition and piety. Because science is not yet able to generate secure, functional knowledge and preserve it for the generations to come, it is tradition that assumes this role, albeit in an imperfect form. Tradition secures the transmission of knowledge and increases the chances of survival of the tribe in the rather inhospitable nature: 'Thus, of all his qualities, truth to tradition is the most important, and a society which makes its tradition sacred has gained by it an inestimable advantage of power and permanence. Such beliefs and practices, therefore, which put a halo of sanctity round tradition and a supernatural stamp upon it, will have a "survival value" for the type of civilization in which they have been evolved.'[52] Malinowski thus described the religious belief in a positive manner as inevitable for the survival of humankind in the context of those societies which still have not reached the adequate level of scientific knowledge because '[r]eligious faith establishes, fixes, and enhances all valuable mental attitudes, such as reverence for tradition, harmony with environment, courage and confidence in the struggle with difficulties and at the prospect of death'.[53]

Malinowski, however, injected a psychological explanation into this mostly functionalist description inspired by Durkheim[54] and subsequently developed further by the so-called British school of social anthropology. This explanation follows in the footsteps of Tylor's animism, although with significant alterations. On the most basic level, Malinowski assumed that 'religion arose as a response to emotional stress',[55] because people are unable to cope with the fact of their own mortality. This is the reason the concept of the soul is eventually introduced as that part of the human being which survives the death of his or her physical body. This concept, however, can provide only fleeting consolation because people are constantly confronted with death and decay. Thus, they remain torn between the fear of complete destruction and a hope for a new life, and it is at this junction that religion comes into play:

> And here into this play of emotional forces, into this supreme dilemma of life and final death, religion steps in, selecting the positive creed, the comforting view, the culturally valuable belief in immortality, in the spirit independent of the body, and in the continuance of life after death. In the various ceremonies at death, in commemoration and communion with the departed, and worship of ancestral ghosts, religion gives body and form to the saving beliefs. Thus the belief in immortality is the result of a deep emotional revelation, standardized by religion, rather than a primitive philosophic doctrine. Man's conviction of continued life is one of the supreme gifts of religion, which judges and selects the better of the two alternatives suggested by self-preservation – the hope of continued life and the fear of annihilation. The belief in spirits is the result of the belief in immortality. The substance of which the spirits are made is the full-blooded passion and desire for life, rather than the shadowy stuff which haunts his dreams and illusions. Religion saves man from a surrender to death and destruction, and in doing this it merely makes use of the observations of dreams, shadows and visions. The real nucleus of animism lies in the deepest emotional fact of human nature, the desire for life.[56]

Similarly as was the case with Freud, a certain form of compensational fantasy plays a role in the emergence of religion and, to put it in very simple terms, 'Malinowski thus believed religious behaviour could be *explained* by the inability of humans – simply as biological systems – to adapt easily to the idea of death'.[57] Malinowski's strategy of explanation of religious phenomena is usually considered reductionistic,[58] but Malinowski himself, quite like the author of the Sisyphus-fragment discussed in Chapter 2, denied the factual truth of religion,[59] but not its social usefulness.[60]

Another scholar from the first half of the twentieth century that professed some sympathy for the naturalistic paradigm and reductionistic explanations of religion *via* human psychological mechanisms is Paul Radin, Polish émigré just like Malinowski. He drew inspiration from his compatriot and Freud to argue that the essence of religion may be identified with a specific feeling that is 'the emotional correlate of the struggle for existence in an insecure physical and social environment'.[61] Radin followed the assumption that in the original environment, humans are facing many dangers which are directly threatening their life. They must fight for survival, brave the caprices of weather that would put Lear's storm to shame, suffer the lack of food and dangers in the form of stronger predators from the animal world; in the social sphere, they face constant conflicts among tribes competing for natural resources. According to Radin, the state of constant, potentially life-threatening danger must be counterbalanced by psychological means, and this psychological reaction to the harshness of the world stands behind the emergence of religion:

> The correlate of economic insecurity, we have seen, is psychical insecurity and disorientation with all its attendant fears, with all its full feeling of helplessness, of powerlessness, and of insignificance. It is but natural for the psyche, under such circumstances, to take refuge in compensation fantasies. And since the only subject matter existing in that primal dawn of civilization was the conscious struggle of man against his physical and economic environment, and his unconscious struggle against his animal-mental equipment as stimulated by his reflective consciousness, the main goal and objective of all his strivings was the canalization of his fears and feelings and the validation of his compensation dreams. Thus they became immediately transfigured, and there emerged those strictly religious concepts so suggestively discussed by the well-known German theologian Rudolf Otto in his work called *Das Heilige*. Being a theologian and a mystic he naturally misunderstood the true nature of these concepts and of their genesis.[62]

The influence of the majority of the abovementioned authors on Radin is quite evident. There is the role of fear, uncertainty and vulnerability; Freudian motif of compensational fantasy; even the reductionistic explanation of religion and the dénouement of its origins in the basic psychological functions of humankind. His critique of Rudolf Otto appropriately documents the fundamental difference between the naturalistic and protectionist paradigm in the study of religions: While naturalism denies that the religious experience has a corresponding correlate of an exclusively religious nature, protectionism, on the contrary, always presumes such correlation, which also allows protectionism to strictly deny reduction and explanation in the study of religions.

4.1.3 Sociological theories: Marx, Simmel, Durkheim

In contrast with the psychological theories I have just discussed, the approaches introduced in this section on the one hand belong to the naturalistic paradigm, whose main goal is the explanation of religion through its reduction to non-religious constitutive elements, but on the other the explanation focuses more on the society than on an individual. Although the Marxist interpretation of religion is only marginally discussed in the study of religions' handbooks and texts,[63] it is necessary to mention it at least in passing, one of the reasons being the fact that due to the political development in Europe after the Second World War, Marxist theory was officially 'canonized' in all communist countries. Marx discussed religion especially in his short essay *Critique of Hegel's Philosophy of Right* (*Zur Kritik der Hegelschen Rechtsphilosophie*, 1843), famous for its definition of religion as the 'opium of the people'.[64] First, Marx emphasized the social aspect of the issue at hand – man is not 'abstract being squatting outside the world', but '[m]an is the world of man – state, society'[65] – only to find later the essence and origin of religion in an inverted consciousness of the world which arises in order to preserve class differences and its concomitant power structures:

> This state and this society produce religion, which is an inverted consciousness of the world, because they are an inverted world. Religion is the general theory of this world, its encyclopaedic compendium, its logic in popular form, its spiritual *point d'honneur*, its enthusiasm, its moral sanction, its solemn complement, and its universal basis of consolation and justification. It is the fantastic realization of the human essence since the human essence has not acquired any true reality. The struggle against religion is, therefore, indirectly the struggle against that world whose spiritual aroma is religion. Religious suffering is, at one and the same time, the expression of real suffering and a protest against real suffering. *Religion is the sigh of the oppressed creature, the heart of a heartless world, and the soul of soulless conditions. It is the opium of the people.*[66]

Marx thus explained religion as a by-product and a weapon of the class struggle, which was adroitly used by capitalists and bourgeoisie to pacify the proletariat. In his explanation, Marx reduced religion to non-religious elements (i.e. to a reflection of socio-economic relations) which meets the conditions to classify this theory as belonging to the naturalistic paradigm.[67] Entirely obvious is also Marx's effort not only to explain religion but also his wish to eliminate it, simply because it stands in the way of humanity's true happiness: 'The abolition of religion as the *illusory* happiness of the people is the demand for their real happiness. To call on them to give up their illusions about their condition is to call on them to give up a condition that requires illusions. The criticism of religion is, therefore, in embryo, the criticism of that vale of tears of which religion is the halo.'[68]

Another sociologist who at the beginning of the twentieth century put emphasis on the social aspect of religion is Georg Simmel. In a short article from 1905, he defended the basic assumption of the naturalist paradigm, namely that religion is to be explained by its reduction to non-religious phenomena.[69] In order to engage with the explanation of religion successfully, Simmel also pointed out that individual religion is secondary and social relationships primary,[70] anticipating thus Durkheim's views:

> I do not mean that the religion was first, and that the sociological relations borrowed their attribute from it. I believe, rather, that the sociological significance arises without any regard for the religious data at all as a purely inter-individual, psychological relation, which later exhibits itself abstractly in religious faith. In faith in a deity the highest development of faith has become incorporate, so to speak; has been relieved of its connection with its social counterpart. Out of the subjective faith-process there develops, contrariwise, an object for that faith. The

faith in human relations which exists as a social necessity now becomes an independent, typical function of humanity which spontaneously authenticates itself from within.[71]

According to Simmel, faith, or rather, elementary 'trust' between two individuals, is the inevitable necessary condition for and a building block of every sustainable social system. This interpersonal trust is eventually internalized and conceptualized abstractly as 'trust' or 'faith' in a deity who represents its perfect object. Although the investigation of religion has been rather at the fringes of Simmel's primary scholarly focus, it is interesting that he anticipated fundamental ideas of one of the most influential sociological works centred on religion, namely Émile Durkheim's *Elementary Forms of Religious Life* (*Les formes élémentaires de la vie religieuse*, 1912).

Durkheim shared with Simmel both the thesis that the 'social' (as opposed to 'individual') is primary (it has priority over both religion and individual psychology) and its correlate, namely that it is possible to explain religion by non-religious (in this case, social) phenomena. Durkheim was heavily influenced by Wilhelm Wundt, who attempted to study morality in a uniquely empiric way.[72] He was also influenced by his Parisian teacher, Fustel de Coulanges, who pointed out in his work *Ancient City* (*Cité antique*, 1864) the intertwining of social and religious sphere in ancient Greece and Rome.[73] As for the likes of Tylor or Frazer, Durkheim dealt with their theories critically, without necessarily resorting to naming them directly. The French sociologist implicitly accused them of turning history and religious ethnography into a 'weapon against religion' (*machine de guerre contre le religion*) and argued that from the sociological perspective 'a human institution cannot rest upon an error and a lie' (*une institution humaine ne saurait reposer sur l'erreur et sur le mensonge*); indeed, 'there are no religions which are false. All are true in their own fashion; all answer, though in different ways, to the given conditions of human existence.'[74]

Although Durkheim perceived religion as 'true' in the sense that it reflects and co-creates social structures, he denied its metaphysical claims, just as his colleagues associated with the journal *L'Année sociologique* (e.g. Henri Hubert or Marcel Mauss) did.[75] Durkheim's view on coexistence of science and religion is explicitly discussed in the closing sections of his *Elementary Forms of Religious Life*:

> That is what the conflict between science and religion really amounts to. It is said that science denies religion in principle. But religion exists; it is a system of given facts; in a word, it is a reality. How could science deny this reality? Also, in so far as religion is action, and in so far as it is a means of making men live, science could not take its place, for even if this expresses life, it does not create it; it may well seek to explain the faith, but by that very act it presupposes it. Thus there is no conflict except upon one limited point. Of the two functions which religion originally fulfilled, there is one, and only one, which tends to escape it more and more: that is its speculative function. That which science refuses to grant to religion is not its right to exist, but its right to dogmatize upon the nature of things and the special competence which it claims for itself for knowing man and the world.[76]

Although Durkheim admitted that scientific knowledge, from a certain point of view, replaced knowledge of religious provenance, his position is not completely disapproving when compared with most authors of the psychological theories in the previous section of this chapter. Another difference lies in Durkheim's staunch refusal of the question of historical origins of religion. Tylor, Frazer and Freud formulated dynamic diachronic models which embraced the idea of progressive evolutionism, while Durkheim considered the question of historical origins of religion as non-scientific.[77] He tried instead to identify constantly present causes that would explain the emergence of religion, which render his model rather static and functionalist. The third difference between Durkheim and the Tylor-Frazer-Freud triad is Durkheim's definition of religion. Durkheim refused the definition of religion that would make use of the concept of supernatural beings as a *definiens* and presented his own definition emphasizing social aspects of religious life; religion was, in his view, a reflection of the society unified by shared morality.[78]

Despite all these differences, I do believe that Durkheim may be classified as a representative of the naturalistic paradigm in the study of religions. Although he has been labelled with various terms by historians of the study of religions, the *opinio communis* considers Durkheim to be a reductionist;[79] occasionally, we find also non-reductionistic interpretations of his work.[80] Durkheim explained religion as a symbolic representation of specific social structures, especially those of moral provenience – society is 'universal and eternal objective cause of these sensations *sui generis* out of which religious experience is made',[81] religion reflects society's ideal structure, it is 'a natural product of social life',[82] in a certain way, it renders the inner structure of society visible and understandable to its members. However, in Durkheim's work, the term *sui generis* has a different meaning than in later scholarship, especially in Otto's works: what is *sui generis* is emphatically not a religious experience as such, but rather it is the society, or that which Durkheim called 'social facts' (*faits sociaux*) or 'collective consciousness' (*conscience collective*).[83]

4.2 Protectionist paradigm in the study of religions until 1945

Following this brief introduction to the most influential figures associated with the naturalistic paradigm in the late nineteenth and early twentieth century, I will now focus on a much more numerous group consisting of the main protagonists of the protectionist paradigm, which means that their theories, directly or indirectly, deny the possibility of an explanation of religious experience and its reduction to more basic constitutive elements of non-religious character. These authors usually refuse in strictest terms the meaningfulness of the question of the origins of religion and they are often highly critical of evolutionism. I will first deal briefly with the beginnings of the modern comparative study of religions; then I will discuss selected scholars standing between the study of religions and biblical studies; and, finally, I will conclude with first critics of evolutionism and animism from the turn of the nineteenth and twentieth centuries.

4.2.1 Comparative approach: Müller, Chantepie de la Saussaye, Tiele

Max Müller, a prominent German linguist (an Indologist), who later worked in the United Kingdom, is commonly considered to be the founder of the comparative approach in the study of religions.[84] His approach to religion stood in opposition to evolutionism and to naturalistic attempts to explain religion that are present in Tylor's, Frazer's or Freud's work. Müller's theoretical-methodological assumptions were based on a comparative perspective and its inspiration may be found in the method of comparative Indo-European linguistics,[85] which took in the nineteenth-century decisive steps towards a reconstruction of the Indo-European language family and connected Indian, Classical and Christian heritage on a linguistic level. The comparative approach is considered by Müller to be the correct method not only in the study of religions, but also in the whole area of 'higher knowledge'.[86] Müller himself did not stop with hollow theoretical declarations, but he also initiated and edited the monumental book series *Sacred Books of the East*, which included modern translations of all relevant texts of eastern religious traditions.[87] Müller was also an expert on the philosophy of Immanuel Kant (whose crucial work *Critiques of Pure Reason* he translated into English) and he followed the preeminent German philosopher intellectually by introducing a new mental faculty in addition to Kant's well-known triad of sensibility (*Sinnlichkeit*), understanding (*Verstand*) and reason (*Vernunft*). The function of this newly postulated faculty is crucial for religious experience because it enables such experience to be possible in the first place:

> There is in man a third faculty, which I call simply the faculty of apprehending the Infinite, not only in religion, but in all things; a power independent of sense and reason, a power in a certain sense contradicted by sense and reason, but yet a very real power, which has held its own from the beginning of the world, neither sense nor reason being able to overcome it, while it alone is able to overcome in many cases both reason and sense. According to the two meanings of the word religion, then, the science of religion is divided into two parts; the former, which has to deal with the historical forms of religion, is called Comparative Theology; the latter, which has to explain the conditions under which religion, whether in its highest or its lowest form, is possible, is called Theoretic Theology.[88]

After this theoretical introduction, Müller focused on comparing individual religious traditions under the umbrella of 'comparative theology' because he believed that the study of religions must exhaust comparative theology first in order to ascend to theoretical theology. The comparative analysis followed the same goals as comparative linguistics, i.e. typology and identification of common features of individual religious traditions and – if possible – reconstruction of the original elements inherent to most religious traditions. However, in principle, Müller's methodology could not have led to a reductive explanation of religious experience, because religious experience is naturally present in human mental systems and based on the existence of already mentioned 'faculty of apprehending the Infinite' (Müller eventually came to consider the Infinite as *definiens* of religion).[89] It is therefore necessary to presume also the objective existence of this Infinite, which assumed various shapes and forms in various individual religious traditions. The task of comparison is not to reduce religion to non-religious elements and to explain it away; rather, its task is to purify religion from posterior secular sediments and deformations.[90] Further, its task is also to identify the seeds of truth that can be found in all religions,[91] even though Müller on occasion claimed that this religious truth is present in a unique and most immediate way in Christianity. Müller, who is unanimously labelled in secondary literature as devout *homo religiosus*,[92] did not leave anyone in doubt with respect to the answer to the question of what should be the main goal of the study of religions:

> The Science of Religion will for the first time assign to Christianity its right place among the religions of the world; it will show for the first time fully what was meant by the fullness of time; it will restore to the whole history of the world, in its conscious progress towards Christianity, its true and sacred character.[93]

As one of the founders of the study of religions, Müller followed goals that were completely different to those of the authors I introduced as representatives of the naturalistic paradigm. The study of religions for him boils down to comparative theology which is to reveal the seeds of truth in all world religions (but fully realised only in Christianity) and to theoretical theology which makes religious experience possible in the first place by discovering in human minds the new faculty for apprehending the Infinite. If we are to speak with respect to Müller about the explanation of religious experience at all, then this explanation must be understood in the context of protectionist paradigm, as it is based on postulating the existence of a special mental faculty whose function only makes sense if we presuppose also the objectively existing 'Infinite' as the origin and source of all religions. As Eric Sharpe concluded, Müller 'believed that the future held promise of a new form of religion, derived not from historical Christianity as he knew it, but from all the various repositories of truth that are to be found scattered over the face of the earth. It will be the "true religion of humanity", since humanity is the sphere of divine revelation; and it will be the essential result of the historical process, leading beyond Christianity, though in some sense perhaps still to be called Christianity.'[94] The ultimate goal of Müller's 'Science of Religion' is thus to facilitate the establishment of a liberal ecumenic project consisting in a spiritual renewal of Christianity, which could in some way be able to integrate the 'seeds of truth' of the other religious traditions.[95]

Another significant figure of the comparative approach is Pierre Chantepie de la Saussaye, one of the first professors of this newly established academic discipline (since 1878 a professor for *Religionsgeschichte* at the University in Amsterdam)[96] and editor and co-author of the important *Handbook of the History of Religions* (*Lehrbuch der Religionsgeschichte*, first edition 1887), in which he introduced the term 'phenomenology' in the domain of the study of religions, although this reference is curiously absent in the second and third editions of this book.[97] Chantepie de la Saussaye did not yet use this term with a strictly philosophical meaning (as Husserl did later on). In his *Handbook*, the term only served for designation for the comparative perspective which did not follow individual religious traditions in their historical development, but rather followed them synchronically from the perspective of a typology of ideas, ritual practices, etc.[98] An important indication for understanding of his methodology is the fact that Christianity is excluded from this comparison, quite like the Old and New Testament were excluded from Müller's *Sacred Books of the East*. While in Müller's case it was the result of pressure on the side of institutionalized Christianity, Chantepie de la Saussaye simply decided to exclude Christian religion from his handbook *sponte sua* and he explained the reasons for this decision in the introduction to his book. On the one hand, he refused (at least nominally) to subordinate comparative study of religions to theology; on the other, he hastened to add the following:

> Others reverse this relation and look upon Christian theology as a subdivision only of the science of religion. Although this is perfectly right in form, still theology can hardly submit to it; for even when it is not reactionary, but works with Protestant freedom, it cannot surrender, without self-destruction, the character of its biblical and ecclesiastical teachings, which constitute the greatest part of its encyclopaedia. The science of religion, and the science of the Christian religion must follow, therefore, separate paths, and have separate objects in view.[99]

Chantepie de la Saussaye immediately added that he did not have a total mutual isolation of both disciplines in mind,[100] but the role he assigned to the study of religion is analogous to the role philosophy played in the early Christian thought, that is to say, it is subordinate to theology. Study of religions serves only as a *praeparatio evangelica* to facilitate the understanding of the Christian doctrine and to make missionary efforts more effective,[101] which clearly demonstrates the apologetic or confessional character of Chantepie's undertaking and constitutes a reason for associating this author with the protectionist paradigm. After all, Chantepie de la Saussaye never attempted to explain religion by its reduction to constitutive non-religious elements – quite to the contrary, the very existence of religion served for him as a proof of god's existence.[102]

The third significant author of the early comparative study of religions is another Netherlander, Cornelis Petrus Tiele, who worked at the newly established Department for the History of Religions in Leiden after the reform of the Dutch universities and the (formal) separation of theological faculties (Amsterdam, Groningen, Leiden, Utrecht) from the Dutch reformed church in 1877.[103] His outlines for inner stratification of the study of religions is much indebted to Müller's work. Tiele also differentiated two fundamental branches of the study of religions: (1) 'morphology', which is more or less analogous to Müller's comparative theology and follows the historical development of individual religious traditions and aims to produce their mutual comparison; and (2) 'ontology', which deals with the origins and the 'essence' of religion and as such is not dissimilar to Müller's theoretical theology.[104]

Just as Müller, Tiele assumed inner unity of religious experience, which makes it possible to study it scientifically;[105] just as Müller, Tiele further assumed that, in principle, there is no conflict between science and religion;[106] and, finally, just as Müller, Tiele worked with the concepti of the Infinite as the source and the origin of religious experience, the only difference being that Tiele located the Infinite 'inside' of human beings, not outside of them.[107] Tiele taught that the evidence for the existence of the

Infinite lies beyond the reach of the scientific study of religion,[108] however, he also claimed that our perception of the Infinite simply *cannot* be an illusion:

> But, though not called upon to prove the truth of religion, our science is not entitled to pronounce it an illusion. This would not only be an unwarrantable conclusion, but it would make human existence an insoluble riddle, it would brand mankind as crazy dreamers, it would pronounce the source of all the best work they have ever done in this world to be sheer folly.[109]

Tiele thus *a priori* refused to even consider a reductionistic explanation of religion, not only because of the theoretical reasons (the existence of the faculty for apprehending the Infinite), but also due to the pragmatic consequences of such a step. It is inconceivable to him that innumerable human multitude could be mistaken for vast periods of time. In the conclusion of his most significant work, which he originally delivered as Gifford's lectures in the years 1896 and 1897, Tiele openly proclaimed the purpose of the study of religions as a scientific discipline:

> Let it do its own duty in throwing light upon the part that religion has ever played in the history of mankind, and still plays in every human soul. And then, without preaching, or special pleading, or apologetic argument, but solely by means of the actual facts it reveals, our beloved science will help to bring home to the restless spirits of our time the truth that there is no rest for them unless 'they arise and go to their Father'.[110]

Tiele, in the same manner as his contemporaries Müller or Chantepie de la Saussaye, did not harbour any doubts that the establishment of the study of religions as a discipline should lead to a deeper religious experience and he even indicated the direction these newly conquered depths should take, namely towards a reformation and reformulation of Christianity in order for it to become an unshakeable foundation for world ecumenism. As Arie Molendijk noted, despite the academic reform in the Netherlands, which was already mentioned, in Tiele's view 'science of religion was expected to fulfil (most of) the tasks of the old theology and to show the superiority of Christian religion. On the basis of an evolutionary scheme, Tiele was even tempted to speculate about the development of liberal Protestantism into the religion of mankind'.[111]

4.2.2 Biblical studies: Strauss, Renan, Robertson Smith, Delitzsch

We saw that Chantepie de la Saussaye tried to achieve a thorough division of labour between the Christian theology and the study of religions and he strictly differentiated the two. However, this artificial severance of the two fields was not met with approval in all corners of the liberal Protestant theology. In this context, it is necessary to at least briefly mention the so-called Tübingen School (or rather, the movement that was later labelled as biblical *Religionsgeschichtliche Schule*, originally associating scholars working mainly at the university in Göttingen).[112] One of their predecessors is David

Friedrich Strauss who, in his book *Life of Jesus* (*Das Leben Jesu*, 1835) as early as in the first half of the nineteenth century, formulated both positive[113] and negative[114] criteria to differentiate myth from historical truth in order to allow scholars to reliably reconstruct the figure of historical Jesus based on evangelic texts. The French analogy to Strauss' book was no less scandalous. Renan's treatise bearing the same title (*La vie de Jésus*, 1863) followed identical goals and did not even exempt the most important event of Christianity – the resurrection of Jesus. When Renan described how there came a cry from Jesus' grave informing that Jesus no longer lies in his grave, he only laconically stated that it is necessary to search for the origins of 'legends' about Jesus' resurrection in historical accounts of the life of his apostles because 'for the historian, the life of Jesus ends with his last sigh'.[115] Renan, however, did not share Müller's or Tiele's conviction of the compatibility of scientific (in his case also historical) approach and religion:

> Let us allow religions to proclaim themselves unassailable, since otherwise they will not gain due respect from their adherents; but let us not subject science to the censorship of a power that has no scientific character. We will not confound legend with history; but neither will we try to banish legend, for it is the form which the faith of humanity of necessity assumes.[116]

A wider comparative perspective encompassing religions of the Near East was presented by William Robertson Smith, who became famous mostly for his *Lectures on the Religion of the Semites* (first edition published in 1889).[117] He introduced the results of the German historical-critical Biblical studies to British audience in a shape that was moulded by the methods of the liberal Protestant theology. On the level of professional academia, his opinions earned him a heresy charge in 1876, his professorship in Aberdeen was taken from him and after a lengthy trial he was convicted for denying Moses' authorship of *Deuteronomy*.[118] The interest in comparative approach to religion was motivated by the efforts of Robertson Smith to reform religion and he felt he acted in direct continuity with the reformation efforts within the Catholic Church in the fifteenth and sixteenth centuries. This may be demonstrated on a simple example.

Based on observations obtained during his six-month stay in the Near East, Robertson Smith reached a conclusion that the primordial sacrificial feast was originally a celebration of the link between god and a man (both in 'totemism' and the ancient Judaism), but that it later lost its original function.[119] Eventually, this function has been reinvented again by Jesus, only to be later lost again in Catholic formalism of the rite. According to Robertson Smith, the study of religions has the potential to discover and restore the original function of sacrifice by historically oriented study, although he denied that he would do as much as to aboard the question of the existence or non-existence of god(s):

> The question of the metaphysical nature of the gods, as distinct from their social office and function, must be left in the background till this whole investigation is completed. It is vain to ask what the gods are in themselves till we have studied them in what I may call their public life, that is, in the stated intercourse between

them and their worshippers which was kept up by means of the prescribed forms of cultus. From the antique point of view, indeed, the question what the gods are in themselves is not a religious but a speculative one [...].[120]

However, this 'declaration of neutrality', to which I will return in Chapter 9, is hardly a convincing one. Robertson Smith's primary motivation was not a 'neutral' research of religion; rather he intended to reform and propagate religious views, which connects this British author again with the protectionist paradigm. Robertson Smith did not offer any explanation of religion, because for him, religion is simply a real lived experience with god and sacred, a conclusion shared by virtually all of his modern interpreters: 'As a firm and constant believer in the ultimate divine inspiration of the Bible, Smith intended to pursue historical scholarship in order to get to the deeper spiritual, "inner" core of revelation that he felt was hidden beneath the "outer" layers of scribal composition, redaction, and editing added over the centuries.'[121] Other scholars pointed to the fact that Robertson Smith even made explicit a direct parallel between the function of the study of religions as a scientific discipline and the function of the Protestant reformation in history of Christianity.[122] Accordingly, the main goal of the study of religions is revival and rejuvenation of religion, which, as I have shown, has been also the position of Müller and Tiele.

On the continent, it is possible to find a similar theoretical position formulated in the same manner and with a clear ideological motivation in the works of Friedrich Delitzsch, who brought to attention a number of parallels between Babylonian and ancient Jewish religion. Delitzsch characterized historical-critical comparison in the study of religions as 'purifying process' that must never endanger,[123] but only strengthen 'true religion':

> But on the other hand, let us not blindly cling to antiquated and scientifically discredited dogmas from the vain fear that our faith in God and our true religious life might suffer harm! Let us remember that all things earthly are in living motion and that standing still means death. Let us look back upon the mighty, throbbing force with which the German Reformation filled the great nations of the earth in every field of human endeavor and human progress! But even the Reformation is only one stage on the road to the goal of truth set for us by God and in God. Let us press forward toward it, humbly but with all the resources of free scientific investigation, joyfully professing our adherence to that standard perceived with eagle eye from the high watch-tower and courageously proclaimed to all the world: 'The further development of religion.'[124]

If we ponder the initial position and goals of both Delitzsch and Robertson Smith, it is apparent that they must be classified as representatives of the protectionist paradigm, since both saw in the (comparative) study of religions a tool for the intellectual reformation of the Christian religion which would be analogous to the German reformation of the sixteenth century. Understandably, the question of the ultimate origins of religion is never posed by any of these authors because, in their view, religious experience comes into being by virtue of the interaction between the human and the divine, and religion is emphatically not something that could be reduced to a compensational fantasy, mirror of economic relations, or unsuccessful attempt to rule the world.

4.2.3 First critics of evolutionism: Lang, Marett, Schmidt

A direct critical reaction to reductive evolutionistic approaches introduced earlier in this chapter was led mainly by three authors – Andrew Lang, Robert Ranulph Marett and Wihelm Schmidt. In his works, Andrew Lang rejected Tylor's theory as 'materialism',[125] since he was acutely aware of the consequences brought by the evolutional scheme of the naturalistic paradigm – for Tylor and Frazer, religion is nothing more than an obsolete stage of human culture that should be superseded by the golden age of scientific progress. The following excerpt from Lang's work *The Making of Religion* (first edition published in 1898) is important because it clearly formulated the dichotomy between the naturalistic and protectionist paradigm which runs through the entire history of the study of religions:

> It is important, then, to trace, if possible, the origin of these two beliefs [*scil.* faith in God and immortality of soul]. If they arose in actual communion with Deity (as the first at least did, in the theory of the Hebrew Scriptures), or if they could be proved to arise in an unanalysable *sensus numinis*, or even in 'a perception of the Infinite' (Max Müller), religion would have a divine, or at least a necessary source. To the Theist, what is inevitable cannot but be divinely ordained, therefore religion is divinely preordained, therefore, in essentials, though not in accidental details, religion is true. The atheist, or non-theist, of course draws no such inferences. But if religion, as now understood among men, be the latest evolutionary form of a series of mistakes, fallacies, and illusions, if its germ be a blunder, and its present form only the result of progressive but unessential refinements on that blunder, the inference that religion is untrue—that nothing actual corresponds to its hypothesis—is very easily drawn.[126]

Andrew Lang thus differentiated between the naturalistic paradigm, in which religion is reduced to non-religious elements, explained away and found lacking any corresponding objective reality as its source, (be it God, the Sacred or the Infinite), and the protectionist paradigm in which, on the contrary, this objectively existing religious reality is presupposed. In accordance with fundamental theses of these approaches, Lang, as a representative of the protectionist paradigm, refused the question of the origins of religion because we know nothing about the first 'religious' human being;[127] according to him, 'dogmatic decisions about the origin of religion seem unworthy of science.'[128] Lang's own solution was informed by his general interest in parapsychology, which he understood as a scientific experimental psychology and not as a pseudoscientific discipline that we are most likely to image under this term nowadays. Led by supposedly incontrovertible evidence for parapsychological phenomena, he concluded that 'very probably there exist human faculties of unknown scope; that these conceivably were more powerful and prevalent among our very remote ancestors who founded religion; that they may still exist in savage as in civilised races, and that they may have confirmed, if they did not originate, the doctrine of separable souls. If they do exist, the circumstance is important, in view of the fact that modern ideas rest on a denial of their existence.'[129] Lang thus did not introduce any particular intellectual faculty for apprehending the Infinite, as Müller or Tiele did, but remained satisfied with the assumption that, because of the existence of parapsychological phenomena, it is not possible to rule out the existence of such a faculty. Therefore, it is also not possible to explain religion 'materialistically', i.e. it is not possible to reduce religion to non-religious elements (as, for example, in his view Tylor did, or attempted to do).[130]

Somewhat different critique than Lang's has been offered by Robert R. Marett, who was one of the first advocates of the so-called 'pre-animism' or 'animatism', i.e. a theory according to which it is futile to seek the origins of religion in personal supernatural beings, since it is to be found rather in a mysterious force (*mana*) with exclusively non-personal character.[131] Although Marett is sometimes categorized next to Frazer as a representative of the naturalistic paradigm and an advocate of the explanatory theory of religion,[132] this characterization is not entirely accurate. His is a functional explanation of the primary forms of religion,[133] which has more in common with the later social-functionalist school of British anthropology than with Tylor and Frazer. Marett, after all, explicitly declared that he has 'not sought to explain so much as to describe',[134] and one of the modern commentators of his work pointed out with no small amount of irony that Marett's work is based on an unshakable belief that a reformed Christian is the jewel crown of all creation and the highpoint of the evolutionary process.[135]

Another critic of 'materialism' in the study of religions, closely following Andrew Lang especially with his theory of the 'original monotheism' which presupposed that monotheism and the belief in the 'high God' (in contrast to belief in 'low gods', e.g. the spirits of the ancestors or demons) stood at the beginning of all religion, was Wilhelm Schmidt. As a member of the missionary association *Societas Verbi Divini* (since 1888) and as a catholic priest, Schmidt scorned Tylor's and Frazer's 'materialistic evolutionism' and complained of an 'outbreak of materialism and Darwinism' in the domain of the study of religions and of the 'evolutionist natural science [which] puts all that is low and simple at the beginning, all that is higher and of worth being regarded only as the product of a longer or shorter process of development'.[136] It is precisely the methodology advocated by Tylor or Frazer at the turn of the nineteenth and the twentieth centuries that Schmidt deplored:

> Its significance for the methods of the history of religion has already been dealt with. As regards the spirit in which the inquiries were conducted, it meant an increasing inability to grasp the deeper essence of religion, to give due value to its higher forms, and a tendency to overestimate the outward elements and underestimate, or entirely neglect, the spirit. All things considered, this meant that the historical study of religion suffered almost more than it had done in the previous period.[137]

If it is possible to speak about thematization of the origins of religion in Schmidt's work at all, it is only possible to understand them as 'primeval revelations'

(*Uroffenbarung*).¹³⁸ The theological and apologetical aspect of his work is quite apparent and even much more explicit than in the case of Lang or Marett.¹³⁹ Reaction to evolutionism of all the authors mentioned here belongs firmly to the protectionist paradigm of the study of religions, since it denies any other explanation of religion than theological, which is to say that the origins of human religious experience have to be found in the interaction between humankind and the divine.

5

Naturalism and protectionism in the study of religions (2): The rise and fall of phenomenology

The realms of human personality and human values are often invaded by a scientism which insists upon only one method of knowing and one type of knowledge. One of the weightiest arguments for those who want to preserve human personality and its values against the imperatives of science is the demonstration that any form of reduction falls short of the aim of a student of religion, which is to do justice to that religion's true nature.

Joachim Wach[1]

The previous chapter introduced briefly the most significant theoretical-methodological approaches to religion from the turn of the nineteenth and twentieth centuries. Scholars belonging to the naturalistic paradigm aimed to explain religious experience away by means of its reduction to non-religious elements, thus proclaiming religion (either directly or indirectly) an illusion. On the contrary, representatives of the protectionist paradigm rejected such a reduction as impossible in principle. They saw the origins of religious experience in objectively existing domain of the sacred (God, the Sacred, the Infinite) and they perceived the emerging study of religions as a tool for reformation and 'purification' of individual religious traditions, especially Christianity. My aim in this chapter is to follow the development of the study of religions further into the twentieth century and demonstrate that the naturalistic paradigm became largely abandoned over time and protectionism gained the upper hand, becoming a methodological 'standard' reigning supreme in the majority of scholarship in the field of the study of religions, especially in the variety of phenomenological approaches. I will also identify a numerous and influential group of historically highly significant scholars in the field who (intentionally or otherwise) rejuvenated an important facet of the early Christian discourse concerning the relationship between philosophy and Christian religion. Almost all representatives of the classical phenomenology of religion argued in favour of the autonomy of the religious experience and its irreducibility to non-religious constitutive elements. They also put emphasis on the method of epistemic justification *per hominem* which, in the twentieth century, did not require miracles or martyrdom for the purposes of ascertaining the truth values of religious propositions, but underwent a transformation into the *condition sine qua non* which dictated that a researcher in the field of the study of religions should also be a believer himself or herself; or alternatively, it transformed into the thesis that the final verdict for the assessment of the results of the study of religions may only be made by believers themselves. In the period after the Second World War, many scholars of the study of religions followed the phenomenological approach, however, at the same time, a new opposition to this approach appeared, an opposition that did not return to the naturalistic paradigm, but attempted to reform the dominant phenomenology of religion and to find a balanced position between the historiographical and phenomenological approach to religious experience.

5.1 The emergence of classical phenomenology

The term 'phenomenology of religion' is considerably vague and is sometimes used to label a somewhat divergent mixture of scholars,[2] who are, however, connected by a number of shared assumptions. This justifies, at least to a certain extent, its heuristic use. The term was first used in the field of the study of religions by Chantepie de la Saussaye, who employed it only as a label for descriptive typology, i.e. an approach that did not purport to study religious traditions primarily in their diachronic, historical development, but rather aimed to build a basic inventory of individual constitutive elements of religious systems (e.g. ritual, modalities of worship of a deity, prayer etc.) and to describe synchronically their manifestations in individual religious traditions. The oldest phase of phenomenology, attested in the works of Nathan Söderblom and Rudolf Otto, is mainly connected with the introduction of the 'Sacred' (or the 'Holy') as a key term for the study of religions. Classical phenomenology of religion has been founded by the Norwegian-Dutch duo Brede Kristensen and Gerardus van der Leeuw and some of their methods were used also by various German authors of the likes of Max Scheler, Heinrich Frick, Gustav Mensching and Friedrich Heiler. Eventually, phenomenology has been transformed into its distinctive and very popular form by Joachim Wach and especially Mircea Eliade.

5.1.1 Discovery of the Sacred: Söderblom and Otto

The discussion of theoretical-methodological assumptions of Nathan Söderblom and Rudolf Otto has to start with a brief reference to the work of Friedrich Schleiermacher, since some of the basic theses of their approach may be traced back to the great German philosopher and theologian. The continuity of Schleiermacher's thought in Söderblom's and Otto's works is quite explicit – in the year 1899, on the occasion of the hundredth anniversary of the publication of Schleiermacher's *Reden über die Religion*, Söderblom delivered in Uppsala his introductory professorial lecture with the title *The Meaning of Schleiermacher's Speeches on Religion* (*Bedeutung von Schleiermachers Reden über die Religion*).[3] In the same year, Otto edited and published the new edition of Schleiermacher's *Reden über die Religion*. Schleiermacher announced the return to the epistemic justification *per hominem* through establishment of a special *conditio sine qua non* with respect to any meaningful study of religion. For Schleiermacher, this requirement consists in a previous direct religious experience on the part of any and every religious scholar,⁴ which essentially amounts to a thesis that there exists a special group of people (namely the believers themselves) that is uniquely privileged to study religion. Their personal religious experience serves as a prerequisite and a touchstone for all the propositions that would try to describe this experience.

In the second speech of his main wok (*Über das Wesen der Religion*), Schleiermacher demarcated the domain of religion against the domain of metaphysics and morality, and he refused the opinion shared by many of his contemporaries, according to which religion is only as an imperfect compound of the aforementioned disciplines. Schleiermacher claimed that religion is related to nature, however, not the finite nature, but infinite one. The same applies for the domain of human action (i.e. the domain of ethics), in which morality is related to freedom, but religion to necessity. The essence of religion is not thought (it belongs to metaphysics), nor action (it belongs to morality), but intuition (*Anschauung*) and feeling (*Gefühl*).⁵ The interconnection of these two modalities creates religious experience and a 'sacred instinct' that forms the basis of religion.

Söderblom and Otto adopted these views with slight modifications. For them, religious experience is an irreducible domain *sui generis*,⁶ and both authors introduced here the term 'the Holy' (or 'the Sacred'), whose 'discovery' was proclaimed 'the biggest achievement of the study of religions in the last hundred years'.⁷ Although the term 'the Holy' is canonically connected to Otto's publication bearing the same title (*Das Heilige*, first edition published in 1917), Söderblom already considered the Holy as the foundation of all religion in an entry with a same name (*Holiness*) in Hastings' *Encyclopaedia of Religion and Ethics* (first edition published in 1913). Söderblom argued that 'Holiness is the great word in religion; it is even more essential than the notion of God' while adding that '[r]eal religion may exist without a definite conception of divinity, but there is no real religion without a distinction between holy and profane'.⁸

Nathan Söderblom was ordained a priest in 1893 and since 1914 he held the position of archbishop of the Swedish evangelical church in Uppsala;⁹ in 1930, he became laureate of the Nobel prize for peace that recognized his contribution to ecumenical movement; his thought and work was significantly influenced by personal mystical experiences.¹⁰ He saw the personal communication between God and human beings as the core of religious experience and clearly refused Durkheim's theory of religion and any other social-reductionistic attempts to explain religion.¹¹ Söderblom followed Lang's and Schmidt's theses about the primacy of the monotheistic religion and about the 'high God'. However, the presence of such a deity in non-Christian religions he assessed from a normative Christian viewpoint: 'Although it is apparent that these [high gods] are more significant than spirits and ghosts, they lack the value for the true religion.'¹² The use of the term '*true* religion' alone is a sufficient indication of Söderblom's normative approach and he even further emphasized that 'the only early monotheism in the world that is worthy of this name is the biblical faith in the revelation in its perfection'.¹³

While it is possible to find only rather veiled and implicit references to the exclusive position of Christianity among other religious traditions in Tiele's, Robertson Smith's or Müller's work, Söderblom operated quite openly from the position of a Christian theologian. He did not assess other religions on their own merits and from the perspective of their historical development but applied normative Christian criteria according to which all other religions possess at best only a partial 'truth' which has been, to a certain extent, revealed by God also in the non-Christian religious traditions. He thus argued similarly as Justin Martyr, who also assumed that (Greek) philosophy possesses at best only a partial 'truth' to the extent to which it took part in the God's Word:

> All forms of religion are united in a common group of phenomena, and this union corresponds to the prophetic and Christian belief in a divine self-communication also outside the 'chosen people' and Christendom. It may be difficult to decide what it is in a certain form of religion that constitutes its trait of revelation from a Christian point of view. And it becomes impossible if we employ an intellectualistic view. But a measure of revelation, i.e. of divine self-communication, is present wherever we find religious sincerity. That has been expressly declared by the belief in revelation within and without Christianity.[14]

Söderblom further concluded that it is 'the Christian mission that started the worldwide spiritual process from which a victorious awareness of God as a common property of all humanity should arise, process that drives this awareness towards perfection'.[15] In contrast to Daniel Chantepie de la Saussaye, the Swedish theologian thus did not consider it necessary to draw a demarcation line between the study of religions and theology[16] – the study of religions or the history of religions should serve (as it does in, for example, Tiele's work) to prove God's existence in its own kind;[17] the history of religions operate in an imperialistic way in which other religious traditions are not *a priori* rejected as superstitions or 'paganism' because they do participate, to a certain extent, on the divine revelation via 'the Holy' which is perceived as 'the communication of the God with himself'. However, Söderblom did not have any doubts that this revelation is fulfilled in its entirety only and exclusively in Christianity – as Walter Capps put it, Söderblom showed a clear 'commitment to the normative status of biblical revelation'.[18] For him, revelation of the Holy is 'an experience that cannot be explained reductively nor grasped rationally',[19] therefore it is appropriate to include him with other representatives of the protectionist paradigm.

Söderblom's contemporary Rudolf Otto influenced the study of religion in the twentieth century as few other scholars did; his book *The Idea of the Holy* (*Das Heilige*, 1917) was praised as 'undoubtedly the single most influential work in the history of religions';[20] his role in the establishment of the phenomenology of religion is hard to overstate as '[a]ll phenomenologists of religion are somehow pupils of Otto'.[21] Otto's rather slim volume, first published in 1917 and subsequently reprinted in dozens of editions, formulated the fundamental theses of the protectionist paradigm in the study of religions perhaps more clearly than any other work in the field. Otto assumed that the Holy is fundamental and irreducible religious essence that manifests itself as a specific 'feeling' labelled by our German theologian as 'numinosity' (*das Numinöse*).[22] As he goes on describing this mental state, it is 'perfectly *sui generis* and irreducible to any other; and therefore, like every absolutely primary and elementary datum, while it admits of being discussed, it cannot be strictly defined. There is only one way to help another to an understanding of it. He must be guided and led on by consideration and discussion of the matter through the ways of his own mind, until he reaches the point at which the numinous in him perforce begins to stir, to start into life and into consciousness.'[23]

The Holy is then an *a priory* term,[24] but – as Gregory Alles observed – Otto turned Kant's philosophy on its head because in Kant's view, experience is the result of perceptions being run through *a priori* categories, while in Otto's thought the relationship is reversed: Experience is the primary datum and its conceptualization serves to create main categories for understanding and classifying religious experience.[25] Because the numinous feeling and its modalities (e.g. *mysterium tremendum* as the feeling of fear which is felt by the creation facing its creator; *mysterium fascinans* as the feeling of awe towards Being and its creator; *mysterium augustum* as an exalted contemplation of Being etc.) are, in principle, inaccessible to scientific research, they can be analysed only by a person who already has a previous experience with the Holy, i.e. only and exclusively believers themselves. Otto (just as Schleiermacher) openly demanded from his reader to recall this experience, and if he or she is not able to do so, they should stop reading the book.[26]

This demand may be, in my opinion, understood as a return to the epistemic justification *per hominem* as it was identified by early Christian authors in Chapter 3. The truth value of a certain proposition describing religious experience is no longer justified by miracles or by perfectly moral behaviour; however, Otto's concept somewhat resembles the modality of epistemic justification via spiritual inspiration. It is the believer *qua* believer alone who is called to judge and analyse the response of humankind to the Holy which is revealing itself in various modalities of the numinous feeling. Otto, just as Müller or Tiele, assumed that there is a specific mental faculty which mediates the experience with the Holy to a believer and he called this faculty 'divination'.[27] Otto, just as Söderblom, was entirely convinced that this experience reached its utmost fulfilment in Christianity, which essentially amounts to an introduction of a normative, hierarchical scale of various religious traditions which participate to a lesser or a greater degree in 'the Holy' and thus participate to a lesser or a greater degree in its divine revelation. The Holy 'lives' and is present in all religions; however, '[i]t is pre-eminently a living force in the Semitic religions, and of these again in none has it such vigour as in that of the Bible'.[28]

Otto further claimed that the harmony of the rational and the irrational in religion is a touchstone for evaluating different religious traditions, and, unsurprisingly, he reached the conclusion that 'Christianity, in this as in other respects, stands out in complete superiority over all its sister religions'.[29] However, some scholars argued that Otto's goal was not necessarily to defend Christianity; he rather aimed to 'defend religion in general against anti-religious critique'.[30] The most important aspect of Otto's thought for my purposes is his clear rejection of the possibility of applying a scientific approach to religion, and although the following passage is rather lengthy, I find it convenient to quote it in full, as it amounts to one of the best statements of the fundamental theses of the protectionist paradigm:

> The religious consciousness itself rises against this desiccation and materialization of what in all religion is surely the most tender and living moment, the actual discovery of and encounter with very deity. Here, if anywhere, coercion by proof

and demonstration and the mistaken application of logical and juridical processes should be excluded; here, if anywhere, should be liberty, the unconstrained recognition and inward acknowledgement that comes from deep within the soul, stirred spontaneously, apart from all conceptual theory. If not natural science or metaphysics, at least the matured religious consciousness itself spurns such ponderously solid intellectualistic explanations. They are born of rationalism and engender it again; and, as for genuine divination, they not only impede it, but despise it as extravagant emotionalism, mysticality, and false romanticism. Genuine divination, in short, has nothing whatever to do with natural law and the relation or lack of relation to it of something experienced. It is not concerned at all with the way in which a phenomenon, be it event, person, or thing came into existence, but with what it *means*, that is, with its significance as a sign of the holy. The faculty or capacity of divination appears in the language of dogma hidden beneath the fine name *testimonium Spiritus Sancti internum*, the inner witness of the Holy Spirit limited, in the case of dogma, to the recognition of Scripture as Holy.[31]

Indeed, Otto 'protests against the entire reductionist theory of religious phenomena to simple psychological mechanisms';[32] the introduction of the Holy as rationally, scientifically and logically inaccessible term 'has the purpose to negotiate independence for religion and prevent it from being derived from non-religious phenomena'.[33] It may be concluded that both Söderblom and Otto belong squarely to the protectionist paradigm in the study of religions, since religion in their view cannot be explained in a reductive way; 'materialism' or 'natural science' do not have any place in the field of the study of religions; religious experience is not an illusion, but a natural reaction of humankind to the objectively existing domain of the Holy, and the possibility of this religious experience is established via 'revelation' (Söderblom) or a specific human mental faculty of 'divination' (Otto). Normative evaluation of individual religious traditions and the elevation of Christianity as a perfect religion reveals that both scholars are liberal-Protestant apologists first and religious scholars second. In addition to the rejection of reductionistic theories, Otto explicitly formulated the requirement of 'living faith' as the primary requisite of any scholar working in the field of the study of religions, which, to a certain extent, represents a return to the epistemic justification *per hominem* discussed in Chapter 3.[34]

5.1.2 Founders of the Classical Phenomenology: Kristensen and Van der Leeuw

Nathan Söderblom and Rudolf Otto promoted the vision of the study of religions as a discipline *sui generis* that had no ambition to explain religion away, but rather to understand it with the help of intuitive insight into the essence of the Sacred. For Otto, the reduction of religion to non-religious elements is *ex definitione* excluded because religion can be studied only by a believer through his or her own experience of the Sacred (and for such a person any reductive explanation is out of the question).[35] This line of thought was followed by two important historians of religions who worked primarily in the Netherlands and shaped phenomenology of religion into its 'classical' form in the first half of the twentieth century. Brede Kristensen, a Norwegian who has been awarded professorship of the comparative study of religions at the University of Leiden after Tiele left his position, followed with certain modifications Otto's concept of the Sacred[36] and defended also the central thesis of modified epistemic justification *per hominem* according to which it is necessary for scholars in the field of the study of religions to be themselves believers:

> It is evident that in the philosophical determination of the essence of religion, we make use of data which lie outside the territory of philosophy, outside our knowledge. We make use of our own religious experience in order to understand the experience of others. We should never be able to describe the essence of religion if we did not know from our own experience what religion is (not: what the essence of religion is!). This experience forces itself upon us even in purely historical research. That has already been demonstrated by the mutual relation of the three areas of study. A rational and systematic structure in the science of religion is impossible. Again and again a certain amount of intuition is indispensable.[37]

Kristensen, however, formulated an additional principle that can be characterized as a return to epistemic justification *per hominem* in the study of religions. Together with Otto, he refused 'rational and systematic structure' of religious experience; he demanded that every scholar of the study of religions be a believer; he postulated autonomy of the discipline and its programmatic isolation from other modalities of human knowledge; he perceived the study of religions as the domain of human knowledge that is primarily based on introspection and intuitive knowledge as opposed to the methods commonly used in natural sciences. Moreover, the Norwegian scholar explicitly demanded scholars in the field of the study of religions should always and automatically assume that a believer *qua* believer is always right, no matter what he or she claims about his or her religion. Kristensen did not stop here and insisted that '[e]very religion ought to be understood from its own standpoint, for that is how it is understood by its own adherents';[38] as a corollary, then, '[f]or the historian only one evaluation is possible: "the believers were completely right"',[39] because '[i]f the historian tries to understand the religious data from a different viewpoint than that of the believers, he negates the religious reality. For there is no religious reality other than the faith of the believers'.[40] Kristensen 'intended to counteract a generation of confident efforts, like Tylor's or Frazer's, to *explain* religion, and indeed to "explain it away": "reductionism"'.[41] His argumentative strategy is rather simple: Naturalistic paradigm always presents an interpretation of religion that cannot ever be accepted by a believer. The faith of a believer (from his or her own point of view) is certainly *not* a compensational fantasy or a reaction to dangerous environment and its source is *not* a mere fear from death or the desire to control the nature. In other words, for the standpoint of a believer, his or her faith or religious belief is not an illusion. Should we then, together with Kristensen, *a priori* assume that the only possible interpretation of religious experience is the one which will be accepted by believers, it follows that the study of religions can never explain religion reductively but can only try to approach it by description and understanding.

Phenomenology of religion, in its classical form, was formulated by Kristensen's student Gerardus van der Leeuw (Kristensen was the supervisor of his dissertation).[42] Van der Leeuw was (just as Söderblom) a theologian and ordained a pastor in 1916.[43] He shared almost identical assumptions with all other already mentioned authors: Van der Leeuw commended Otto's *The Idea of the Holy* as 'one of the most remarkable books ever written'[44] and his own concept of the religious 'power' or 'force' (*Macht*) may be seen as a variation on Otto's concept of the Holy.[45] He approvingly referred to Otto also in the context of unequivocal refusal of the naturalistic paradigm and applauded him for 'relentless and repeated warnings against "epigenesis" in any form' and for his 'continued defense of the independence and autonomy of religious experience against any attempt to derive it from other motives'.[46] He followed Kristensen and Otto also in requiring scholars in the field of the study of religions to be believers themselves – in his inaugural lecture at the University of Utrecht in 1918, he stated that '[i]t must be demanded from the scholar in the field of religion that he be religious himself'.[47]

Van der Leeuw formulated two basic methodological assumptions of the classical phenomenology of religion. It is the principle of *epoché* and phenomenological bracketing that should follow 'direct insight' into the essence of religious phenomena (*Wesensschau*) and 'intuitive empathy' (*Einfühlung*). Already in his early works, he firmly opposed the methodology of natural sciences and any attempts of reductive explanation of religion, which is also apparent from his characterisation of the method of intuitive empathy: 'The identification of causal relations is of no use here (one could not "relive" them), but we have to delve into the connections of the stream of consciousness, which cannot be grasped by attempts to quantify, count and measure it from the outside. It is only possible to understand it from the inside, we have to let this unbroken whole act on us in its entirety.'[48] When Van der Leeuw described a phenomenologist in work, he emphasized that he always has to proceed 'intuitively, not analytically, he is not dealing with empirically tangible experiences, but with experiences that can be understood directly in their general essence.'[49] Not causal connections (i.e. *a fortiori* no explanation), but the understanding structural relations (in continuity with Jaspers, Van der Leeuw used consistently the term *verständliche Zusammenhänge*)[50] are what enables scholars of the study of religions to do any meaningful work in their field. This understanding of the structural relations is achievable only through intuition or direct insight and Van der Leeuw himself confessed that this methodological view of the study of religions makes it closer to art than (natural) sciences.[51]

In accordance with the abovementioned tendencies of Van der Leeuw's thought is also his division of sciences, thematized mostly by the work *Introduction to Theology* (*Inleiding tot de theologie*, 1935). This book was analysed in detail by Jacques Waardenburg, one of the most significant experts of Van der Leeuw works, who reached the conclusion that in the context of the entire system of sciences, Van der Leeuw differentiated disciplines that aim to explain (*erfassende Ereigniswissenschaft*) and disciplines that aim to understand (*verstehende Erlebniswissenschaft*), while on the top of the hierarchy of sciences sit theology, which purports to grasp of the 'ultimate meaning'.[52] Waardenburg concluded that '[t]heology, for Van der Leeuw, functions as the norm ("queen") of all sciences',[53] a proposition which resembles closely the Christian subordination of philosophy in relation to revelation as attested in early Christian authors, Augustine or Thomas Aquinas. Natural sciences are not able to offer the ultimate explanation; they suffer from their own inner limitations and the realization of the fact that (natural) sciences can only ever produce provisional, falsifiable knowledge indicates, according to Van der Leeuw, that faith is necessary to obtain a higher level of knowledge. Although Van der Leeuw often made mention of the principle of *epoché* (also in the sense of bracketing the truth values of religious propositions), his modern interpretations generally agreed that his reception of Husserl's philosophy was lamentably shallow and Van der Leeuw never really adhered to the principle of *epoché*.[54] Consider, for instance, his appeal in the concluding sections of his *opus magnum Religion in Essence and Manifestation*:

> Understanding, in fact, itself presupposes intellectual restraint. But this is never the attitude of the cold-blooded spectator: it is, on the contrary, the loving gaze of the lover on the beloved object. For all understanding rests upon self-surrendering love. Were that not the case, then not only all discussion of what appears in religion, but all discussion of appearance in general, would be quite impossible; since to him who does not love, nothing whatever is manifested; this is the Platonic, as well as the Christian, experience.[55]

Van der Leeuw further emphasized, contrary to Tylor's, Frazer's and Freud's, that 'phenomenology knows nothing of any historical "development" of religion, still less of an "origin" of religion. Its perpetual task is to free itself from every non-phenomenological standpoint to retain its own liberty, while it conserves the inestimable value of this position always anew.'[56] The key thesis of the protectionist paradigm, namely a thorough refusal of the possibility of explanation of religion in a reductionistic way, is unambiguously adopted by Van der Leeuw, and, as Ivan Strenski concluded, 'Van der Leeuw seeks to do a job that is *descriptive*, not *explanatory*. [...] That is to say, that we will only meet with disappointment if we seek *explanations* from phenomenologists like Van der Leeuw'.[57] His phenomenological project could be seen as an intermediary stage between the 'factual' philological and historical theology on the one side and the dogmatic-systematic theology that is 'illuminating the truth' on the other.[58] In brief, the study of religions as Van der Leeuw constituted it is 'a doxology to the God Christians worship'.[59]

5.1.3 Phenomenology in Germany: Scheler, Frick, Heiler

Further development in the phenomenology of religion continued in the German-speaking world in the direction set out by Rudolf Otto. One of the first representatives of philosophically more erudite phenomenology of religion was Max Scheler, who focused on the topic of religion mainly in the second part of his work *On the Eternal in Man* (*Vom Ewigen in Menschen*, 1921). He criticized psychological explanatory theories which, according to Scheler, reduce religion to a 'collection of psychic phenomena, which required to be described, casually explained, and at best conceived teleologically (from the biological aspect) as a particular stage in man's adaptation to his environment'.[60] Against this 'atheistic, explanatory religious psychology' Scheler argued in favour of the phenomenology of religion,[61] and he did, just like all the other authors mentioned so far in this chapter, emphasize the role of the modified version of epistemic justification *per hominem*:

> Since it is of the *essence* of a religious object that it can attest its possible reality only through and in an act of *faith*, all those who do not possess the appropriate belief in a religious reality fail to satisfy the *precondition* for empirically knowing and observing the action of the religious object on the *psyche*. To give an example, it is clear that nobody who does not possess *belief* in the Real Presence of Christ in the Sacrament can seek even to *describe* the psychic experiences induced by a Catholic's pious assistance at the holy Mass.[62]

Heinrich Frick, the author of *Comparative Religion* (*Vergleichende Religionswissenschaft*), a rather slim volume published in an influential summarizing series *Sammlung Göschen* in 1928, adopts the concept of the sacred as a basis for his work,[63] and just as Söderblom or Otto, he is convinced that although other religious traditions can participate on the sacred, the sacred is revealing itself entirely only in Christianity: 'The awe with respect to that which is under us, which recognizes as divine also the lowly, pain and death; that which worships even sin and transgression as the promotion of the Holy – that is ultimate and highest, that is Christianity.'[64] With respect to the relationship between theology and the study of religions, Frick advocated the same solution as Söderblom or Van der Leeuw did: 'If the comparative study of religions remains within its strictly defined bounds, not only does it not present any danger for theological reflection, but rather represents an indispensable part of modern theology.'[65] Indeed, one may easily guess what these 'strictly defined bounds' mean – the study of religions as *ancilla theologiae*, i.e. the study of religions that is subservient to theological interest and confessional apologetics, either in missionary work or as providing a seemingly 'scientific' proof that Christianity is the religion *non plus ultra* among other religious traditions.

Friedrich Heiler, together with Wilhelm Schmidt one of the few representatives of the Roman Catholic confession,[66] taught and worked at the University in Marburg (just as Otto) and was significantly influenced by the thought of Nathan Söderblom, whose Gifford's lectures he published in German under the title *The Living God* (*Der Lebendige Gott im Zeugnis der Religionsgeschichte*, 1942). He also met Söderblom personally in Uppsala in 1919, where he presented a cycle of lectures *The Essence of Catholicism* (*Wesen des Katholizismus*).[67] Heiler's significant early work is his dissertation *The Prayer* (*Das Gebet*, published as a monograph in 1919), defended in the same year as Otto's *The Idea of the Holy* (*Das Heilige*) was published. Already here the German phenomenologist formulated the requirement for the scholar of religions to be religious himself or herself, arguing that 'who never felt on his own a religious impulse will never penetrate into the world of religion, so rich in miracles and enigmas.'[68] Essential for the phenomenological approach was to become his late synthesizing work *The Manifestations and Essence of Religion* (*Erscheinungsformen und Wesen der Religion*, 1961), a work that may be considered one of the last monographs focused on the classical phenomenology of religion and a book that completes the 'trilogy' of important works of German provenience related to the phenomenology of religion and indebted to Otto's legacy.[69]

Most instructive for my purposes is the introduction from the last mentioned Heiler's work, where he outlined necessary requirements that any scholar in the field of the study of religions had to fulfil. With respect to methodology, Heiler considered the phenomenological approach the only possible one for any successful research of religion.[70] He did not, however, propose only specific scientific methodology, but also required certain personal qualities of his fellow scholars: In the first place, 'reverence for all true religions';[71] in the second place, Heiler demanded 'personal religious experience';[72] in the third place, there is a requirement to accept religion as *a priori* true and to reject any form of reductive explanation:

> The third requirement is *to take seriously the truth-claims of religions*. Religion can never be understood correctly if we explain it away as superstition, illusion or a bogeyman. [...] Every study of religions is, after all, theology, insofar as it has to do not only with psychological and historical phenomena, but also with the experience of otherworldly realities.[73]

A competent researcher in the field of the study of religions is thus only the researcher that is himself or herself religious. It is not surprising that his modern interpreters argued that, for Heiler, the study of religion is simply 'liberal philosophical theology',[74] and he tried to use the phenomenological method as 'a substitute proof for the existence of God'.[75] The affiliation of all the authors discussed in this section to the protectionist paradigm need no further elaboration.

5.1.4 The Atlantic connection: Wach and Eliade

Another significant figure representing the protectionist paradigm rooted in German phenomenology of religion was Joachim Wach, who studied under Friedrich Heiler in Munich.[76] Many researchers focusing on the history of the study of religions considered him to be one of the 'founding fathers' of the study of religions in the United States,[77] where he emigrated to escape Nazism. For many years, he worked at the University of Chicago and together with his future successor Mircea Eliade founded so-called 'Chicago school' which, to a significant extent, shaped the discourse of the study of religions in the United States of America. As with all previously mentioned authors, Wach's inspiration by Otto is clear,[78] since the German *émigré* defined religion as the 'experience of the Sacred' and argued (just as Scheler did) that '[a]n examination of definitions of religion is beyond our scope. However, the most workable one still appears to be short and simple: "Religion is the experience of the Holy." This concept of religion stresses the objective character of religious experience in contrast to psychological theories of its purely subjective (illusionary) nature which are so commonly held among anthropologists'.[79] Although he did not explicitly name authors of these 'psychological theories', it is apparent that he had the likes of Tylor, Frazer or Radin in mind. His disdain for reductive approaches in the study of religions knows no bounds:

Nothing is more embarrassing than the helpless attempt to interpret religious texts or monuments by someone who does not know what awe and holy shiver and for whom these attestations of humankinds search for the unification with the ultimate Truth are only outward attestations of a sensibility of a 'mentally ill' or backward-thinking people.[80]

Wach adopted *verbatim* also Otto's inner division of the Holy into its individual modalities (*mysterium tremendum, fascinans, augustum* etc.) and insisted that this religious experience 'will ultimately defy any attempt to describe, analyse, and comprehend its meaning scientifically'.[81] Not only that – Wach simply *a priori* postulated that phenomenological hermeneutics 'has an eternal right over against all rationalism in the understanding of religious expressions',[82] and the requirement of empirical verification of hypotheses has been rejected already in his earlier texts as an inadequate basis for the study of religions.[83] If the 'scientific', i.e. empiric falsification (or verification) is rejected, it is necessary to ask what kind of method a scholar in the study of religions should use to reach his or her goal. Wach again, in continuity with Otto, accepted the latter's concept of the 'sense for perceiving the Holy' (*sensus numinis*) and fought against any suggestion of a reductive explanation of religious phenomena which could threaten to demask religion as an illusion.[84]

Wach, quite like all the aforementioned authors, required personal religious experience as a necessary condition for successful work in the field of the study of religions; he specifically asked for 'an adequate emotional condition [...], not indifference, as positivism in its heyday believed [...], but rather an engagement of feeling, interest, *metexis*, or participation';[85] in a different text, Wach, in continuity with Schleiermacher or Kristensen, repeated that 'we must learn from our own personal religious life in order to encounter the foreign';[86] in continuity with German *Religionsgeschichtliche Schule*, Söderblom and Otto, he endorsed a normative hierarchical organization of individual religions and it is not surprising that Christianity is again placed on the symbolical pedestal.[87] For a better understanding of Wach's approach to the study of religions, it is convenient to cite a section in which he openly described what all other scholars belonging to the protectionist approach actually thought, but only a few of them explicitly acknowledged. Wach namely claimed that it is simply impossible to assume a 'neutral position' in the study of religions with respect to epistemic justification or truth values of religious propositions:

> The West has to relearn from Kierkegaard that religion is something toward which 'neutrality' is not possible. It is true that dangers accompany the appeal to emotions and the arousing of passions. Yet emotions and passions do play a legitimate role in religions. It is precisely here that the *raison d'être*, the best justification, for the comparative study of religions can be and must be found. It is an error to believe that comparative studies must breed indifference. They contribute toward gaining the perspective, as well as of discernment and understanding.[88]

Wach's central theoretical-methodological positions therefore differed little from those of other representatives of the protectionist paradigm (Müller, Tiele, Robertson

Smith, Delitzsch): 'It is the task of theology to investigate, buttress, and teach the faith of a religious community to which it is committed, as well as to kindle zeal and fervor for the defense and spread of this faith, it is the responsibility of a comparative study of religion to guide and to purify it.'[89] As one of Wach's recent commentators concluded, 'study of religions serves on the one side as a proof of natural revelation and on the other side it should lead all religions participating on this revelation to a special revelation in Jesus Christ as the highest form of the self-revelation of God'.[90]

In the final part of this brief introduction to the 'classical' phenomenology of religion, I have to turn to one of the most significant representatives of this approach, Mircea Eliade.[91] If Otto's work *Das Heilige* was pronounced to be one of the most important books of the study of religion, Eliade is consistently labelled as one of the most influential figures of this discipline.[92] Although the word 'history' is frequently occurring in his most significant works (e.g. *Traité d'histoire des religions*, work originally written in Romanian and subsequently translated into French, or his *opus magnum* in three volumes, *Histoire des croyances et des idées religieuses*)[93] and Eliade in some places argued in favour of a division between the study of religions and theology while putting emphasis on empiric approach,[94] current consensus among scholars considers Eliade to be a full-fledged phenomenologist of religion,[95] while some critics perceived his stated interest in empiric and historically contextualized research as a hollow declaration whose only goal is to conjure an impression of a scientific approach.[96]

For Eliade, the study of religion in its individual historical traditions is only a starting point. The true goal of the scholar should be focused on an identification of so-called 'hierophanies' (manifestations of the Sacred) in these historical traditions, analysing them by means of 'creative hermeneutics'[97] and identifying in them the shared and strictly ahistorical essence. Eliade pushed *ad absurdum* the thesis of his predecessors about religion being an autonomous reality *sui generis* – for Eliade, not only religion, but also his own method of studying religion is an autonomous reality *sui generis*.[98] Eliade is not primarily a historian, but phenomenologist, and it is possible to attest in his thought the same characteristics of this approach as in all already mentioned representatives of the protectionist paradigm, mainly the rejection of methods of the natural sciences in the study of religions.[99] Beside the explicit continuity with Otto's *a priori* concept of the Holy,[100] Eliade argued against any form of reduction of religion to non-religious elements:

> But admitting the historicity of religious experience does not imply that they are reducible to non-religious forms of behavior. Stating that a religious datum is always a historical datum does not mean that it is reducible to a non-religious history – for example, to an economic, social, or political history.[101]

With respect to the requirement of faith (or some form of religiosity) on the part of scholars working in the field of the study of religions as a necessary condition for their work, Eliade came with a completely radical solution – a human being is simply identified as *homo religiosus*, no matter if he or she accepts the label or not. If Freud, Frazer or Tylor explained religion by reduction to non-religious elements, then Eliade turned this relation on its head and claimed that even people who do not consider themselves religious are latent believers anyway, only they are not aware of their inner faith and unconsciously search for harmony with the Sacred in their attempts to escape from the horrors of 'history', only to find secondary and derived forms of the Sacred in activities such as reading of books or watching movies (by getting lost in their stories),[102] or even in the 'American way of life'.[103] According to Eliade, the study of religions is not a descriptive scientific discipline, but it rather has a 'soteriological function'[104] – it reveals the Sacred and aims to reform and renew the modern, secularized individual.[105] It is clear from what has been said that both Wach and Eliade belong to the protectionist paradigm of the study of religions, however, it is important to emphasize that Eliade, in contrast to Wach and many other scholars in the field of the phenomenology of religion, did not promote a single religious tradition (Christianity) at the expense of others.

5.2 Phenomenology and its critics after 1945

Although phenomenologists of religion active in the first half of the twentieth century often differed among themselves in particularities, all of them shared basic tenets of the protectionist paradigm, i.e. the view of religion as a phenomenon *sui generis* and establishment of the study of religions as a scientific discipline *sui generis*; stringent rejection of reductionistic explanation of religious experience; refusal of even considering applying theoretical-methodological procedures of natural sciences in the study of religions; focus on introspection, empathy (*Einfühlung*) and understanding (*Verstehen*); neglect for historical anchoring of the specifics forms of religious life; last but not least, a return to a modified version of epistemic justification *per hominem* which dictates, on the one hand, that scholars must be religious themselves in order to even begin to work competently in the field of the study of religions and, on the other hand, the claim that the verdict of the believers is the ultimate deciding factor in assessing truth values of propositions that are related to the religion of those believers.

Phenomenology became the dominant approach in the study of religions in the first half of the twentieth century, a fact that is appreciated even by its later critics. In 1973, Theo van Baaren noted that in the years 1920–1940, Gerardus van der Leeuw and Rudolf Otto completely defined theoretical-methodological discussion in the study of religions and '[t]heir combined influence is still strong';[106] Lammert Leertouwer in the same year concluded that 'it is still phenomenology of religion, at least on the continent of Europe, which is accounted *the* method of systematic science of religion, in spite of the fact that precisely problems of methods are little attended to by phenomenologists'.[107] A couple of years later, Lauri Honko spoke with respect to phenomenology about its 'methodological imperialism' and although he argued that 'Father Wilhelm Schmidt, Rudolf Otto, Gerardus van der Leeuw and Mircea Eliade no longer rule [methodology of the study of religions]',[108] the Finnish scholar was, in 1979, still expressing a mere wish rather than describing the actual state of affairs.

Although it is true that since the end of the 1970s, the phenomenology of religion gradually became the target of a small group of methodological reformers, in 1984,

Frank Whaling could still argue in summarizing the theory and methodology of the study of religions that 'the general phenomenological concerns of *epoché* and *Einfühlung* have been fairly widely accepted as underlying principles of religious studies in general and comparative religion in particular'.[109] This may be attested also on an institutional and personal level. The organization and decision-making processes connected with the congresses of the *International Association for the History of Religions* (IAHR) during the years 1950–1970 were almost exclusively in the hands of the scholars affiliated with the phenomenological approach.[110] I will now briefly introduce the most significant directions of the theoretical-methodological discussion in the study of religions in the period from the end of the Second World War approximately to the year 1980, with special focus on the reception of the phenomenological approach introduced in the previous section.[111]

5.2.1 Historical approach: Pettazzoni, Bianchi

I have shown in the preceding section that the phenomenological approach often wilfully ignored historical conditionality of religious experience and attempted to grasp the essence of religious phenomena. This methodological directive, connected mainly to names such as Van der Leeuw and Eliade, provoked a critical reaction and a substantial part of theoretical-methodological discussion in the period between 1950–1980 was marked by a conflict between the phenomenological and historical approach.[112] In this respect, it is possible to consider the Italian duo Raffaele Pettazzoni and Ugo Bianchi as the most significant representatives of the historical approach. They criticized phenomenology mainly for its ahistoricity, its emphasis on intuition as a methodological key for understanding religion, and especially for the merger of theology and study of religions, or, rather, a contamination of the supposedly impartial scientific research by normative and apologetic goals.[113]

However, the historical approach did not completely distance itself from phenomenology and rather called for integration of these two main branches of the study of religions (i.e. systematic and historical approach).[114] With respect to the difference between the naturalistic and protectionist paradigm, it is important to emphasize that that there are practically no attempts to introduce reductive explanation in the works of representatives of the historical branch, whether we take into consideration the very beginnings of this approach in the nineteenth century when 'many historians [of religion] regarded description of the facts as tantamount to an explanation, so that there was often no stimulus to further analysis',[115] or its more developed form in the twentieth century. Indeed, Ugo Bianchi explicitly pointed out that 'historian of religions must beware of the "reductionist" temptation, and of the tendency to give facile explanations'.[116] Historical approach thus cannot mark the return to the naturalistic paradigm and to reductionistic explanation of religious phenomena. Rather, it criticized bias and the lack of historical anchoring of the phenomenological approach and called for an integration of both of these branches of research in the field of the study of religions.

5.2.2 British school of social anthropology: Radcliffe-Brown, Evans-Pritchard

If there is an obvious place to look for continuation of the naturalistic paradigm in the study of religions, then it would possibly be in the British anthropology which, after all, could follow in the footsteps of its founders of the likes of Tylor, Frazer and Malinowski. However, even a cursory evaluation of the main protagonists of their institutional heirs shows the opposite. During the first half of the twentieth century, the so-called British School of Social Anthropology completely abandoned the reductive explanatory ambitions of its predecessors and used social-functionalist methods with emphasis on fieldwork. In the manifesto of the British School of Social Anthropology, Alfred Radcliffe-Brown expressed himself very clearly when he, in contrast to his predecessors, argued that the social anthropology does not 'deal with origins but with social functions of religions, i.e. the contribution that they make to the formation and maintenance of a social order'.[117] This position has been shared by his contemporary, E. E. Evans-Pritchard, who dedicated a whole monograph to critical evaluation of the naturalistic paradigm and its fundamental early proponents:

> What use as a guide to field research are Tylor's and Müller's and Durkheim's theories of the genesis of religion? It is the word genesis on which emphasis is placed. It was because explanations of religion were offered in terms of origins that these theoretical debates, once so full of life and fire, eventually subsided. To my mind, it is extraordinary that anyone could have thought it worth while to speculate about what might have been the origin of some custom or belief, when there is absolutely no means of discovering, in absence of historical evidence, what was its origin. And yet this is what almost all our authors explicitly or implicitly did, whether their theories were psychological or sociological [...].[118]

According to Evans-Pritchard, it makes no sense to ask for an explanation of the origins of religion because such question lies outside of the capabilities of the scientific scrutiny – this is the fundamental thesis of structural-functionalist methodology that eventually 'came to dominate social anthropology until the 1960s'.[119] If the earliest period of the British anthropology was marked by the attempts of explaining religion reductively, a competing approach started to gain more ground in the period between the two World Wars abandoned all reductive explanation and focused more on partial hypotheses oriented on the function of religion in a specific social groups. Evans-Pritchard was aware of the basic conflict between the naturalistic and protectionist paradigm and, as is natural for a Catholic convert,[120] he tenaciously rejected any attempts to explain religion away. As Daniel Pals stated, according to the British anthropologist, a 'scholar without any personal religious commitment is unlikely to succeed in it. For the study of religion is not entirely like other disciplines. Scholars who reject all religion will inevitably be looking for an explanation that reduces it, for some theory – biological, social, or psychological – that will explain it away. The believer, on the other hand, is a person much more likely to see religion – including other people's religions – from the inside and to try to explain it on terms that are its own'.[121]

Although I cannot pursue here in any great detail the transformations of the British anthropology in the post-war era, its most significant figures, such as Evans-Pritchard's student Mary Douglas or Victor and Edith Turner shared the fight against the reductionism of Tylor or Frazer. Timothy Larsen argued, quite correctly in my opinion, that anthropology played very different roles for the older and for the newer generations of British social anthropologists: By studying anthropology, Tylor lost his Christian faith; by studying anthropology, the Turners found theirs. Frazer used comparative perspective to question the truth of Christianity; Mary Douglas, on the contrary, tried to use it to strengthen this truth.[122] The explicit refusal of reductionism and the frequent use of modified category of 'the Sacred' may be found also in Roy Rappaport's work, considered to be a modern classic of ecological anthropology.[123] Just as in case of the historical approach represented by Pettazzoni and Bianchi, it is not possible to speak about the return to naturalism and explanation in the works of those above-mentioned protagonists of anthropology of religion.

5.2.3 Transformations of post-classical phenomenology: Bleeker, Widengren, Smart

One of the last representatives of the classical phenomenology and defenders of Van der Leeuw's legacy was Jouco Bleeker,[124] an important figure in the field of the study of religions also because of his position in IAHR (secretary from 1950 to 1965) and co-editorship of *Historia Religionum* (1969–1971).[125] Bleeker affiliated himself with the protectionist paradigm and denied the possibility of a reductionistic explanation simply because 'a religio-historical explanation should never be a reduction of religion to non-religious factors, either anthropological, or psychological, or sociological'.[126]

In agreement with Söderblom, Kristensen and other representatives of classical phenomenology, he held the opinion that besides good knowledge of historical data, scholars in the field of the study of religions should follow 'the principle of Nathan Söderblom, who declared that in order to understand the religion of the African negroes one should learn to think black'.[127] Bleeker eventually elaborated on this line of thought in a little less controversial manner by stating that 'the true evaluation of methods [in the study of religions] would be to retain only those methods which let religious people themselves testify their faith'.[128] This simply means that the believers are again identified as the last instance passing judgment on the results generated by an academic study of religions. From his speech on the occasion of the opening of the IAHR Congress in 1975 it is apparent that, according to Bleeker, the study of religions should not, as a scientific discipline, limit itself to generation of knowledge about religion, but that it should play an active, supporting role in the spiritual revival of the secular world into a new religious sensibility, albeit he argued in favour of this idea in a rather indirect form:

> Let us not forget that we are living in a period in which religion and cultural values are compelled to fight for their very existence. The question arises: What will be the future of religion and of our civilization? Science cannot corroborate, nor can it

renew a faltering faith and a decaying culture. Nor can the history of religions. But it could make its contribution to the solution of the crisis by presenting a clear picture of the intrinsic value of religion. The history of religions, studied impartially and critically, shows that religion always has been one of the noblest possessions of humanity, and that it has for the most part served to spiritualize culture. This is a truth which might bring new hope to the present generation, a generation which is struggling for more spiritual certainty and for a culture permeated by the ideas of justice and peace.[129]

Bleeker here clearly defended the fundamental theses of the protectionist paradigm and he may be cited as one of the last important representatives of the classical phenomenological approach to religion. Geo Widengren, the second editor of the already mentioned two-volume work *Historia Religionum*, advocated rather different form of phenomenological research. He is the author of one of the last large handbooks of phenomenology – his *Phenomenology of Religion* (*Religionsphänomenologie*)[130] was published in German in 1969 (first edition in Swedish, 1945) to wide positive acclaim.[131] Widengren differentiated phenomenology as (1) *systematics*, which does not take the historical development or social and psychological influences into consideration, but it offers structural typology of individual significant spheres which are recurrent in individual religious traditions (e.g. myth, sacrifice, ritual, prayer, issue of the existence of evil, eschatology, apocalypse etc.), and (2) *history of religions*, which describes the development of individual religious traditions diachronically. In contrast to the 'classical' phenomenology, Widengren abandoned the *Wesensschau* as a methodological principle and did not entertain any spectacular metaphysical claims.[132] According to modern interprets of his work, his is a 'harmless comparative approach',[133] and some scholars rightfully concluded that 'Widengren and Heiler cannot be further apart in their understanding of the phenomenological method'.[134] After all, Widengren himself criticized one of the cornerstones of the classical phenomenology, namely Otto's concept of the Holy.[135] He also had serious doubts with respect to the possibilities of application of the widely accepted phenomenological 'suspension of judgement' (*epoché*) in the field of the study of religions.[136]

Although Widengren could be credited with a return from the 'classical' phenomenological method back to the comparative perspective that would be analogous to Müller's concept of comparative theology or Tiele's morphology of religious experience, this Swedish scholar programmatically denied the possibility of explaining religious experience by reduction to non-religious elements, which is the fundamental premise of the naturalistic paradigm. Widengren correctly connected evolutionism with the attempt at an explanation of the origins of religion, but in his interpretations he did not differentiate much between 'origin' in the sense of historical origins of religion (i.e. when and in what circumstances did the 'first' religion emerge?) and 'origin' in the sense of psychological origins of religion (i.e. which psychological mechanisms are responsible for the emergence and transmission of religious representations and ideas?). The question of 'origins', which Widengren perceived rather in the sense of 'historical origins', is simply refused as unscientific:

The origin of religion lies beyond that which can be explored scientifically – we can only have a very imprecise notion of the oldest imaginable forms of religion. The attempt to find the origin of religion must be abandoned in the same way as the old evolutionistic methods.[137]

Another author who attempted to reform phenomenology 'from the inside' was Ninian Smart. With respect to the history of the phenomenology of religion, Smart differentiated 'pure typological phenomenology' (in short, typology) and 'metaphysical phenomenology'.[138] Authors such as Chantepie de la Saussaye, Tiele or previously mentioned Geo Widengren belong to the first category, while Otto, Van der Leeuw, Kristensen, Heiler or Eliade belong to the second one. Smart understood his own approach to operate within the first category as an attempt to establish more dynamic phenomenology (Bleeker already tried to accomplish this with his conception of *entelecheia*)[139] and he did not shun from criticizing the main representatives of 'metaphysical phenomenology'.[140] Just as Widengren, however, he refused explanatory reductionism of the naturalistic paradigm.[141] Although Smart dedicated a whole chapter to the issue of explanation,[142] an 'explanation' for him did not mean reduction of religious experience to non-religious phenomena, but something that he labelled 'intra-religious explanation', i.e. explanation of one religious phenomenon by another religious phenomenon. This method was thought to overcome and reform the traditional, static phenomenology and Smart was highly suspicious of the possibility of establishing a (reductive) 'extra-religious explanation', although he indicated that these two modes of explanation could possibly create a 'symbiotic' relation in the future.[143]

5.2.4 The study of religions as ecumenical theology: Frick, Benz, Heiler, Cantwell Smith

The initiatives that focused on reforming the phenomenology of religion were not the only theoretical-methodological proposals in the period from 1950–1980. Beside it, there were also authors who inclined to rather different goals, goals that were established already by the ecumenical Parliament of the World's Religions, first convened in 1893 in Chicago with an explicitly stated aim to 'unite all Religion against all irreligion'.[144] Heinrich Frick, who was already mentioned in one of the previous sections of this chapter, asked himself in his intervention at the first modern IAHR congress in 1950 if the solemnly proclaimed (although in practice hardly existent) 'neutrality' of the scientific research in the field of the study of religions is adequate from a methodological standpoint or even morally justifiable.[145] He answered the question negatively and proposed that 'our congress should be more involved in rising above the mere neutral information and research,'[146] of course ideally in the service of the wider goals of ecumenical theology.

During the IAHR congress in 1965, Ernst Benz proposed that the study of religions should fulfil the same tasks as the ecumenical Christian theology in bringing individual Christian denominations closer together – according to Benz, the study of religions should be ecumenical movement of all world religions,[147] and the author himself as a liberal Protestant theologian has been convinced that 'the history of religions and the history of the development of the religious consciousness must be seen as coterminous with the history of salvation. If the revelation in Christ is really the fulfilment of time, then it must also be the fulfilment of the history of religions'.[148]

In an essay from 1959, Friedrich Heiler highlighted the hidden unity of all religions (behind manifestations and phenomena of individual religions, there is the one 'true religion') and by comparing individual religious traditions he came to a conclusion that is the opposite of Frazer's. If, for Frazer, analogies between Christian ideas and rituals and 'pagan' religions of the Antiquity represented a line of potential critique, for Heiler, this unity is an indication for the 'truth of religion'.[149] Heiler triumphantly closed his text with the following message as far as the aims and methods of the study of religions are concerned:

> A new era will dawn upon mankind when the religions will rise to true tolerance and co-operation in behalf of mankind. To assist in preparing the way for this era is one of the finest hopes of the scientific study of religion.[150]

Heiler claimed outright that *scientific* study of religion should become ecumenical theology in order to fulfil its mission. Wilfred Cantwell Smith, beside Joachim Wach and Mircea Eliade one of the most influential scholars of the study of religions in North America, held virtually the same views. Fully in accordance with the protectionist paradigm, he *a priori* demanded that whenever the question of truth values of propositions related to the specific religions, believers affiliated with this or that particular religion should have the last word:

> For I would proffer this as my second proposition: that no statement about a religion is valid unless it can be acknowledged by that religion's believers. I know that this is revolutionary, and I know that it will not be readily conceded; but I believe it to be profoundly true and important.[151]

Such methodological requirement is not revolutionary at all, as this chapter purported to show, but Cantwell Smith was right in claiming that these special requirements formulated by him and other fellow scholars of religion were not accepted without any resistance. Proposals with similar theological-ecumenical message were sometimes harshly criticized, as can be attested for example in the protest declaration against the infiltration of apologetical theology into the scientific study of religions, which Zwi Werblowsky, a defender of the scientific and naturalistic approach to religion, circulated during the IAHR congress in Marburg (1960) in the form of a list of basic theses that should regulate the study of religions.[152] One year earlier, he stated, with a healthy dose of irony, the following:

> When we hear and read the many statements on this topic [*sc.* methodology of the study of religions], one often has the feeling that all the world torn apart by hate, discord, mutual distrust and hideous passions of all kinds needs is the gentle light of religion and the radiance of its spirit of soft wisdom and tolerance to return to the path of reason and true human progress.[153]

5.2.5 The Groningen Group: Van Baaren, Drijvers, Waardenburg

A systematic critique of the phenomenological methodology was introduced in the 1970s by the so-called Groningen Group, a loose collection of scholars dissatisfied with the current state of the theoretical-methodological discussions in the study of religions. Among its most significant representatives were Theo van Baaren and Jacques Waardenburg. Van Baaren criticized phenomenology because of its dissociation from the historical and cultural environment in which individual religions are situated;[154] Lammert Leertouwer rejected *a priori* postulated central terms of phenomenology of religion, especially 'the Holy' (Otto) or 'Power' (Van der Leeuw) as 'mystifications' without any corresponding representation in reality;[155] Han Drijvers subjected to critique the epistemic justification *per hominem* which presumed that the final arbiter of the truth values of propositions related to individual religions are only and exclusively the believers of those religions.[156]

The problematic nature of this methodological assumption was brought to attention also previously by other scholars: Ugo Bianchi, in addition to the obvious impossibility of applying this principle to ancient religions, pointed out that believers often have only very unclear ideas about the tenets of the religions they profess;[157] Zwi Werblowsky further argued that the 'the faith of the believer' can be a touchstone only when we strive to understand the subjective view of that particular believer – whenever we try to explain religious phenomenon 'objectively' (as it is in the case of reductive explanation in the context of the naturalistic paradigm), believer's opinion will not play any role in such an explanation.[158]

The synthesis of the most significant line of critique of the classical phenomenology has been delivered mainly by Jacques Waardenburg, who refused the *sui generis* approach to religious experience ('There is no legitimate scholarly reason to consider data which have a religious meaning to people as constituting a separate realm, just as there is no legitimate scholarly reason to consider what is called religion in different cultures and societies to as constituting an autonomous reality.');[159] intertwining of theology and the study of religions ('... classical phenomenology has in fact played an ideological role within the study of religion...');[160] and value judgements ('...religion has not only been considered a value category in itself, but also that it has been presupposed that religion is and ought to remain generally existing and universally human.').[161] Waardenburg ultimately reached the conclusion that 'a religious view of religion makes phenomenology of religion out to be less a product of scholarship than a world view and perhaps a form of religion itself'.[162]

Although the Groningen group managed to subject classical phenomenology to a serious critique, it was not immediately clear what should replace it. Waardenburg's own ideas turned again to a 'reformation' of phenomenology (so-called 'new style' phenomenology) which would replace the supposed 'objective' meanings by subjective ones, emphasizing the role of intentionality in their making and proposing to study religion as a 'system of signification'.[163] Waardenburg did not pronounce a final verdict on the possibility of reductive explanation, but Theo van Baaren intentionally omitted the question of 'origins' of religion from the discussion.[164] The methodological crisis at the turn of the 1970s and 1980s is best captured in the words of Michael Pye who on the one side agreed that the era of the epistemic justification *per hominem* is probably over, but on the other side it was anybody's guess as to which theoretical-methodological approach could or should replace it:

> We must continue to be haunted by the possibility of a more general theory of the meaning of depth-structures of religion [...] which must be expected in some ways to supersede or even to contradict the self-understanding of at least some of those involved. Unfortunately no methodologically clear lines of approach seem to have emerged in this area yet, and it remains an urgent problem.[165]

5.3 Conclusion: Elimination of the naturalistic paradigm in the study of religions

In conclusion of Chapters 4 and 5, I hope to have shown that, with the exception of a brief period at the turn of the nineteenth and twentieth century when Tylor, Frazer or Freud formulated their psychological theories of the emergence of religion and Durkheim his sociological theory in the context of the naturalistic paradigm, the modern study of religions for the larger part of its history lied under the sway of the protectionist paradigm, especially in the decades when the phenomenology of religion dominated the field.[166] Raphael's *Transfiguration* may again serve as a convenient visual representation of a large part of history of the study of religions in the nineteenth and twentieth centuries. Although a handful of scholars and authors active mostly during the belle époque attempted to explain religion by its reduction to non-religious phenomena, their fate was, in a broader context, the same as the fate of the apostles trying to cure the boy possessed by a demon. A significant number of their contemporaries, especially the advocates of the phenomenology of religion, were convinced that, just as Jesus must descend from the mountain to heal the boy who cannot be cured solely by secular wisdom, the sacred supernatural blaze in the form of the commitment of religious faith on the side of the scholar of religions and his or her commitment to showing absolute respect to the standpoint of believers was necessary to guide the methodology of the study of religions. The painting captures also another assumption of the protectionist paradigm – just as the two halves of the painting are separated from each other by means of light and composition, the *sui generis* model of the study of religions in the context of the protectionist paradigm is separated from the 'secular wisdom', especially from the methods of natural sciences. Raphael's work even accurately depicts their mutual hierarchical relationship (from the point of view of protectionists) – religion and the study of religions as a discipline that describes religion stands at the top, while all other disciplines are situated below it. Indeed, Wach's claim that 'any form of reduction falls short of the aim of a student of religion, which is to do justice to that religion's true nature', serving as the epigraph to this chapter, encapsulates best the methodological positions of protectionists.

The dominance of the protectionist paradigm in the study of religions continued in the 1980s in spite of a wider and stronger chorus of critics who were, however, unable to replace phenomenology with another methodological programme. A summarizing essay that mapped psychological theories of religion from the years 1945–1985 concluded that '[t]heir common goal is to "understand" (*verstehen*) religious experience, not by means of reductive causal explanation, but by "reliving" the experience emphatically';[167] a summary of socio-anthropological studies focusing on the same period came to an identical result: 'It is a fair generalization that many anthropological studies of religion are not concerned with the explanation of religion but with the role of religion in the explanation of society'.[168] In the 1970s in the Old Continent and at the beginning of the 1980s in the North America, however, a significant opposition[169] to the protectionist paradigm has formed and the chasm between the naturalists and protectionists became so wide that in 1985 it caused a split even on an institutional level, when a group of scholars (Donald Wiebe, Luther Martin and Thomas Lawson) left the *American Academy of Religion* (AAR) and founded *North American Association for the Study of Religion* (NAASR).[170] The reason for such a decision was AAR's more or less open endorsement of the protectionist paradigm which had a corollary in 'the Academy's negative, if not hostile, behavior toward other, scientifically oriented, associations committed to the study of religions phenomena'.[171] This group of scholars then prepared the ground for the return of the explanation to the study of religions, especially in the form of the cognitive science of religion (CSR), whose significance will be analysed with respect to its methodology, terminology and practice in the following chapters.[172]

6

Cognitive science of religion (1): Methodology

We need a method if we are to investigate the truth of things.

Descartes[1]

In the first part of this work, comprising the previous five chapters, I have presented the naturalist and the protectionist paradigm in the study of religions by focusing on its origins in the Presocratic philosophy and earliest Christian literature and following its developments in the modern study of religion in the late nineteenth and first half of the twentieth century. The second part of this work, comprising the next four chapters, including this one, will deal primarily with the cognitive science of religion, an approach introduced in the early nineties that, in a sense, rehabilitates naturalist and primarily reductionist strand in the field of the study of religions. In contradistinction to the naturalist approaches of the belle époque, this modern take on naturalism is firmly grounded in rigorous empirical and experimental research made possible by the developments in cognitive and evolutionary psychology. If the first part of the work has been largely guided by a historical approach, in the following chapters I will move in a more systematic manner and illustrate the role of the cognitive science of religion in three distinct areas of interest – methodology, terminology and practical application. In this chapter, I will focus on methodology and interdisciplinarity and show that the theoretical and methodological changes in the study of religion have significant parallels in other domains of science – in this case, I will consider methodological consilience in the fields of ethics and the study of religions.

Over the past several decades, the scientific study of morality and religion has witnessed a major paradigmatic shift with respect to methodologies used in the explanation of these complex aspects of human behaviour. I will argue that both fields suffered from a set of very similar defects, impeding deeper understanding of the cognitive and emotional processes required for an adequate analysis of the phenomena pertaining to the domains of morality and religion. Two of these defects are central. First, much of the scholarly discussion in the twentieth century has been dominated by the view I term 'methodological isolationism', that is, an assumption that special theoretical and methodological procedures are needed in order to understand moral and religious behaviour; alternatively, some thought that moral and religious phenomena are not liable to any rational analysis whatsoever. This thesis has been advanced not only in both ethics and the study of religion in particular, but also more generally for the whole of social sciences. Second, until recently, the theory of evolution by natural selection played virtually no role in the explanation of moral and religious phenomena. What is more, many scholars thought that evolutionary theory is not only irrelevant, but dangerous, since it threatens to undermine received wisdom on these subjects; at times, it has even been argued that some peculiarities of human moral and religious behaviour directly contradict the predictions of evolutionary theory. In what follows, I will provide a concise historical overview of these methodological issues and sketch some of the solutions advanced by Evolutionary Ethics and Cognitive Science of Religion.

6.1 Methodological isolationism

Methodological isolationism in the study of religions has been already introduced in some detail in the previous two chapters, since it is a trademark feature of the protectionist paradigm. Here, I will only provide a few clarifications and supplements. Methodological isolationism in the realm of religious studies can be traced back to Friedrich Schleiermacher, whose collection of five essays, published anonymously in 1799 under the title *On religion*, exerted profound influence on many subsequent scholars (esp. Nathan Söderblom and Rudolf Otto). The main purpose of these essays is stated clearly by the author himself in a letter to the censor of the text Friedrich Samuel Gottfried Sack: 'My ultimate goal has been to properly depict and lay foundations for the independence of religion from everyday metaphysics'.[2] For Schleiermacher, the essence of religion is not found in thinking (which belongs to metaphysics) or action (which belongs to morals), but rather consists in intuition (*Anschauung*) and feeling (*Gefühl*). While this might look like an innocent attempt to demarcate the domain of religion from other modalities of human thought and action, it is, in effect, one of the earliest attempts to shield the study of religion from any interference from every other type of human knowledge; as Daniel Pals rightly notes, Schleiermacher is trying 'to isolate a realm of feeling – and within it that one type of feeling which is absolute dependence – as the singular band of human experience which belongs alone and unassailably to religion'.[3]

Max Müller, widely considered to be one of the founding fathers of the comparative study of religion, used slightly different strategy to inaugurate religion as an independent phenomenon insulated from any possibility of reductionist explanation. After differentiating between 'comparative theology', studying historical manifestations, and 'theoretical theology', studying what Ivan Strenski termed 'religion-as-such',[4] Müller postulates the existence of general mental faculty, which allows people to conceive the Infinite under most variegated names and in ever changing forms; the faculty, which is not only independent from understanding (*Verstand*) and sense (*Sinn*), but, by their nature, stands in harshest opposition to them.[5] For Schleiermacher, religion is merely independent from other human faculties; for Müller, it already stands in opposition to them.

Another important figure of modern religious studies influenced heavily by Schleiermacher, whose *On Religion* he edited for the centennial edition, is Rudolf Otto. In 1917 he published *The Idea of the Holy*, which could be considered a classic early twentieth-century piece of methodological isolationism in the domain of religious studies. Otto, following Schleiermacher,[6] claims that a meaningful discussion of religion is reserved for people who are themselves religious – the reader of his book is invited to bring into memory the moment of strong religious excitement; failure to comply results in a kind recommendation not to read further.[7] Following this remarkable opening, Otto proceeds to introduce the 'Sacred' as an ineffable and mysterious essence of religion, ontologically and epistemologically distinct from all other (profane) human experiences. Needless to say, *sacrum* as an a priori category eventually came to dominate the discussion of religion for many subsequent decades.

Instrumental in this development has been Mircea Eliade, arguably the most influential scholar of religion in the twentieth century, who draws directly on Otto's concept of the 'Sacred'[8] and perpetuates the distinction between the essence of religion and its historical manifestations introduced by Müller. Eliade is charitable enough to grant that religions can be studied by various historical, social and psychological approaches, yet these barely scratch the surface of the phenomenon, because the essence of religion is not amendable to scientific explanation.[9] The 'Sacred' cannot be explained, only understood through the study of hierophanies, since it is 'absolutely heterogeneous' to the profane.[10] Brede Kristensen, an influential phenomenologist of religion, summarized this view in no ambiguous terms, proclaiming *sacrum* to be 'self-subsistent and absolute; it is beyond all our rational criticism'.[11]

Several provisional conclusions may be drawn from this short overview and the material presented in the previous two chapters. By presenting religion as a *sui generis* phenomenon which cannot be studied by conventional scientific means, methodological isolationism in the study of religion not only insulated inherently complex religious behaviour from other modalities of human activity, but, on the meta-theoretical level, established itself as impermeable to any form of criticism. From *sui generis* religion, *sui generis* study of religion; or, as Russell McCutcheon has aptly noted, 'a discursive strategy of containment and exclusion'.[12] If we turn our attention to the study of morality, an analogous form of methodological isolationism appears with respect to factual and normative judgments. Normative judgments, the backbone of every conceivable ethical system, have been pronounced fundamentally different from descriptive statements dealing with matters of fact. It is remarkable that this schism has been endorsed (albeit in different forms) by both analytical philosophy and existentialism.[13]

Analytical critique harks back to David Hume's well-known complaint about the illicit shift from descriptive to prescriptive judgments and ensuing 'is–ought' dichotomy has become a commonplace in many subsequent accounts of ethics, in spite of the fact that Hume does not provide anything resembling a proof for the incommensurability of factual and normative statements, but only notes that the move from 'is' to 'ought' is, without further argument, highly suspicious *non sequitur*.[14]

> In every system of morality, which I have hitherto met with, I have always remark'd, that the author proceeds for some time in the ordinary way of reasoning, and establishes the being of a God, or makes observations concerning human affairs; when of a sudden I am surpriz'd to find, that instead of the usual copulations of propositions, is, and is not, I meet with no proposition that is not connected with

an ought, or an ought not. This change is imperceptible; but is, however, of the last consequence. For as this ought, or ought not, expresses some new relation or affirmation, 'tis necessary that it shou'd be observ'd and explain'd; and at the same time that a reason shou'd be given, for what seems almost inconceivable, how this new relation can be a deduction from others, which are entirely different from it.[15]

While Hume brought deserved attention to an important issue, George E. Moore, whose critical appraisal of neo-Hegelian thought marked the birth of analytic philosophy, provided the proof (or so he thought, anyways).[16] In his *Principia Ethica*, Moore tried to show that every attempt to 'naturalize' ethics, consisting in an identification of 'good' (moral predicate *non plus ultra*) with some natural property (e.g. 'pleasure'), is bound to fail, because it cannot withstand an 'open question' argument. Open question is simply a question that does not have a trivial answer, for instance, the question 'Is bachelor an unmarried man?' is, for every competent speaker of English, not an open question, because the answer is trivially 'yes'. It does not make any good sense asking whether bachelors are really unmarried. Yet within the moral sphere, it always makes good sense asking whether any natural property 'x' is really good.

For the British philosopher, 'good' is simply 'good',[17] unanalysable and principally undefinable property; any claims to the contrary are committing 'naturalistic fallacy'. With respect to the theory and methodology of the study of religion it is worth emphasizing that for Moore, the key property of the good is its 'nonnaturalness', while the difference between natural and nonnatural properties is that 'natural properties exist in time while nonnatural properties do not'.[18] The subject of ethics (the good), in this view, is an ahistorical, atemporal and indefinable entity, very much resembling in these respects the sacred of the phenomenologists of religion. Furthermore, it is important to note that large parts of *Principia Ethica* are conceived as an argument against the spectre of social Darwinism embodied in the philosophy of Herbert Spencer.[19] Spencer, in Moore's view, has been unconsciously committing naturalistic fallacy when he tried to derive normative statements from purely descriptive theory, namely Darwin's theory of evolution. A brief quote by Moore makes this abundantly clear:

> The survival of the fittest does not mean, as one might suppose, the survival of what is fittest to fulfil a good purpose – best adapted to a good end: at the last, it means merely the survival of the fittest to survive; and the value of the scientific theory, and it is a theory of great value, just consist in shewing what are the causes which produce certain biological effects. Whether these effects are good or bad, it cannot pretend to judge.[20]

The combined double whammy of Hume's and Moore's critique created a seemingly unbridgeable gap between facts and values. If the study of religion has been trying to isolate religious experience as something unique, the study of morality, it seems, has been working towards the same goal with respect to moral phenomena. In Wittgenstein's *Tractatus Logico-Philosophicus*, whose importance for the analytic tradition of philosophy can hardly be overstated, the subject of ethics is described in the very terms scholars of religion used for the description of the 'Sacred'; moral sphere of human existence becomes a thing-in-itself, divorced from other domains of knowledge and unamendable to the application of proper scientific methodology, ineffable and transcendental.[21] For Wittgenstein, '[i]f there is a value which is of value, it must lie outside all happening and being-so. [...] Hence also there can be no ethical propositions. [...] It is clear that ethics cannot be expressed. Ethics is transcendental'.[22]

Of course, it can be objected that motives for methodological isolationism in the study of religion (quite often ideological and apologetic) and in the study of morality (usually stemming from the careful analysis of the language) are different. I will gladly concede that much, yet I am not concerned here with psychology, but the effects methodological isolationism had on further developments – and with this perspective in mind, ethics did not fare much better than the study of religion; as Patricia Churchland lamented with respect to Moore's naturalistic fallacy, 'separation of science and moral philosophy established itself as orthodoxy'.[23] To anticipate some of the conclusions, Evolutionary Ethics does not necessarily claim to solve the 'is–ought' problem, but it does claim that morality is certainly something that 'can be expressed', not a transcendental phenomenon *sui generis*. While it is fallacious to draw axiological conclusions from observations of facts without a strong argument to justify this move, it is equally as fallacious to think that evolutionary theory is irrelevant to our understanding of moral phenomena, just because there is no consensus on the solution to the 'is–ought' problem.[24]

Existentialist line of thought arrives at the same conclusions through different means. For analytical philosophy, the difficulty lies in the peculiar nature of the language of morals; for existentialists and their forerunners, the issue lies largely with human nature. Friedrich Nietzsche, the most important source of inspiration for twentieth century existentialism, has been essential for this development, summarizing his position thus:

> You have heard me call for philosophers to place themselves *beyond* good and evil – to rise *above* the illusion of moral judgment. This call is the result of an insight that I was the first to formulate: there are absolutely no moral facts. What moral and religious judgments have in common is the belief in things that are not real. Morality is just an interpretation of certain phenomena or (more accurately) a *mis*interpretation.[25]

For Nietzsche, then, morality is only an illusion; all there is are moral interpretations of non-moral phenomena and it is telling that his thesis lumps together morality and religion. Canonical positions for twentieth-century atheist existentialism have been further formulated by Martin Heidegger and Jean-Paul Sartre. Heidegger famously proclaimed that the 'essence of Dasein lies in its existence';[26] Sartre concluded in a similar manner that 'existence precedes essence'.[27] Yet this assumption, central as it is for existentialist thought, entails one necessary conclusion, namely, the rejection of any notion of 'human nature'. Since Nietzsche pronounced God to be dead (Heidegger and Sartre will not object to this conclusion),[28] on what foundation could the morality possibly rest? If there is no human nature for any sort of moral principles to be ingrained in and no God to act as a paragon of moral conduct or an originator of moral rules, morality cannot be much more than what Nietzsche already proclaimed it to be – an illusion.

Sartre takes great pleasure in ridiculing the naïve morality of the *Belle époque*, acting as if nothing changes if the God does not exist.[29] For an existentialist, everything changes, because now, she is not able to consult heavenly authorities in moral decisions. Human beings are free; they are condemned to freedom, because they cannot escape the necessity of choice, but they can never find any justification for it. Although Sartre, at the end of his *opus magnum*, promised a book on morality – a promise on which he failed to deliver – even there he makes it clear that the main outcome of the existentialist psychoanalysis is to make us forget about any objective values.[30]

For Wittgenstein, ethics is transcendental; for Sartre, it is all but that, yet for both, morality is a special domain of human experience insulated from all the others. In a move that has become almost all-too-predictable by now, Heidegger explicitly argues that his existentialist project is completely insulated from other scientific disciplines, stating that '[t]he missing ontological fundament cannot be replaced, even if we incorporate anthropology and psychology into general biology'.[31] Incidentally, that is exactly what Sociobiology or evolutionary psychology, essential in the development of both Evolutionary Ethics and Cognitive Science of Religion, is about.

After surveying very briefly methodological isolationism in the study of religion and philosophy of morality, I turn to one of its most influential proponents in the ranks of natural scientists, Stephen Jay Gould and his theory of nonoverlapping magisteria.[32] In a sense, Gould epitomizes the tendencies for special pleading with respect to methodology of both fields discussed above, since he marries together religion and morality, presenting them as fundamentally different from the objects of study of natural sciences. As he goes on explaining, 'the net, or magisterium, of science covers the empirical realm: what is the universe made of (fact) and why does it work this way (theory). The magisterium of religion extends over questions of ultimate meaning and moral value'.[33] I leave aside the fact that Gould's definition of religion is deeply flawed – as Steven Weinberg quipped, 'the great majority of the world's religious people would be surprised to learn that religion has nothing to do with factual reality';[34] of concern here is the positively advocated split of human knowledge and experience into two incommensurable parts.

Although Gould does not claim that the magisteria are completely separate in all possible aspects, he does claim that they do not overlap 'in the important logical sense that standards for legitimate questions, and criteria for resolution, force the magisteria apart on the model of immiscibility'.[35] Therefore, the domain of religion/morality cannot interfere with the domain of science and by the same token religion/morality cannot be appropriately explained by science. By joining together morality and religion and framing them as essentially insulated from scientific analysis, Gould achieved a pinnacle of methodological isolationism and *sui generis* pleading. What is more, this position has been enthusiastically embraced by most respected scientific journals and remains a mainstay in scientific circles all around the world.[36] As Sam Harris notes after an analysis of the use of the word 'religion' in *Nature* editorials from the 2000–2010 period, 'Nature's editors have generally accepted Stephen J. Gould's doomed notion of 'nonoverlapping magisteria' – the idea that science and religion, properly constructed, cannot be in conflict because they constitute different domains of expertise'.[37] Indeed, the separation of the magisterium of science and the magisterium of religion is, in a sense, a win–win situation, since under its basic assumptions religions should not interfere with science (a position welcomed by a host of scientists) and natural sciences should not be used to explain religion away (a position welcomed by protectionists).

6.2 Religion, morality and evolution

Yet even if it would be granted, for the sake of an argument, that the phenomena of morality and religion are amendable to scientific analysis involving empirical testability of theoretical claims, it would seem that Darwin's theory of evolution is particularly ill-suited to accomplish anything, since important aspects of both moral and religious behaviour appear to be, at least *prima facie*, at best inconsistent, at worst straight up contradictory to the evolutionary theory. With respect to religion, it is possible to differentiate the objections to the applicability of evolutionary theory in two classes, some coming from the believers themselves, others resulting from a scientific point of view. Religious traditions often tackle questions of ultimate meaning of human life and evolution is effectively a blind mechanical process of random genetic mutation and non-random survival of individuals, completely devoid of any higher meaning. Incidentally, the first official reaction of the Catholic Church, formulated at the Council of Cologne just one year after the publication of Darwin's *On the Origin of Species*, disqualifies evolutionary theory precisely because it suggests that humans are not God's purposeful creations, but come into being by a mere 'spontaneous mutation' (*spontanea immutatione*).[38] Creation stories in various religious traditions are usually imbued with meaning and highly teleological in nature; on the contrary, evolution is 'meaningless' and blind. Thus, religious belief remains a major obstacle to the acceptance of the evolutionary theory by much of the populace in United States of America as well as in Europe.[39]

More importantly, a second set of objections can be formulated on purely scientific grounds. Many aspects of religious behaviour consist of actions, which seem to be costly to the actor in terms of evolutionary currency (fitness). How is it possible that behaviour seemingly detrimental to one's fitness is so widespread and persistent? How to make sense of purposeful waste of time (e.g. prayer), resources (e.g. religious offerings), health (e.g. rituals involving self-mutilation)[40] and genetic legacy (e.g. celibacy and castration)?[41] If it is assumed that genetics can influence human behaviour by building brains which make humans more or less liable to such wasteful behaviour, then genetic factors coding for the positive dispositions of individuals to indulge themselves in these activities should be weeded out under selection pressure. Yet this type of behaviour seems endemic in most religious traditions of the world, creating a challenge for anyone attempting to use the explanatory potential of evolutionary theory on religious phenomena.

With respect to morality, the prospects of the application of evolutionary theory seem even bleaker. Again, the problem appears to be twofold. First, many important building blocks of morality consist of actions that *prima facie* fail to incur an adaptive benefit to the actor. Reciprocity and fairness, altruism and caring for others seem to enhance the well-being of others at the cost to the perpetrator of these behaviours; they are costly in evolutionary terms, therefore the genes coding for these predispositions should be pruned out under the selection pressure. Second, even if we set aside the thorny issue of 'is–ought' dichotomy and simply assume that values can be, in principle, glimpsed from the workings of nature, what would those moral rules look like? Given the ostentatious indifference of nature to the well-being of her creatures, wouldn't these moral precepts contradict everything that is pre-theoretically considered to be moral? Would it make any good sense to speak about 'morality'? In the intellectual discourse of the nineteenth century, this problem has been recognized by many major philosophical figures, notwithstanding the fact that some authors formulated these theses without any reference, or even in direct opposition to Darwin's evolutionary theory.[42]

For instance, Arthur Schopenhauer, in an attempt to deconstruct the idea of the 'best of all possible worlds', endorsed by Leibniz, describes the character of nature in quite graphic terms as 'stomping ground of agonized and frightened beings surviving only by one consuming the other, where therefore every predator is a living grave for thousand others and his self-preservation is a chain of tormenting deaths...'.[43] Nietzsche, reflecting on sheer impossibility of the fundamentals of Stoic ethical system, which prompts one to live 'according to nature', wrote the following:

> So you want to *live* 'according to nature?' Oh, you noble Stoics, what a fraud is in this phrase! Imagine something like nature, profligate without measure, indifferent without measure, without purpose and regard, without mercy and justice, fertile and barren and uncertain at the same time, think of indifference itself as power – how could you live according to this indifference? Living – isn't that wanting specifically to be something other than this nature?[44]

Finally, John Stuart Mill drafted this unappealing portrayal of nature even before Darwin's *On the Origin of Species* had been published in 1859:

> In sober truth, nearly all things which men are hanged or imprisoned for doing to one another, are nature's every day performances. [...] Nature impales men, breaks them as if on the wheel, casts them to be devoured by wild beasts, burns them to death, crushes them with stones like the first Christian martyr, starves them with hunger, freezes them with cold, poisons them by the quick or slow venom of her exhalations, and has hundreds of other hideous deaths in reserve [...] All this, nature does with the most supercilious disregard both of mercy and of justice, emptying her shafts upon the best and noblest indifferently with the meanest and worst; upon those who are engaged in the highest and worthiest enterprises, and often as the direct consequence of the noblest acts; and it might almost be imagined as a punishment for them. She mows down those on whose existence hangs the well-being of a whole people, perhaps the prospects of the human race for generations to come, with as little compunction as those whose death is a relief to

themselves, or a blessing to those under their noxious influence. Such are Nature's dealings with life.[45]

What James Adams noted while commenting on Mill's *On Nature* holds firmly for all these thinkers: 'In order to establish that "nature" ... does not define a standard of value, Mill needs only establish some discrepancy between natural processes and moral behavior. But Mill's argument puts forth a much stronger claim: "the natural" considered as a moral standard is not simply incommensurate with human morality, but it is in virtually every respect positively antagonistic to it.'[46] This essentially amoral view of nature does not pertain only to the realm of nineteenth-century philosophy but extends to Darwin's close personal associates.

Thomas Henry Huxley, a passionate advocate of Darwin's ideas, for instance, dedicated a whole set of lectures to the topic of the relationship between evolutionary theory and ethics, and his conclusion has been unequivocal. Evolution and human morality stand against each other as irreconcilable rivals, natural selection knows only the 'law of the strongest'[47] and the only moral that could possibly be drawn from the observation of the process of natural selection is ultimate selfishness and unbounded cruelty. Huxley consequently considers evolution to be 'headquarters of the enemy of ethical nature';[48] virtue 'involves a course of conduct which, in all respects, is opposed to that which leads to success in the cosmic struggle for existence'; ultimately, 'the ethical progress of society depends, not on imitating the cosmic process, still less in running away from it, but in combatting it.'[49] Since Darwin's own ideas about the evolutionary origin of morality have been somewhat obscure,[50] combining group selection ideas, 'expanding moral circle' theory not unlike the one Singer proposed a century later,[51] and cultural determinism, the solution to the puzzle of altruistic behaviour has begun to unravel only in the sixties and seventies of the twentieth century.

In 1964, William Hamilton proved mathematically that a mutant allele coding for a disposition for altruistic behaviour towards kin will successfully replicate within a gene pool, pointing out that 'for a gene to receive positive selection it is not necessarily enough that it should increase the fitness of its bearer above the average if this tends to be done at the heavy expense of related individuals, because relatives, on account of their common ancestry, tend to carry replicas of the same gene; and conversely that a gene may receive positive selection even though disadvantageous to its bearers if it causes them to confer sufficiently large advantages on relatives.'[52] While the notions of 'inclusive fitness' and the 'gene-point-of-view' have been a major success, Hamilton's rule in fact accounted only for a fraction of the sum of altruistic behaviour observed in our species, since humans do not act altruistically only towards kin, but also towards other, often genetically unrelated individuals.

Another piece of the puzzle has been supplied by Robert Trivers, who proposed, albeit on a much weaker mathematical foundation than Hamilton, the theory of reciprocal altruism: In a population in which there is a high frequency of interaction between any two individuals, where an individual habitually cooperates with a small and stable group of other individuals, and where at least a rough underlying symmetry between the costs and benefits of the altruistic actions, measured in inclusive fitness, is present, reciprocal altruism between genetically unrelated individuals can be expected to emerge.[53] What the theory lacked in mathematical rigour has been supplied by other means. In a series of famous computational simulations of iterated Prisoner's dilemma,[54] Robert Axelrod demonstrated that a simple strategy cooperating on the first move and copying the behaviour of the other player on all subsequent turns outcompeted all other strategies, notably the 'evil' ones designed to defect and exploit 'nicer', more cooperative ones, while further diachronic simulations showed it to be evolutionary stable under certain conditions.[55] Although subsequent experiments identified other strategies to be even more successful,[56] for Trivers, as he himself noted, the paper had 'almost biblical proportions, since it "proved" non-kin cooperation not only possible, but, under certain conditions, stable'.[57]

Successful as it was in expanding the scope of an evolutionary explanation of the altruistic behaviour, Hamilton's kin altruism and Trivers' reciprocal altruism still did not cover all observable altruistic behaviour in humans, since we often help even non-kin unable to reciprocate the favour. Richard Alexander resolved the issue by introducing the concept of indirect reciprocal altruism, in which, as he explains, 'the return is expected from someone other than the recipient of the beneficence. This return may come from essentially any individual or collection of individuals in the group. Indirect reciprocity involves reputation and status, and results in everyone in a social group continually being assessed and reassessed by interactants, past and potential, on the basis of their interactions with others.'[58] Altruistic acts directed towards non-kin who cannot reciprocate back then serve as costly signalling of the well-being. Amotz and Avishag Zahavi, who expanded Alexander's main ideas in what eventually became the 'handicap principle', note in summarizing the main thesis: '[W]aste can make sense, because by wasting one proves conclusively that one has enough assets to waste more. The investment – the waste itself – is just what makes the advertisement reliable.'[59] What an individual pays for the performance of an altruistic act eventually brings forth fruits in the form of increased reputation (which entails higher chance on direct cooperation, in which both participants end up better off) and better chances in sexual selection by females.

All these developments eventually became formalized,[60] and much of the pre-1976 research popularized by Richard Dawkins in his immensely influential book *The Selfish Gene*.[61] In the end, the undisputable fact of altruistic behaviour in humans does not threaten evolutionary theory; quite to the contrary, many facets of it can be understood within the evolutionary framework. Yet with regard to the relationship of the evolutionary theory and morality, it seemed that human altruism, the cornerstone of morality, is not just explained, but explained away: What we commonly identify as altruistic behaviour is only a slightly amusing spectacle of clueless individuals acting as directed by selfish genes, their miniature biological overlords.

As William Hamilton noted in reflecting upon his papers on the kin selection, '[i]n many people, perhaps even a majority, reading them leads to an instant automatic wish for both the evidence and the idea to go away'.[62] The depiction of nature as a cruel force impervious to the pain and suffering it brings about has not been shattered. George C. Williams, after a critical assessment of authors trying to make nature look benign, noted that 'biology would have been able to mature more rapidly in a culture not dominated by Judeo-Christian theology and the Romantic tradition'[63] and summarized his lifelong held position on these topics succinctly in the paper ominously entitled *Mother Nature is a Wicked Old Witch*, in which he endorses Huxley *verbatim*, using his call-to-arms against the immoral nature as an introductory quote.[64] Richard Dawkins comes to similar conclusions, stating that '[i]f there is a human moral to be drawn, it is that we must teach our children altruism, for we cannot expect it to be part of their biological nature';[65] parting words of *The Selfish Gene* urge the readers to 'turn against our creators' and 'rebel against the tyranny of the selfish replicators'.[66] For all the advances in the evolutionary understanding of altruism, Dawkins picks up the argument where Huxley left it almost a century earlier – as Daniel Dennett observed (though certainly not with respect to Dawkins), '[f]rom the outset, there have been those who thought they saw Darwin letting the worst possible cat out of the bag: nihilism'.[67] Because of these developments, I find it useful to clear up some conceptual muddles with respect to 'selfish genes' first, then sketch the paradigmatic methodological shift effectuated by Evolutionary Ethics, Cognitive Science of Religion, and their precursors.

6.3 Selfish genes

'Selfish gene' was supposed to be a useful metaphor, but it became much more. Due to insufficient differentiation between genes and individuals, acknowledged by Dawkins himself in the new introduction to the thirtieth anniversary edition of *The Selfish Gene*,[68] the image of nature bringing forth creatures relentlessly selfish at core stuck. Consider a single example, provided by one of the central figures of Evolutionary Ethics, Jonathan Haidt. While commenting on religion, he notes that '[b]y making people long ago feel and act as though they were parts of one body, religion reduced the influence of individual selection (*which shapes individuals to be selfish* [italics mine]) and brought into play the force of group selection (which shapes individuals to work for the good of their group)'.[69] Setting aside the problematic inclusion of group selection as a significant force in human evolution, which is a topic of much contention today and its proper discussion would extend well beyond the aims of this chapter,[70] 'individual' selection certainly does not shape individuals to be (uniquely) selfish. It shapes them to be altruistic (in addition to being egoistic and nepotistic).

The meaning of the terms 'selfish' and 'altruistic', as used in common parlance, always implies notions of intentionality and motivation; at the same time, both terms are used in theoretical biology to denote behaviour increasing or decreasing inclusive fitness. Therefore, it is essential to appreciate the difference between the proximate motivation of altruistic behaviour (usually mediated by emotions) and ultimate resulting consequences on fitness of the acting individual, as introduced under varied terminology by Alexander ('genotypic' vs. 'phenotypic' egoism),[71] de Waal ('vernacular' vs. 'evolutionary' egoism)[72] or Henrich & Henrich ('proximate' vs. 'ultimate' levels of explanation).[73] Failure to respect different levels of analysis leads to a fallacy, which, as Frans de Waal comments, assumes that 'since natural selection is a cruel, pitiless process of elimination, it can only have produced cruel and pitiless creatures';[74] likewise, Matt Ridley noted that we can have selfish genes and yet be altruistic individuals.[75]

Theoretical advances described very briefly above eventually led to the paradigmatic change in methodology with respect to the study of morality and religion. To summarize the argument so far, originally, both domains (and, by extension, their academic study as well) have been considered *sui generis*, unsuitable for a proper scientific analysis. Furthermore, it has been thought that evolution by natural selection could not possibly contribute to the explanation of moral and religious phenomena. Both of these objections have been effectively challenged by Harvard biologist Edward O. Wilson in 1975 with the publication of *Sociobiology*.[76]

6.4 Rediscovery of human nature

Arguing against the *sui generis* claim of the study of both religion and morality, Wilson introduced the notion of 'consilience', that is, methodological and conceptual unification of natural and social sciences with a principal requirement of the empirical testability. While this process of integration has been maturing in 'hard sciences' already for some time, as Wilson notes, 'physical sciences have been relatively easy; the social sciences and humanities will be the ultimate challenge',[77] largely because methodological isolationism did not operate only in the fields of ethics and religious studies, but also on a more general level of social sciences as a whole. By mid-century, the divergence has become so large that scientist-turned-novelist C. P. Snow noted that he 'was moving among two groups – comparable in intelligence, identical in race, not grossly different in social origin, earning about the same incomes, who had almost ceased to communicate at all, who in intellectual, moral and psychological climate had so little in common that instead of going from Burlington House or South Kensington to Chelsea, one might have crossed an ocean'.[78] Snow has been writing more narrowly about the schism between literary intellectuals and scientists, yet his observations about the split of human knowledge into 'two cultures' would be applicable to the relationship between social and natural sciences as well.

The philosophical pedigree of this position could be traced back to the philosopher Wilhelm Dilthey, who argued that 'spiritual sciences' (*Geisteswissenschaften*) and 'natural sciences' (*Naturwissenschaften*) are bound to use different methodologies in order to be successful in achieving their objectives.[79] Soon enough, this idea permeated socio-cultural sciences. While the influence of Dilthey's ideas on Franz Boas, who became one of the leading figures of American anthropology, is all but evident, Boas has been prepared to acknowledge at least a possibility that 'similarities in the behavior of man [...] may arise independently on account of the sameness of the mental structure'.[80] Most of his contemporaries, students and followers have not been so charitable. Robert Lowie, another founding figure of American anthropology, argued clearly for the *sui generis* nature of culture:

> Culture is a thing *sui generis* which can be explained only in terms of itself. This is not mysticism but sound scientific method. The biologist, whatever metaphysical

speculations he may indulge in as to the ultimate origin of life, does not depart in his workday mood from the principle that every cell is derived from some other cell. So the ethnologists will do well to postulate the principle, *Omnis cultura ex cultura*. This means that he will account for any given cultural facts by merging it in a group of cultural facts or by demonstrating some other cultural fact out of which it has developed.[81]

Further, *sui generis* claims have been often coupled with an emphatic rejection of 'human nature'; for instance, Ruth Benedict, one of Boas' students, writes in 1934:

> Man is not committed in detail by his biological constitution to any particular variety of behaviour. The great diversity of social solutions that man has worked out in different cultures in regard to mating, for example, or trade, are all equally possible on the basis of his original endowment. Culture is not a biologically transmitted complex.[82]

European tradition did not lag too far behind; Émile Durkheim, holder of the first academic chair of sociology, parallels Lowie almost *verbatim*:

> The society is a reality *sui generis*; it has its own specific nature that cannot be found, or cannot be found in the same form, in the rest of the universe.[83]

Finally, Clifford Geertz, arguably one of the most influential anthropologists of the twentieth century, reaffirms the central tenet of cultural determinism thus:

> [T]here is no such thing as a human nature independent of culture. Men without culture [...] would be unworkable monstrosities with very few useful instincts, fewer recognizable sentiments, and no intellect: mental basket cases. As our central nervous system – and most particularly its crowning curse and glory, the neocortex – grew up in great part in interaction with culture, it is incapable of directing our behavior or organizing our experience without the guidance provided by systems of significant symbols. [...] Without men, no culture, certainly; but equally, and more significantly, without culture, no men.[84]

Yet if we ponder for a moment that 'culture was probably not a vastly greater factor in human social practices than in bonobo or baboon social practices, for example, until humans have been around for roughly 150,000 years'[85] and couple it with the fact that 'anatomically modern' *Homo sapiens* evolved 300,000 to 200,000 years ago,[86] one might wonder as to how these 'unworkable monstrosities' survived the intermittent tens of thousands of years. Geertz's convoluted rhetoric aside, the combined dogma of methodological isolationism, rejection of the notion of 'human nature' and resulting cultural determinism, christened by Leda Cosmides & John Tooby as 'Standard Social Science Model',[87] became so firmly embedded in the social sciences that James Wilson, an early proponent of Evolutionary Ethics, noted rather sardonically that 'the study of culture has in general produced two conclusions: first, culture is everything, nature nothing; and second, no universal moral rules exist in all cultures'.[88] Moreover, with the emergence of post-structuralism and post-modernism, the idea of scientific progress has been challenged, legitimacy of scientific methodology called into question, and cultural determinism revived under the guise of social constructionism.[89]

No wonder, then, that E. O. Wilson has been considered nothing short of a heretic, 'a racist, a sexist, a capitalist imperialist' and his work 'a right-wing plot, a blueprint for the continued oppression of the oppressed'.[90] Evolutionary Ethics and Cognitive Science of Religion had to overcome no small amount of resistance: Robert Frank noted that he has 'always encountered a few people in every audience who become hostile at the mere mention of biological forces playing a role in human choices';[91] Pascal Boyer stated in a similar fashion that there is 'a widespread reluctance to this type of argument [sc. that evolutionary biology is an essential component for any prospects for understanding human behavior] in cultural anthropology, which often takes for granted that "culture" is an autonomous level of reality, which cannot be "reduced" to psychological or biological constraints'.[92]

How did a Harvard entomologist manage to generate enough negativity to essentially start a trench war between natural and social scientists that lasted for decades (and is still going on)? Simply put, Wilson suggested two things, both highly uncomfortable for significant parts of the social side of the academia. First, just as there is no 'alternative' and 'traditional' medicine, only medicine that works (i.e. evidence-based medicine) and 'medicine' that does not work,[93] there are, with respect to methodology, no 'natural' and 'social' sciences, only theories that are backed by evidence and theories that are not. And if social sciences continuously produced theories untestable by confrontation with empirical evidence, the solution does not amount to resorting to *sui generis* special pleading, but construction of better, testable theories. Second, existence does not, with all due respect to existentialist thinkers, precede essence; culture is not, with all due respect to cultural anthropologists, unconstrained by our evolved dispositions – members of our species are not infinitely malleable pieces of clay. These erroneous baselines, converted on a cognitive level into a behaviourist doctrine of anti-mentalism and on a cultural level into a theory of cultural determinism, must be rejected and replaced with the deep understanding of the evolutionary history of our species that constrains our mental equipment and consequently constrains also 'varieties of culture'.

These general claims can be easily transposed on the study of religion and morality and Wilson himself comments on both (albeit in considering religion, his claims are very inchoate). With respect to morality, Wilson essentially laid down main assumptions of what later on became Evolutionary Ethics, as Jonathan Haidt noted on multiple occasions.[94] The phenomenon of human morality is a result of complex interactions of emotions and their conscious reflection, which eventually creates axiological standards. Consequently, if we want to understand the nature of our moral judgments, we have to identify the origin and functional mechanisms of emotions underlying our morality. If one then accepts the assumption that emotions are essentially products of the brain functioning and brain itself an organ of the human body subjected to selection pressure, evolutionary biology becomes an indispensable tool for analysing morality.[95] Disheartened by the less-than-stellar track record of philosophers, Wilson argues that 'it is time for ethics to be taken from the hands of philosophers and biologized';[96]

elsewhere, he somewhat disparagingly notes that 'discussions of ethics should not rest upon the freestanding assumptions of contemporary philosophers who have evidently never given thought to the evolutionary origin and material functioning of the human brain'.[97] What goes for morality goes for the study of religion as well: 'The same reasoning that aligns ethical philosophy with science can also inform the study of religion';[98] religion, in Wilson's view, 'emerged on an ethical basis and has been used to defend moral maximes'.[99]

6.5 Methodological consilience

Emphatic rejection of methodological isolationism in favour of methodological consilience has been fully endorsed by central figures of both Evolutionary Ethics and Cognitive Science of Religion. Neither social science in general, nor study of religion and morality in particular, can be *a priori* isolated other disciplines, if only because religion and morality involve highly complex patterns of human behaviour. Accordingly, proponents of Evolutionary Ethics announce that 'drawing on converging data from neuroscience, evolutionary biology, experimental psychology, and genetics, and given a philosophical framework consilient with the data, we can now meaningfully approach the question of where values come from';[100] others, entirely in line with the consilient research programme, conclude that '[i]nquiry into our moral nature will no longer be the proprietary province of humanities and social sciences, but a shared journey with natural sciences'.[101] Likewise, in the Cognitive Science of Religion, the 'intimate link between the natural and the human sciences'[102] is being emphasized and entire chapters with titles such as *Towards a consilience* advance Wilson's central thesis and methodological requirements.[103] The focus on interdisciplinary character, as opposed to earlier protectionism, is not only explicitly stated,[104] but can be seen in practice in an extraordinarily varied conflux of researchers and scholars with widely divergent professional backgrounds. Anthropologists, evolutionary biologists, economists, psychologists, philosophers, neuroscientists and primatologists are all working in concert, united by the common theoretical framework.

The core methodological principle of this approach states that any relevant explanation of both religious and moral phenomena requires what Pascal Boyer called 'rich psychology',[105] that is, resolute abandonment of the behaviourist stimulus-response analysis and the concomitant ban on the use of any more complex cognitive and emotional mechanisms than a general-purpose learning process in explaining behaviour. Max Friedländer understood this with respect to the study of art as early as 1946, when he noted that '[a]rt being a thing of the mind, it follows that any scientific study of art will be psychology. It may be other things as well, but psychology it will always be'.[106] In a similar manner, Steven Pinker rephrases the famous dictum of Theodosius Dobzhansky, noting that 'nothing in culture makes sense except in the light of psychology';[107] finally, driving home the same point, Todd Tremlin writes that '[t]he flaws of traditional explanations for religion result from considering culture (religion) before the psychology (religious ideas) that makes it possible'.[108] The same reasoning would, of course, apply for the study of morality.

Further, if it is accepted that cognitive and emotional mechanisms play a crucial role in constituting morality and religion, it is vital to understand their origins. Assuming that our cognitive and emotional make-up is the product of our brain functions,[109] and recognizing the simple fact that the brain, just like any other organ we possess, has been shaped into its current form by the gradual process of random genetic mutations and the pressure of natural selection, it becomes clear that in order to account for the architecture of our brains, we have to reconstruct its development throughout the evolutionary history of our species. In short, psychology has to become evolutionary psychology.[110]

The analysis of evolutionary roots of morality and religion has yielded slightly different results. The emerging consensus in Evolutionary Ethics considers mechanisms underlying behaviour that would be pre-theoretically considered 'moral' as generally adaptive; as Jonathan Haidt notes, 'morality, like language, is a major evolutionary adaptation for an intensely social species, build into multiple regions of the brain and body, that is better described as emergent than as learned yet that requires input and shaping from a particular culture'.[111] With respect to religious behaviour, two alternatives have been put forward. One of them considers religion to be generally adaptive,[112] yet the majority of scholars is leaning to the other alternative, which considers religion to be what Stephen Jay Gould named 'spandrel' or 'exaptation'[113] and what today is usually called 'by-product', that is, phenotypic characteristic that is not adaptive *per se*, but evolved as a secondary outcome of some other adaptive characteristic(s). In this view, religion is originally a non-adaptive outcome of a combination of some of our adaptive cognitive mechanisms, especially folk theories, theory of mind and agency detection systems.[114] This is a topic for some further debate and both positions need not be mutually exclusive. For instance, Ilkka Pyysiäinen and Marc Hauser argued that 'although religion did not originally emerge as a biological adaptation, it can play a role in both facilitating and stabilizing cooperation within groups, and as such, could be the target of cultural selection'.[115] More importantly, both alternatives are attesting to the vital importance of evolutionary thinking in the study of religion and both account for the puzzling features of religion we encountered earlier – under the premises of the 'religion-as-adaptation' hypothesis, individually costly religious behaviour could be seen as hard-to-fake signalling, bolstering within-group cooperation; in view of the 'religion-as-by-product' hypothesis, the costs of the religious beliefs and actions are offset by intrinsic value of adaptive mental systems at the conflux of which the religious behaviour originates.

The rejection of the behaviourist methodology, coupled with evolutionary considerations of religious and moral behaviour, has had important consequences with respect to the notion of 'human nature', so staunchly rejected by both philosophical existentialists and cultural anthropologists. James Wilson notes demands that '[m]oral and political philosophy must begin with a statement about human nature';[116] in a recent major account of the evolutionary origins of morality based on the idea of 'social selection', Christopher Boehm puts it even more bluntly: 'Humans are moral because we're genetically set up to be that way.'[117]

Even though Cognitive Science of Religion had in its early days emphasized cognitive mechanisms without paying much attention to their evolutionary origins –

for instance, Lawson and McCauley have 'rejected nativist accounts of the universal principles underlying religious ritual systems', yet, considering further developments in the field, almost prophetically add that 'it would be premature at best to hold that biology is irrelevant',[118] it soon became clear that evolutionary perspective is all but necessary in order to account for the religious phenomena (major turn-of-the-century synthetic appraisals of CSR have 'evolution' already in the very title).[119] Both disciplines assume that natural selection has endowed our species with a set of distinct dispositions: Morality is mediated primarily by moral emotions (shame, guilt, or sense of fairness and justice); the central concepts of religious beliefs, counter-intuitive agents, are made not only possible, but also highly salient and successful in cultural transmission by virtue of diverse mental systems with different degrees of domain specificity, most notably belief-desire psychology, (hyperactive) agency detection system and folk theories of physics and biology.

It is important to note that this does not mean that human beings are somehow 'genetically determined' to acquire a distinct sense of morality or a set of religious ideas and behaviours irrespective of cultural influence.[120] Unlike many social scientists, early sociobiologists (and, later, evolutionary psychologists) never claimed that 'culture' plays no role in explanations of religious or moral phenomena. Rather, they emphasized the ways in which cultures are constrained by our evolved mental architecture.[121] Many analogies and metaphors have been put forward to elucidate the interaction of nature and nurture; Robert Frank offers the 'gyroscope' metaphor, where 'that nature's role is to have endowed us with a capacity that is much like a gyroscope at rest; and that culture's role is to spin it and establish its orientation';[122] Scott Atran uses the 'conduit' metaphor, in which 'humankind's evolutionary landscape greatly reduces the many possible sources of religious expression into structures that seem always to reappear across history and societies';[123] according to Boehm, 'cultural glove fits the genetic hand';[124] Marc Hauser uses the linguistic analogy of the 'principles and parameters' approach with human nature setting up the principles and culture fine-tuning the parameters.[125] In fact, Chomsky's description of P&P could be directly transposed into the domains of religion and morality. He explains that '[t]he P&P approach aims to reduce descriptive statements to two categories: language-invariant, and language-particular. The language-invariant statements are principles (including the parameters, each on a par with a principle of UG); the language-particular ones are specifications of particular values of parameters', while noting that '[t]he parametric option available appears to be quite restricted'.[126] Likewise, in the realm of morality and religion, we would find invariants shared by all possible religions and moral systems (e.g. counter-intuitive agents; ban on indiscriminate killing), while cultural environment, 'restricted' by the architecture of our minds, provides particulars (e.g. what are the counter-intuitive agents like; conditions which, if satisfied, render the killing morally permissible). This integrated methodological approach allows us to appreciate both a large degree of cross-cultural variation and the notion of evolved human nature.

Developments in the fields of primatology, developmental psychology and neuroscience provide both empirical support for central claims sketched above and testimony to the idea of interdisciplinary methodological consilience. Some building blocks of morality are present in great apes,[127] and while I do not see the prospect of identifying anything worth calling 'religious behaviour' in any other species than ours likely to succeed, some efforts have been made even in this respect.[128] Further, developmental psychology seems to support the idea of an innate capacity for acquiring morality and religious beliefs: even small children underdetermined by cultural input express a remarkable capacity for the experience of moral emotions and the acquisition of religious ideas.[129] Finally, the advances in neuroimaging, coupled with a functionalist account of human mind, integrate the research on morality and religion with neurosciences.[130]

Most importantly, the methodology in Cognitive Science of Religion and Evolutionary Ethics is firmly based in the general requirement of empirical testability. When we read in one of the turn-of-the-century appraisals that 'cognitive science of religion must rely on empirical observations and data from actual experiments',[131] this principle might seem too trivial and self-understood to be even worth spelling out, if it would not be the case that for the most part of the twentieth century, empirical testability (or explanatory account of moral and religious phenomena, as opposed to hermeneutics or silence) has been thought to be either impossible or uncalled for.

6.6 The return of naturalism

In spite of the fact that the main premises of both Cognitive Science of Religion and Evolutionary Ethics emerged only in the past two decades, both research programmes have already achieved extraordinarily fast growth. As Scott James puts it, '[f]or good or ill, the process of "biologicizing" ethics is under way';[132] with respect to the Cognitive Science of Religion, Thomas Lawson noted as early as 2006 that CSR is 'no longer a gleam in the eye of its earlier visionaries', but 'established and an increasingly substantial program of scientific inquiry',[133] a conclusion that is even truer today than it was ten years ago. Methodological consilience, an emphasis on empirical testability of claims coupled with evolutionary accounts of the architecture of human mind, rediscovery of the 'human nature', balanced position in the 'nature-nurture' debate, and a preference for causal explanatory accounts have become indispensable tools in attempts to account for our moral and religious dimension. Just as Socrates 'called the philosophy down from heavens' (*philosophiam devocavit e caelo*),[134] combined efforts of the Evolutionary Ethics and Cognitive Science of Religion called morality and religion down from their transcendental lodgings, placed their fundaments firmly in evolutionary history of our species and integrated their study with other domains of human knowledge.

Following the very basic outline of the cognitive science of religion and its most important theoretical and methodological assumptions, it is, in my opinion, incontrovertible that CSR firmly belongs to the naturalist paradigm in the study of religion, since its primary aim is to explain religion (or, rather, its particular and sometimes quite disjointed constitutive elements) in a reductive fashion by means of the identification of cognitive mechanisms. Moreover, CSR clearly rejects in the strongest terms any methodological isolationism and a *sui generis* approach advocated by the protectionist paradigm.

7

Cognitive science of religion (2): Terminology

When nobody asks me about it, I know. But when I would want to explain it to the one who asks, I don't know.

Augustinus Aurelius[1]

In the previous chapter, I showed how the cognitive science of religion draws on and renews the naturalist paradigm with respect to theory and methodology. Cognitive approach refuses methodological isolationism that understands human religious experience as a domain *sui generis*; it attempts to explain religion reductively with the help of cognitive mechanisms that play a major role in the acquisition and transmission of religious ideas in the culture; and, finally, it strongly rejects any version of the epistemic justification *per hominem* and concludes that the believers themselves are often not able to supply coherent and meaningful explanation of their beliefs and practical activities, such as rituals. A comparison with the parallel developments in the field of evolutionary ethics demonstrated the interdisciplinary nature of the cognitive revolution, highlighted important similarities in results that have been reached and invited us to ask anew the question about the relationship between morality and religion. This chapter focuses on a particular terminological problem, namely the definition of religion.

7.1 On the advantage and disadvantage of definition for the life (of religious studies)

After much ink spilled over thousands upon thousands of pages and no *communis opinio* in sight, the quest for the definition of religion seems to be doomed to failure from the onset. We find ourselves in a situation where there is no consensus even on whether there is a consensus on the pre-theoretical (!) use of the term 'religion';[2] likewise, there is no generally accepted answer to the question of whether the definition of religion is even possible, and if so, whether it is necessary for the constitution of the scientific study of religion.[3] Yet, in spite of the obvious difficulties, the problem of the definition of religion should not be swept under the rug as idle theorizing, for two quite distinct reasons.

Firstly, several scholars have rightly drawn attention to a seemingly trivial fact that has nonetheless serious ramifications, namely, that the definition of religion is a miniature theory of religion.[4] Unless the study of religion wants to resign on formulating even the most basic theoretical assumptions and join Paul Feyerabend in his methodological anarchism,[5] it will eventually have to state the premises of its scientific programme, and a definition of the very subject-matter that is being studied surely belongs to these premises. If we resign from attempting to provide at the very least an approximate definition, not only will the study of religion fail to demarcate the object of its study but it will also be at pains to formulate its basic theoretical postulates.

Secondly, the question of the definition of religion is emphatically not just armchair philosophy, but has important social consequences.[6] International and territorial laws habitually operate with the term 'religion' – many of these grant the 'freedom of religion' or the strict separation of Church and state (what today amounts in practice to the separation of religion and state), which has far-reaching consequences for the public education system,[7] the tax-exempt status of religious organizations[8] and the status of the conscientious objector.[9] In fact, legal scholars themselves at times search in vain for a solution to the definitional problem in the texts of specialists – and who else should be considered a specialist in answering the question 'What is religion?' than a tenured professor at one of the many departments of religious studies throughout the world. Even so, they find nothing resembling a general consensus, which eventually prompts them to state with a considerable degree of irony that 'academia has the luxury of discussion on whether the term "religion" is hopelessly ambiguous, lawyers and jurors often do not'.[10] Although I largely agree with the 'science-for-science' stance (that is, the main objective of science is the acquisition of knowledge, the public utility of which is only secondary), and while the study of religion should certainly not be politically motivated, it should nevertheless reflect on the possible social consequences of the theories it proposes.

Finally, it is worth considering the possibility that the apparent failure to define religion might not be due to the nature of the term 'religion' but results from our often critically unchallenged presuppositions of what a definition should achieve and how it operates.[11] Yet this is essentially a philosophical question. Consequently, I believe that some light could be shed on the problem of the definition of religion by examining the implicitly assumed, but rarely explicitly stated philosophical background behind the definitions of religion. In what follows, I will first review the scholarly literature associated with the cognitive science of religion and reconstruct what might be considered a 'cognitive definition of religion'; then provide some historical context, especially in regard to what I term the 'Tylor–Durkheim dichotomy' and to recent social constructionist approaches; and finally evaluate the worth of a definition of cognitive provenience in the face of the difficulties and challenges posed by previous definitional practices.

7.2 Definition of religion and CSR

What follows is a sample selection of assertions concerning the nature of religion, reconstructed from the works of leading scholars associated with the cognitive science of religion (CSR), which, although by no means exhaustive, I consider representative of this particular theoretical approach (italics are mine):

- 'All religions do share a feature: ostensible communication with *humanlike, yet nonhuman, beings* through some form of symbolic action.'[12]
- 'For the purpose of discussion here, "religion" designates a shared system of beliefs and actions concerning *superhuman agency*.'[13]
- 'Religion is about the existence and causal powers of *nonobservable entities and agencies*.'[14]
- 'Roughly, religion is (1) a community's costly and hard-to-fake commitment (2) to a *counterfactual and counterintuitive world of supernatural agents* (3) who master people's existential anxieties, such as death and deception.'[15]
- '"Religion" is a concept that identifies the *personalistic counter-intuitive representations* and the related practices, institutions, etc. that are widely spread, literally believed, and actively used by a group of people in their attempts to understand, explain and control those aspects of life, and reality as a whole, that escape common sense and, more recently, scientific explanation.'[16]
- 'For the present purposes, let us simply say that religion consists of any set of shared beliefs and actions appealing to *supernatural agency*.'[17]
- '*Superhuman agents* are a force to be reckoned with; at least that's what religion seems to be about. Religion involves doing rituals and other sorts of activities that are predicated on presumptions about what kind of beings supernatural agents are.'[18]
- 'For my purposes, religion refers to the collection of beliefs related to the *existence of one or more gods*, and the activities that are motivated by those beliefs.'[19]

Further, it has to be noted that the work considered by many to be foundational for the cognitive approach to religion,[20] Lawson and McCauley's *Rethinking Religion*, defines ritual *qua* religious ritual precisely on the condition of the inclusion of supernatural agents: '*All religious rituals involve superhuman agents* at some point or other in their representation. ... Every structural analysis of a religious ritual must include a superhuman agent in at least one of the rituals embedded in the ritual under analysis. This is to say that *all religious rituals either directly involve or presuppose the participation of the gods*.'[21] Closer examination of these statements reveals some remarkable facts:

1. Firstly, barring some minor differences, every single assessment of the nature of religion cited above explicitly identifies superhuman, supernatural or counter-intuitive agents as a *differentia specifica* of religion: A belief or an action can be considered religious if and only if it entails the involvement of counter-intuitive agents. Since the acceptance of this principle is virtually unanimous in the CSR, I find it justified to speak about a 'cognitive definition of religion' with the concept of counter-intuitive agents operating as its *definiens*. I understand this definition to be an ideal type reconstructed on the basis of the statements about the nature of religion found in the works of authors affiliated with CSR, although differences will necessarily be present between individual scholars and some would probably deny being in the definitional business at all, which brings us to the next point.

2. Secondly, it is not without interest to observe the presentation of the varieties of the cognitive definition of religion – scholars generally proceed very carefully, with cautious, almost idiosyncratic qualifications such as 'for the purpose of discussion here', 'roughly', 'for the present purposes', 'that's what religion *seems* [italics mine] to be about', 'for my purposes'. If we consider (1) and (2) jointly, it would seem that scholars operating in the cognitive tradition all agree on a very robust *definiens* of religion, yet at the same time, the majority of them deliberately try to downplay the importance of the definition by suggesting that it is nothing more than an *ad hoc* construction of comparatively small value for the theory. While this peculiar instance of 'cognitive dissonance' would merit further attention, I will presently focus on the reconstructed definition itself, not on the concomitant cautionary qualifications of scholars who introduce it.
3. Thirdly, it would seem, at least *prima facie*, that this allegedly novel (some would say even revolutionary) approach to the study of religion returns all the way back to Edward Burnett Tylor and his animistic 'minimal definition' of religion as a belief in spiritual beings. Jonathan Z. Smith even argues that 'religion's *sine qua non* ... is held consistently, whenever the issue of definition is explicitly being raised, to be "beliefs and practices that are related to superhuman beings".'[22] One could reasonably ask whether the whole field of the cognitive science of religion is not just too much ado about nothing and its claims to originality void.
4. Lastly, the definition proposed by the CSR, with its emphasis on the role of evolutionary and cognitive constraints on the acquisition and transmission of cultural concepts, is not congruent either with the prevalent definitional approach, which uses the theoretical tools of language games and family resemblances and considers 'religion' to be an unbound and/or socially constructed category, or with the social functionalist definition proposed almost a century ago by Durkheim as a direct critical response to Tylor's animism mentioned above. I will therefore examine the Tylor–Durkheim dichotomy concerning the essentialist definition of religion, the crux of which, as we will see, is closely related to the central concept of the CSR; then provide an overview of the non-essentialist approaches to the definition of religion; and, finally, sketch the main theoretical underpinnings of the cognitive definition of religion.

7.3 Essentialism: Tylor–Durkheim dichotomy

I find it instructive to start a discussion on essentialist definitions in the study of religion by looking at one of their very first instances in Plato's dialogue *Euthyphro*.[23] Socrates asks Euthyphro, an Athenian priest and self-professed expert in 'all things religious' (τῶν θείων [...] καὶ τῶν ὁσίων τε καὶ ἀνοσίων),[24] a seemingly trivial question: What is piety? Without any hesitation, Euthyphro answers with an ostensive definition – piety is what he himself is currently doing, namely prosecuting his father for a crime – yet Socrates is unfazed by the answer. After all, he is not asking for an example or even a list of pious or impious actions, but the criterion according to which one could identify any action as pious or impious (ἐκεῖνο αὐτὸ τὸ εἶδος ᾧ πάντα τὰ ὅσια ὅσιά ἐστιν).[25] Euthyphro tries again with various other proposals,[26] but Socratic dialectical machinery renders every definition untenable and the dialogue eventually ends without any definitive answer as to the nature of piety. The methodological prerequisite for a definition is nonetheless clear: Every definition has to include the identification of a necessary and sufficient property for any criterion that demarcates clearly the term in question.[27]

If we now turn our attention to the competing definitions of religion proposed by Tylor and Durkheim, we will find the essentialist paradigm to be present in both, in spite of the unmistakable differences – Tylor's definition is rather intellectual, Durkheim's affective and functional;[28] Tylor's is more exclusive (that is, compared to our pre-theoretical understanding, it brings under the umbrella of 'religion' less than is expected), Durkheim's more inclusive (marks as 'religion' more than is pre-theoretically expected).[29] When Tylor considered primitive cultures in one of the foundational texts of modern anthropology, he came to the conclusion that we cannot do without at least a 'rudimentary definition of religion', which he found in 'the belief in Spiritual Beings' or the doctrine of 'Animism'.[30] As Samuel Preus notes, this belief 'constitutes not only the fundamental common denominator of religious history but of primitive society as a whole'.[31] In other words, the belief in spiritual beings constitutes the essence of religion. Deceivingly simple, this definition amassed a large following, but not without sharp criticism from the founding father of another discipline of the humanities, the sociologist Émile Durkheim.

Durkheim argues that the Tylorian definition of religion as a belief in spiritual beings is untenable, because there exists a set of beliefs and actions which would undoubtedly be pre-theoretically considered as 'religious', yet (according to Durkheim) lack the necessary and sufficient property that Tylor singled out as the *definiens* of religion, that is, belief in supernatural beings. The set in question, namely Buddhism, is (in the interpretation of the French sociologist) clearly an atheistic religion, by virtue of which the definition proposed by Tylor happens to be falsified.[32] I leave aside evaluation of the integrity and accuracy of Durkheim's depiction of Buddhism, on which even the specialists seem to be at odds,[33] or the question of whether there is such a thing as Buddhism in itself. What is important to note is that Durkheim's argumentation comes dangerously close to the fallacy of false dichotomy,[34] since the French sociologist seems to be constructing his position in polar opposition to Tylor's, as if these two proposals were the only ones permissible. Tylor's definition singles out spiritual beings as the *definiens* of religion; Buddhism is atheistic; Buddhism is pre-theoretically clearly to be considered a religion; therefore Tylor's definition is untenable; *therefore* Durkheim's definition is true. I find it convenient to refer to this line of discussion as the Tylor–Durkheim dichotomy, whose crux lies in the concept of spiritual beings as being either necessary (Tylor) or arbitrary (Durkheim) to the definition of religion, its borderline case being the interpretation of Buddhism.

Durkheim's own proposed definition of religion is a combination of an essentialist and functionalist approach, considering religion to be a 'system of beliefs and practices related to sacred things – that is, things set apart and forbidden – beliefs and practices which unite all those who adhere to them in a single moral community, called a church'.[35] There is, of course, no mention of gods or supernatural beings, yet the definition is no less essentialist in nature than Tylor's, only the criterion by which it is possible to recognize an instance of religion as such is not the belief in spiritual beings, but an analytical category of the sacred[36] in conjunction with its moral function in the society. For Durkheim, religion is what religion does; and religion seems to constitute and regulate many important social relations while providing the participants with a specific moral code. This move then allows Durkheim to include Buddhism, in concert with our pre-theoretical expectations, in the herd of religions. Before introducing a cognitive solution to the Tylor–Durkheim dichotomy, a brief introduction to the variety of social constructionist approaches to the definition of religion is in order.

7.4 'Naïve' social constructionism

Though definitions of religion have traditionally been based on an essentialist definition introduced by the philosophers of classical antiquity and upheld throughout most of Western intellectual history, the tide started to turn decisively in the second half of the twentieth century. The change can once again be traced back to its philosophical pedigree, where the philosophy of late Wittgenstein played a major role. Abandoning his earlier 'picture theory' of perfect parallelism between language and the world, between atomic formulae and atomic facts (though Wittgenstein never quite succeeded in explaining what these atomic facts actually are),[37] exposed in the *Tractatus*, late Wittgenstein proposes a new theory of meaning based on the concept of 'language games', where the meaning of the words is constituted solely by their use by competent speakers of a particular natural language. It is worth quoting the crucial passage from *Philosophical Investigations* in full:

> Consider for example the proceedings that we call 'games'. I mean board-games, card-games, ball-games, Olympic games, and so on. What is common to them all? – Don't say: 'There *must* be something common, or they would not be called "games"' – but *look and see* whether there is anything in common to all. – For if you look at them you will not see something that is common to all, but similarities, relationships, and a whole series of them at that. [...] And the result of this examination is: we see a complicated network of similarities overlapping and criss-crossing: sometimes overall similarities, sometimes similarities of detail. [...] I can think of no better expression to characterize these similarities than 'family resemblances' [...] For how is the concept of a game bounded? What still counts as a game and what no longer does? Can you give the boundary? No. You can *draw* one; for none has so far been drawn. (But that never troubled you before when you used the word 'game').[38]

Now, suppose that the term 'religion' is, in this important respect, of the same quality as the word 'game'. If this obtains, it would not be surprising at all that there is no essential quality or specific difference which would constitute a general criterion for clear demarcation of the term. At the same time, this does not mean that the concept is completely arbitrary, for Wittgenstein views the 'family resemblance' of particular words grouped under one collective term as an interconnected semantic network, which somehow unites all the particular instances of the collective, such as 'game' or 'religion'. This would mean that the problem, after all, does not lie with the word 'religion', but with our asking for an essentialist definition where none could possibly be found.

A historically influential critique of the essentialist concept of the definition of religion, though initially unrelated to Wittgenstein's philosophy, has been put forward by Wilfred Cantwell Smith in his work *The Meaning and End of Religion*.[39] Cantwell Smith analyses the use of the notion 'religion' (as well as other general labels, such as 'Christianity', 'Buddhism' or 'Hinduism') throughout history and comes to the conclusion that these terms went through some rather radical semantic changes. Originally, the term 'religion' denoted inner faith, but later became a somewhat sterile external reification of the phenomenon itself in what Smith calls 'cumulative tradition'. The consequences of this historical analysis are clear – the term 'religion' is not only ambiguous, but often misleading.[40] Using the language of Wittgenstein, the term means different things to different people depending on the particular language game they happen to be playing.

This line of thought gained a large following in the second half of the twentieth century, up to a point where the essentialist definitions of religion are now deemed to be untenable by a large majority of scholars and definitions making use of the concepts of 'family resemblances', 'unbound categories' and 'polythetic classes' abound,[41] often complemented with attempts to compile specific lists of 'family resemblance networks' for 'religion'.[42] Yet it is quite reasonable to inquire critically as to the mutual relation between particular items on the list of family resemblances or in a polythetic class, since it would seem that only the following two interpretations are possible: Either there is some connection between the items on the list, a special something which glues them together and imposes mutual compatibility and cohesion (if so, how is it different from an 'essence'?); or there is no such connection and all the items within the polythetic class are randomly assigned, having no inner coherence (if so, the proponent of this thesis would be hard pressed to explain that a term like this can be effectively used by competent speakers of a particular natural language). Both interpretations have their defenders,[43] but the answer to this problem may not lie in epistemic, but in pragmatic considerations.

7.5 Power-based social constructionism

I have termed the social constructionist approach to the definition of religion discussed in the preceding section 'power-innocent' or 'naive' to differentiate it from an alternative approach that, on the one hand, shares some of the basic premises (especially the rejection of essentialism), but, on the other hand, is very different in one important respect. While for Wittgenstein the question of power relations lurking behind the semantics of natural languages simply does not arise, for the 'power-based' strain of the social constructionist approach to the definition of religion, the question of power distribution is clearly the central issue. As with the other approaches discussed above, 'power-based' social constructionism also has important philosophical predecessors.

One of them is undisputedly Friedrich Nietzsche, since the concept of power (or will to power) is omnipresent in his late writings.[44] In the twentieth century, this line of thought was further developed especially in the French postmodernist cultural milieu and is strongly connected with the work of Michel Foucault and Pierre Bourdieu.[45]

The central thought of this vein of social constructionism is best expressed in the arbitrariness of classification, articulated simply and eloquently in the discussion of the categorization of animals in a Chinese encyclopaedia dreamed up by Borges[46] and cited in Foucault's landmark publication *The Order of Things* from 1966.[47] Classifications and associated thought patterns, lying largely outside of our conscious evaluation, which are culture-specific and prone to diachronic change, constitute the 'cultural *a priori*' which Foucault termed 'episteme'. Yet, unlike Wittgenstein, who, drawing on Augustine, sketches in the very first paragraph of the *Philosophical Investigations* the idyllic way of the transfer of meaning from one generation to another,[48] Foucault identifies an intimate connection between the constitution of knowledge and the distribution of power, which permeates all his subsequent work. To take just one instructive example, in *Madness and Civilization*, Foucault shows how the deep changes in the concept of 'madness' from the renaissance to the seventeenth century are promoted for largely pragmatic, not epistemic, reasons, in order to isolate the irrational element from self-proclaimed rational society. Conceptual change, in a mutually reinforcing fashion, goes hand in hand with the practice of what Foucault termed 'internment', which, being an 'institutional creation specific to the seventeenth century' and therefore clearly culture-specific and relative to the classical age,[49] serves the powers that be to collect and segregate elements contrary to the ideals of the society. Pierre Bourdieu expressed the essence of this approach by a simple slogan: 'No more innocent words.'[50] Language games are emphatically not games, but battles and wars where words are used as weapons to secure power and domination.

Turning to 'power-based' social constructionism in the study of religion, this theoretical approach finds its 'power-innocent' counterpart deficient in two different ways. Firstly, as we have already seen, it could be objected that the use of the term 'religion' under the premises of a language game approach could result in a situation where anything and everything could be labelled as 'religion',[51] depending on whether there is a connecting feature in between various family resemblances. If there is such a feature – John Hick, for instance, identifies it as 'ultimate concern',[52] it is not immediately clear in which sense this approach is different from an essentialist definition. Yet if we rule out the common denominator of the set of family resemblances and settle with the 'grab-bag' use, where particular items are unconnected, bearing no relation one to another, then the definition itself becomes so vague that it is probably not worth having in the first place.

Yet a more urgent objection to 'naïve' social constructionism is this: It is possible to agree with Cantwell Smith, for instance, that the term 'religion' does not adequately describe the phenomenon itself, yet 'naïve' social constructionism and its innocent language games miss the crucial part of the equation, namely the connection of name-giving with power distribution. This view is most eloquently voiced with respect to the study of religion by Russell McCutcheon and Timothy Fitzgerald, and with respect to the phenomenon of religion itself by the late Gary Lease, although it could be argued that the study of religion is merely mirroring discursive practices of its object of study, since 'scholars of religion are handmaids to what we can only understand as the self-evidently beneficial, universalizing power of religion and religious experiences'.[53]

Under this interpretation, the line between religion and the study of religion is blurred, since both are understood as systems designed to safeguard a particular network of power structures. Fitzgerald notes that 'language is not simply a natural free-flowing system that spontaneously erupts into new usages'; quite to the contrary, 'uses of language are connected to power and control';[54] McCutcheon demonstrated in his discussion of *sui generis* approaches to religion, one of the most prominent theoretical and methodological systems in the twentieth-century study of religion, that 'such methods and theories are entrenched in unrecognized issues of discursive demarcation, power, and control';[55] finally, for Lease, religion itself is a 'political manifestation' of the distribution of power, an 'imperialistic totalitarianism' which stretches the world onto the rack of conceptual schemata created solely for the purposes of imprisonment and control:

> In both the short and the long run, religions are human constructions, systematic series of stories about humans and the chaos surrounding them. [...] These fabrications provide straightjackets into which people should/must place their lives: they enslave. Religions thus become the most finely tuned examples of power structures, patterns of force which control human lives and dictate how they are to be conducted. Make no mistake about it: religions are about power, about power to be given you and about the power which controls you.[56]

'There is no religion', contends Lease,[57] only power structures that manipulate the contents of the term itself to their own idiosyncratic benefits. And the study of religions, as it is habitually conducted, is probably nothing more than the projection of the same power structures and ideological propaganda under the veil of academic *gravitas*.

Given the difference between 'power-innocent' and 'power-based' social constructionism, a cognitive definition of religion may be interpreted as responding to two quite distinct claims: First, against both modes of social constructionism, the CSR shows that the category of 'religion' is not completely arbitrary because its *definiens*, the concept of minimally counter-intuitive agents, is fundamentally constrained by our evolved mental architecture, and therefore not 'socially constructed' in the postmodern sense of the term; second, with respect to the second mode of social constructionism, the CSR suggests that negative consequences of the relationship between religion, the study of religion, and power structures can be, if not completely avoided, then at least significantly minimized by strict adherence to methodological principles based on the empirical testability of hypotheses.

7.6 Cognitive definition of religion

To sum up, in order for the definition of religion by the CSR to contend successfully in the current definitional discourse, it has to address the following issues: (1) In what sense is the definition of religion endorsed by the CSR – self-proclaimed to be 'one of the most exciting developments in the study of religion during the past fifteen years'[58] – different from Tylor's definition of religion proposed almost 150 years ago? (2) Given the similarities with Tylor's definition, how does the CSR respond to the challenge raised by Durkheim and his followers, namely that it seems that there are traditions we would pre-theoretically call religious, yet apparently do not entertain the concept of spiritual or supernatural beings? (3) Since the CSR definition is, in an important sense, universalistic (some would even call it essentialist), it needs to be shown that the social constructionist approach to religious phenomena is at the very least incomplete in non-trivial aspects, or that it is simply mistaken. (4) The CSR needs to answer the claim of the 'power-based' strain of social constructionism that the foundation of religion is the management and distribution of power. I believe that all of these questions can be answered by scrutinizing more closely the basic theoretical and philosophical assumptions of the cognitive approach to religion.

7.6.1 Philosophical and theoretical background

It has been shown that the philosophical forefathers of the essentialist definition of religion form part of a long tradition going all the way back to Plato; in the domain of non-essentialist definitions, 'power-innocent' social constructionism is closely related to the work of the late Ludwig Wittgenstein, while 'power-based' social constructionism is connected with Nietzsche's work and the later efforts of French postmodernism and post-structuralism. With respect to the cognitive approach, a case could be made for the seminal influence of the philosophy of Immanuel Kant and the well-recognized influence of Noam Chomsky's work.

Kant's philosophy can best be seen as an attempt to make peace between continental rationalists, who advocated the existence of innate ideas, and insular empiricists, who proposed the blank slate theory of the human mind.[59] Kant acknowledges the existence of innate principles according to which we generate experiential contents; they are, however, neither Platonic absolutes nor mere culturally determined Humean habits, but stand somewhere 'in between'. They are general or universal in a certain sense, since it is supposed that every neurologically healthy member of our species possesses them (in Kant's philosophy, they are *rules*; for the cognitive approach, they are better thought of as statistically relevant *propensities*), yet they are not absolute, but applicable only to the experiential content they help to generate. For Kant, the central question of the *Critique of the Pure Reason* is this: How are synthetic *a priori* judgments possible?[60] How can something be at the same time non-trivial and knowable *a priori* (that is, before any experience)? The answer to this question is, in my opinion, one and the same for both Kant and the cognitive approach: If we assume an active, constitutive, and formative role for our minds with respect to the generation of experience, it is quite possible that something can be both non-trivial and *a priori* knowable, namely the categorical framework our minds impose on the objects of our senses and thoughts. The best explanation, which comprises only two sentences in the German original, is provided by Kant himself:

If intuition (*Anschauung*) must conform to the constitution of the objects, I do not see how we could know anything of the latter *a priori*; but if the object (as object of the senses) must conform to the constitution of our faculty of intuition (*Anschauungsvermögen*), I have no difficulty in conceiving such a possibility. Since I cannot rest in these intuitions if they are to become known, but must relate them as representations to something as their object, and determine this latter through them, either I must assume that the *concepts*, by means of which I obtain this determination, conform to the object, or else I assume that the objects, or what is the same thing, that the experience in which alone, as given objects, they can be known, conform to the concepts. In the former case, I am again in the same perplexity as to how I can know anything *a priori* in regard to the objects. In the latter case the outlook is more hopeful. For experience is itself a species of knowledge which involves understanding (*Verstand*); and understanding has rules which I must presuppose as being in me prior to objects being given to me, and therefore as being *a priori*. They find expression in *a priori* concepts to which all objects of experience necessarily conform, and with which they must agree.[61]

What Kant did on a general level in philosophy, Chomsky did in particular for linguistics.[62] For Chomsky, language is simply too complex to be explained properly by invoking the idea of the mind as a passive receptacle of the contents of experience operating by 'associative learning'. On the contrary, if we want to understand language acquisition, we have to postulate the existence of the 'language faculty', which we understand to be some array of cognitive traits and capabilities, a particular component of the human mind/brain'.[63] What Kant did not know, and Chomsky did not care too much about, yet what must be dealt with in order to understand the theoretical underpinnings of the CSR is the answer to the question about the origins of the architecture of the brain and its various subsystems, which is provided by evolutionary psychology and has been forcefully articulated in a manifesto penned by Leda Cosmides and John Tooby in the introduction to their influential collection of essays aptly entitled *The Adapted Mind* (edited jointly with Jerome Barkow). Cosmides and Tooby are in complete agreement with both Kant and Chomsky, when they claim that '[a]ll humans tend to impose on the world a common encompassing conceptual organization, made possible by universal mechanisms operating on the recurrent features of human life',[64] but provide a rationale for the existence of the specialized automated systems that play a constitutive role in the creation of knowledge and experience: Domain-specific inference systems or modules are adaptations selected for by natural selection throughout the course of human evolution.[65] These modules generate automatically what have been called 'cross-cultural universals',[66] representations that are automatically generated in neurologically healthy humans. Thus a universalistic bent already present in Tylor's definition is vindicated and explained by the conceptual framework that originated in broad strokes in Kant's philosophy and gained momentum thanks to recent advances in the cognitive sciences, launched by Chomsky's ground-breaking work in linguistics in the late fifties.[67]

It has to be noted that the modular approach to the human mind, characterized by the triplet of domain specificity, information encapsulation and localization of function,[68] introduced in linguistics by Chomsky and further expanded by Cosmides and Tooby to the 'massive modularity' thesis, has come under severe criticism, ranging from 'a common academic parody of Chomsky... proposing innate modules for bicycling, matching ties with shirts, rebuilding carburetors, and so on',[69] to more serious considerations of the limits of massive modularity.[70] Compelling alternatives have been proposed as early as 1996, when Steven Mithen proposed a three-stage evolution of the human mind, where the evolutionarily oldest general-purpose learning mechanism first undergoes domain specialization, followed by the integration of different domains and the emergence of 'cognitive fluidity', which seems to provide for a reasonable compromise between modularity and interactivity.[71] Further advancements in neurocognitive research will undoubtedly yield new discoveries which will further improve our knowledge of the cognitive processes gauging more closely the number of modules, the extent of their function, and their possible integration, yet it seems clear that – contrary to the reigning presuppositions of the larger part of the twentieth century – the structure of the mind matters. As Joseph LeDoux puts it, 'the brain does indeed learn different things using different systems... which is consistent with the nativist view of innate learning modules and inconsistent with the behaviorist notion of a universal learning function'.[72]

7.6.2 Cognitive definition and the Tylor-Durkheim dichotomy

The cognitive approach, in my opinion, has succeeded in a reconceptualization of the Tylor–Durkheim dichotomy by greatly increasing the accuracy of the original term in question, 'spiritual beings'; in a later modification of Tylor's definition by Melford Spiro, religion is 'an institution consisting of culturally patterned interaction with culturally postulated superhuman beings'.[73] It has been pointed out numerous times, and rightly so, that terms such as 'spiritual', 'supernatural' or 'superhuman' are hopelessly vague and ambiguous.[74] The CSR solves this problem by the introduction of the concept of 'counter-intuitive agents', where the central notion of 'counter-intuitiveness' is well-defined in terms of 'folk theories' of physics, biology and psychology firmly grounded in evolutionary psychology. The practical application of this concept with respect to Buddhism has been taken up by Ilkka Pyysiäinen. Using the conceptual background of the CSR, the Finnish scholar has been able to present a plausible case for Buddhism as a religion containing a large number of counter-intuitive agents; in his own words, 'Buddha and the buddhas most clearly belong to the category of counter-intuitive beings, and ... Buddhism thus need not be problematic with regard to a global concept of religion'.[75] Reformulated in this way, Buddhism is no longer the magic bullet argument that Durkheim once took it for.

7.6.3 Cognitive definition and social constructionism

Varieties of social constructionism therefore seem to be mistaken in the belief that essentialist definitions of religion are defective in principle. The concept of (minimally) counter-intuitive agents used by the CSR could be viewed as a cross-cultural universal,[76] well-tailored for our cognitive systems in being 'weird' enough to matter for memory recall and, by extension, cultural transmission, yet not 'too weird' to allow for rich inference potential. In a sense, the CSR is set to replace the false dichotomy of naïve essentialism on the one hand and free-for-all social constructionism on the other with a synthetic approach recognizing relatively stable sets of constraints, which are generated by our cognitive architecture designed during the evolutionary history of our species, as well as deep intercultural variation among religious concepts, beliefs and practices.

Concerning 'power-based' social constructionism in particular, the response of the CSR is different with respect to the relation of power and religion itself and the relation of power and the study of religion. Concerning the latter, Ivan Strenski is probably right in noting that '[i]t is frankly ludicrous to imply that the academic study of religion, so meager in its resources, has hegemonically imposed a concept of "religion" on the wretched of the earth, as some of our comrades believe'.[77] This is not to contest the claim that religious studies can, and often are, used for political purposes. Nevertheless, it could be argued that the CSR (as opposed to, say, *sui generis* approaches to religion) minimizes the risk of potentially unwanted misuse of the academic study of religion for political ends via the adoption of a proper scientific methodology, including empirical testing, experimentation and the rejection of inherently flawed analytic categories (such as the 'Sacred') and reformulation of potentially ambiguous ones ('gods' or 'supernatural beings').

Concerning the relation of power and religion itself, the CSR does not deny the interrelation of power and religion,[78] but does not place it in the focus of its scientific endeavours either. Further, an argument could be made for the chronological primacy of religious concepts free from power relations in society. These concepts do not seem to be purposefully invented to cement power relations desirable for their inventors. Rather, they are generated naturally as by-products of the architecture of the human brain, with the possibility of political (mis)use as an optional, secondary development. Somewhat simplistically, the difference between 'power-based' social constructionism and the CSR could be viewed as a difference in accent demonstrated via the distinction of two interconnected, yet in many respects autonomous, systems of thought. The first system, evolutionarily older, operating quickly and automatically on the basis of evolved cognitive modules, generates inferences and causal relations, biased to believing and confirming (as opposed to critically examining). The second system, evolutionarily younger, operating slowly and consciously, houses executive functions and accounts for deliberate action and thought.[79] The focus of the CSR lies with the first system because of its instrumental role in the generation of representations which seem to be a *conditio sine qua non* for any subsequent development of the beliefs and practices we term 'religious'. The second system is then responsible for the conscious manipulation of religious concepts (e.g. to fulfil political needs or strengthen the existing or desired power distribution). As Todd Tremlin aptly points out, 'if a ubiquity of gods is indeed the case, then it would seem that ... gods are in fact foundational and it is *religion* that is instrumental'.[80]

7.7 Has the cognitive science of religion (re)defined 'religion'?

I have tried to show in this chapter that:

1. In spite of the cautionary tone of scholars affiliated with the CSR, it is possible to reconstruct a 'cognitive definition of religion'.

2. Owing to paradigmatic theoretical changes, this cognitive definition of religion solves the Tylor–Durkheim dichotomy by replacing the hopelessly ambiguous concept of 'spiritual', 'superhuman' or 'supernatural' beings within the empirically testable concept of counter-intuitiveness.
3. The theoretical framework of the cognitive approach, especially the concept of cross-cultural species-specific universals generated naturally by the architecture of the human mind, answers the objections of social constructionism against any form of 'essentialism'.
4. While the CSR acknowledges that power relations might play a significant role in many religions, an explanatory theory of religion based solely on power relations is at best incomplete, since it is unlikely to explain adequately the origin of religious concepts.

Is it fair to conclude that the cognitive science of religion solved once and for all the problem of the definition of religion? Probably not. However, its discussion of the definitional problem showed on the terminological level the potential and possibility to define on a much more rigorous basis the term 'supernatural beings', which is essential for a study of religion irrespective of whether we accept it as a *definiens* of religion or not. Even more importantly, I hope to have shown that the cognitive science of religion rests deeply embedded in the naturalist paradigm. Protectionist definitions via empirically untestable 'faculties for the perception of the Infinite' of Müller or Tiele or nebulous and ill-defined *sacra* of Otto or Eliade are abandoned in favour of relatively narrowly-defined concepts and notions that are liable to empirical testing.

8

Cognitive science of religion (3): Practical application

For the love of God, let no one read and interpret Homer according to any 'theory'!
Otmar Vaňorný[1]

In the two previous chapters, I have attempted to describe the metamorphoses of the naturalistic paradigm in the context of the cognitive science of religion in domains of method and terminology. In this chapter, I turn to a particular problem, much discussed both in classical philology and study of religions, namely the invocation of the Muse in Homer and Hesiod. Over the past several decades, the invocation of the Muse in archaic Greek epic poetry has been studied in some detail from various modern theoretical perspectives.[2] The main aim of this chapter is to offer a comprehensive interpretation of these invocations that is based on advances in the cognitive science of religion. The argument shall proceed in three steps. The first section collates primary data for the analysis, presenting and commenting on all relevant mentions of the Muse in Homeric epics and Hesiod. The second section consists of an overview of the most important hypotheses concerning the origin and function of such invocations. The third section briefly introduces the cognitive science of religion and applies some of its theoretical concepts to invocations of the Muse in the earliest Greek poetry.

Before discussing the primary data, two brief remarks are necessary. With respect to Homeric epics, Albin Lesky famously wrote that their meaningful scholarly analysis requires as a *sine qua non* at the very least a provisional answer to the 'Homeric question'.[3] With all due respect to the great Austrian classicist, I do not find this issue very pressing in the cognitive analysis of invocations, as cognitive structures and mechanisms evolve at a snail's pace and would be the same for (say) a court poet in the twelfth century BCE and a vagrant singer of tales in the eighth century BCE. I have therefore adopted a phenomenological ἐποχή of sorts with respect to the manifold complex problems related to the composition of Homeric epics, presupposing, however, their origin in oral poetry, a point that does not seem controversial in current scholarship.[4] The second remark pertains to the number of Muses and the consistent use of the singular in the following text. Homer informed us that there are nine Muses (Μοῦσαι δ' ἐννέα),[5] and we find the same information confirmed in Hesiod, who (unlike Homer) also provided us with a list of their personal names.[6] Since it may be safely assumed that the respective domains of competence of the Muses, known from later tradition, are far from established in the oldest Greek poetry,[7] I will consistently use the singular form 'Muse' with an implied collective meaning.

8.1 The Muse in Homer and Hesiod: Primary data

In Homeric epics, the Muse is explicitly mentioned 14 times.[8] The number of mentions grows to 15 if we include the very first verse of the *Iliad*, where the vocative θεά undoubtedly refers to our goddess. In Hesiod's *oeuvre*, we find 17 explicit references.[9] We may provisionally divide these into invocations *sensu stricto* and mere mentions. In invocations *sensu stricto*, the singer addresses the Muse directly, which is carried out grammatically through the use of the vocative case of the nominal form and the imperative mood of the verbal form. Mere mentions indirectly reference the Muse in the third person, with the exception of a single locus in Hesiod, discussed below.

8.1.1 Invocations *sensu stricto*

Major invocations *sensu stricto* are embedded within the proems introducing each Homeric epic.[10] I am assuming here that the proems are genuine,[11] given their close structural and functional similarities.[12] The central theme of each epic is introduced by a substantive in the accusative (μῆνιν, ἄνδρα) followed by a verbal form in the imperative mood (ἄειδε, ἔννεπε), an address to the Muse in the vocative (θεά, Μοῦσα), a relative proposition presenting the poem's main theme, and the conclusion of a repeated direct address to the Muse, in the form of either a question (τίς τάρ σφωε θεῶν ἔριδι ξυνέηκε μάχεσθαι) or a renewed invitation to sing (τῶν ἁμόθεν γε, θεά, θύγατερ Διός, εἰπὲ καὶ ἡμῖν). In both cases, the singer clearly considers himself[13] an intermediary, receiving instruction from the Muse and communicating it on to the audience.

An invocation *sensu stricto* is also found at the beginning of both fully extant works by Hesiod, although the philological considerations of the proem to the *Theogony* in particular are more complicated than those in the Homeric epics. The textual integrity of its first 115 verses has often been doubted,[14] but the majority of more recent scholarship on the topic has argued for unity,[15] whether on the basis of structural[16] or grammatical analysis.[17] The invocation of the Muse in Hesiod's *Theogony* is embedded within the larger frame of a hymn in which the Muse is not only directly addressed but also celebrated as a deity. It is probably impossible (and of dubious heuristic value) to attempt an exact demarcation of the various elements in the first 115 verses of the *Theogony* (proem, hymn, invocation, etc.),[18] yet scholars usually place the invocation *sensu stricto* as beginning at verse 104,[19] or alternatively 114.[20] A significantly shorter invocation of the Muse is also found in the first few lines of Hesiod's *Works and Days*.[21] In both invocations, as in the two Homeric ones, the singer is depicted as being fully reliant on the Muse in his endeavours.

The invocations *sensu stricto* also include several verses prefacing the 'Catalogue of Ships' in the second book of the *Iliad*.[22] Introducing probably one of the epic's oldest segments,[23] this invocation of the Muse is significant in establishing a contrast between the κλέος of mortals and the divine knowledge offered by the Muse. The exact semantic extension of the term κλέος in verse 486 has been the subject of a lively scholarly discussion. For some, it denotes a 'lower' degree of knowledge;[24] for others, it represents 'oral tradition' or 'traditional poetry' based on information obtained by hearsay (and therefore in opposition to information authenticated by the goddess);[25] for others still, the two lines comparing human and divine knowledge betray a well-developed religious feeling of the sacred (as distinct from the profane).[26] Regardless of the interpretation one would choose, the invocation prefacing the Catalogue of Ships brings yet another instance of the singer's professed dependence on the Muse.

In addition to the invocations discussed above, the *Iliad* also includes so-called 'minor' invocations,[27] spanning no more than three lines in length and parallel in structure, with the formulaic ἔσπετε νῦν μοι Μοῦσαι Ὀλύμπια δώματ' ἔχουσαι introducing most of them. The singer always asks a specific question and invites the Muse to provide an answer.[28] In Hesiod's *Theogony*, we find two instances of minor invocations.[29] It may be concluded that all invocations *sensu stricto* depict the poet as heavily reliant on the Muse as a source of unerring information, this information being indispensable for his poetic activity.

8.1.2 Other mentions

In addition to direct addresses to the Muse, we find the earliest Greek epic poetry contains several sections commenting indirectly on the process of poetic creation and discussing the relationship between the singer and the goddess. In the *Odyssey*, this is found particularly in the descriptions of Demodokos,[30] a blind singer at the court of Alkinoös, king of the Phaiakians, and Phemios, a bard working his art at Odysseus' palace in Ithaka. In Hesiod's poetry, we find valuable commentary in the famous *Dichterweihe* episode[31] at the beginning of the poet's *Theogony*.

The description of Demodokos in the eighth book of the *Odyssey* corroborates the conclusions reached in the above discussion of direct invocations. It is the Muse who grants the singer the ability to compose and sing the songs (δίδου δ' ἡδεῖαν ἀοιδήν)[32] – one could argue that in the context of the oral poetry there is little difference between composition and actual delivery of the poem – and it is the Muse who inspires the poet (Μοῦσ' ἄρ' ἀοιδὸν ἀνῆκεν ἀειδέμεναι).[33] Several hundred verses later, Odysseus himself again repeats that the Muse 'taught' the singers their songs (σφέας οἴμας Μοῦσ' ἐδίδαξε).[34] The divine origin of poetry is further established by Demodokos' capacity to sing about the events that occurred at Troy κατὰ κόσμον,[35] in spite of the fact that he was never present there (and even if he had been, it would not have been of much value to him, as he was blind).

The emerging picture of the passive poet serving as a mouthpiece for the Muse is, at least *prima facie*, somewhat put into question by the words uttered by Phemios during Odysseus' slaughter of the suitors. In order to defend himself in course of the raging μνηστηροκτονία, Phemios begs Odysseus to spare him, as with his song the bard pleases both mortals and immortals. One puzzling aspect is the two lines in which Phemios says, in Lattimore's translation, 'I am taught by myself, but the god has inspired in me the song-ways of every kind' (αὐτοδίδακτος δ' εἰμί, θεὸς δέ μοι ἐν φρεσὶν οἴμας

| παντοίας ἐνέφυσεν).[36] How is it possible for Phemios to plausibly claim both that he is αὐτοδίδακτος – a term that would seem to imply complete independence – and that he is inspired by the goddess, especially if, as we have seen, invocations *sensu stricto*, minor invocations, and the description of Demodokos all make it very clear that the poet is completely dependent on the Muse? Some scholars have accepted these lines in their apparent incompatibility with other claims by the poet of the Homeric epics and concluded that 'Homer is ambivalent as to whether the poet is an independent artist or a medium of the Muses',[37] while others have seen in Phemios' assertion a 'claim of artistic originality'[38] or argued for a compromise that takes the poetic art to be partly learned and partly granted by the Muse.[39]

I believe that closer inspection of the context of Phemios' utterance may well solve the apparent contradiction between Phemios' claims on the one side and the direct invocations and descriptions of Demodokos on the other. Silvio Accame in 1963 showed that αὐτοδίδακτος here could not possibly mean 'self-taught' in the sense of 'independent of external influence'.[40] Phemios uttered these words under a direct threat to his life, facing an enraged Odysseus who had casually murdered almost everyone else in sight. What sense would it make for Phemios to argue in this situation that he is 'self-taught'? Quite to the contrary, the adjective αὐτοδίδακτος is here better understood as meaning 'not taught by other mortals' (but by the immortals, namely the Muse), because it is precisely his special relationship with the divinity that provides him with a plausible argument for why he should be spared.

I now turn to Hesiod's *Dichterweihe*[41] because this section of the *Theogony* is both very important, as Hesiod talks directly about himself, as opposed to the Homeric epics, where insight into the singer's creative process is indirectly 'mirrored' in Demodokos and Phemios,[42] and also very puzzling, as some lines seem to indicate that the Muse does not always tell the truth but also has the capacity to lie. In accordance with the evidence mustered from the Homeric epics, the Muse 'breathed a divine voice into me [Hesiod]' (ἐνέπνευσαν δέ μοι αὐδὴν θέσπιν)[43] and 'taught Hesiod beautiful song' (αἵ νύ ποθ''Ησίοδον καλὴν ἐδίδαξαν ἀοιδήν).[44] The puzzling part comes with the much-discussed lines 'we know how to say many false things similar to genuine ones, but we know, when we wish, how to proclaim true things'.[45] That the Muse tells the truth (ἴδμεν δ' εὖτ' ἐθέλωμεν ἀληθέα γηρύσασθαι) is unproblematic, but what of her capacity to lie – and to lie in such a particular way that the lie is indistinguishable from the truth (ἴδμεν ψεύδεα πολλὰ λέγειν ἐτύμοισιν ὁμοῖα)? What exactly is meant by the expression ψεύδεα ἐτύμοισιν ὁμοῖα?

Many scholars have argued that these 'false things similar to genuine ones' are, in fact, the Homeric epics, either because they contain some factually incorrect information[46] or because their main purpose (namely, to celebrate the famous deeds of great heroes) is so distant from the world of Hesiod and his shepherd audience that it cannot be 'genuine'.[47] Alternatively, the Homeric epics are not 'genuine' because they contain genealogies of their heroes and thus establish and perpetuate social divisions between aristocratic rulers and ordinary folk (including Hesiod and his audience).[48] Other scholars have argued that knowledge communicated by the Muse, a daughter of Mnemosyne (Memory), cannot possibly be false and consequently that the expression ψεύδεα ἐτύμοισιν ὁμοῖα denotes not lies but the 'memory' of evil or insignificant deeds.⁴⁹ Some have read the lines in a religious context and claimed that the portrayal of the Muse as capable of speaking things both true and false is nothing more or less than an expression of the singer's piety.⁵⁰ Others have simply accepted the words at face value and concluded that the Muse indeed sometimes lies.⁵¹

I tend to accept the interpretation of Bruce Heiden, who recently studied all relevant occurrences of the adjective ὁμοῖος in Greek texts of the Archaic age and came to the conclusion that the term did not signify similarity but rather identity. For him, 'the Muses did not tell Hesiod that they spoke two separate and different things, both lies (*Theogony* 27) and truth (*Theogony* 28). Hard though it may be to understand, the Muses told Hesiod that they spoke only the truth, because even their lies were somewhat equivalent to the truth. [...] the Muses' speech appears to broadcast a threat to listeners or readers who might find the Muses' songs unbelievable and dismiss them as mere lies.'⁵² According to this interpretation, then, Hesiod's Muse (quite like the goddess of the Homeric epics) does not lie. Rather, what Hesiod signals here is that at times, to an uneducated audience (such as shepherds) it might *seem* that the Muse is lying, but this is always due to a fault in the receiver, not the transmitter.⁵³ Hesiod's concept of the Muse is then in its important aspects similar if not identical to the concept introduced in the Homeric epics: the goddess is depicted as a source of unerring information and the poet is substantively reliant on this information in the process of poetic creation.

I am aware of the fact that the rapprochement sketched above between the Homeric epics and Hesiod might raise some eyebrows. After all, the discussion of the 'lying Muse' in Hesiod brought views that Hesiod might be 'the first critic of Homer'.⁵⁴ If we bracket the differences not directly relevant to the topic at hand,⁵⁵ some scholars claimed that Hesiod 'describes a much more personal relationship between himself and the Muses'⁵⁶ and this much may be accepted, but I find unwarranted the arguments that the invocation of the Muse⁵⁷ or the self-understanding of the poet⁵⁸ in Hesiod is substantially different from that found in the Homeric epics. In fact, central aspects of the relationship between the Muse and the poet are strikingly similar between the two poets.⁵⁹ For both the author(s) of the Homeric epics and Hesiod, the Muse is introduced within the marked context of the poems' opening sequences, and for both it is the Muse who 'teaches' the poet to sing and, while it might be difficult to assess the exact nature of their relationship and the level of the singer's autonomy, the Muse is unequivocally portrayed as the unerring source of the poet's information.

It is true, however, that the relationship between the Muse and the singer in the earliest Greek epic poetry underwent a clear shift in emphasis in twentieth-century classical scholarship. Especially in the first half of the twentieth century, the singer was repeatedly constructed as a completely passive instrument, a megaphone of sorts for the Muse.⁶⁰ Historically, we find this interpretation as early as Democritus, who claimed that any and all valuable poetry is created only μετ' ἐνθουσιασμοῦ καὶ ἱεροῦ πνεύματος,⁶¹ which was canonically the view of Plato, for whom poets are nothing more or less than 'interpreters of the gods'.⁶² This view further established that the singers are completely dependent on the Muse,⁶³ and for some scholars even Hesiod's proem does not constitute an exception.⁶⁴ Simply put, the 'classical conception of the Muse' argued that the goddess 'deprives a human being of his senses and uses him as the witless mouthpiece of divine utterance'.⁶⁵

A strong opposition against this arguably overly simplistic theory began to form in the second half of the twentieth century. Scholars started to realize that the interpretation of poetic creativity expounded by Democritus and Plato was not immediately applicable to Homeric and Hesiodic poems and amounted to a serious anachronism.[66] In a new appraisal of the relationship between the poet and Muse, the singer started to appear significantly more autonomous. It was resolutely denied that he was only a passive mouthpiece and the relationship between the Muse and the poet was described as 'open'.[67] The two protagonists are seen as engaging in a collaborative enterprise[68] and, as Irene de Jong summarized, more recent scholarship on the nature of poetic creativity in archaic Greece testified to 'an interesting development leading towards the emancipation – indeed the self-assertion – of the narrator *vis-à-vis* his god'.[69]

Setting aside occasional attempts to fall back on the thesis of the poet's complete dependence on the Muse,[70] I find it important to emphasize that abandoning Democritus and Plato's notion of 'divine possession' and the overall interpretation of the relationship between the poet and Muse in which the former is allowed to play a much more significant active part does not in any way violate the assumption that the singer is nevertheless reliant on the Muse as a source of information and that she remains the dominant partner in the relationship and a *sine qua non* of archaic Greek epic poetry.

8.2 The interpretations of the invocations: *Status Quaestionis*

Having completed the collation of and brief commentary on primary data, consisting of the invocations and mentions of the Muse in the Homeric epics and Hesiod's poems, I now turn to a brief overview of the variety of interpretations proposed by classical scholars. This step is necessary not only to do justice to the wealth of scholarship on this topic, but also because the cognitive approach presented in Section 8.3 of this chapter has direct bearing on several items discussed in the current section. It must be mentioned that these interpretations are by no means mutually exclusive and scholars quite often subscribe to several of them simultaneously.

8.2.1 Librarian interpretation

Some of these approaches may be mentioned only in passing, simply because their plausibility has collapsed under the weight of progress in classical scholarship. With respect to the Homeric epics, Gilbert Murray, for instance, associated the Muse with the invention of writing and on the basis of this connection he thought that the invocations marked difficult or memory-heavy sections in the poem that required the singer to consult some written notes.[71] As summarized by one of his less enthusiastic early critics, 'what Murray means is that we have here a long catalogue of diverse facts on which the poet consults the Muses and that the Muses represent his book'.[72] Since the oral origin of the Homeric epics has been proven beyond any doubt, the Muse can hardly represent a book.[73]

8.2.2 Topical interpretation

The topical interpretation of invocations of the Muse asserts that these instances in the poems are of a purely literary character; the singer is the sole creative force in the composition and his address to the Muse is completely artificial in nature.[74] One would not, of course, wish to deny that invocation of the Muse eventually became a stock motif in the epic genre of the European literary canon, spanning from Virgil[75] through Dante[76] to Milton[77] and onwards, but the topical interpretation is not readily applicable to Homer and Hesiod simply because the inner logic of the motif or *topos* dictates that for any motif M, the first instance of M cannot be topical in itself, because a motif becomes a motif only in the context of some earlier, pre-existing tradition. If we then accept as true that the Homeric epics and Hesiod's works are among the first documents in European literature and certainly the first to feature invocations of the Muse (which is uncontroversial), those invocations cannot be interpreted topically as they only establish the motif for later epic poetry.[78]

8.2.3 Etymological interpretation

Etymological observations have their own intrinsic value,[79] but the conflation of a term's etymology with an account of the origin and function of the concept embodied by this term is unlikely to produce a meaningful explanation. By means of an example, Calvert Watkins, in a flurry of comparative linguistics, reconstructed the Indo-European basis of the Greek word Μοῦσα as *mon-tu-h$_2$, itself containing the root *men-, signifying 'active mental force, thinking, perceiving, remembering'. This much is uncontroversial, but one is left to wonder whether this observation warrants the conclusion that the 'inspiration of the divine Muse is only a personification of the trained mind of the poet'.[80] Equating the invocation of the Muse with 'personification' raises doubts in itself;[81] it could further be asked how the 'trained mind of the poet', a subjective mind, could produce statements that are, at least declaratively, absolute in nature.[82] Moreover, the argument itself is a clear *non sequitur*, because the mere fact that the etymology of term T is X does not enable us, without further effort, to deduce that T is X, plain and simple.

8.2.4 Social interpretation

Moving on to more fruitful approaches, several scholars have understood an invocation of the Muse to be a functional element addressed primarily to the audience and used in order to strengthen the singer's social standing. The upside of this interpretation is that it finds direct support in the Homeric epics and Hesiod's works. For instance, Odysseus notes in the eighth book of the *Odyssey* that 'with all peoples upon the earth singers are entitled to be cherished and to their share of respect, since (οὕνεκα) the Muse has taught them her own way, and since she loves all the company of singers'.[83] The causal force of οὕνεκα clearly signals that the social prestige and authority of the singers is due to their association with and instruction by the Muse. In Hesiod's *Theogony*, the *Dichterweihe* likewise depicts the Muse handing over to the poet a sceptre as a symbol of power and authority.[84] Furthermore, in the proem to the *Theogony* the Muse is also portrayed as a patron of the rulers (or judges).[85] This association has produced many different interpretations,[86] and yet it seems unproblematic that the connection between the Muse and rulers (or judges) endows Hesiod in particular and the poet in general with additional authority. Kathryn Stoddard argued that the association of rulers (or judges) with the Muse is present already in the *Dichterweihe* and 'what Hesiod has done in these two passages of the proem of his *Theogony* is to establish for himself a double legitimacy'.[87]

The authority and legitimacy generated by associating the Muse and singers in the Homeric epics and Hesiod then serves as an 'excellent alibi for creative intervention', since 'each of the poet's innovations automatically gains the status of divine truth in virtue of its origin in divine inspiration'.[88] Additionally, the association with the Muse further shields the poet from any adverse reactions from the audience.[89] This functional aspect of the invocation is indeed plausible and '[i]t is not surprising poets should accept the doctrine of divine inspiration',[90] yet one might ask why the audience should accept it. Even if we assume that invoking the Muse strengthened the singer's social standing, the precise mechanism of why this should be the case is left unexplained. The cognitive account of invocation presented in Section 8.3 of this chapter will attempt to provide some provisional answers.

8.2.5 Rhetorical interpretation

A different scholarly approach to such invocations claims that the Muse served to alert the audience to specific parts of the song and to capture attention. Of course, we shall not find any explicit confirmation of this functional hypothesis in the primary data (the Homeric and Hesiodic epics are not treatises on poetics), yet even some ancient authorities understood invocations in this way, as evidenced by Aristotle,[91] a Hellenistic scholiast on Homer,[92] as well as Quintilian.[93] Modern 'rhetorical' interpretations, heavily influenced by Aristotle and Quintilian, then argued that the invocation of the Muse prefacing the Catalogue of Ships serves as a *captatio benevolentiae* of sorts.[94] In this view, other invocations mark sections of the song that are either technically demanding and require heightened attention from the audience[95] or containing important developments in the dramatic plot.[96] As is the case with the interpretation that saw in the invocations a means to enhance the singer's social standing, the interpretation of invocations as a rhetorical device is plausible, but it is not entirely clear how mentioning the Muse would be able to effectively raise the audience's attentiveness, especially given the fact that Indo-European poetry knew also direct pleas for attentiveness.[97] A provisional answer will be proposed in Section 8.3 of this chapter.

8.2.6 Religious interpretation

The last interpretation to be discussed in this section is what I would like to term the 'deflationist' interpretation, taking the invocations in the Homeric epics and Hesiod's work at face value. Whatever other functions it might serve, an invocation of the Muse is, first and foremost, not a literary artifice introduced in order to raise the audience's attentiveness or improve the singer's social status and legitimize the contents of his work,[98] but an expression of genuine religiosity. This possibility has been at times emphatically denied, and some scholars have argued that 'the invocation is only due to a sacred tradition and is not organically connected with the following epic tale' and 'is no longer connected with the cult of a special deity, nor recited at its festival';[99] invocations therefore 'cannot be safely approached as genuine appeals, but only as the ossified remains of such appeals'.[100] Other have suggested that the genuineness of even the very first invocations of the Muse is 'problematic' and 'we may doubt whether anyone "truly believed in" the Muses or divinely authorized speech'.[101]

In the second half of the twentieth century, interpretations of the invocations as an authentic religious experience became more and more favoured, largely as a consequence of the abandonment of methodological colonialism and rejection of the reformed Christian religion as the canon against which all other religious traditions were to be measured.[102] Scholars slowly but surely started to consider the view that 'Homer's invocations of the Muse seem to be based on a real religious experience'[103] and while Hesiod's *Dichterweihe* might seem slightly more artificial, recent scholarship defended the authenticity of religious experience found in the proem to the *Theogony* as well.[104] In this interpretation, then, invocations in the earliest Greek epic poetry 'spring[s] from a real, religious belief'.[105]

8.3 Cognitive approach to invocations

Following the review of primary data (Section 8.1 of this chapter) and some of the most common scholarly interpretations (Section 8.2 of this chapter), I shall now propose a cognitive approach to invocations of the Muse in the earliest Greek epic poetry. In particular, I will use recent findings from the cognitive science of religion in an attempt to shed some light on the possible origin of these invocations and investigate their relationship with several of the interpretations introduced above. A cognitive approach to some aspects of the Homeric epics has been fruitfully applied especially by Elizabeth Minchin, who argued that 'Homer's narrative is for the most part founded and generated by cognitive structures which organize the memory storage not only for singers, like Homer, in an oral tradition, but of all individuals'.[106] While the present study shares some important theoretical assumptions with Minchin's work, in contradistinction to her emphasis on memory (and therefore transmission), I would like to focus on the acquisition of the concept of the Muse and use specific conceptual tools developed by the cognitive science of religion. First, however, I must present, very briefly, the basic theoretical assumptions of the cognitive approach in general.

For a large part of the twentieth century, humanities and social sciences were dominated by the culturally deterministic 'standard social science model' (SSSM).[107] The SSSM was based on an essentially behaviourist psychology which considered the mind to be a blank slate equipped only with a general-purpose associative-learning mechanism which passively internalizes whatever cultural inputs the individual is exposed to. The creation, acquisition and transmission of ideas and beliefs is therefore fully determined by the particular cultures the individual interacts with and, assuming the basic tenets of the SSSM, it is therefore futile to search for any universals in human behaviour and thinking. During the 1970s, several key figures challenged this predominant model of cultural determinism by highlighting the role of implicit knowledge and cognitive mechanisms in the acquisition and transmission of cultural concepts.

Dan Sperber analysed symbolism as a 'cognitive mechanism' and argued that 'the basic principles of the symbolic mechanism are not induced from experience but are, on the contrary, part of the innate mental equipment that makes experience possible';[108] Edward O. Wilson demonstrated the importance of our evolved biology in the study of social organization and cultural representations;[109] and Richard Dawkins introduced the notion of the 'meme' as an analogue to the gene as a unit of cultural selection.[110] Setting aside obvious differences, what all three authors shared is an interest in explaining why and how cultural concepts, representations and beliefs are created, acquired and transmitted, as well as a strong conviction that one key to this explanation is the architecture of the human mind as shaped by evolution through natural selection.[111]

Thus, in contradistinction to the SSSM, the cognitive approach assumes that the human mind is a collection of domain-specific modules shaped by evolution through natural selection.[112] These modules have evolved to solve specific tasks presented to the individual by his or her environment with the single goal of increasing the individual's fitness and assuring the replication of his or her genes in the next generation. The cognitive model therefore views the evolved architecture of the human mind as an active factor, significantly constraining the acquisition and transmission of cultural representations and actions. To put it simply, the architecture of our minds makes us more receptive to some ideas and less receptive to others; cultural input is significantly filtered by our cognitive hardware. Now if the 'mind is [...] what the brain does, and not even everything it does'[113] and the brains of all neurologically healthy members of our species are roughly the same (simply because they have been subject to the same evolutionary pressures), then it follows that some features of cultural representations, namely those that are constrained the most by the architecture of our minds, should be cross-culturally recurrent, that is to say, universal.[114]

While a substantive account of the development of the cognitive science of religion (CSR) lies far beyond the scope of this chapter,[115] it will suffice to say that the CSR draws on the aforementioned general theories of culture (especially on Sperber's 'epidemiology of beliefs') and seeks to account for the origin, acquisition and transmission of religious beliefs and actions in particular. In what follows, I will briefly discuss three specific concepts developed within the CSR (hyperactive agency detection, minimal counter-intuitiveness and strategic information) and subsequently use them to formulate a cognitive account of invocations of the Muse in the earliest Greek poetry.

The hyperactive agency detection device is an evolved cognitive module whose primary function – as the name suggests – is the detection of agents in our environment.[116] An 'agent' is defined as an entity to which we ascribe mental states and teleological (goal-oriented) behaviour. Calling the agency detection module 'hyperactive' simply means that the module may often be triggered by minimal cues and that it generates many false positives – that is to say, human beings often detect agents when there are none present. It is also important to emphasize that the module's hyperactivity is not anything pathological; agency detection in neurologically normal members of our species is hyperactive by default because the evolutionary cost of false positives (measured in the currency of the individual's overall fitness) is, on average, much lower than the cost of a failure to identify an agent when one is present.

To illustrate this by means of a simple example, Stewart Guthrie compared the evolutionary costs and benefits of mistaking a bear for a boulder and *vice versa*.[117] If I mistake an oddly shaped boulder for a bear, I might get scared and I am immediately prompted to inspect the situation in more detail, eventually realizing that I have detected an agent (bear) where there is none. I lost a few seconds of my precious time and some extra energy. If, on the other hand, I mistake a bear for a boulder and do not initiate the appropriate action (e.g. running for a tree or playing dead, depending on your preference), I might lose my life. Since the cost of a false positive in agent detection is low and a failure to detect an agent may often be fatal, evolutionary pressures in our environment have tuned our agency detection to a high sensitivity.

If we turn from detection of agency in general to specific types of agents, we may discuss another concept developed by the CSR, namely 'minimal counter-intuitiveness'.[118] First, a counter-intuitive concept is a concept that violates our intuitive, hard-wired assumptions about how different classes of objects (or, to use Boyer's term, ontological categories)[119] work. For instance, by identifying an object in my environment as a 'person', I expect that object to behave as an agent, that is to say, I expect it to have a mind and an underlying belief-desire psychology as well as to engage in teleological behaviour. Similarly, if I classify an object as a 'tool', I expect it to be man-made and to serve a specific function (but I do not expect it to have a mind or agency).

Second, a minimally counter-intuitive concept is a concept that conforms to most of our intuitive expectations (generated automatically by virtue of belonging to a specific ontological category) and violates only a few of them. As Justin Barrett has summarized, minimally counter-intuitive concepts 'constitute a special group of concepts that largely match intuitive assumptions about their own group of things but have a small number of tweaks that make them particularly interesting and memorable. Because they are more interesting and memorable, they are more likely to be passed on from person to person. Because they readily spread from person to person, [they] are likely to become cultural (that is, widely shared) concepts.'[120]

As this brief outline of minimal counter-intuitiveness makes clear, the Muse in the Homeric epics and Hesiod's works may be unequivocally categorized as a minimally counter-intuitive concept. She falls under the heading of the ontological category 'person', as she is portrayed as obviously anthropomorphic: the Muse communicates with the singer, is actively involved in matters of human beings, and is subject to familiar emotional states (e.g. anger at Thamyris).[121] All of this renders the Muse-concept intelligible and potentially inference-rich. What sets her apart from the most conspicuous other members of the 'person' ontological category, namely human beings, is her immortality, potential to be not readily visible, and, most importantly, her full access to strategic information.[122]

Put simply, strategic information is any sort of information that is relevant for any specific individual, whether socially or otherwise. For instance, I may be very interested in knowing whether my love interest or boss likes me (making the information strategic for me), but I might be much less interested in knowing whether my neighbours bought a new television or what my distant relative ate for dinner yesterday (making the information non-strategic). What counts as 'strategic information' is completely subjective and relational – piece of information *I* may be strategic for individual *P* and at the same time non-strategic for person *Q*.

Now that the concept of 'strategic information' has been outlined, we may, following Boyer, formulate two main principles: First, we presume that other people's access to strategic information is neither perfect nor automatic – that is to say, human beings always know less than they would like to know. Let this be called the 'principle of imperfect access'. Second, supernatural beings are usually conceptualized as having far greater epistemic powers than human beings have, with access to information that is not readily available (qualitatively or quantitatively) to us mortals. In some cases, these beings even have access to the complete set of all information available, of which the entirety of strategic information forms a subset. Let this be called the 'principle of full access'.

Turning to the Homeric epics and Hesiod, we can clearly demonstrate both that the Muse is portrayed as a key element in the transfer of information to the singer and that she has full access to information, as defined above. Unlike many other Olympian gods susceptible to lies and tricks,[123] the Muse is consistently portrayed by Homer and Hesiod as omniscient.[124] More importantly, one of the rare instances of a *communis opinio* in Homeric and Hesiodic scholarship is the observation that the nature of the poetic inspiration bestowed on the poet by the Muse consists primarily of the transfer of information. As observed by W.W. Minton, 'the poet does not ask for help or guidance in "how" he shall tell his story; there is no suggestion of a plea for "inspiration", only for information'.[125] Even in Homeric minor invocations, discussed above, we always find the poet asking the Muse to produce specific factual information,[126] not Alcman's charms and dancing.[127]

It is now time to put all the pieces of the puzzle together. Elizabeth Murray is one of the few scholars to have considered seriously the possibility that the Muse in the earliest Greek poetry represents in some way the very nature of the creative process, which, as we have seen, may be characterized as a steady flow of information from the Muse to the poet. She wrote that 'whatever else the Muses stand for they symbolize the poet's feeling of the dependence on the external: they are personifications of his inspiration'.[128] It is important to emphasize here the fact that the source of information is deemed to be external to the poet, an observation made by other scholars as well – not only with respect to the Homeric epics and Hesiod's works,[129] but also with respect to the nature of poetic creativity in general.[130]

Given the predominantly oral context of the earliest extant epic Greek poetry, I find it plausible to assume the following statements to be true:

1. The singer(s) of the Homeric epics and Hesiod felt during their performances that poetic inspiration came from outside themselves as a kind of external force.

2. For the singer(s) of the Homeric epics and for Hesiod, this poetic inspiration consisted of the transfer of information from the external source to themselves.
3. *Pace* Gilbert Murray, no written documents of any kind played a role in the process of poetic creativity and performance.

If these three propositions hold true, we may assume that the external source of information on which the poet depends belongs to the ontological category 'person'. This is to say that the source is conceptualized as an agent exhibiting teleological behaviour and a belief-desire psychology through the operation of the hyperactive agency detection device, which facilitates identification of the external source of information as an agent.[131] This agent further exhibits a handful of counter-intuitive features, chiefly full access to strategic information, immortality, and (if we may so surmise) occasional invisibility. The Muse as a concept therefore falls within the set of minimally counter-intuitive agents since she retains high inference potential coupled with several counter-intuitive elements. This kind of concept is salient (highly attractive to our cognitive systems) and not readily falsifiable,[132] which considerably elevates its chance of being acquired and transmitted throughout the cultural environment. In short, the Muse of the Homeric epics and Hesiod's works may be understood as originating in the process of conceptualizing the external source of information on which the singers felt they depended.

How does the cognitive take on the origin of the Muse-concept relate to the scholarly interpretations briefly described in Section 8.2 of this chapter? Since minimally counter-intuitive concepts are prime candidates for worship as deities, the case for invocations as genuine appeals seems to be strengthened. Of course, not every minimally counter-intuitive concept is necessarily a religious concept, but we do possess some external evidence for a cult of the Muse in Greece and the close connection between poetry and prophecy also lend some support to the genuineness of the appeals.

Pausanias informs us that the cult of the Muses was established by Ephialtes and Otos at Helicon,[133] which would seem to suggest that the cult of the Muses existed even well before Hesiod.[134] Their worship was not limited to Boeotia, as Pausanias also knew about a sanctuary of the Muses near the Temple of Artemis at Troizen, built by one Ardalos, son of Hephaistos.[135] Plutarch referred to him as a 'priest' (ἱερεύς),[136] and in his dialogue *De Pythiae oraculis* we find mentions of a cultic place of the Muses at Delphi.[137] It is clear that the particulars of these reports may be questioned, but they do attest to the tradition of the cultic veneration of the Muse in Antiquity.

Further support for the genuine religiosity of the appeals to the Muse may be found in the close connection between poets and prophets. Both epic poetry and the majority of prophetic utterances share a metrical structure (dactylic hexameter), and on the lexical level it may be noted that Hesiod's Muse knows both future and past (τά τ' ἐσσόμενα πρό τ' ἐόντα),[138] very similarly to Kalchas the prophet in the *Iliad* (τά τ' ἐόντα τά τ' ἐσσόμενα πρό τ' ἐόντα).[139] According to one recent interpretation, the expression γαστέρες οἶον in Hesiod's *Dichterweihe* refers to mantic inspiration[140] and some have argued that such expressions as θέλξις attest to the 'primitive connexion of poetry and magic'.[141] It has been observed that the formal structure of invocations of the Muse bears a striking resemblance to a prayer,[142] and a strong connection of poets with prophecy has been attested not only for archaic Greek epic poetry,[143] but also cross-culturally.[144]

With respect to the 'social' and 'rhetorical' interpretations of invocations, the conclusions reached here suggest that the origins of the Muse-concept are not *primarily* to be found in the poet's desire to enhance his social standing and establish authority *vis-à-vis* his audience, nor to create a poetic device to raise his audience's attentiveness or signal important changes in the dramatic plot. Invocations originate in the poet's feeling of dependence on an external source of information and this source is conceptualized through our common cognitive machinery into the form of the Muse as a counter-intuitive agent. This does not mean, however, that the *secondary* effects of these genuine appeals to the divinity may not have been precisely what the 'social' and 'rhetorical' interpretations assume them to be. In fact, it has been demonstrated that the perceived presence of supernatural beings (or, in the parlance introduced here, minimally counter-intuitive agents) invariably has a significant impact on human behaviour.[145]

8.4 Conclusion

The purpose of this chapter has been to demonstrate the possibilities of the practical application of the theories and concepts produced by the cognitive science of religion on a particular problem, and thusly complement the previous theoretical and terminological discussions. The interpretation of the invocation of the Muse in earliest Greek poetry produced here belongs firmly to the naturalist paradigm, since it aims at a reductive explanation of the origins of the concept of the Muse by means of indicating cognitive mechanisms that play a significant role in the origination, acquisition and transmission of this concept. The poet (at least in the context of the oral poetry) subjectively feels that the subject matter of the song in its specific metrical form (information) is coming to him 'from the outside'; for the Greece of the Dark Ages, it is trivially true that this information can come only from another 'person' ('person' is here understood as an ontological category); the subjective perception that is coming from another 'person' activates the cognitive module for agency detection (HADD); because information is taken to be strategic and its producer as infallible, it follows that the information cannot originate with mere mortals, since these do not have unlimited access to strategic information and are not infallible; Muse is constituted as a minimally-counterintuitive agent with unlimited access to strategic information; Muse as a concept is therefore, because of these specific attributes, salient in acquisition and transmission of cultural concepts and her implied presence during the performance heightens the attention of the audience and establishes the authority of the bard.

9

Conclusion: A return of the prodigal son?

Who can be wise, amazed, temp'rate and furious,
Loyal and neutral in a moment? No man.

Shakespeare[1]

This work intended to show that the operating space of the theory and methodology of the study of religions is, quite like the space of Raphael's *Transfiguration*, divided into two separate and mutually incompatible parts. Naturalistic paradigm, whose first formulations may be attested at the very beginning of the European thinking, is based on an assumption that religious experience is to be explained reductively by means of psychological or social mechanisms. Religion in the context of naturalistic paradigm is therefore always in some sense an 'illusion' and the divinity exists only as a mental concept that lacks any extension. The second important assumption of the naturalistic paradigm is virtually uniform use of the epistemic justification *per rem*, which is to say that any specific person and his or her special properties or attributes may not serve as truth-makers of any proposition (that does not speak about said person and said properties, of course).

Protectionist paradigm, appearing already in the earliest Christian literature, assumes, to the contrary, that it is impossible to explain the human religious experience reductively, because its ultimate source and origin is the (objectively existing) divinity. As Walter Baetke canonically put it, 'all true religions naturally believe in the reality of the object of religion. For any deeply religious person, it is not only a mere idea or representation, but a living reality. In this faith lies the firm basis as well as the mystery of every religion. We could say: The man's faith is the correlate to the reality of the divinity – one is conditioned by the other.'[2] Further, I have attempted to show that the protectionist paradigm in the early Christian literature makes ample use of the epistemic justification *per hominem*. This is to say that the truth-maker of propositional contents of central theses of early Christianity is a specific person and its special attributes and properties, such as the ability to work miracles, superior moral behaviour or direct access to the perfect knowledge via prophecy or divine inspiration. Earliest Christianity, of course, at times uses also epistemic justification *per rem* (e.g. in the form of natural theology or philosophy), but it has been shown that the justification *per hominem* takes precedence. Whenever the two modalities of epistemic justification come into conflict, the justification *per hominem* (usually in various forms of 'revelation') always trumps all-too-human, and therefore fallible, reason and experience.

Following the discussion of the first formulations of the naturalistic and protectionist paradigm in the Antiquity, I focused on the method and theory of the studies of religion in the nineteenth and twentieth century and tried to identify explicit or implicit allegiances of the most influential theorists of religion to either naturalism or protectionism by observing their answers to the question about the possibility of explaining religion reductively. It has been shown that, a few leading authors at the turn of the century (Marx, Tylor, Frazer, Freud and, to a certain extent, Durkheim) notwithstanding, the academic study of religions has been dominated by the protectionist paradigm, which denies the possibility of explaining religion reductively. Moreover, in the phenomenology of religion (most notably in its 'classical' version) we have identified a return to the reformed version of the epistemic justification *per hominem*, that is realized in the assumption that a scholar of religion should be religious himself or herself, as well as in the assumption that it is up to the believers or members of a particular religion, as insiders, to decide the truth or falsity of the propositions that are speaking about their religion.

In the second part of this work, I moved from a historical to a more systematic perspective and focused primarily on the cognitive science of religion, at a methodological level, terminological level and at a level of practical application. Cognitive science of religion unequivocally belongs to the naturalistic paradigm in the study of religions, since its main aim is the reductive explanation of the religious experience to non-religious building blocks. Theory and methodology of the cognitive approach is based on empirically testable hypotheses. As such, it stands in opposition to the phenomenology of religion (arguably historically the most important current of the protectionist paradigm), which was based on ill-defined, *a priori* postulated notions ('the Infinite', 'the Sacred' etc.) and on the method of almost mystical vision of the essences hidden behind individual religious phenomena (*Wesensschau*, Eliade's hierophanies, etc.).

While the protectionist paradigm assumes the position of methodological isolationism, which considers religion to be a *sui generis* domain of human experience and the appropriate research thereof must, consequently, use methods *sui generis*, the cognitive approach is methodologically founded on the idea of consilience with other domains of scholarly research, which manifests itself in the rapprochement of the Study of Religions and various natural sciences (such as evolutionary biology or neurosciences). A comparison with the development of ethics presented in Chapter 6 demonstrated the interdisciplinary dimension of the cognitive revolution as well as the fact that both evolutionary ethics and the cognitive science of religion reach very similar conclusions: to explain moral judgement as well as the religious experience, the evolutionary history of our species plays an important role, during which specific cognitive mechanisms originated under the influence of particular selection pressures, and the analysis of these mechanisms is a *sine qua non* for even attempting to answer scientifically the question about the origins of human morality and religion.

On the terminological or definitional level, the use of minimally counter-intuitive agents for a minimal definition of religion also indicates that the cognitive science of religion is clearly anchored in the naturalistic paradigm. In contradistinction to the *a priori* postulated terms with unclear intensions and extensions (e.g. 'the Sacred', 'power', 'the infinite'), minimally counter-intuitive agents are clearly defined and empirically testable concepts that simply presuppose that the cognitive apparatus of humankind is very sensitively tuned to a specific group of mental representations, namely those that in most respects conform to our implicit expectations about a particular ontological group of objects; on the other hand, however, transgress or subvert these expectations in a handful of respects. This ratio makes minimally counter-intuitive concepts sufficiently understandable and inference-rich, but the occasional counter-intuitive feature causes them to be much more memorable and salient and therefore the best candidates for cultural acquisition and transmission.

Following the methodological and terminological bases of the cognitive science of religion, I demonstrated on the level of practical application how these insights may be used to further our understanding. The attempted cognitive interpretation of the invocation of the Muse in Homer and Hesiod showed the reductive-explanatory modus operandi of the cognitive science of religion: the invocation of the Muse in earliest Greek epic poetry originated with help of specific cognitive mechanisms (such as HADD) that identify the external source of the strategic information as an agent, while the perfect access to this strategic information (Muse knows everything) rules out the possibility that this agent could be a human being, since humans have only limited access to information. Muse as a minimally counter-intuitive agent in possession of the strategic information then reflects bard's experience of externalized inspiration during a creative poetic process.

The distinction between naturalism and protectionism in the Study of Religion presented in this book is far from being original. Already Andrew Lang or Father Schmidt in their critical assessment of the 'evolutionism' of Tylor or Frazer contrasted reductive explanations (that view religion as ultimately an illusion) and other, more religiously 'attuned' approaches (as Germans say) that presuppose that human religious experience is a reflection of an objectively existing divine reality, be it the Infinite, the Sacred or (Christian) Creator God. Jacques Waardenburg speaks about 'idealists' (i.e. protectionists) and 'realists' (i.e. naturalists);[3] Frank Whaling argued that '[i]t would be futile to suggest that the personal equation has no bearing upon the questions a scholar asks, the theories and methods that he employs to answer them, or the conclusions that he draws';[4] more recently, Russell McCutcheon differentiated the scholars in the field of the Study of Religions into 'critics' (i.e. naturalists) and 'caretakers' (i.e. protectionists).[5]

That being said, the incommensurability of the naturalist and protectionist paradigm in the study of religions remains strangely understated – a large majority of scholars (working in both paradigms!) has been always convinced that the academic study of religions must follow the principle I would like to provisionally name 'declaration of neutrality'. In the context of phenomenological approaches, this principle has been stated in terms of *epoché*, i.e. the suspension of judgment or 'bracketing' with respect to the truth values of believers' most important propositions. However, this methodological maxim has been only declaratively present and in practice never applied, since 'classical' phenomenologists of religion always required of scholars personal faith as a necessary condition for a successful treatment of the subject at hand.[6] It is more surprising to find the declaration of neutrality in works of researchers not only unconnected with the phenomenological approaches, but even strongly critical thereof. Main figures of the Groningen group, for instance, claimed that 'the student [of religion] gives an objective and impartial description and explanation of the religious phenomena' and '[n]either does he give a moral or other evaluation of these phenomena, nor does he inquire into the truth of them';[7] systematic science of religion 'only studies religions as they are empirically and disclaims any statements concerning the value and truth of the phenomena studied'.[8] Ugo Bianchi, an important proponent of the historical approach and a critic of phenomenology likewise claimed that '[t]he history of religions has then no confessional or anti-confessional bias, [...] [n]or has it any grounds for incompatibility with, or dependence on, the philosophy of religion [...] or theology as such'.[9]

One would be indeed pushed hard to argue against these propositions advocated by phenomenologists, since strictly descriptive approach of historically-based study of religions or anthropology of religions does allow for a more or less neutral description of the phenomena observed. Much stranger is the acceptance of the declaration of neutrality on part of the proponents of the cognitive approaches to religion, who only rarely discuss the question of the truth or falsity of religious actors' beliefs – they rather emphasize, in contrast with the cultural evolutionism of Comte, Tylor, Frazer or Freud, that even if it would be possible to prove without reasonable doubt that religion is an illusion, it would not have a large net effect on the believers, since our cognitive endowment that makes specific religious ideas successful in the cultural transmission is not going to change anytime soon.[10] Whenever the question of the possible consequences of the cognitive science of religion on the truth value or epistemic justification of believers' deeply held convictions is raised, it is in the context of the appropriation of the results of their research by so-called 'New Atheism',[11] while the reactions to this appropriation were rather dismissive. By way of example, when Daniel Dennett published in 2006 his monograph *Breaking the Spell*, one of the leading outlets of cognitivists, *Method & Theory in the Study of Religion* (MTSR),[12] dedicated the entire volume to its reviews, much of those rather combative, with Armin Geertz arguing that *Breaking the Spell* is a 'catastrophe' and its author has done 'a disservice to the entire neuroscientific community'.[13]

The ways cognitivists handle possible philosophical or normative consequences of their theory of religion is relatively straightforward and we may provisionally name the move 'deistic charade'. Blaise Pascal wrote after his 'second turning to Jesus' in 1654 on a small sheet of paper his 'manifesto' and then had it sewn it into his coat. One of the principal theses encapsulated a simple distinction: '*God of Abraham, God of Isaac, God of Jacob*; not the god of philosophers and scientists'.[14] The deistic charade then comprises the inversion of Pascal's thesis: Whenever any particular religion (usually Christianity) seems to be running the risk of being explained away, many scholars working in the cognitive science of religion imperceptibly move from the God of Abraham, Isaac and Jacob to the god of the philosophers and the scientists, since this *deus otiosus*, a bloodless and gutted abstraction, stands firmly and squarely outside of the domain that can be meaningfully investigated by scientific means. From this move it is necessary to conclude that the cognitive science *qua* science must assume, at worse, agnostic stance in the questions of God's existence or non-existence. Justin Barrett puts it as follows: 'I find cognitive science of religion independent of whether someone should or should not believe in God. Whether God (or most other gods) exists cannot be proven or disproven by science. Metaphysical concerns such as this remain in the domain of philosophy."[15]

The problem of the deistic charade lies in the fact that the cognitive science of religion itself, with its concept of the minimally counter-intuitive agents, posits that individual religions (in this case, Christianity) spread and keep themselves alive because their believers believe in Jesus and his resurrection, the efficacy of intercessory prayer, an endless line of saints ready to help and intervene in their lives and the mystery of transubstantiation, and emphatically not in a nebulous, ill-defined and powerless philosophical abstraction with no effect whatsoever on their lives which is the deistic god.[16] It remains ironic that it was precisely the cognitive science of religion that showed as much in different guises, as a 'tragedy of a theologian'[17] or in the concept of the 'theological incorrectness'.[18] A representative sample of Christians do not read Heidegger before going to sleep in order to fully appreciate Tillich's concept of faith as the 'ultimate concern';[19] and they certainly do not show themselves interested in Bultmann's project of 'demythologization'.[20] The response of the vast majority of Christians in these matters would be the one of a certain Ramon E. Morales, who in the *Los Angeles Times* offered his lay view on any possible 'demythologization':

> It is ludicrous for the Jesus seminar to state that their 'findings' do not act to tear down any people's faith. They claim that the Jesus didn't speak the words attributed to him, he didn't perform any miracles and that he didn't physically resurrect after his death. Since most of the New Testament theology is dependent on at least one of those three things, that leaves us following some wimpy do-gooder who got in trouble with the law and was crucified. Not much point in that.[21]

If this line of argumentation makes a caricature out of religion by reducing it to a version of philosophical theism, competing argumentative strategy inverts this relationship and makes a caricature out of scientific methodology. According to this view, the cognitive science of religion 'is no threat to Christian belief, since it can handily be *complemented* by a theological account of the development of religion'.[22] Justin Barrett, for instance, proposes to complement it by denying the randomness of genetic mutations, that is to say, by denying the foundation of Darwin's theory of evolution, on which the evolutionary-cognitive paradigm is based;[23] Nancey Murphy argued that God communicates with humans directly 'by orchestrating events in our brains at the quantum level to produce subtle effects on our thoughts, imaginations, and emotions'.[24] All of this is certainly possible, just like it is possible to complement the inventory of celestial bodies of the solar system with a teapot (as Bertrand Russell ironically proposed)[25] or complement the inventory of our universe with invisible and undetectable flying spaghetti monster (as Bobby Henderson would have it).[26] These 'complements' would, however, blunt the indispensable tool of the scientific method, namely Occam's razor.[27] If it stands, as I think it does, that the cognitive science of religion is and must be based on the requirements of empirical verification or falsification of its propositions[28] and its congruence a consilience with the bulk of knowledge produced by natural sciences,[29] it is not immediately clear why or how could or should its reductive explanations of religious phenomena be complemented with anything, be it a complement of theological or any other provenience.

A short parallel from the history of natural sciences might shed some light on the crux of the issue at hand. In 1909 Albert Einstein published an important text entitled *On the development of our views on the nature and composition of radiation* (*Über die Entwicklung unserer Anschauungen über das Wesen und die Konstitution der Strahlung*), in which he briefly touched upon the problem of the existence of aether.[30] In the nineteenth century, when it was empirically established that the light exhibits the properties of interference and diffraction, a conclusion became unescapable that light has to be understood as a wave. The movement of waves, however, requires the existence of a medium, in which the wave can propagate. And since light propagates also in vacuum, it has been necessary to assume that there is, also in vacuum, some special matter that makes this propagation of light possible. This mysterious medium must have been present even in translucent solid bodies, like glass! The scholars in the nineteenth and at the beginning of the twentieth century have not been able to demonstrate empirically the existence of this medium (let us note here the famous experiments by Michelson and Morley), they simply presupposed it, since other empirical observations identified light with a wave and from the observation of other types of waves (e.g. acoustic ones) it was clear that the wave motion requires a medium through which it propagates.

An analogical argument with respect to the human religious experience makes its appearance as early as Cicero's *On the Nature of Gods* (*De natura deorum*).[31] One of the characters of this philosophical dialogue first emphatically states that there is on the face of the Earth no nation or people that would not believe in and worship some god, even *sine doctrina*, which is to say, naturally. Since by way of empirical observation we conclude that all nations and peoples believe in some deities, then as it would be quite remarkable for all humankind to be collectively and perpetually mistaken, it follows that (at least some) gods necessarily exist. In both cases related by Cicero and Einstein, the starting point is the empirical observation: light exhibits wave-like characteristics; from other observations we know that waves always propagate in a medium; therefore, it is necessary to postulate the existence of luminiferous aether as the medium in which light can propagate. By the same token, in the argument related by Cicero, all people do have some religious experience and since it is impossible that the humankind would suffer from a sort of inescapable shared delusion, it is necessary to presuppose the existence of divinities, sacred or some sort of a transcendental reality, which makes this religious experience possible.[32] Both arguments are based on abductive reasoning or the inference to the best explanation. On the one hand, we are forced to presuppose an entity whose existence we cannot prove directly (aether; divinities) and by doing this our theory postulates a strong ontological commitment; on the other hand, it seems that there is not better solution available.

Should we now return to Einstein's text, we will find that in the following paragraph the celebrated physicist considers the hypothesis of luminiferous aether to be overthrown.[33] The reason is rather simple: the quantum description of light, that the man himself presented in 1905 in the explanation of the photoelectric effect, for which he received in 1921 the Nobel prize in physics. This description namely does not require the existence of any medium through which the light would propagate. We can now ask whether this means that Einstein 'proved' the non-existence of aether and the answer has to be a robust 'no'. What he did achieve, however, is showing that the very hypothesis of aether is unnecessary, and the principle of Occam's razor dictates that we accept the theory that postulates the lowest number of empirically untestable entities or relations; or, to use Quine's term, lowest number of ontological commitments.[34] This principle then may be applied to cognitive science of religion as well. Pascal Boyer in his already classical turn-of-the-millennium account *Religion Explained* (2001) reaches the following conclusion:

> I have explained religion in terms of systems that are in all human minds and that do all sorts of precious and interesting work but that were not really designed to produce religious concepts of behaviors. There is no religious instinct, no *specific* inclination in the mind, no particular disposition for these concepts, no special religion center in the brain, and religious persons are not different from nonreligious ones in essential cognitive functions. Even faith and belief seem to be simple by-products of the way concepts and inferences are doing their work for religion in much the same way as for other domains.[35]

One may surely argue that Boyer failed to provide a convincing and all-encompassing explanation of religion. But if we understand his central theses not as achieved objectives but as future aims and aspirations of the study of religions and methodological guidelines for the cognitive science of religion, then it is hardly possible to square this approach with any variant of normative neutrality. If we presuppose that religious experience is a by-product of evolutionarily shaped cognitive structures and it is (or will be, in the future) possible to explain it reductively, Occam's razor forces us to cut out every and any ontological commitment that is not absolutely crucial in the explanation – and in the case of the cognitive science of religion, this ontological commitment is the existence of deities or sacred, just like aether in the case of the quantum theory of light. It is worth emphasizing again that this does not, in any way, shape or form, prove the non-existence of any transcendental reality; it only shows the redundancy of entertaining such a proposition for those scholars who are abiding by the naturalist paradigm in the field of the study of religions.[36]

The aim of this work was not to prove the truth or falsity of particular propositions entertained by adherents of Christianity or any other religion (as does New Atheism), not even to focus more closely on the relationship between religion and science on a more general level.[37] The twofold aim of this book work was to show that (1) the study of religions is – quite like Raphael's *Transfiguration* – cleaved into two mutually exclusive paradigms, namely the naturalist and the protectionist; and to show that (2) the cognitive science of religion rediscovered the naturalist paradigm in the study of religions following the long period of the dominance of protectionist approaches, albeit I have argued that some notable scholars advancing the CSR (for example, Justin Barrett) do not accept philosophical consequences which a naturalist programme like CSR necessarily entails.[38] Over thirty years ago, Donald Wiebe in discussion with Robert Segal wrote that '[t]here is no question that Segal is right to claim that reductionist interpretations of religions are the only ones possible for sceptics (nonbelieving interpreters) if they are to remain nonbelieving interpreters. However, this argument cuts both ways: the opposite holds for the devotees if they are to remain believers."[39] This remains profoundly true today and if the cognitive science of religion on one hand embraces the naturalist paradigm of reductive explanations and on the other some of its prominent champions argue that its results do not have any implications whatsoever on the epistemic justification of propositions crucial to particular religious traditions, the resulting picture is not very far removed from the one painted by the anonymous artist of Horatius' *Ars poetica*:

> *What if a Painter, in his art to shine,*
> *A human head and horse's neck should join;*
> *From various creatures put the limbs together,*
> *Cover'd with plumes, from ev'ry bird a feather;*
> *And in a filthy tail the figure drop,*
> *A fish at bottom, a fair maid at top:*
> *Viewing a picture of this strange condition,*
> *Would you not laugh at such an exhibition?*[40]

Notes

1 Introduction: Methodological schism in the study of religions

1. Kierkegaard, *Entweder – Oder*, 155: 'Ich bin durchaus kein Freund von Bildern; die neuere Literatur hat sie mir in hohem Maße verleidet; denn es ist bald dahin gekommen, daß mich, sooft ich auf ein Bild stoße, unwillkürlich eine Furcht befällt, der wahre Zweck desselben möchte sein, eine Dunkelheit des Gedankens zu verbergen.' Translation author's own.
2. Schopenhauer, *Die Welt als Wille und Vorstellung* (ZA I, 7).
3. Schopenhauer, *Die Welt als Wille und Vorstellung* (ZA I, 221–335).
4. Cf. the use of Velásquez' *Las Meninas* by Foucault (1966: 19–31).
5. This circumstance has been deftly leveraged by Napoleonic propaganda to justify its imperial cultural politics. At the beginning of the nineteenth century, Raphael's *Transfiguration*, together with scores of other artistic treasures, has been moved from Rome to the newly founded Parisian *Musée Napoleon* (see Rosenberg (1985/86: 191)).
6. Gombrich (1986: 143); De Vecchi (2002: 336).
7. For an overview of older interpretations of the *Transfiguration*, see Lütgens (1929). Even Wölfflin (1983: 161–62) identified in the lower half of the painting a hand of one of Raphael's apprentices.
8. Gould (1982: 479) argued in favour of Raphael's exclusive authorship as follows: If we assume that the painting is unfinished (as we rightly should, since it has been confirmed by the restoration), then if any of Raphael's students had decided to complete it, we would not find any unfinished spots on the painting; we do find unfinished spots on the painting; therefore Raphael is its exclusive author; Q.E.D.
9. Vasari, *Vite* (vol. II: 116): 'si fa giudizio commune de gli artefici che questa opera, fra tante quante egli ne fece, sia la più celebrata, la più bella e la più divina'. Unless indicated otherwise, translations of non-English texts are mine.
10. Mt. 17.1–20; Mk 9.1–28; Lk. 9.28–43. The transfiguration of Christ is also described in apocryphal *Acta Joannis* 90.1–91.1.
11. Schneider (1896: 16).
12. King (1982: 156).
13. Preimesberger (1987: 90); Jungić (1988: 81); Kleinbub (2008: 371).
14. Preimesberger (1987: 107).
15. Jungić (1988: 81).
16. Cranston (2003: 18).
17. Campbell and Cole (2010: 388).
18. Aristoteles, *Poetica* 1451a30–35.
19. Bradner (1956: 8).
20. Richardson, *An Essay on the Theory of Painting*, 31: 'O divine Raphael! Forgive me if I take the liberty to say I cannot approve in this particular of that amazing picture of the transfiguration [...].'

21 Goethe, *Italienische Reise* (HA XI, 389): 'Die Transfiguration des letzteren wurde mitunter sehr strenge getadelt und die *Disputa* das Beste seiner Werke genannt . . .'. In a later entry of his *Reisebericht* (ibid., 453–54), Goethe returned to Raphael's *Transfiguration* and argued for a unity of both halves: 'Wie will man nun das Obere und Untere trennen? Beides ist eins: unten das Leidende, Bedürftige, oben das Wirksame, Hülfreiche, beides aufeinander sich beziehend, ineinander einwirkend.'
22 Rosenberg (1985/6: 199).
23 Burckhardt (1855: 905): 'ein Wagestück, das wahrlich nicht Jedem zu rathen ware.'
24 Nietzsche, *Geburt der Tragödie* (KSA I, 39–40).
25 Oberhuber (1962).
26 Schneider (1896: 11–12); Preimesberger (1987: 98) argued that the moon, reflected in the pool of water next to the foot of the sitting Apostle with the opened book in the lower left corner of the picture, alludes to Islamic crescent.
27 Mt. 16.18: σὺ εἶ Πέτρος, καὶ ἐπὶ ταύτῃ τῇ πέτρᾳ οἰκοδομήσω μου τὴν ἐκκλησίαν καὶ πύλαι ᾅδου οὐ κατισχύσουσιν αὐτῆς.
28 Gombrich (1986: 145–46).
29 Mk 9.29: τοῦτο τὸ γένος ἐν οὐδενὶ δύναται ἐξελθεῖν εἰ μὴ ἐν προσευχῇ. The addition καὶ νηστείᾳ ('and by fasting') is most likely a later interpolation that the editors of the Greek text of the New Testament (Nestle and Aland) do not accept, Latin Vulgate (eds Weber and Gryson), however, prints *hoc genus in nullo potest exire nisi in oratione et ieunio*.
30 King (1982: 152–54).
31 Jungić (1988: 81).
32 Mt. 17.9; Mk 9.9; Lk. 9.36.
33 Mt. 17.17: ὦ γενεὰ ἄπιστος καὶ διεστραμμένη, ἕως πότε μεθ᾽ ὑμῶν ἔσομαι; ἕως πότε ἀνέξομαι ὑμῶν;
34 Mt. 17.20: ἐὰν ἔχητε πίστιν ὡς κόκκον σινάπεως, ἐρεῖτε τῷ ὄρει τούτῳ Μετάβα ἔνθεν ἐκεῖ, καὶ μεταβήσεται, καὶ οὐδὲν ἀδυνατήσει ὑμῖν.
35 Mk 9.23–24.
36 For this interpretation, see especially Kleinbub (2008), who, however, identified the contrast of faith and earthly wisdom in the lower half of the painting. A vertical slice running through the middle of this lower section represented for him a 'confrontation between the empirically minded, who are bent on external explanations, and those of higher spiritual wisdom, who reject the material world of the senses' (ibid., 376).
37 Preimesberger (1987: 99).
38 Kleinbub (2008: 375).
39 Cranston (2003: 20).
40 Xenophon, *Memorabilia* 1.1.2: θύων τε γὰρ φανερὸς ἦν πολλάκις μὲν οἴκοι, πολλάκις δὲ ἐπὶ τῶν κοινῶν τῆς πόλεως βωμῶν, καὶ μαντικῇ χρώμενος οὐκ ἀφανὴς ἦν.
41 Latte (1958: 172): 'Θεοὺς νομίζειν ist viel eher, was etwa *pratiquer* für einen Katholiken ist.' See also Babut (1974c: 11): 'L'expression grecque qui traduit la croyance en l'existence des dieux (θεοὺς νομίζειν) a d'abord signifié exclusivement « honorer les dieux comme le veut la coutume » (νόμος) – seule exigence des dieux de la Grèce à l'égard de leurs fidèles.'
42 Drobner (2011: 126); compare also Frend (2008: 106).
43 Terentius, *Heauton timorumenos*, v. 797.
44 Guthrie (1993), in the subtitle of his otherwise brilliant book *Faces in the Clouds*, proudly heralds 'a new theory of religion', but the central conclusion of his argument, namely that 'religion is anthropomorphism' (ibid., 178), may be found in the fragments

of Xenophanes dated to sixth century BCE. When Ilkka Pyysiäinen (2003a: 55) claimed that Durkheim's focus on the social dimension of religion was a radical innovation, one may consider the fact that the so-called Sisyphus fragment explained away religion in a socio-functionalistic manner already in the fifth century BCE.
45 To give just one example, Davies (1989: 31–32) connected the Sisyphus fragment with the ideas of James Frazer, an analogy that is far from being persuasive, see preceding note.
46 Cf. e.g. Plantiga (2000); Swinburne (2005); Moser (2008); Moser and McFall (2012).
47 When Burkert (1996) attempted to apply selected sociobiological concepts into the field of ancient religions, the reactions to this pioneering work (for an overview, see Saler 1999: 388–89) led Daniel Dennett (2006: 264) to remark that '[o]ne of the causes for dismay is seeing how gingerly [Burkert] thinks he must tiptoe around the hair-trigger sensitivities of his fellow humanists when he introduces these dreaded biological notions into their world'. However, the works like Larson (2016) and some others are starting to show that Classics is not as methodologically conservative as one may have originally thought and that these 'dreaded biological notions' do indeed make their way into the Humanities.
48 Diogenes Laertius, *Vitae philosophorum* 9.1 = DK 22 B 40.
49 Nietzsche, *Also sprach Zarathustra* (KSA IV, 311–12): 'Lieber Nichts wissen, als Vieles halb wissen! Lieber ein Narr sein auf eigne Faust, als ein Weiser nach fremdem Gutdünken! Ich – gehe auf den Grund: – was liegt daran, ob er gross oder klein ist? Ob er Sumpf oder Himmel heisst? Eine Hand breit Grund ist mir genug: wenn er nur wirklich Grund und Boden ist! – eine Hand breit Grund: darauf kann man stehn. In der rechten Wissen-Gewissenschaft giebt es nichts Grosses und nichts Kleines.' – 'So bist du vielleicht der Erkenner des Blutegels? fragte Zarathustra; und du gehst dem Blutegel nach bis auf die letzten Gründe, du Gewissenhafter?' – 'Oh Zarathustra, antwortete der Getretene, das wäre ein Ungeheures, wie dürfte ich mich dessen unterfangen! Wess ich aber Meister und Kenner bin, das ist des Blutegels Hirn: – das ist meine Welt! Und es ist auch eine Welt! Vergieb aber, dass hier mein Stolz zu Worte kommt, denn ich habe hier nicht meines Gleichen. Darum sprach ich "hier bin ich heim". Wie lange gehe ich schon diesem Einen nach, dem Hirn des Blutegels, dass die schlüpfrige Wahrheit mir hier nicht mehr entschlüpfe! Hier ist mein Reich! – darob warf ich alles Andere fort, darob wurde mir alles Andre gleich; und dicht neben meinem Wissen lagert mein schwarzes Unwissen. Mein Gewissen des Geistes will es so von mir, dass ich Eins weiss und sonst Alles nicht weiss: es ekelt mich aller Halben des Geistes, aller Dunstigen, Schwebenden, Schwärmerischen.' English translation by A. del Caro.

2 Naturalistic paradigm: Critical reflexion of religion in Presocratic philosophy

1 Lucretius, *De rerum natura* 1.66–71: *primum Graius homo mortalis tollere contra* | *est oculos ausus primusque obsistere contra,* | *quem neque fama deum nec fulmina nec minitanti* | *murmure compressit caelum, sed eo magis* | *acrem irritat animi virtutem, effringere ut arta* | *naturae primus portarum claustra cupiret.* English translation by W. E. Leonard.
2 A direct influence of Presocratics on the nineteenth- and twentieth-century study of religions is limited, but far from being non-existent. As e.g. Drechsler and Kattel (2004:

117–18) showed, Feuerbach has been substantially influenced by Xenophanes. For an overview of the concept of 'histories of mentalities', see Hutton (1981). Histories of mentalities, not unlike Foucault's *episteme*, are not necessarily concerned with direct causal connections of ideas between different authors and historical epochs, but rather focus on the implicitly shared mental networks that constrain the thought and ideas of any particular epoch. It would be factually untrue to claim that Presocratic philosophers exercised any significant influence on the formation of modern religious studies in the nineteenth and twentieth centuries, but it would be very hard to deny that they effectively formulated and introduced the (proto-)naturalistic approach to religion into the Western culture.
3   An exception to the rule, Meslin (1973: 19–25) dealt, however briefly, with the period of Antiquity.
4   Preus (1987: 3).
5   Waardenburg (1999: 117).
6   Strenski (2006: 9–60).
7   As Boyer (2001: 9) pointed out, a free choice of religion is a comparatively modern convenience.
8   See Vernant (1957), reprinted *in* Vernant (1996: 373–402), and esp. Nestle (1966). For a good modern overview, Fowler (2011) may be consulted.
9   See e.g. Herodotus, *Historiae*, 2.53: οὗτοι δέ εἰσι οἱ ποιήσαντες θεογονίην Ἕλλησι καὶ τοῖσι θεοῖσι τὰς ἐπωνυμίας δόντες καὶ τιμάς τε καὶ τέχνας διελόντες καὶ εἴδεα αὐτῶν σημήναντες. Even the fiercest critics of the Homeric poems had to admit that their role in Greek education has been second to none; cf. Xenophanes (DK 21 B 10, ἐξ ἀρχῆς καθ' Ὅμηρον ἐπεὶ μεμαθήκασι πάντες, DK 21 B 10) and Plato (*Respublica*, 606e2-3, τὴν Ἑλλάδα πεπαίδευκεν οὗτος ὁ ποιητής).
10 Homerus, *Ilias*, 1.1: Μῆνιν ἄειδε θεὰ Πηληϊάδεω Ἀχιλῆος.
11 Homerus, *Odyssea*, 1.1: Ἄνδρα μοι ἔννεπε, Μοῦσα, πολύτροπον.
12 Homerus, *Ilias*, 2.484–86.
13 Hesiodus, *Theogonia*, 22–23.
14 Detienne (2000).
15 Patočka (1996: 27).
16 Homerus, *Odyssea*, 1.32–34: οἶον δή νυ θεοὺς βροτοὶ αἰτιόωνται. | ἐξ ἡμέων γάρ φασι κάκ' ἔμμεναι· οἱ δὲ καὶ αὐτοὶ | σφῇσιν ἀτασθαλίῃσιν ὑπὲρ μόρον ἄλγε' ἔχουσιν.
17 Hesiodus, *Theogonia*, 27.
18 Diogenes Laertius, *Vitae*, 1.119.
19 Pindarus, *Isthmia*, 2.6.
20 This selection intentionally omits several important Presocratic thinkers who on the one hand criticized many features of Homeric religion, such as Heraclitus – cf. Adomenas (1999) and, more recently, Most (2013) for his attitude to religion – but on the other hand they did not attempt to provide any explanatory theory of religion. I decided to focus exclusively on those Presocratics who not only criticized selected facets of Greek religion, but also tried to explain its origins.
21 Eisenstadt (1974: 143) argued that Xenophanes' critique of Greek pantheon is to be understood as 'amused detachment' and the philosopher from Colophon supposedly 'warmly approved of the forms and practice of traditional Greek religion' (ibid., 147). Gemelli Marciano (2005: 125) placed Xenophanes' critique of Homer and Hesiod in the context of him being, amongst other things, a wandering rhapsode who was more interested in attacking his professional opponents rather than putting forward a serious intellectual and philosophical critique of religion. Feyerabend (1986b: 214)

refused Xenophanes' critical reception of Homeric deities as unjustified, since according to him Homer did not make any claims for possessing absolute truth in his songs (which is, in itself, a strikingly mistaken view).

22 García López (1986: 49), Halfwassen (2008: 49) and Carrasco Meza (2010: 56) all agreed in considering Xenophanes' critical interpretation of ancient Greek representations of gods as one of the most devastating in all of the Antiquity.
23 With the exception of the so-called Lebedev fragment, all English translations of the fragments are those of J. H. Lesher (his translation of the fragment B 12 has been slightly modified).
24 Edwards (1991).
25 For moral functions of Homeric gods, see Yamagata (1994: 3–21).
26 Carrasco Meza (2010: 56) considered the critique of questionable ethical standards of Homeric gods to be 'una "premisa" de todo su "systema"' and argued for Pythagorean and Orphic influences. For Babut (1974a: 111–12) and Álvarez Salas (2011: 263), fragments B 11 and B 12 are not starting points, but rather the consequences of Xenophanes' rationalistic approach that would deem the attribution of humanlike characteristics to gods to be incorrect *simpliciter*, irrespective of whether these characteristics are of ethical or any other nature.
27 Sextus Empiricus, *Adversus mathematicos*, 9.193 = DK 21 B 11.
28 Sextus Empiricus, *Adversus mathematicos*, 1.289 = DK 21 B 12.
29 Drechsler and Kattel (2004: 117).
30 Clemens Alexandrinus, *Stromata*, 5.109 = DK 21 B 14.
31 Wittgenstein (2001: 190).
32 Clemens Alexandrinus, *Stromata*, 5.110 = DK 21 B 15.
33 Babut (1974a: 115); Babut (1974c: 25).
34 Burnet (1920: 129). Babut (1974b: 425 *et passim*) likewise denied that Xenophanes would have formulated a 'positive theology'.
35 Jaeger (1947: 49), see also Gerson (1990: 17). Burnet's and Jaeger's interpretation has been juxtaposed already by Vlastos (1952: 101), later also by Kirk, Raven and Schofield (2004: 215).
36 Guthrie (1962: 375); Barnes (1982: 92); Kirk, Raven and Schofield (2004: 218–19). Halfwassen (2008: 276) argued that one has to differentiate between 'exclusive monotheism' (i.e. 'there is only one god') and 'inclusive monotheism' (i.e. 'one god is reigning over other deities which are his aspects or parts'). Halfwassen himself (ibid., 278) considered Xenophanes to be an exclusive monotheist.
37 Herschbell (1983: 130–31); Gemelli Marciano (2005: 127).
38 Athenaeus, *Deipnosophistae*, 11.462c = DK 21 B 1.
39 Clemens Alexandrinus, *Stromata*, 5.109 = DK 21 B 23.
40 Deichgräber (1938: 31). The problem with this interpretation lies in the fact that Deichgräber is basing it exclusively on the expression ἀμφὶ θεῶν in DK 21 B 34, but in other instances of the use of the plural 'gods' his solution does not hold water.
41 Wiśniewski (1994: 100–1).
42 Halfwassen (2008: 285).
43 For the analysis of Xenophanes' use of Homeric language see Torres-Guerra (1999). Granger (2007: 405–6) explains Xenophanes' use of verse as a means to reach the widest possible audience.
44 Polar expressions are attested already for Indo-European, see West (2007: 99–104). Elsewhere, I tried to show that Lucretius' critique of the gods is not incompatible with

his invocations of Venus in the *prooimion* of *De rerum natura*, cf. Franek (2011). After all, in Goethe's *Faust* (HA III, 18), the plural 'gods' is used by the Almighty himself.

45 Those who considered Xenophanes a pantheist, as e.g. Guthrie (1962: 382–33) did, usually relied on Aristotle's testimony (τὸ ἓν εἶναι φησι τὸν θεόν, *Metaphysica*, 986b21–25). It is possible, however, that this mention might have been 'contaminated' by merging Xenophanes with Parmenides and the 'Elean school', see Kirk – Raven – Schofield (2004: 221). Finkelberg (1990: 113) saw in Xenophanes an influence of Anaximander's philosophy, while Halfwassen (2008: 290) cast doubts on the interpretation of Xenophanes as a pantheist because of the ontological separation of the world from god. God is thought to be immobile himself; but the world is in motion (moved by none other than god); therefore, god is not identical with the world.

46 Lebedev (2000).

47 According to Feyerabend (1986a: 211), Xenophanes did not offer 'Kritik', only 'bloße Verneinung'.

48 *Scholia BLT Eustathii ad Homerum* Λ 27 = DK 21 B 32 (transl. J. H. Lesher): ἥν τ᾽Ἶριν καλέουσι, νέφος καὶ τοῦτο πέφυκε, | πορφύρεον καὶ φοινίκεον καὶ χλωρὸν ἰδέσθαι. Lesher (2012: 81) considered clouds to be the primary explanatory device in the realm of natural and meteorological phenomena. For a detailed analysis of Xenophanes' naturalistic explanation, as compared with Hesiod's approach, see Álvarez Salas (2011: 264–72).

49 Burnet (1908: 141). These lines have been omitted in the third edition of Burnet's *Early Greek Philosophy*, see Burnet (1920: 128). Needless to say, Xenophanes has been labelled as 'atheist' by several authors of the Antiquity, but these reports are late and untrustworthy. Neanthes of Cyzicus reports that Xenophanes has been driven out of his country because of 'impiety' (ἐβεβλῆσθαι τῆς πατρίδος διὰ τὴν ἀσέβειαν αὐτοῦ) and Byzantine Lexicon *Suda* called him 'an enemy of gods' (θεοῖς ἐχθρός); for these testimonies see Winiarczyk (1984: 181). On the other hand, Xenophanes has been (according to Aristotle) one of the first to blame Homer and Hesiod for impiety: ἀσεβοῦσιν οἱ γενέσθαι φάσκοντες τοὺς θεοὺς τοῖς ἀποθανεῖν λέγουσιν (Aristoteles, *Rhetorica*, 1399b5 = DK 21 A 12), cf. also Winiarczyk (1992: 217).

50 Vlastos (1952: 104).

51 Feyerabend (1986b), for instance, termed Xenophanes' god 'Denk-, Seh-, Hör- und Intelligenzmonstrum' (ibid., 210), 'Intelligenzbestie' (ibid., 218) or 'Gottesmonstrum' (ibid., 221).

52 On occasion, scholars voiced dissenting opinions. Ramnoux (1984: 198), for example, assumed 'l'existence d'une tradition monothéiste savante, développée en marge des cultes et traditions populaires ou civiques' inspired by Xenophanes. Kirk, Raven and Schofield (2004: 216) even argued that Xenophanes' religious reform had 'deep impact on ordinary people', quoting Heraclitus, Empedocles, Aeschylus and Euripides in support of this thesis. One would be hard pressed, however, to consider the aforementioned Greeks 'ordinary people'. Rather, I agree with Grant (1952: 43), according to whom Xenophanes' critique of Homeric gods 'did not have much effect on the thought of ordinary Greeks, for we do not hear of reactions against the criticism or the critics'.

53 Kahn (1997: 254).

54 McGibbon (1965: 389), for instance, argued that Democritus believed in gods endowed with supernatural powers. However, as Eisenberger (1970: 148–51) pointed out, Democritus used the adjective θεῖος in as a metaphor and the fragments B 175, B 217 or B 234 are to be taken in an ethical or political, not in a religious sense; similar

conclusions have been reached by Vlastos (1945: 580–81). Most puzzling is the form εὔχετο in the fragment B 166. McGibbon (1965: 393–94) translates it with the English verb 'to pray', Eisenberger (1970: 152) with 'to wish for'. Given the pre-eminence of the *do ut des* principle in Graeco-Roman religion, both meanings are simultaneously present and the fragment on its own does not allow us to reach any wide-reaching conclusions about Democritus' religiosity; cf. also Babut (1974c: 55–56).

55 Henrichs (1975: 103) considered the anthropological speculation to be 'less sophisticated' and Guthrie (1965: 478) likewise gave precedence to the atomistic hypothesis, which is, in his view, 'more interesting and individual'.

56 English translations of Democritus' fragments are those of C. C. W. Taylor, with the exception of Hermippus (A 78, transl. mine), Clement of Alexandria (A 79, transl. W. Wilson) and Lucretius (A 75, transl. M. F. Smith).

57 Sextus Empiricus, *Adversus Mathematicos*, 9.24 = DK 68 A 75.

58 Philodemus, *De pietate* 5a, p. 69 Gomperz = DK 68 A 75. In the Diels – Kranz edition, this fragment (found in the Herculaneum papyri, *PHerc*. 1428, *frg*. 16) appeared in the 'A' section, i.e. as an indirect *testimonium*. Henrichs (1975: 104) showed, on the basis of linguistic and subject-matter criteria, that the fragment may be safely attributed to Democritus, i.e. it should be relegated to section DK's 'B' (direct quotations).

59 Sextus Empiricus, *Adversus Mathematicos*, 9.19 = DK 68 B 166.

60 Cicero, *De natura deorum*, 1.12.29 = DK 68 A. It is important to keep in mind that when Cicero rebuked Democritus for his apparently equivocal use of a specific term, he did so from a standpoint of an open critique, which does add an element of tendentiousness and bias. Ciceronian solution did, however, find some advocates even among the modern scholars. For instance, McGibbon (1965: 392) argued that Democritus used the term εἴδωλα equivocally – sometimes to denote gods, sometimes to denote the thin atomic films which emanate from these gods.

61 See e.g. DK 68 B 123, a fragment that mentions both terms (more exactly: it defines one through the other).

62 Sextus Empiricus, *Adversus Mathematicos*, 9.19 = DK 68 B 166.

63 Clemens Alexandrinus, *Stromata*, 5.88. = DK 68 A 79.

64 Hermippus, *De astrologia*, 1.16.122, p. 26, 13 Kroll-Viereck = DK 68 A 78.

65 Guthrie (1965: 482) claimed that this terminological inconsistency is the consequence of Democritus' split between 'intellectual loyalty to materialism' on the one side and the commitment to certain religious and aesthetic values on the other. For Vlastos (1945: 581, n. 24), εἴδωλα are 'aetiological explanation of the popular belief in the gods, and nothing more'. The addition ἀπὸ τῆς θείας οὐσίας in Clement is then, according to Vlastos, Clement's own interpretation stemming from anachronistic contamination of Democritus' thought with Epicurean philosophy.

66 Barnes (1982: 460).

67 Eisenberger (1970: 142) considered the fragment B 166 'glaubwürdig' as well.

68 See also Babut (1974c: 49): 'les images ne *sont* pas dieux, elles font naître l'*idée* de dieux, et il n'existe *rien* de divin en dehors d'elles.'

69 Barnes (1982: 461).

70 Cf. Hourcade (2000: 99): 'L'enterprise mise en oeuvre par Démocrite, dans son approche plus générale des images divins, entends [...] dénoncer le caractère illusoire de la croyance en l'existence de dieux à forme humaine, mais aussi expliquer un tel phénomène.' I do not believe that the qualification 'mais aussi' is necessary. Democritus criticized religion precisely by making use of the naturalistic explanation thereof.

71 Philostratus, *Vitae Sophistarum*, 1.501 Olearius = DK 88 A 1.

72 A 'traditional' interpretation of this fragment is offered by Guthrie (1971: 243), who claimed not only that Critias has been the author of the fragment, but also that the contents are representative of Critias' personal opinions.
73 Kahn (1997: 248). Whitmarsh (2014: 109) even considered the fragment to be 'arguably the most important single document in the history of ancient atheism'.
74 Sextus Empiricus, *Adversus Mathematicos*, 9.54. Santoro (1994: 426) rightly observed that the cautious δοκεῖ seems to signal Sextus' uncertainty regarding Critias' atheism.
75 For a contrary opinion, see Whitmarsh (2014: 112): 'There are no decisive signs that the play is satyric rather than tragic: no satyrs, no low humour or parody. It is not impossible, but nothing in the fragment necessitates that conclusion, or even makes it probable.'
76 Holzhausen (1999: 287–88) read (with Mss.) γνῶναι, I print DK's <θεῶν>.
77 Dihle (1977: 41) read τὰ πάντα *in lieu* of τε ταῦτα (DK); Kahn (1997: 248, n. 2) accepted this emendation.
78 Diggle (1996: 103) read *in lieu* of Mss. ἥδιστον an ironic κύδιστον. I see no reason for this. The introduction of the divinity (despite being a 'lie') is ἥδιστον in that it strengthens the observance of the laws on part of the general populace and thus makes the society better.
79 Holzhausen (1999: 290) read τοιοίδε περιέστησαν ἀνθρώποις φόβοι, since (according to him) δέος refers to religious awe and φόβος to fear. I prefer DK's text.
80 English translation is that of Charles Kahn.
81 For a basic overview of these discussions, see Sutton (1981: 35) and Davies (1989: 24–28).
82 Pseudo-Plutarchus, *Placita philosophorum*, 880e4–10: καὶ Εὐριπίδης δ' ὁ τραγῳδοποιὸς ἀποκαλύψασθαι μὲν οὐκ ἠθέλησε, δεδοικὼς τὸν Ἄρειον πάγον, ἐνέφηνε δὲ τοῦτον τὸν τρόπον· τὸν γὰρ Σίσυφον εἰσήγαγε προστάτην ταύτης τῆς δόξης καὶ συνηγόρησεν αὐτοῦ ταύτῃ τῇ γνώμῃ· 'ἦν' γάρ 'χρόνος' φησίν 'ὅτ' ἦν ἄτακτος ἀνθρώπων βίος | καὶ θηριώδης ἰσχύος θ' ὑπηρέτης'.
83 Dihle (1977: 37 *et passim*).
84 Winiarczyk (1987: 45).
85 Yunis (1988: 46).
86 TrGF, frg. 1007c: {—} λ]άθρα δὲ τούτων δρωμένων τίνας φοβῇ; | {—} τοὺς μείζονα βλέποντας ἀνθρώπων θεούς. It is important to emphasize that Yunis (1988: 41–2) presented his conclusions as provisional, noting that similarities in the subject-matter in both fragments are far from being a conclusive argument for them belonging to the same play.
87 Following Dihle, Kahn (1997: 249) argued for Euripides' authorship and thought this conclusion to be widely accepted. That is an overstatement; compare e.g. Sutton (1981) and Davies (1989). Santoro (1994) did not address the problem of authorship directly, but her analysis of the fragment makes it clear that she did not put Critias' authorship in doubt. Bremmer (2007: 16–17) referenced the most recent edition of Euripides' fragments (TrGF 2.658, ed. Kannicht) and agreed with its attribution of the fragment to Critias. Similar conclusions have been reached by Whitmarsh (2014: 112), according to whom 'the hypothesis that the play was originally attributed to Critias and subsequently reallocated to the more famous Euripides (who already had a reputation for atheism) seems *prima facie* more plausible than the reverse'.
88 Other Critias' fragments do not contain any overt traces of atheism and even those doxographers or historians who considered Critias an unscrupulous and cruel man (e.g. Xenophon) never mentioned his 'atheism', although they had the best of reasons to do so.

89 Sutton (1981: 38).
90 Davies (1989: 28). Santoro (1994: 424, 429) added that the tone of the fragment is (in line with the tradition of the satyr play) burlesque and therefore rather unsuitable for a presentation of a serious philosophical hypothesis attempting to work out origins of human society and religion. This observation, on its own, is nonetheless insufficient for concluding that 'Sisyphus' could not have represented Critias' own ideas.
91 TrGF, frg. 286; cf. Riedweg (1990) for a detailed analysis.
92 Hobbes, *Leviathan*, 89.
93 Guthrie (1971: 244). Compare Voltaire, *Oeuvres complètes* (X, 403): 'Si les cieux, dépouillés de son empreinte auguste, | Pouvaient cesser jamais de le manifester, | Si Dieu n'existait pas, il faudrait l'inventer. | Que le sage l'annonce, et que les rois le craignent. | Rois, si vous m'opprimez, si vos grandeurs dédaignent | Les pleurs de l'innocent que vous faites couler, | Mon vengeur est au ciel: apprenez à trembler. | Tel est au moins le fruit d'une utile croyance.'
94 However, as O'Sullivan (2012: 178) observed, 'concealing the truth [. . .] is elsewhere presented favourably in Classical Greek literature' and it is not 'an unequivocal evil in Greek thought'.
95 For instance, O'Sullivan (2012: 185) did not, in any way, deny that, for the author of the Sisyphus fragment, religion is an illusion ('. . . it is true that the speaker in Critias fr. 19 presents the link between the human and the divine as an illusion . . .'). He did claim that this fact does not necessarily have to result in the wholesale rejection of religion, precisely on counts of its social utility. Whitmarsh (2014: 114), who apparently did not appreciate the difference between truth and social utility, accused O'Sullivan from contaminating Classics with religious propaganda by claiming that his paper is a 'pungent reminder [. . .] that Classics is not always the secularised discipline we have been led to think since the nineteenth century'.
96 Guthrie (1971: 242).
97 For Babut (1974c: 50), Prodicus 'tout comme Démocrite . . . se borne à rechercher l'origine de l'*idée* de dieux, en laissant totalement de côté la question de leur existence, comme si elle ne méritait pas l'examen.' I find this conclusion to be mistaken. Prodicus (indeed, just like Democritus) answered the question about the existence of gods precisely by identifying their 'true' (that is to say, human, all-too-human) origin.
98 I follow the Greek text printed by Mayhew (2011: 46), since it is more complete and (unlike DK) contains *apparatus criticus*. The English translations are those of R. Mayhew, except for Cicero (B 5, transl. H. Rackham).
99 I follow the Greek text printed by Mayhew (2011: 46).
100 Henrichs (1975: 108) first translated the expression θεοὺς οὔτ' εἶναί φησιν οὔτ' εἰδέναι as '[Prodicus] maintains that the gods of popular belief do not exist and that he does not recognize them'. A year later, he preferred the translation with an emphatic negation '. . . he maintains that the gods do not exist and that they lack knowledge' (see Henrichs (1976: 20)). This interpretation is accepted and defended also by Mayhew (2011: 184).
101 DK indicated a *lacuna* between the words εὐσέβειαν and ἐγγυώμενος. I see no good reason for this.
102 Bańkowski (1962: 12); Guthrie (1971: 227); García López (1986: 60); Winiarczyk (1990: 10).
103 Plato, *Leges*, 889e3–5.
104 Henrichs (1984: 141); Guthrie (1971: 239); Bremmer (2007: 15); Mayhew (2011: 180–81).

105 This, obviously, seems already quite close to 'Euhemerism'; see Roubekas (2017) for an excellent overview.
106 Guthrie (1971: 241) provided a compelling example from Euripides' *Bacchae*: Dionysus is first described as an 'inventor' of wine (ὁ Σεμέλης γόνος | βότρυος ὑγρὸνπῶμ' ηὗρε, *Bacchae* 278-79), yet, just a few verses later, he is the very wine he was supposed to 'invent' (οὗτος θεοῖσι σπένδεται θεὸς γεγώς, *Bacchae* 284). Henrichs (1984: 145) suggested that this portion of Euripides' play has been inspired by Prodicus, which would, of course, undermine Guthrie's argumentation. Lefkowitz (1989: 74-75) argued that Euripides himself did not accept Prodicus' hypothesis about the origin of religion; Harrison (1990: 196-98) heard further echoes of Euripides and Prodicus in Lucretius' *De rerum natura*, 5.13-21.
107 Kahn (1997: 261).
108 Mayhew (2011: 176) argued that Sextus' comments are based on Epicurus' lost work *On nature* (Περὶ Φύσεως), whose twelfth book supposedly contained the very first *index atheorum* of the Antiquity.
109 Guthrie (1971: 241) claimed that the *communis opinio* of ancient doxographers and philosophers was that Prodicus has been an atheist. Henrichs (1976: 21; 1984: 141, 157) has been more reluctant to proclaim Prodicus an atheist; Winiarczyk (1990: 6-7) also denied that Prodicus was an atheist and considered the question itself 'misleading' ('falsch'). One may agree with Winiarczyk in his emphasis on differentiating carefully between Prodicus' own interpretation of religion, the reception of Prodicus by later doxographers, modern notions of 'atheism' and the risk of committing anachronisms by applying a modern concept to an ancient author. Yet in the case of Prodicus, all these point to the same direction and Winiarczyk's own interpretation, according to which Prodicus has been unaware of the consequences of his theory, sounds rather unconvincing. On 'atheism' in Ancient Greece, see further Roubekas (2014).
110 Nietzsche, *Der Antichrist* (KSA VI, 182): 'Ein Volk, das noch an sich selbst glaubt, hat auch noch seinen eignen Gott. In ihm verehrt es die Bedingungen, durch die es obenauf ist, seine Tugenden – es projicirt seine Lust an sich, sein Machtgefühl in ein Wesen, dem man dafür danken kann. Wer reich ist, will abgeben; ein stolzes Volk braucht einen Gott, um zu opfern... Religion, innerhalb solcher Voraussetzungen, ist eine Form der Dankbarkeit. Man ist für sich selber dankbar: dazu braucht man einen Gott.' English translation by T. Wayne.
111 Fumerton (2002: 205). For a detailed discussion of the concept, see e.g. Swinburne (2001).
112 Aristoteles, *Metaphysica*, 1011b25-27: δῆλον δὲ πρῶτον μὲν ὁρισαμένοις τί τὸ ἀληθὲς καὶ ψεῦδος. τὸ μὲν γὰρ λέγειν τὸ ὂν μὴ εἶναι ἢ τὸ μὴ ὂν εἶναι ψεῦδος, τὸ δὲ τὸ ὂν εἶναι καὶ τὸ μὴ ὂν μὴ εἶναι ἀληθές.
113 Sextus Empiricus, *Adversus mathematicos*, 7.111 = DK 28 B 1 (ll. 26-30): χαῖρ', ἐπεὶ οὔτι σε μοῖρα κακὴ προὔπεμπε νέεσθαι | τήνδ' ὁδόν (ἦ γὰρ ἀπ' ἀνθρώπων ἐκτὸς πάτου ἐστίν), | ἀλλὰ θέμις τε δίκη τε. χρεὼ δέ σε πάντα πυθέσθαι | ἠμὲν Ἀληθείης εὐκυκλέος ἀτρεμὲς ἦτορ | ἠδὲ βροτῶν δόξας, ταῖς οὐκ ἔνι πίστις ἀληθής.
114 This view is defended by Granger (2007: 416), who argued that 'in contrast with Xenophanes, they [*sc*. Parmenides and Empedocles] may be in sympathy with the old poetic tradition and its reliance upon the Muses'.
115 Diogenes Laertius, *Vitae philosophorum*, 8.62 = DK 31 B 112: χαίρετ'· ἐγὼ δ' ὑμῖν θεὸς ἄμβροτος, οὐκέτι θνητός | πωλεῦμαι μετὰ πᾶσι τετιμένος, ὥσπερ ἔοικα, | ταινίαις τε περίστεπτος στέφεσίν τε θαλείοις.

116 Sextus Empiricus, *Adversus mathematicos*, 7.125 = DK 31 B 3: ἀλλὰ θεοὶ τῶν μὲν μανίην ἀποτρέψατε γλώσσης, | ἐκ δ' ὁσίων στομάτων καθαρὴν ὀχετεύσατε πηγήν | καὶ σέ, πολυμνήστη λευκώλενε παρθένε Μοῦσα, | ἄντομαι, ὧν θέμις ἐστὶν ἐφημερίοισιν ἀκούειν, | πέμπε παρ' Εὐσεβίης ἐλάουσ' εὐήνιον ἅρμα. Compare Babut (1974c: 35): 'Même si l'on ne veut voir là qu'un trait purement conventionnel, il reste que le philosophe réserve expressément leur place aux dieux, dans sa construction du monde . . .'. For a detailed analysis of the invocation of the Muse in Empedocles, see Picot – Berg (2013: 11–12).
117 Diogenes Laertius, *Vitae philosophorum*, 8.69: Ἱππόβοτος δέ φησιν ἐξαναστάντα αὐτὸν ὡδευκέναι ὡς ἐπὶ τὴν Αἴτνην, εἶτα παραγενόμενον ἐπὶ τοὺς κρατῆρας τοῦ πυρὸς ἐναλέσθαι καὶ ἀφανισθῆναι, βουλόμενον τὴν περὶ αὑτοῦ φήμην βεβαιῶσαι ὅτι γεγόνοι θεός, ὕστερον δὲ γνωσθῆναι, ἀναρριπισθείσης αὐτοῦ μιᾶς τῶν κρηπίδων.
118 Cicero, *De natura deorum*, 1.5.10 (English translation by H. Rackham).
119 Guthrie (1962: 148).
120 Barnes (1997: 207).
121 Braun (1971: 242).

3 Protectionist paradigm: Early Christian literature between faith and reason

1 Donne, *The Trinity*, 250.
2 For a convenient anthology of relevant texts pertaining to the 'faith' vs. 'reason' dichotomy, see Helm (1999).
3 Freeman (2009: 176).
4 Moores (1995: 160).
5 Van Winden (1977: 190): 'Comme interlocuteur Justin est donc favorable à la philosophie. Mais la discussion elle-même n'est pas favorable à la philosophie. Car Justin se laisse convaincre par le viellard que le Platonisme ne contient pas la vérité. En d'autres termes, ce passage aussi a un caractère anti-philosophique.'
6 Chadwick (1993: 237). Félix (2014: 438) reached a similar conclusion and claimed that Justin 'buscará mostrar con claridad la racionalidad del cristianismo, por el camino de la semejanza con la cultura helenística'.
7 Tertullianus, *De carne Christi*, 5.4: *Crucifixus est dei filius; non pudet, quia pudendum est. Et mortuus est dei filius; credibile est, quia ineptum est. Et sepultus resurrexit; certum est, quia impossibile.*
8 Sider (1980: 418).
9 Bochet (2008: 271): '[. . .] l'usage du paradoxe n'est pas une mise en cause de la raison; plus radicalment même, il en est une exigence'.
10 Labhardt (1950: 166 *et passim*). Similarly, Frend (2008: 361) highlighted Tertullian's 'utter rejection of pagan society and pagan philosophy'.
11 Kaufmann (1991: 173).
12 Fumerton (2002: 205). For a good discussion of current philosophical theories of epistemic justification, see Swineburne (2001). I am using Fumerton's rather basic definition on purpose, since the discussion of the earliest Christian literature in modern philosophical terms (such as internalism vs. externalism) would be anachronistic.

13 Justinus Martyr, *Apologia prima*, 53.1-3: Πολλὰς μὲν οὖν καὶ ἑτέρας προφητείας ἔχοντες εἰπεῖν ἐπαυσάμεθα, αὐτάρκεις καὶ ταύτας εἰς πεισμονὴν τοῖς τὰ ἀκουστικὰ καὶ νοερὰ ὦτα ἔχουσιν εἶναι λογισάμενοι, καὶ νοεῖν δύνασθαι αὐτοὺς ἡγούμενοι ὅτι οὐχ ὁμοίως τοῖς μυθοποιηθεῖσι περὶ τῶν νομισθέντων υἱῶν τοῦ Διὸς καὶ ἡμεῖς μόνον λέγομεν, ἀλλ' οὐκ ἀποδεῖξαι ἔχομεν. τίνι γὰρ ἂν λόγῳ ἀνθρώπῳ σταυρωθέντι ἐπειθόμεθα, ὅτι πρωτότοκος τῷ ἀγεννήτῳ θεῷ ἐστι καὶ αὐτὸς τὴν κρίσιν τοῦ παντὸς ἀνθρωπείου γένους ποιήσεται, εἰ μὴ μαρτύρια πρὶν ἢ ἐλθεῖν αὐτὸν ἄνθρωπον γενόμενον κεκηρυγμένα περὶ αὐτοῦ εὕρομεν καὶ οὕτως γενόμενα ἑωρῶμεν [...]. English translation by M. Dods & G. Reith.

14 Tertullianus, *Apologeticum*, 46.1: *ostendimus totum statum nostrum, et quibus modis probare possimus, ita esse sicut ostendimus, ex fide scilicet et antiquitate diuinarum litterarum, item ex confessione spiritalium potestatum.*

15 Guerra (1991: 109) singled out the following five warrants: (1) scripture, (2) reason, (3) superior moral behaviour, (4) spiritual testimony and (5) tradition. It is not entirely clear what he understands under the heading 'reason', but it seems that the term refers to a 'natural theology' of sorts, comprising knowledge about God independent of revelation. While it is true that early Christian authors sometimes do argue along these lines, it will be shown that, at best, natural theology can provide only secondary support for their claims. I took the liberty of replacing category with another warrant, namely demonstration of supernatural power in miracle works, which is clearly used by many early Christian authors as means of epistemic justification. Modified and rearranged, the list of warrants I use is the following: (1) miracles, (2) superior moral behaviour, (3) spiritual testimony and divine inspiration, (4) scripture and the fulfilment of prophecies, and (5) tradition.

16 Van der Loos (1960: 241-51).

17 This is emphasized even in standard textbooks, cf. Ehrman (2012: 182-84). Elsewhere, Ehrman (2009: 85) claimed that 'supernatural proofs of Jesus' identity were strictly off limits in Matthew, in John they are the principal reason for Jesus' miraculous acts'; Kee (1986: 80) also notes that 'Jesus [...] presents himself as the instrument of miracle only in order to meet the needs of the sick and the demon-possessed. He will not act in order to corroborate his own authority'. All this might be true, yet *from the point of the view of the reader*, it is completely inconsequential that in Mark or Matthew Jesus is portrayed as discouraging the 'divulgation' of his miraculous deeds, since the reader knows about them from the text itself and identifies him therefore as the Messiah.

18 The best recent systematic study of Jesus' miracles is Zimmermann (2013).

19 Mt 4.23-4.

20 Mt. 7.28-9.

21 This is clear also from the following two chapters (Mt. 8.1-9.38), displaying a wide array of miracles performed by Jesus in different domains. As Keener (1999: 258) noted, 'Matthew 8:1-17 shows Jesus' authority over sickness; 8:23-8 shows his authority over nature, demons, and paralysis; and 9:18-34 demonstrates his authority over disabilities and death.' The link between miracles and authority is established also by Turner (2008: 226, 'Matt. 8-9 presents selected specific miracles in order to demonstrate Jesus' authority') and France (2007: 302).

22 Mt. 10.20.

23 Cf. Keener (1999: 335): 'those cities that witnessed many miracles yet did not respond with wholesale repentance demonstrate their folly' and France (2007: 437): 'when those who have been privileged to witness Jesus' ministry in their own communities

fail to respond, they must expect to face a more serious judgment than the notorious pagan cities which had no such special revelation.'
24 Jn 2.11.
25 I find this to be uncontroversial *communis opinio*. As Kee (1986: 129) summarized, '[t]he ability to perform wonders, including healings, figures importantly in Paul's *apologia* for his apostolic ministry', cf. also Schnelle (2014: 149). Kelhoffer (2001: 183) likewise concluded that '[a]lready by the time of Paul's writings, miracles had become an established part of the Christian tradition, a means of authenticating a particular leader's authority'.
26 Gal. 3.4–5.
27 Gal. 3.4–5. All English translations of the New Testament books are those of New Revised Standard Version.
28 1 Cor. 2.4–5. According to Fee (1987: 95), this 'demonstration of the Spirit and of power' does not necessarily reference exclusively miracles; Fitzmyer (2008: 173), drawing on Bauer's *Lexicon to the New Testament*, translated δύναμις here as 'miracle-working power'.
29 1 Cor. 4.20.
30 2 Cor. 12.12. Contrary to other cited sections of 1 Cor., Paul's intention to legitimize his apostolic authority *via* miracles is here unequivocal, compare Barnett (1997: 581): '[a]lthough Acts 18 records no miracle of Paul during his sojourn in Corinth, the amplifying phrase "signs, wonders and miracles" demands that a significant manifestation of miraculous activity occurred there at the hands of the apostle.'
31 Rom. 15.18–19. Moo (1996: 892–93) argued that these 'words and deeds' do not have to be exclusively miracles, but those were certainly a part of it, since ἐν δυνάμει σημείων καὶ τεράτων is 'standard biblical phraseology for miracles, the former term connoting the purpose of the miracle and the latter its marvelous and unusual character'.
32 For Piñero and Del Cerro (2004: 91), the main difference between canonical and apocryphal miracles lies in their perceived 'utility'. In canonical texts, almost all miracles are 'useful' (*útiles*), in a sense of helping directly the person afflicted by disease, demon, death, etc. In apocryphal literature, there are many miracles that are not 'useful' in this sense (*inútiles*) – however, it may be plausibly argued that the usefulness of the miracles considered by Piñero and Del Cerro as 'useless' lies precisely in the demonstration of godly power as an extremely effective means of conversion; their function is to epistemically justify the content of apostle's teaching.
33 Infancy Gospel of Thomas, 9.3, ibid., 18.2.
34 Gospel of Nicodemus, 5.1.
35 See e.g. Acts of Andrew, 4.2 or Acts of John, 30.2. For an overview of the miracles in the apocryphal *Acts*, including a valuable discussion of the 'competition' between Christian and pagan miracle workers, see Bremmer (2002).
36 Acts of John, 39.2.
37 Acts of John, 42.2.
38 Acts of Peter, 16.2–3: *Iam plurima turba fraternitatis reuersa est per me et per quae signa fecisti in nomine meo. Habebis autem agonem fidei ueniente sabbato et conuertentur multo plures de gentibus et de Iudaeis in nomine meo in me contumeliatum, derisum, consputum. Ego enim me tibi praestabo petenti [te] signa et prodigia, et conuertes multos, sed habebis contrarium Simonem per opera patris sui. Sed omnia eius adprobabuntur carmina et magica figmenta. Nunc autem noli cessare, et quoscumque tibi misero in nomine meo fundabis.* The *agon fidei* takes place in Acts of Peter, 25–8; ibid., 31–2.

39 On the topic of exorcisms (and other miracles) performed by ordinary Christians, see esp. Kelhoffer (1999), who presupposed a 'resounding boom [*sc.* of ordinary believers as workers of miracles] in the early centuries of the Christian movement' and Kollmann (1996: 375–76), arriving to a virtually identical conclusion: 'Für das frühe Christentum läßt sich eine breite Bewegung von Wandermissionaren nachweisen, die ihre Legitimität und die Art ihres Auftretens entscheidend von der im Kern authentischen Aussendungstradition *Lk* 10,1–12par ableiteten. Die wesentlichen Charakteristika sind neben Verkündigungstätigkeit ein Bewirken von Dämonenaustreibungen und Krankenheilungen...'.

40 Justinus Martyr, *Apologia secunda*, 6.6: δαιμονιολήπτους γὰρ πολλοὺς κατὰ πάντα τὸν κόσμον καὶ ἐν τῇ ὑμετέρᾳ πόλει πολλοὶ τῶν ἡμετέρων ἀνθρώπων, τῶν Χριστιανῶν, ἐπορκίζοντες κατὰ τοῦ ὀνόματος Ἰησοῦ Χριστοῦ, τοῦ σταυρωθέντος ἐπὶ Ποντίου Πιλάτου, ὑπὸ τῶν ἄλλων πάντων ἐπορκιστῶν καὶ ἐπᾳστῶν καὶ φαρμακευτῶν μὴ ἰαθέντας, ἰάσαντο καὶ ἔτι νῦν ἰῶνται, καταργοῦντες καὶ ἐκδιώκοντες τοὺς κατέχοντας τοὺς ἀνθρώπους δαίμονας.

41 Theophilus Antiochenus, *Ad Autolycum*, 2.8.

42 Tertullianus, *Apologeticum*, 46.4: *Nomen hoc philosophorum daemonia non fugiunt.*

43 Origenes, *Contra Celsum*, 1.46: Πεπλήρωται δὲ ὁ νόμος καὶ οἱ προφῆται τῶν παραπλησίων παραδόξων τῷ ἀναγραφέντι περὶ τοῦ Ἰησοῦ παρὰ τῷ βαπτίσματι περὶ τῆς περιστερᾶς καὶ τῆς ἐξ οὐρανοῦ φωνῆς. Σημεῖον δὲ οἶμαι τοῦ τότε ὀφθέντος ἁγίου πνεύματος ἐν εἴδει περιστερᾶς τὰ ὑπὸ τοῦ Ἰησοῦ παράδοξα γεγενημένα, ἅτινα διαβάλλων Κέλσος φησὶν αὐτὸν παρ' Αἰγυπτίοις μεμαθηκότα πεποιηκέναι. Καὶ οὐκ ἐκείνοις γε μόνοις χρήσομαι ἀλλὰ γὰρ κατὰ τὸ εἰκὸς καὶ οἷς οἱ ἀπόστολοι τοῦ Ἰησοῦ πεποιήκασιν. Οὐκ ἂν γὰρ χωρὶς δυνάμεων καὶ παραδόξων ἐκίνουν τοὺς καινῶν λόγων καὶ καινῶν μαθημάτων ἀκούοντας πρὸς τὸ καταλιπεῖν μὲν τὰ πάτρια παραδέξασθαι δὲ μετὰ κινδύνων τῶν μέχρι θανάτου τὰ τούτων μαθήματα. Καὶ ἔτι ἴχνη τοῦ ἁγίου ἐκείνου πνεύματος, ὀφθέντος ἐν εἴδει περιστερᾶς, παρὰ Χριστιανοῖς σῴζεται ἐξεπάδουσι δαίμονας καὶ πολλὰς ἰάσεις ἐπιτελοῦσι καὶ ὁρῶσί τινα κατὰ τὸ βούλημα τοῦ λόγου περὶ μελλόντων. English translation by H. Chadwick.

44 Cf. Larmer (2011: 46): 'The claim that Jesus fulfilled the Old Testament prophecies of a coming Messiah and that his miracles are confirmation that in him the Messiah has arrived was regarded by first- and second-century Christian apologists as the strongest argument for Christianity'; Kollmann (2011: 66): 'Wundergeschichten dienten, daran kann wenig Zweifel bestehen, im Rahmen der urchristlichen Missionstätigkeit dazu, die Hoheit Jesu zu erweisen und die Konkurrenz aus dem Felde zu schlagen. Sie wollen zum Glauben an Jesus animieren und bedienen sich einer in der antiken Welt üblichen Form der Werbung.'

45 1 Cor. 15.5–8.

46 As Hauck (1988: 249) noted, the unreliability of witnesses is one of the objections that achieved topical status in pagan criticisms of the early Christian movement.

47 1 Cor. 15.32.

48 Again, this seems to be an unproblematic *communis opinio*. For Meunier (2006: 331), 'avant d'être un bon théologien ou un fournisseur de concepts, il [*sc.* Paul] est un homme voué au Christ. Telle est aux yeux des Pères la source de son authorité theologique.' Dassmann (2009: 244), having especially Paul in mind, argued that '[e]l prestigio de los apóstoles queda reforzado por su martirio en Roma...'. Already Frend (2008: 85–6) highlighted the fact that 'Paul passionately believed that suffering, beatings and death were the symbol of his own right to be called an apostle. [...]

In Paul's mind suffering for the faith and the task of witnessing to it were equally urgent and inextricably interwoven.'
49 2 Cor. 11.16–12.10.
50 Ignatius Antiochenus, *Ad Trallianos*, 10: Εἰ δέ, ὥσπερ τινὲς ἄθεοι ὄντες, τουτέστιν ἄπιστοι, λέγουσιν, τὸ δοκεῖν πεπονθέναι αὐτόν, αὐτοὶ ὄντες τὸ δοκεῖν, ἐγὼ τί δέδεμαι, τί δὲ καὶ εὔχομαι θηριομαχῆσαι; Δωρεὰν οὖν ἀποθνῄσκω. Ἄρα οὖν καταψεύδομαι τοῦ κυρίου.
51 Ignatius Antiochenus, *Ad Romanos*, 4.1: Σῖτός εἰμι θεοῦ καὶ δι' ὀδόντων θηρίων ἀλήθομαι, ἵνα καθαρὸς ἄρτος εὑρεθῶ τοῦ Χριστοῦ.
52 Ignatius Antiochenus, *Ad Smyraeos*, 5.1–2: Ὃν τινες ἀγνοοῦντες ἀρνοῦνται, μᾶλλον δὲ ἠρνήθησαν ὑπ' αὐτοῦ, ὄντες συνήγοροι τοῦ θανάτου μᾶλλον ἢ τῆς ἀληθείας· οὓς οὐκ ἔπεισαν αἱ προφητεῖαι οὐδὲ ὁ νόμος Μωσέως, ἀλλ' οὐδὲ μέχρι νῦν τὸ εὐαγγέλιον οὐδὲ τὰ ἡμέτερα τῶν κατ' ἄνδρα παθήματα.
53 Brent (2007: 44–60).
54 It is not possible to survey martyrological literature systematically here. For a classical account of early Christian martyrdom, see Frend (1965) and esp. recent volumes by Candida Moss (2010; 2012; 2013).
55 Nietzsche, *Der Antichrist* (KSA VI, 234).
56 *Martyrium Polycarpi*, 15.1–2: μεγάλης δὲ ἐκλαμψάσης φλογός, θαῦμα εἴδομεν οἷς ἰδεῖν ἐδόθη· οἳ καὶ ἐτηρήθημεν εἰς τὸ ἀναγγεῖλαι τοῖς λοιποῖς τὰ γενόμενα. τὸ γὰρ πῦρ καμάρας εἶδος ποιῆσαν ὥσπερ ὀθόνη πλοίου ὑπὸ πνεύματος πληρουμένη, κύκλῳ περιετείχισεν τὸ σῶμα τοῦ μάρτυρος. καὶ ἦν μέσον οὐχ ὡς σὰρξ καιομένη ἀλλ' ὡς ἄρτος ὀπτώμενος ἢ ὡς χρυσὸς καὶ ἄργυρος ἐν καμίνῳ πυρούμενος. καὶ γὰρ εὐωδίας τοσαύτης ἀντελαβόμεθα ὡς λιβανωτοῦ πνέοντος ἢ ἄλλου τινὸς τῶν τιμίων ἀρωμάτων. English translation by M. W. Holmes.
57 *Martyrium Polycarpi*, 16.1–2: θαυμάσαι πάντα τὸν ὄχλον, εἰ τοσαύτη τις διαφορὰ μεταξὺ τῶν τε ἀπίστων καὶ τῶν ἐκλεκτῶν, ὧν εἷς καὶ οὗτος γεγόνει ὁ θαυμασιώτατος Πολύκαρπος, ἐν τοῖς καθ' ἡμᾶς χρόνοις διδάσκαλος ἀποστολικὸς καὶ προφητικὸς γενόμενος ἐπίσκοπός τε τῆς ἐν Σμύρνῃ καθολικῆς ἐκκλησίας. πᾶν γὰρ ῥῆμα ὃ ἀφῆκεν ἐκ τοῦ στόματος αὐτοῦ καὶ ἐτελειώθη καὶ τελειωθήσεται.
58 Tertullianus, *Apologeticum*, 50.13: *Etiam plures efficimur, quotiens metimur a uobis: semen est sanguis christianorum!* Epistemic justification and martyrdom is explicitly linked in also Origen's work. As Frend (2008: 392) noted, '[t]he *Exhortation to Martyrdom* represents Origen as the rebel. In words which echo Josephus, *Against Apion* (1.8.42), he claims that Christianity was true because people were prepared to die for it.'
59 *Martyrium Montani*, 14.9: *hoc enim est propter Christum pati, Christum etiam exemplo sermonis imitari et esse probationem maximam fidei. O exemplum grande credendi!*
60 Moss (2012: 23).
61 *Didache*, 11.3–6: Περὶ δὲ τῶν ἀποστόλων καὶ προφητῶν κατὰ τὸ δόγμα τοῦ εὐαγγελίου, οὕτως ποιήσατε. Πᾶς δὲ ἀπόστολος ἐρχόμενος πρὸς ὑμᾶς δεχθήτω ὡς κύριος· οὐ μενεῖ δὲ εἰ μὴ ἡμέραν μίαν· ἐὰν δὲ ᾖ χρεία, καὶ τὴν ἄλλην· τρεῖς δὲ ἐὰν μείνῃ, ψευδοπροφήτης ἐστίν. Ἐξερχόμενος δὲ ὁ ἀπόστολος μηδὲν λαμβανέτω εἰ μὴ ἄρτον, ἕως οὗ αὐλισθῇ· ἐὰν δὲ ἀργύριον αἰτῇ, ψευδοπροφήτης ἐστίν. English translation by M. W. Holmes.
62 Hager (1978: 76–77). Cf. also Scaglioni (1972: 186), who even generalized this observation to apply to the entire early Christianity: 'Secondo una linea di attenzione che era già comunissima tra gli scrittori cristiani, viene colpita qui – in primo luogo – l'inefficienza morale della sapienza mondana del filosofo.'

63 Aristides Athenaeus, *Apologia*, 11.7: ὅθεν λαμβάνοντες οἱ ἄνθρωποι ἀφορμὴν ἀπὸ τῶν θεῶν αὐτῶν ἔπραττον πᾶσαν ἀνομίαν καὶ ἀσέλγειαν καὶ ἀσέβειαν καταμιαίνοντες γῆν τε καὶ ἀέρα ταῖς δειναῖς αὐτῶν πράξεσιν.
64 Athenagoras, *Legatio pro Christianis*, 20.1.
65 Athenagoras, *Legatio pro Christianis*, 20.4; ibid., 21.4: τί τὸ σεμνὸν ἢ χρηστὸν τῆς τοιαύτης ἱστορίας, ἵνα πιστεύσωμεν θεοὺς εἶναι τὸν Κρόνον, τὸν Δία, τὴν Κόρην, τοὺς λοιπούς; [...] οὐ καταβάλλουσι τὸν πολὺν τοῦτον ἀσεβῆ λῆρον περὶ τῶν θεῶν; Οὐρανὸς ἐκτέμνεται, δεῖται καὶ καταταρταροῦται Κρόνος, ἐπανίστανται Τιτᾶνες, Στὺξ ἀποθνῄσκει κατὰ τὴν μάχην—ἤδη καὶ θνητοὺς αὐτοὺς δεικνύουσιν—ἐρῶσιν ἀλλήλων, ἐρῶσιν ἀνθρώπων· English translation by W. R. Schoedel.
66 Clemens Alexandrinus, *Protrepticus*, 2.33.6-7: Τούτους ὑμῶν αἱ γυναῖκες προσκυνούντων τοὺς θεούς, τοιούτους δὲ εὐχέσθων εἶναι τοὺς ἄνδρας τοὺς ἑαυτῶν, οὕτω σώφρονας, ἵν' ὦσιν ὅμοιοι τοῖς θεοῖς τὰ ἴσα ἐζηλωκότες· τούτους ἐθιζόντων οἱ παῖδες ὑμῶν σέβειν, ἵνα καὶ ἄνδρες γενήσονται εἰκόνα πορνείας ἐναργῆ τοὺς θεοὺς παραλαμβάνοντες.
67 One might add Justinus Martyr, *Apologia prima*, 21 & *Apologia secunda*, 12. For a detailed study of Justin's critique of pagan gods, see Munier (1988: 94–96), who concluded that 'Justin reprend aussi et amplifie l'argument des transformations morales opérées par le christianisme, qui avait servi à Aristide, pour prouver la vérité et la sainteté de la religion chrétienne'; see further also Theophilus Antiochenus, *Ad Autolycum*, 1.9; ibid., 3.3; or Tatianus, *Oratio ad Graecos*, 8–11 et passim.
68 Already Kühneweg (1988: 113) highlighted the general argument from superior moral behaviour in early Christianity by claiming that 'die Praxis [ist] ein so wesentliches Element des Christentums, kann sie auch als Argument für seine Wahrheit dienen'.
69 Rev. 1.1–2.
70 As Mounce (1998: 42) pointed out, the Greek text does not make it clear whether the transfer of information moves on the line God – Jesus – Angel – John, or the term ἄγγελος denotes here Jesus as a 'messenger' of God.
71 Cf. Aune (1983: 248): 'Paul often designates himself an "apostle", but never a "prophet." Modern scholars, however, are quite willing to categorize him as a prophet. From the standpoint of early Christianity, the role of apostle appears to have been a functional equivalent of the OT prophet.'
72 Gal. 1.1.
73 Gal. 1.11–12. Compare Moo (2013: 67): 'The denial of any human involvement in Paul's apostolic status is echoed in his later claim that his gospel was not of human origin (1:11–12). The most likely reason for this concern is that the agitators were attempting to undermine Paul's authority with the Galatians by arguing that his status and teaching depended on the Jerusalem apostles, whose views (as represented by the agitators) should therefore trump Paul's. Paul not only highlights this denial by placing it before his reference to his divine commissioning; he also repeats the point for emphasis.'
74 1 Cor. 2.10.
75 1 Cor. 2.15.
76 Homerus, *Ilias*, 2.485–86.
77 2 Cor. 3.5–6.
78 See e.g. Tertullianus, *De praescriptione haereticorum*, 22.3, 8–10: *Quis igitur integrae mentis credere potest aliquid eos ignorasse quos magistros Dominus dedit, indiuiduos*

habens in comitatu in discipulatu in conuictu, quibus obscura quaeque seorsum disserebat, illis dicens datum esse cognoscere arcana quae populo intellegere non liceret? [...] *Dixerat plane aliquando:* Multa habeo adhuc loqui uobis, sed non potestis modo ea sustinere, *tamen adiciens:* Cum uenerit ille spiritus ueritatis, ipse uos deducet in omnem ueritatem, *ostendit illos nihil ignorasse quos omnem ueritatem consecuturos per spiritum ueritatis repromiserat. Et utique impleuit repromissum, probantibus actis apostolorum descensum spiritus sancti.*

79   Morgan-Wynne (1984: 176).
80   Irenaeus, *Adversus haereses*, 3.1.1: *Postea enim quam surrexit Dominus noster a mortuis, et induti sunt supervenientis Spiritus sancti virtutem ex alto, de omnibus adimpleti sunt, et habuerunt perfectam agnitionem.*
81   Farkasfalvy (1968: 323).
82   Justinus Martyr, *Apologia prima*, 31–53. For a detailed analysis of this argument in Justin's works, see Skarsaune (1987). De Vogel (1978: 370) highlighted the fact that for Justin, the ultimate argument in favour of the truth of Christianity is precisely the fulfilment of prophecies, not the 'philosophical' (impersonal) argumentation: 'The argument of the fulfilment of the prophecies is for him "proving", not any argument from Greek philosophy. This is a remarkable fact, but it is true.'
83   Justinus Martyr, *Dialogus cum Tryphone*, 7: Τίνι οὖν, φημί, ἔτι τις χρήσαιτο διδασκάλῳ ἢ πόθεν ὠφεληθείη τις, εἰ μηδὲ ἐν τούτοις τὸ ἀληθές ἐστιν; Ἐγένοντό τινες πρὸ πολλοῦ χρόνου πάντων τούτων τῶν νομιζομένων φιλοσόφων παλαιότεροι, μακάριοι καὶ δίκαιοι καὶ θεοφιλεῖς, θείῳ πνεύματι λαλήσαντες καὶ τὰ μέλλοντα θεσπίσαντες, ἃ δὴ νῦν γίνεται· προφήτας δὲ αὐτοὺς καλοῦσιν. οὗτοι μόνοι τὸ ἀληθὲς καὶ εἶδον καὶ ἐξεῖπον ἀνθρώποις, μήτ᾽ εὐλαβηθέντες μήτε δυσωπηθέντες τινά, μὴ ἡττημένοι δόξης, ἀλλὰ μόνα ταῦτα εἰπόντες ἃ ἤκουσαν καὶ ἃ εἶδον ἁγίῳ πληρωθέντες πνεύματι. One may well ask, with Jossa (2003: 172), whether these lines are fiction or historical reality: 'Non sappiamo se sia stata effettivamente la realtà dei fatti o se siamo in presenza soltanto di un finzione letteraria.'
84   Tertullianus, *Apologeticum*, 20.2-3: *Quicquid agitur, praenuntiabatur; quicquid uidetur, audiebatur* [...] *Dum patimur, leguntur; dum recognoscimus, probantur. Idoneum, opinor, testimonium diuinitatis ueritas diuinationis.* English translation by S. Thelwall.
85   Guerra (1991: 117).
86   Kaufman (1991: 172).
87   Irenaeus, *Adversus haereses*, 2.28.2: *Scripturae quidem perfectae sunt, quippe a Verbo Dei et Spiritu ejus dictae.*
88   Sesboüé (1981: 886–87): 'Ainsi donc non seulement la prophétie est une preuve de l'événement, mais l'événement à son tour devient une preuve de la prophétie: le Verbe incarné est envoyé tel qu'il avait été annoncé.'
89   Aune (1983: 126–29).
90   Grant (1952: 171).
91   *1 Clement* 42.1–4: Οἱ ἀπόστολοι ἡμῖν εὐηγγελίσθησαν ἀπὸ τοῦ κυρίου Ἰησοῦ Χριστοῦ, Ἰησοῦς ὁ Χριστὸς ἀπὸ τοῦ θεοῦ ἐξεπέμφθη. Ὁ Χριστὸς οὖν ἀπὸ τοῦ θεοῦ, καὶ οἱ ἀπόστολοι ἀπὸ τοῦ Χριστοῦ· ἐγένοντο οὖν ἀμφότερα εὐτάκτως ἐκ θελήματος θεοῦ. [...] Κατὰ χώρας οὖν καὶ πόλεις κηρύσσοντες καθίστανον τὰς ἀπαρχὰς αὐτῶν, δοκιμάσαντες τῷ πνεύματι, εἰς ἐπισκόπους καὶ διακόνους τῶν μελλόντων πιστεύειν. In discussion of this section of Clement, Ferguson (2008: 51) interpreted the tradition as 'divine chain of authority'.

92 Irenaeus, *Adversus haereses*, 5, *praefatio*: [...] *et veritate ostensa, et manifestato praeconio Ecclesiae, quod prophetae quidem praeconaverunt, quemadmodum demonstravimus, perfecit autem Christus, Apostoli vero tradiderunt, a quibus Ecclesia accipiens, per universum mundum sola bene custodiens, tradidit filiis suis* [...].
93 Hefner (1964: 304).
94 Tertullianus, *De praescriptione hereticorum*, 20.1–6: *Christus Iesus, Dominus noster,* [...] *quisquis est, cuiuscumque Dei filius, cuiuscumque materiae homo et Deus, cuiuscumque fidei praeceptor, cuiuscumque mercedis repromissor, quid esset, quid fuisset, quam patris uoluntatem administraret, quid homini agendum determinaret, quamdiu in terris agebat, ipse pronuntiabat siue populo palam, siue discentibus seorsum, ex quibus duodecim praecipuos lateri suo allegerat destinatos nationibus magistros. Itaque uno eorum decusso reliquos undecim digrediens ad patrem post resurrectionem iussit ire et docere nationes tinguendas in Patrem et in Filium et in Spiritum sanctum. Statim igitur apostoli – quos haec appellatio missos interpretatur – adsumpto per sortem duodecimo Matthia in locum Iudae ex auctoritate prophetiae quae est in psalmo Dauid, consecuti promissam uim Spiritus sancti ad uirtutes et eloquium, primo per Iudaeam contestata fide in Iesum Christum et ecclesiis institutis, dehinc in orbem profecti eamdem doctrinam eiusdem fidei nationibus promulgauerunt. Et perinde ecclesias apud unamquamque ciuitatem condiderunt, a quibus traducem fidei et semina doctrinae ceterae exinde ecclesiae mutuatae sunt et cottidie mutuantur ut ecclesiae fiant. Ac per hoc et ipsae apostolicae deputantur ut suboles apostolicarum ecclesiarum.* English translation by P. Holmes.
95 Moores (1995); Scott (2009).
96 Justinus Martyr, *Apologia secunda*, 13.3: ἕκαστος γάρ τις ἀπὸ μέρους τοῦ σπερματικοῦ θείου λόγου τὸ συγγενὲς ὁρῶν καλῶς ἐφθέγξατο·
97 Irenaeus, *Adversus haereses*, 2.6.1: *Unde etiamsi nemo cognoscit Patrem nisi Filius, neque Filium, nisi Pater, et quibus Filius revelaverit, tamen hoc ipsum omnia cognoscunt, quando ratio mentibus infixa moveat ea et revelet eis, quoniam est unus Deus, omnium Dominus.*
98 Tertullianus, *Adversus Marcionem*, 1.10.2: *Denique maior popularitas generis humani, ne nominis quidem Moysei compotes, nedum instrumenti, deum Moysei tamen norunt* [...].
99 Tertullianus, *Adversus Marcionem*, 1.10.3: *Ante anima quam prophetia. Animae enim a primordio conscientia dei dos est* [...].
100 Tertullianus, *De resurrectione mortuorum*, 3.1: *Est quidem et de communibus sensibus sapere in dei rebus, sed in testimonium ueri, non in adiutorium falsi, quod sit secundum diuinam, non contra diuinam dispositionem. Quaedam enim et naturaliter nota sunt, ut inmortalitas animae penes plures, ut deus noster penes omnes.*
101 1 Cor. 15.3–4.
102 Meunier (2006: 332).
103 1 Cor. 15.14.
104 Any attempts to 'rationalize' the resurrection of Jesus are bound to fail – one may only recall Athenagoras' (or *pseudo*-Athenagoras'?) treatise *On Resurrection* and the unflattering, yet entirely correct conclusions Grant (1952: 242) drew with respect to it: 'In this example we see the rationalistic tendency of apologetic leading to its absurd conclusion. Athenagoras is thoroughly unrealistic. It is not as a Christian, however, that he goes astray; it is as an amateur philosopher convinced of the validity of his concept of "nature" and of his deductive method.'
105 1 Cor. 1.18–25.

106 Morris (1985: 44).
107 Fee (1987: 66).
108 Garland (2003: 63).
109 For a short outline of Luther's critique of human reasoning unaided by revelation, see Kaufmann (1958: 305–07).
110 Garland (2003: 66).
111 What Scaglioni (1972: 213) concluded with respect to the relationship of 'faith' and 'reason' in Tertullian would be valid for virtually all early Christian apologists and theologians, namely that 'il discorso di Paolo ha inciso profondamente nell'animo di Tertulliano, così che riuscirebbe difficile intenderne la la posizione su questo punto, prescindendo dall'Apostolo'.
112 Justinus Martyr, *Apologia prima*, 46.3: καὶ οἱ μετὰ λόγου βιώσαντες Χριστιανοί εἰσι, κἂν ἄθεοι ἐνομίσθησαν, οἷον ἐν Ἕλλησι μὲν Σωκράτης καὶ Ἡράκλειτος καὶ οἱ ὅμοιοι αὐτοῖς, ἐν βαρβάροις δὲ Ἀβραὰμ καὶ Ἀνανίας καὶ Ἀζαρίας καὶ Μισαὴλ καὶ Ἠλίας καὶ ἄλλοι πολλοί, ὧν τὰς πράξεις ἢ τὰ ὀνόματα καταλέγειν μακρὸν εἶναι ἐπιστάμενοι τανῦν παραιτούμεθα.
113 Wright (1982: 82).
114 Price (1988: 20). Already Piper (1961: 155–56) emphasized the fact that Justin's λόγος is not employed congruently with its previous uses in Greek philosophy: 'While it has often been held that Justin borrowed the concept of the *Logos* from Philo or from Stoicism, a careful investigation will show that at the best he might have received from those philosophies the stimulus for the use of that term. His understanding of its place in human thought and in metaphysics, however, differs greatly from them.'
115 Justinus Martyr, *Apologia secunda*, 10.1–3.
116 Justinus Martyr, *Apologia secunda*, 15.3.
117 This important point is argued for by Pycke (1961), mostly by analysing sections of the *Dialogue*. His conclusion (ibid., 77) runs as follows: 'Justin met avant tout l'accent sur la nécessité de la grâce pour comprendre les Écritures; des raisonnements habiles n'y suffisent pas. L'intelligence des Écritures suppose nécessairement une intervention de Dieu ou du Christ, sans laquelle la doctrine des Écritures pourrait paraître au lecteur absurde et indigne de Dieu.'
118 Löhr (2000: 407). Similar conclusion with respect to Justin's view of philosophy was reached by De Vogel (1978: 381): 'Platonism had only a partial view of the truth and was mixed with error; Christianity was Truth in its fullness. Its relation to philosophy was that of completion and correction.'
119 Droge (1987: 315).
120 Wright (1982: 81, 83).
121 Crépey (2009: 75): '[L]a sagesse humaine ne puisse atteindre qu'une partie de la vérité, non la vérité intégrale que seul le Christ, Raison incarnée, est à même de révéler.'
122 Irenaeus, *Adversus haereses*, 3.25.5: *Quibus religiosior Plato ostenditur, qui eundem Deum et justum et bonum confessus est, habentem potestatem omnium* [...].
123 Schoedel (1959: 24).
124 Irenaeus, *Adversus haereses*, 2.14.7: *Dicemus autem adversus eos: utrumne hi omnes qui praedicti sunt, cum quibus eadem dicentes arguimini, cognoverunt veritatem, aut non cognoverunt? Et si quidem cognoverunt, superflua est Salvatoris in hunc mundum descensio. Ut quid enim descendebat? An nunquid ut eam quae cognoscebatur veritas, in agnitionem adduceret his, qui cognoscunt eam hominibus?* English translation by A. Roberts and W. Rambaut.

125 For an analysis of the notion of 'truth' in Clement, see Klibengajtis (2004). With respect to the notion of 'faith', Osborn (1994: 3–4) differentiated no less than eight different meanings: (1) 'preconception'; (2) 'assent and decision'; (3) 'hearing and seeing'; (4) 'listening to God in the scriptures'; (5) 'first principle'; (6) 'criterion which judges that something was true or false'; (7) 'always on the move, from faith to faith, moving up the ladder of dialectic'; (8) 'source of power and stability'. Slightly less detailed analysis is offered by Peršić (2005: 157–61), who differentiated three main sematic fields: (1) 'attitude of certainty of human spirit in the first, unproved principles from which a proof is derived'; (2) 'firm conviction of reason in what is scientifically proven'; (3) 'taking of what is said in the Bible for true without investigation', while noting that Clement himself criticized the interpretation (3).

126 Wolfson (1942: 223–30) saw in Clement's notion of 'faith' a combination of Aristotelian and Stoic influences. Lössl (2002: 337), however, argued that the influence of Plato and Aristotle is much stronger than the influence of Stoicism of Clement's day. Havrda (2012: 265), in discussion of Clement's use of the term ἀπόδειξις, noted that '[d]espite conceding that faith cannot be proven in terms of Greek logic, and even chastising his opponents for making such a demand, Clement nevertheless attempts to show that the standpoint of faith is logically sound, and even that it has the force of a scientific demonstration.'

127 Zuiddam (2010: 310 *et passim*).

128 Dal Covolo (1998: 243): 'Clemente divide i cristiani in due classi: i «semplici» e gli «gnostici». Non si tratta di una differenza essenziale, ma solo di grado: i primi sono i credenti che vivono la fede in modo comune, gli altri quelli che conducono una vita di perfezione spirituale.'

129 Le Boulluec (1999: 188): 'La «philosophie» des Grecs est certes utile, mais elle doit être dépassée, elle n'est qu'une propédeutique.' Same conclusion has been reached by Rizzerio (1998: 177): '[...] il est évident que le Principe suprême, Dieu, ne pourra jamais être connu uniquement par l'activité de la raison pure. Car le Dieu des chrétiens est plus qu'un simple Principe, il est une "personne" à aimer, l'objet premier de notre liberté.'

130 Clemens Alexandrinus, *Stromata*, 6.2.27.5 *et passim*: ἐπιλείψει γάρ με ὁ βίος, εἰ καθ' ἕκαστον ἐπεξιέναι αἱροίμην τὴν Ἑλληνικὴν διελέγχων φίλαυτον κλοπήν, καὶ ὡς σφετερίζονται τὴν εὕρεσιν τῶν παρ' αὐτοῖς καλλίστων δογμάτων, ἣν παρ' ἡμῶν εἰλήφασιν.

131 Barcala (1976b: 245); Hager (1978: 78–79).

132 Tertullianus, *De resurrectione carnis*, 3.3: *At cum aiunt: 'Mortuum quod mortuum' et 'Viue dum uiuis' et 'Post mortem omnia finiuntur, etiam ipsa', tunc meminero et cor uulgi cinerem a deo deputatum et ipsam sapientiam saeculi stultitiam pronuntiatam* [...].

133 Tertullianus, *De anima*, 2: *Plane non negabimus aliquando philosophos iuxta nostra sensisse; testimonium est etiam ueritatis euentus ipsius. Nonnumquam et in procella confusis uestigiis caeli et freti aliqui portus offenditur prospero errore, nonnumquam et in tenebris aditus quidam et exitus deprehenduntur caeca felicitate, sed et natura pleraque suggerentur quasi de publico sensu, quo animam deus dotare dignatus est.*

134 Tertullianus, *De baptismo*, 2.2: *Quid ergo? Nonne mirandum est lauacro dilui mortem? Si, quia mirandum est, idcirco non creditur, atquin eo magis credendum est: qualia enim decet esse opera diuina nisi super omnem admirationem? Nos quoque ipsi miramur, sed [quia] credimus. Ceterum incredulitas miratur quia non credit: miratur enim simplicia quasi uana, magnifica quasi inpossibilia.* According to Stockmeier

(1972: 243), '[o]hne Zweifel wird hier im Gegenüber von *mirari* und *credere* das Paradox christlichen Glaubens sichtbar [...].'
135 Tertullianus, *De carne Christi*, 5.4: *Crucifixus est dei filius; non pudet, quia pudendum est. Et mortuus est dei filius; credibile est, quia ineptum est. Et sepultus resurrexit; certum est, quia impossibile.*
136 Bauer (1970: 11–12); Peršić (2005: 156); Bochet (2008: 267–71).
137 Barcala (1976a: 357): 'Esta forma de reflexión es la que designamos con el nombre de «dialéctica de los contrarios».'
138 Tertullianus, *De praescriptione haereticorum*, 7.9: *Quid ergo Athenis et Hierosolymis? quid academiae et ecclesiae? quid haereticis et christianis?*
139 Tertullianus, *Apologeticum*, 46.18: *Adeo quid simile philosophus et Christianus, Graeciae discipulus et caeli, famae negotiator et salutis uitae, uerborum et factorum operator, et rerum aedificator et destructor, et interpolator et integrator ueritatis, furator eius et custos?*
140 Stanton (1973: 90); in addition to his examples, see also 2 Cor. 6.14–16.
141 Labhardt (1950: *passim*). Similar interpretations are offered by Quasten (1964: 320–21) and Gilson (1986: 97). Refoulé (1956) and Braun (1971) were far less radical in their interpretation of Tertullian, but even they did not doubt the primacy of faith and revelation over philosophy in his thought. Cruciat (2016) carefully assessed the use of terms *philosophus* and *philosophari* in Tertullian's work and concluded that the great Latin apologist 'esprime una concezione radicalmente negativa della philosophia'. One of the most interesting readings of Tertullian's paradox has been put forward by Williams (2006: 3–21; a reprint of the original 1955 paper).
142 Osborn (1997).
143 Compare D'Alès (1905: 33): '. . . dans la pensée de Tertullien, l'adhésion à la religion chrétienne est un acte éminemment raisonnable' and especially Bauer (1970); Sider (1980) and Bochet (2008). Similar conclusions were reached by Osborn (1997: 48–64).
144 González (1974: 21). See also Lortz (1987: 132): 'Die Wahrheit par excellence liegt aber im Glauben. Wer diesen gesucht und gefunden hat und sich zu eigen gemacht hat, der darf wohl zur Stärkung und Befestigung eben dieses Glaubens noch weiter forschen, aber nicht so, daß dieser Glaube selbst wieder in Frage gestellt würde.'
145 Irenaeus, *Adversus haereses*, 1.22.1.
146 Tertullianus, *De praescriptione haereticorum*, 13.1. For a closer look at the 'rule of faith' in Tertullian, see especially Braun (1962: 446–54); Waszink (1979) and Countryman (1982).
147 This is the view of Farmer (1984) and Ferguson (2001), amongst others.
148 Hägglund (1958: 4): 'Nicht eine im Kampfe gegen die Häresien erfundene oder formulierte Lehrzusammenfassung wird damit gemeint, sondern der Glaube selbst, die Wahrheit selbst, die in der heiligen Schrift, in der Verkündigung des Herrn und der Apostel, geoffenbart und bekanntgemacht worden ist, und in der Taufe einem jeden Christen übergeben und anvertraut wird.'
149 Fernández (2004: 120): 'Cuando el mensaje bíblico parece ir contra razón, la regla de fe tiene una palabra que decir.'
150 Freeman (2005), although focusing on Late Antiquity and Early Middle Ages, provided a good account of this process and his conclusions bears close resemblance to the argument put forward in this chapter (ibid., 335): 'It has never been part of the argument of this book that Christians did not attempt to use rational means of discovering theological truths. The problem was rather that reason is only of limited use in finding such truths.'

151 Beckaert (1961: 62): 'L'évolution historique manifeste bien que la philosophie n'a pas absorbée le christianisme, mais qu'elle s'est résorbée en lui.' Cf. also Grant (1952: 263): 'As regards these basic physical and metaphysical questions, Nestle righlty observes that Christianity was in no way whatever the heir of Greek philosophy.'
152 Augustinus, *De doctrina Christiana*, 2.40.60.
153 This analogy may be found already in Origen, cf. Heine (1993: 90).
154 Augustinus, *De doctrina Christiana*, 2.44.63.
155 Thomas Aquinas, *Summa Theologiae*, Prima pars, Qu. I, A. 1.
156 Thomas Aquinas, *Summa Theologiae*, Prima pars, Qu. I, A. 5.
157 For an interpretation of Pomponazzi as a radical critic of religion, see esp. Pine (1986: 235–74).
158 Petrus Damiani, *Epistula CXIX*, 354.

4 Naturalism and protectionism in the study of religions (1): The beginnings

1 Müller (1893: 8).
2 My selection of authors and works discussed in these two chapters is based primarily on six invaluable volumes mapping the theory and method in the study of religions published in the series *Religion & Reason*, founded by Jacques Waardenburg, cf. Waardenburg (1973 [reprint 1999]; 1974), Whaling (1984; 1985), Antes, Geertz and Warne (2008a; 2008b). I further made ample use of Lanczkowski (1974), who published a collection of texts dealing with the theory and method of the study of religions in the esteemed German series *Wege der Forschung*, as well as other basic works on the history of the study of religions, such as Michaels (1997), Strenski (2006), Pals (2015a), Preus (1987), Sharpe (1986) and Capps (1995).
3 Godfrey-Smith (2003: 239) defined 'paradigm' generally as 'a whole "way of doing science" that has grown up around a paradigm in the narrow sense. In this sense, a paradigm will typically include theoretical ideas about the world, methods, and subtle habits of mind and standards used to assess "good work" in the field'. Curd, Cover and Pincock (2013: 1313) differentiated paradigms in the sense of an 'exemplar' and a 'disciplinary matrix' in the following manner: 'An exemplar is an important scientific theory or piece of research that serves as a model for further inquiry. Disciplinary matrices contain exemplars as one of their elements. They also include heuristic models, ontological and metaphysical assumptions, and methodological principles. In short, paradigms (in the sense of disciplinary matrices) are 'super theories' that underlie and guide an entire tradition of scientific research and theorizing.' I use the term 'paradigm' with the latter meaning, i.e. as a disciplinary matrix.
4 Cf. Boyer (2010: 24): 'People have tried to explain religious belief in terms of infantile thought, as the flight of reason, as the need for explanations, the urge for reassurance, the necessity of social cohesion and the interests of patriarchy. All those things are real, but they are not the explanations, for the thing to be explained is largely an illusion fostered by religious guilds. Science can explain a lot about people's religious thoughts and behaviours, and should not concern itself with explaining what is non-existent.'
5 The categorization is essentially that of Bianchi (1975: 191–200), who differentiated 'psychologism' (e.g. Freud) and 'Marxist sociologism' (e.g. Marx, De Martino). In this chapter, both categories are understood in a wider sense, with 'psychologism' including

also the anthropological speculations on the origins of religion put forward by Tylor and Frazer and 'sociologism' including late Durkheim.
6 Comte is mentioned only rarely in the handbooks and manuals dealing with the history of the study of religions, the notable exception being Preus (1987: 107–30). A detailed analysis of the three stages may be found in Bourdeau (2006); Wernick (2001) discussed at length Comte's concept of the 'religion of mankind'.
7 Comte (1934: 2) specifically mentioned a 'marche progressive de l'esprit humain'. The idea of the three stages of the development of the culture is somewhat indebted to previous Enlightenment theories, esp. to Saint-Simon; see Capps (1995: 61–62).
8 Comte (1934: 2): 'Dans l'état théologique, l'ésprit humain dirigeant essentiellment ses recherches vers la nature intime des êtres, les causes premières et finales de tous les effets qui le frappent, en un mot, vers les connaissances absolues, se représente les phénomènes comme produits par l'action directe et continue d'agents surnaturels plus ou moins nombreux, dont l'intervention arbitraire explique toutes les anomalies apparentes de l'univers.' English translation by H. Martineau, modified.
9 For a brief overview of Comte's most important theses on the reform of the religion, see Bourdeau (2003: 10–20), who noted that Comte's ideas flatly failed to generate the desired response: 'Le moins qu'on puisse dire est que l'histoire n'a pas répondu aux attentes du Grand-Prêtre de l'Humanité' (ibid., 19).
10 See especially Tylor (1903a: 417–502; 1903b: 1–361).
11 Strenski (2006: 93).
12 Tylor (1903a: 70).
13 Strenski (2006: 112).
14 Tylor (1903a: 70–111).
15 Tylor (1903a: 100).
16 Tylor (1903a: 104): 'The lingering survivals of the quaint old formulas in modern Europe seem an unconscious record of the time when the explanation of sneezing had not yet been given over to physiology, but was still in the "theological stage".'
17 Tylor (1903a: 501): 'Yet it is evident that, notwithstanding all this profound change, the conception of the human soul is, as to its most essential nature, continuous from the philosophy of the savage thinker to that of the modern professor of theology. [...] The soul has given up its ethereal substance, and become an inmaterial entity, 'the shadow of a shade'. Its theory is being separated from the investigations of biology and mental science, which now discuss the phenomena of life and thought, the senses and the intellect, the emotions and the will, on a ground-work of pure experience. There has arisen an intellectual product whose very existence is of the deepest significance, a 'psychology' which has no longer anything to do with 'soul'. The soul's place in modern thought is in the metaphysics of religion [...].'
18 Preus (1987: 138): 'The outcome of Tylor's massively documented consideration of mythology and animism will be that religion itself is a survival.'
19 Capps (1995: 82) argued that, according to Tylor, 'the primitive imagination (characterized by the animistic theory of vitality) must be abandoned in favor of a perspective that claims a clearer and more refined scientific accuracy'; Sharpe (1986: 57) similarly came to a conclusion that Tylor found the origin of religion in a 'childish aberration (or at least inadequacy) of thought'.
20 Cf. Kohl (1997: 45): 'Sein Interesse an der Religion war denn auch alles andere als religiös geprägt. Ihre endgültige Überwindung durch die Wissenschaft erschien ihm nur eine Frage der Zeit.' Strenski (2006: 94) likewise concluded that Tylor was 'certainly broadly antagonistic towards religion, [and] found it agreeable to cast

religion in the poorest light possible'; elsewhere, he spoke about Tylor's 'general antipathy to religion' (ibid., 105). Pals (2015a: 16) identified in Tylor's works 'a strong distaste for traditional Christianity, especially Roman Catholicism' and considered the man himself as someone who 'refused to settle any question by an appeal to the divine authority of the Church or the Bible' (ibid., 17).

21 Tylor (1903b: 450).
22 Spencer accepted the theory of animism practically without any objections, but he preferred to call it 'ghost-theory'; see in brief Spencer (1885: 1–7); Spencer (1898: 171–83, 218–25) offers a fuller account. Quite like Tylor, Spencer also considered animism to be erroneous and factually wrong; indeed, in his own words, '[t]he ghost-theory of the savage is baseless', see Spencer (1885: 14). The difference between the two lies in the fact that Spencer, unlike Tylor (and quite like Comte) refused to let go completely of religion, but rather tried to formulate the principles for a sort of an 'agnostic religion', cf. esp. his discussions with Frederic Harrison, reprinted under the title *The Insuppressible Book* in Spencer (1885). Sharpe (1986: 34) showed more understanding for Spencer's unrelenting apology of the evolutionary approaches in the nineteenth century than for his own theories of religion.
23 Widengren (1945: 87): 'die Inkarnation des evolutionistischen Geistes auf dem Gebiet der vergleichenden Religionswissenschaft.'
24 By way of example, one may cite Eliot's modernistic masterpiece *The Waste Land* – in the notes to the poem, Eliot (1952: 50) wrote: 'To another work of anthropology I am indebted in general, one which has influenced our generation profoundly; I mean *The Golden Bough*; I have used especially the two volumes *Adonis, Attis, Osiris*. Anyone who is acquainted with these works will immediately recognise in the poem certain references to vegetation ceremonies.'
25 Tworuschka (2011: 77).
26 Wißmann (1997: 85).
27 Strenski (2006: 142) observed that Frazer (quite like Tylor) made practically no difference between science and technology, which is why he was able to establish the parallel between magic and 'science'.
28 Frazer (1920: 222).
29 Frazer (1920: 237) spoke about a 'tardy recognition of the inherent falsehood and barrenness of magic'.
30 Frazer (1920: xxvi).
31 Cf. Ackerman (1987: 95).
32 Cf. Strenski (2006: 139, 'Frazer quite early rejected religion'); according to Wißmann (1997: 77), Frazer 'in aller Religion nur «superstition» am Werk sehen konnte'; Pals (2015a: 28) considered Frazer an outright atheist. *Pace* Sharpe (1986: 87), according to whom 'Frazer was in fact conventionally Christian all his life, and in no way wanted to see his work applied to the dismissal of religion'.
33 MacLennan (1865) was one of the first authors to describe the phenomenon of exogamy in his work *Primitive Marriage*, which dealt primarily with the tradition of the bride kidnapping; totemism as primitive religion is thematized in his papers originally published in *Fortnightly Review*, see MacLennan (1869; 1870). The fundamental works from the turn of the nineteenth and twentieth century include *Animal Worship and Animal Tribes among the Arabs and in the Old Testament* by Robertson Smith (originally published 1880, reprinted in Robertson Smith 1912: 455–83), Westermarck's discussion of the incest taboo in his *The History of Human Marriage* (see Westermarck 1891: 290–335), Andrew Lang's *Secret of the Totem* (Lang 1905) and especially the synthetizing

four-volume work by Frazer, *Totemism and Exogamy* (Frazer 1910). The concept of totemism as primitive religion has been sharply rejected already in the early twentieth century, cf. e.g. Goldenweiser (1910) and Van Gennep (1920). Freud's works on this topic were therefore somewhat antiquated already in the year of their publication. For an overview of the theory of totemism from MacLennan to Freud, see Jones (2005).

34 Freud (1991: 195) calls the primal tribe the less-than-flattering term 'Darwinische Urhorde'.
35 Freud (1991: 196): 'Eines Tages taten sich die ausgetriebenen Brüder zusammen, erschlugen und verzehrten den Vater und machten so der Vaterhorde ein Ende. Vereint wagten sie und brachten zustande, was dem einzelnen unmöglich geblieben wäre. (Vielleicht hatte ein Kulturfortschritt, die Handhabung einer neuen Waffe ihnen das Gefühl der Überlegenheit gegeben.) Daß sie den Getöteten auch verzehrten, ist für den kannibalen Wilden selbstverständlich. Der gewalttätige Urvater war gewiß das beneidete und gefürchtete Vorbild eines jeden aus der Brüderschar gewesen. Nun setzten sie im Akte des Verzehrens die Identifizierung mit ihm durch, eigneten sich ein jeder ein Stück seiner Stärke an. Die Totemmahlzeit, vielleicht das erste Fest der Menschheit, wäre die Wiederholung und die Gedenkfeier dieser denkwürdigen, verbrecherischen Tat, mit welcher so vieles seinen Anfang nahm, die sozialen Organisationen, die sittlichen Einschränkungen und die Religion.' English translations of Freud's works are those of J. Strachey.
36 Freud (1991: 198): 'Sie widerriefen ihre Tat, indem sie die Tötung des Vaterersatzes, des Totem, für unerlaubt erklärten, und verzichteten auf deren Früchte, indem sie sich die freigewordenen Frauen versagten. So schufen sie aus dem *Schuldbewußtsein des Sohnes* die beiden fundamentalen Tabu des Totemismus, die eben darum mit den beiden verdrängten Wünschen des Ödipus-Komplexes übereinstimmen mußten.' As Preus (1987: 181) noted, the analogy between the child and the wildling is based on Haeckel's thesis 'ontogeny recapitulates phylogeny'.
37 Freud (1975: 129): 'eine Entwicklung [...] die als langsame »Wiederkehr des Verdrängten« zu beschreiben ist.'
38 As Sharpe (1986: 202) dully noted, '*Totem and Taboo* expresses no historical truth whatsoever'.
39 Strenski (2006: 234). Pals (2015a: 72) introduced Freud's theories as prime examples of reductionism in the study of religions.
40 Freud (1989: 587–88): 'Vom Standpunkt der Wissenschaft aus ist es unvermeidlich, hier Kritik zu üben und mit Ablehnungen und Zurückweisungen vorzugehen. Es ist unzulässig zu sagen, die Wissenschaft ist ein Gebiet menschlicher Geistestätigkeit, Religion und Philosophie sind andere, ihr zum mindesten gleichwertig, und die Wissenschaft hat diesen beiden nichts dareinzureden....'
41 Freud (1989: 594–95): 'Den letzten Beitrag zur Kritik der religiösen Weltanschauung hat die Psychoanalyse geleistet, indem sie auf den Ursprung der Religion aus der kindlichen Hilflosigkeit hinwies und ihre Inhalte aus den ins reife Leben fortgesetzten Wünschen und Bedürfnissen der Kinderzeit ableitete. Das bedeutete nicht gerade eine Widerlegung der Religion, aber es war doch eine notwendige Abrundung unseres Wissens um sie und wenigstens in einem Punkt ein Widerspruch, da sie selbst göttliche Abkunft für sich in Anspruch nimmt.'
42 Waardenburg (1999: 361).
43 Freud (1989: 597): 'Was immer Wert und Bedeutung der Religion sein mögen, sie hat kein Recht, das Denken irgendwie zu beschränken, also auch nicht das Recht, sich selbst von der Anwendung des Denkens auszunehmen.'

44 For a good discussion of this work, see the collected volume by O'Neil and Akhtar (2009).
45 Freud (1993: 121): 'Die Götter behalten ihre dreifache Aufgabe, die Schrecken der Natur zu bannen, mit der Grausamkeit des Schicksals, besonders wie es sich im Tode zeigt, zu versöhnen und für die Leiden und Entbehrungen zu entschädigen, die dem Menschen durch das kulturelle Zusammenleben auferlegt werden.'
46 Freud (1993: 133). Pals (2015a: 65), in my opinion correctly, concluded that the supposed difference between 'Illusion' and 'Irrtum' is merely a sophistic world-play; cf. also DiCenso (1999: 37): 'It would seem that the tension between the critiques of religion as illusion and as delusion has been resolved in favor of the latter. But the reclassification of religion as delusion cannot annul the previous arguments that link to religion by virtue of the psychological processes it reflects and to which it responds.'
47 Zinser (1997: 95); Strenski (2006: 247); Pals (2015a: 59).
48 Freud (1993: 136): 'Es liegt nicht im Plane dieser Untersuchung, zum Wahrheitswert der religiösen Lehren Stellung zu nehmen. Es genügt uns, sie in ihrer psychologischen Natur als Illusionen erkannt zu haben. Aber wir brauchen nicht zu verhehlen, daß diese Aufdeckung auch unsere Einstellung zu der Frage, die vielen als die wichtigste erscheinen muß, mächtig beeinflußt. Wir wissen ungefähr, zu welchen Zeiten die religiösen Lehren geschaffen worden sind und von was für Menschen. Erfahren wir noch, aus welchen Motiven es geschah, so erfährt unser Standpunkt zum religiösen Problem eine merkliche Verschiebung. Wir sagen uns, es wäre ja sehr schön, wenn es einen Gott gäbe als Weltenschöpfer und gütige Vorsehung, eine sittliche Weltordnung und ein jenseitiges Leben, aber es ist doch sehr auffällig, daß dies alles so ist wie wir es uns wünschen müssen. Und es wäre noch sonderbarer, daß unseren armen, unwissenden, unfreien Vorvätern die Lösung all dieser schwierigen Welträtsel geglückt sein sollte.'
49 Freud (1993: 151): 'der Infantilismus ist dazu bestimmt, überwunden zu werden.'
50 Paden (2002: 79), cf. also Palmer (1997: 7): 'It is therefore largely Freud's perception of psychoanalysis as falling within the main determinist-scientific tradition – a tradition which included his own teachers and which he extended out to include even greater luminaries like Copernicus, Kepler, Newton, and Darwin – that leads him to maintain that religion and science are fundamentally incompatible. Indeed, such is the antagonism that he sees between them that the following rule applies: anyone who considers himself a medical man and an empiricist has to be an atheist. This was not a choice for Freud but more a matter of logical consistency.'
51 Preus (1987: 196).
52 Malinowski (1948: 22–23).
53 Malinowski (1948: 69).
54 The influence of Durkheim on Malinowski is emphasized by Capps (1995: 98).
55 Bowie (2006: 5).
56 Malinowski (1948: 32–33).
57 Strenski (2006: 273). Stolz (1997: 258) argued in the same vein that Malinowski explained religious ritual as a: 'Coping-Strategie, um mit dem Erlebnis des Todes fertig zu werden; den chaotischen Gefühlen gegenüber, die jetzt aufbrechen, stattet es den Menschen mit einem bestimmten Glauben an ein Jenseits aus und setzt dadurch die lebensbewahrenden und -fördernden gesellschaftlichen Werte und Normen in Kraft.'
58 Cf. Stolz (1997: 262): 'Das Konzept Malinowskis ist reduktionistisch; kulturelle Phänomene (darunter auch die Religion) werden zurückgeführt auf andere, letztlich biologische.'

59 Tambiah (1990: 70), who somehow surprisingly argued that 'it is difficult to maintain that Malinowski was an important thinker on religion', considered his general interpretation of religion not dissimilar to Plato's 'noble lie'. Cf. also Strenski (2006: 263): 'For religion, as for myth, Malinowski, of course, does not believe it to be literally true. [...] But these religious images and concepts are much needed for most people to maintain order and a sense of meaning in their lives. Religion thus provides indispensable "crutches". And since religion functions to maintain social coherence, we need to keep religion on hand – if only for the pragmatic purposes it serves in keeping society from disintegrating.'

60 This is also the view presented by William James, who, following a short discussion of 'medical materialism' in the introduction to his Gifford lectures (James 1922: 13), argued that this approach 'finishes up Saint Paul by calling his vision on the road to Damascus a discharging lesion of the occipital cortex [and] snuffs out Saint Theresa as an hysteric, Saint Francis of Assisi as an hereditary degenerate'. James then asked: 'But now, I ask you, how can such an existential account of facts of mental history decide in one way or another upon their spiritual significance?' (ibid., 14) and responded in a clearly consequentialist manner: In evaluation of any religious tradition and its significance, the only important thing is its function for an individual or for a society as a whole, not its truth or falsity: 'At any rate you must all be ready now to judge the religious life by its results exclusively, and I shall assume that the bugaboo of morbid origin will scandalize your piety no more' (ibid., 21).

61 Radin (1934: 4).

62 Radin (1934: 8–9). In his later works, Radin (1953: 72) reiterated this viewpoint and argued that 'man needs help from supernatural beings because of the existence of an unbalance within his own psyche'.

63 Any discussion of Marxism is relatively rare in the handbooks and textbooks of the history of the religious studies. Whenever discussed, only a few pages are dedicated to it, cf. e.g. Meslin (1973: 64–67); Bianchi (1975: 192–98); Hill (1985: 100–01); Paden (2002: 33–34). One of the few exceptions is Pals (2015a: 113–42), who dedicated an entire chapter to Marx and his views on religion.

64 Raines (2002: 5–6) quite rightly argued that this statement is not necessarily a rebuke. Religion is, for Marx, a reaction to human suffering, yet it is much better to remove the origin of this suffering (class differences) that treat the symptoms with religion. Similar conclusion has been reached by Capps (1995: 40): 'the fact that religion exists is testimony to the need to eliminate all forms and occasions of dehumanization, to correct the social, cultural, and political situation from which religious aspirations spring.'

65 Marx (ME I, 378): 'Aber *der Mensch*, das ist kein abstraktes, außer der Welt hockendes Wesen. Der Mensch, das ist *die Welt des Menschen*, Staat, Societät.'

66 Marx (ME I, 378): 'Dieser Staat, diese Societät produzieren die Religion, ein *verkehrtes Weltbewußtsein*, weil sie eine *verkehrte Welt* sind. Die Religion ist die allgemeine Theorie dieser Welt, ihr enzyklopädisches Kompendium, ihre Logik in populärer Form, ihr spiritualistischer Point-d'honneur, ihr Enthusiasmus, ihre moralische Sanktion, ihre feierliche Ergänzung, ihr allgemeiner Trost- und Rechtfertigungsgrund. Sie ist die *phantastische Verwirklichung* des menschlichen Wesens, weil das menschliche Wesen keine wahre Wirklichkeit besitzt. Der Kampf gegen die Religion ist also mittelbar der Kampf gegen *jene Welt*, deren geistiges *Aroma* die Religion ist. Das *religiöse* Elend ist in einem der *Ausdruck* des wirklichen Elendes und in einem die *Protestation* gegen das wirkliche Elend. Die Religion ist der Seufzer der bedrängten

Kreatur, das Gemüt einer herzlosen Welt, wie sie der Geist geistloser Zustände ist. Sie ist das *Opium* des Volks.' English translation by A. Jolin and J. O'Malley.

67 For a detailed discussion of Marx's reductionism and a contextualization of his thought on the background of previously discussed authors (Frazer; Tylor; Freud), see esp. Pals (2015a: 132–33).

68 Marx (ME I, 379): 'Die Aufhebung der Religion als des *illusorischen* Glücks des Volkes ist die Forderung seines *wirklichen* Glücks. Die Forderung, die Illusionen über seinen Zustand aufzugeben, ist die *Forderung, einen Zustand aufzugeben, der der Illusionen bedarf*. Die Kritik der Religion ist also im *Keim* die *Kritik des Jammertales*, dessen *Heiligenschein* die Religion ist.'

69 Simmel (1905: 360): 'Thus it may help us to an insight into the origin and nature of religion, if we can discover in all kinds of non-religious conditions and interests certain religious momenta, the beginnings of what later came to be religion, definitely and independently. I do not believe that the religious feelings and impulses manifest themselves in religion only; rather, that they are to be found in many connections, a co-operating element in various situations, whose extreme development and differentiation is religion as an independent content of life.'

70 For a sketch of the relationship between the individual and the social, cf. Simmel (1917: 34–50).

71 Simmel (1905: 367).

72 Kippenberg (1997b: 104).

73 Fustel de Coulanges (1900).

74 Durkheim (1960: 3): 'Il n'y a donc pas, au fond, de religions qui soient fausses. Toutes sont vraies à leur façon: toutes répondent, quoique de manières différentes, à des conditions données de l'existence humaine.' English translations of Durkheim are those of J. Ward Swain.

75 Preus (1987: 159): 'religion is no longer "true" in the literal sense of statements it makes about the world and the gods. But religion has been, and may continue to be, socially necessary.' Compare also Mürmel (1997: 211); Sharpe (1986: 82) argued that Durkheim was an 'atheist of Jewish extraction'; Pals (2015a: 83) characterized him as an 'avowed agnostic'.

76 Durkheim (1960: 614): 'Voilà en quoi consiste le conflit de la science et de la religion. On s'en fait souvent une idée inexacte. On dit que la science nie la religion en principe. Mais la religion existe; c'est un système de faits donnés; en un mot, c'est une réalité. Comment la science pourrait-elle nier une réalité? De plus, en tant que la religion est action, en tant qu'elle est un moyen de faire vivre les hommes, la science ne saurait en tenir lieu, car si elle exprime la vie, elle ne la crée pas; elle peut bien chercher à expliquer la foi, mais, par cela même, elle la suppose. Il n'y a donc de conflit que sur un point limité. Des deux fonctions que remplissait primitivement la religion, il en existe une, mais une seule, qui tend de plus en plus à lui échapper: c'est la fonction spéculative. Ce que la science conteste à la religion, ce n'est pas le droit d'être, c'est le droit de dogmatiser sur la nature des choses, c'est l'espèce de compétence spéciale qu'elle s'attribuait pour connaître de l'homme et du monde.'

77 Durkheim (1960: 10): 'la question n'a rien de scientifique et doit être résolument écartée.'

78 Durkheim's definition of religion will be discussed in greater detail in Chapter 7.

79 Bianchi (1975: 21) considered the theories formulated by members of the circle created around the journal *L'Année sociologique* to be clearly reductionistic; same conclusion has been reached by Meslin (1973: 45): 'Cette idée avait été aussi formulée par les sociologues français Hubert et Mauss qui niaient l'existence de sentiments religieux *sui*

generis: seuls existent des sentiments normaux, dont la religion est à la fois produit et l'objet.' Whaling (1984: 212) found in Durkheim's works 'implied reductionism'; Sharpe (1986: 86) even claimed that 'Durkheim was so dominated by the desire to explain away the phenomenon of religion that his theories about the origins of religion are of little consequence'. Similarly, Pals (2015a: 108) argued that 'Durkheim's theory, like Freud's, fits the mold of an aggressively reductionist functionalism; his program essentially reduces religion to something other than what its adherents think it to be.'

80 Strenski (2006: 294–97) proposed both reductionist as well as non-reductionist reading of Durkheim; Yinger (1970: 88) considered Durkheim's theory to be 'basically a functional theory, not an explanation of origins in the historical sense'; according to Paden (2002: 44), Durkheim refused both 'theological' as well as 'materialistic and rationalistic' approach. For a reappraisal of Durkheim and his influence, see now also Paden (2016: 19–43; 177–96).

81 Durkheim (1960: 597): 'Or c'est précisément ce que nous avons tenté de faire et nous avons vu que cette réalité, que les mythologies se sont représentées sous tant de formes différentes, mais qui est la cause objective, universelle et éternelle de ces sensations *sui generis* dont est faite l'expérience religieuse, c'est la société. Nous avons montré quelles forces morales elle développe et comment elle éveille ce sentiment d'appui, de sauvegarde, de dépendance tutélaire qui attache le fidèle à son culte.'

82 Durkheim (1960: 603): 'Ainsi, la formation d'un idéal ne constitue pas un fait irréductible, qui échappe à la science; il dépend de conditions que l'observation peut atteindre; c'est un produit naturel de la vie sociale.'

83 Durkheim (1960: *passim*).

84 For a detailed and rather fascinating account of Max Müller's life, cf. Van den Bosch (2002: 1–183).

85 Müller (1893: 10–11) argued that the science of religion should follow in the footsteps of comparative Indo-European linguistics, for a more detailed account, see Müller (1907: 239–410).

86 Müller (1893: 9).

87 The edition has been completed only after Müller's death and spanned no less than fifty volumes. Müller himself contributed with preparing three of them, including a new edition and translation of the Rigveda. It is worth pointing out that Old and New Testament have been excluded from the series because of vocal protests of Christian Churches (see Tworuschka (2011: 23)). The genesis and the ultimate fate of the series has been mapped in some detail by Molendijk (2016).

88 Müller (1893: 16–17).

89 Müller (1907: 114–40).

90 Müller (1868: xxiv): 'Whenever we can trace back a religion to its first beginnings, we find it free from many of the blemishes that offend us in its later phases.' Capps (1995: 70–71) noted that Müller 'displayed a negative attitude towards what happens to religion in the course of its subsequent development'.

91 Kitagawa (1959: 17) read Müller through phenomenological lens and argued that 'he was concerned with *religio naturalis*, or the original natural religion of reason, and assumed that "truth" was to be found in the most universal essence of religion and not in its particular manifestations'. Similar conclusions have been reached by Tworuschka (2011: 32), according to whom Müller claimed that '[j]ede Religion der Menschheit besitze Körner der Wahrheit, keine ist völlig ohne Wahrheit'; Klimkeit (1997: 37) likewise argued that 'Müller ist überzeugt, daß der Sinn der verschiedenen Religionen insofern konvergiert, als ihnen jeweils die Offenbarung Gottes in je eigener Sprache zugrunde liegt.'

92 Klimkeit (1997: 36, 38). Cf. also Strenski (2006: 66), who considered Müller to be 'unashamedly, if progressive, pious man, motivated by a rich and subtle combination of heart-felt religious and scientific motives'.
93 Müller (1868: xx).
94 Sharpe (1986: 44).
95 For instance, Vedānta represented for Müller a sort of a corrective for the Christianity of his day. As Green (2016: 189) argued, 'Vedānta was not represented as a religion to which one could "convert", but as encapsulating principles that were a necessary complement to and corrective for the Christianity of the times. Understood in this way, Müller was a "Vedāntist" on Vivekananda's terms – insofar as he acknowledged that Vedānta had most adequately expressed the essential principle underlying all religions; yet, at the same time, he was also a Christian – insofar as he found Christ's teachings to be the most congenial particular expression of that general principle.'
96 Michaels (1997: 7).
97 Sharpe (1986: 223) suspected that the reason why the Dutch author in the second and the third edition of his *opus magnum* omitted the term 'phenomenology' was because 'Chantepie was also in some difficulty about reaching a satisfactory synthesis of scientific objectivity and Christian commitment'. Indeed, whenever in the protectionist paradigm the epistemic justification *per rem* ('reason') and the epistemic justification *per hominem* ('faith') come into conflict, the exigencies of faith always trump reason (or science, objectivity etc.).
98 Sharpe (1979: 209) termed his approach 'descriptive phenomenology'.
99 Chantepie de la Saussaye (1897: 6): 'Andere kehren das Verhältniss um und wollen die christliche Theologie nur als Untertheil der Religionswissenschaft gelten lassen. Wiewohl dies formell ganz richtig ist, kann doch die Theologie sich hierzu schwerlich bequemen; denn auch wenn sie nicht reactionär, sondern in protestantischer Freiheit arbeitet, wird sie doch den Charakter der biblischen und kirchlichen Disciplinen, woraus ihre Encyklopädie zum grössten Theil besteht, nicht ohne Selbstauflösung preisgeben können. Die Wissenschaft der Religion und die der christlichen Religion gehen also ihre eigenen Wege und verfolgen ihre eigenen Zwecke.' English translation by B. S. Colyer-Ferguson.
100 Chantepie de la Saussaye (1897: 6): 'Freilich müssen sie einander gegenseitig fördern.'
101 Chantepie de la Saussaye (1897: 6): 'die Missionskunde diese Kenntniss durchaus nicht entbehren kann.' The role of the study of religions in the missionary activities has been emphasized also by Müller (1868: xi).
102 Cox (2006: 106): 'When scientists of religion observe, describe and classify religious phenomena, they actually are recording the revelations of God. For Chantepie, the very existence of religion confirms that God has been at work everywhere and that God has implanted within humans the innate capacity to respond to the divine revelation.'
103 For a more detailed overview of the academic environment of the study of religions in the turn of the nineteenth and the twentieth centuries, see Sharpe (1986: 119–43). For a brief account of Tiele's biography, see Molendijk (2000b: 79–92).
104 Tiele (1897: 27).
105 Tiele (1897: 6): 'The unity which combines the multiplicity of these phenomena is the human mind, which reveals itself nowhere so completely as in these, and whose manifestations, however different the forms they assume on different planes of development, always spring from the same source. This unity renders a scientific classification of religions quite as justifiable as that of language.'

106 Tiele (1899: vi): 'between pure science and true religion nothing but perfect and abiding harmony can prevail.'
107 Tiele (1899: 230): 'The origin of religion consists in the fact that man *has* the Infinite within him, even before he is himself conscious of it, and whether he recognizes it or not.'
108 Tiele (1899: 230): 'Whether this be an illusion or truth we do not at present inquire; nor does the question strictly belong to the scope of our research.'
109 Tiele (1899: 235).
110 Tiele (1899: 262–63).
111 Molendijk (2000a: 22–23). Wiebe (2000: 9–50) argued forcefully that Müller and Tiele were instrumental for a degree of emancipation of the study of religions against theology, but I find this rather puzzling. Their project of the renewal of religions (and, in particular, Christianity) *via* newly established 'scientific' study of religions is well grounded in the protectionist paradigm.
112 For Tübingen school, cf. Harris (1990); for Göttingen, cf. Lüdemann and Schröder (1987).
113 Strauss (1837: 103–05): 'Daß ein Bericht nicht historisch, etwas Erzähltes nicht so geschehen sein könne, wird sich vor Allem daran erkennen lassen, wenn es [...] mit den bekannten und sonst überall geltenden Gesetzen des Geschehens unvereinbar ist. [...] Doch nicht allein mit den Gesetzen des Geschehens, auch mit sich selbst und mit anderen Berichten darf eine Relation nicht im Widerspruch stehen, wenn sie geschichtliche Geltung ansprechen will.'
114 Strauss (1837: 106): 'Ist die Form poëtisch, wechseln die Handelnden hymnische Reden, länger und begeisterter, als sich von ihrer Bildung und Situation erwarten läßt: so sind wenigstens diese Reden nicht als historisch anzusehen. [...] Stimmt der Inhalt einer Erzählung auffallend zusammen mit gewissen, innerhalb des Kreises ihrer Entstehung geltenden Vorstellungen, welche selbst eher darnach aussehen, aus vorgefaßten Meinungen, als nach der Erfahrung gebildet zu sein: so wird ein sagenhafter Ursprung der Erzählung ja nach Umständen mehr oder weniger wahrscheinlich.'
115 Renan (1863: 433): 'Que s'était-il passé? C'est en traitant de l'histoire des apôtres que nous aurons à examiner ce point et à rechercher l'origine des légendes relatives à la résurrection. La vie de Jésus, pour l'historien, finit avec son dernier soupir.'
116 Renan (1857: xxii): 'Laissons les religions se proclamer inattaquables, puisque sans cela elles n'obtiendraient pas de leurs adhérents le respect dont elles ont besoin; mais n'obligeons pas la science à passer sous la censure d'un pouvoir qui n'a rien de scientifique. Ne confondons pas la légende avec l'histoire; mais n'essayons pas de bannir la légende, puisque telle est la forme que revêt nécessairement la foi de l'humanité.' English translation by O. B. Frothingham.
117 Robertson Smith (1927).
118 For a detailed description of the process, Maier (2009: 150–86) may be consulted. As Kippenberg (1997a: 63) stressed, Smith's teacher Julius Wellhausen also understood the potential dangers of the historical-critical approach to the founding texts of the Judeo-Christian tradition and in the year 1882 has been transferred (by his own petition) from Greifswald (where he held the chair of the Old Testament) to Halle (to serve as a chair for Semitic linguistics).
119 Strenski (2006: 130) differentiated in this matter the sacrifice as a *communion* and the sacrifice as *expiation*.
120 Robertson Smith (1927: 24).

121 Strenski (2006: 121). Strenski further added that Robertson Smith studied the development of Judaism into Christianity 'in the spirit of a triumphalist and supercessionist *Heilsgeschichte*' (ibid., 134).
122 Bedianko (1997: 145): 'Smith clearly drew a close parallel between the crisis of the sixteenth century and that of the nineteenth, and believed that the Reformation provided a paradigm for the new work of theologizing required to meet the daily needs of the spiritual life in the nineteenth century.'
123 Delitzsch (1902: 44): 'Und so ist es mir vielleicht gelungen zu zeigen, dass auch unserm religiösen Denken durch das Medium der Bibel noch gar manches Babylonische anhaftet. Durch das Ausscheiden dieser zwar hochbegabten Völkern entstammenden, aber trotzdem rein menschlichen Vorstellungen und durch die Befreiung unseres Denkens vor allerlei festgewurzelten Vorurteilen wird die wahre Religion selbst, die wahre Religiosität, wie sie uns die Propheten und Dichter des Alten Testaments und in erhabenstem Sinne Jesus gelehrt, so wenig berührt, dass sie vielmehr nur um so wahrer und verinnerlichter aus diesem Reinigungsprozesse hervorgeht.'
124 Delitzsch (1903: 38): 'Aber anderseits lasst uns nicht blind festhalten an veralteten, wissenschaftlich überwundenen Dogmen, etwa gar aus Angst, es möchte hierdurch unser Gottesglaube und wahrhafte Religiosität Schaden leiden! Bedenken wir, dass alles Irdische in lebendigem Fluss ist, Stillstehen gleichbedeutend mit Tod. Schauen wir hin auf die gewaltig pulsierende Kraft, mit welcher die deutsche Reformation grosse Nationen der Erde auf allen Gebieten menschlicher Arbeit, menschlichen Fortschritts erfüllt! Aber auch die Reformation ist nur eine Etappe auf dem Wege zu dem uns von Gott und in Gott gesteckten Ziele der Wahrheit. Ihm streben wir nach in Demut, aber mit allen Mitteln der freien Forschung der Wissenschaft, freudig uns bekennend zu der von hoher Warte mit Adlerblick geschauten und hochgemut aller Welt kundgegeben Losung der Weiterbildung der Religion.' English translation by W. H. Carruth.
125 Lang (1898: 49).
126 Lang (1898: 51).
127 Lang (1898: 63): 'What kind of creature was man when he first conceived the germs, or received the light, of Religion? All is guess-work here!'
128 Lang (1898: 330–31).
129 Lang (1898: 66–67).
130 As Sharpe (1986: 61) observed, Lang was among the first authors to use the term *sensus numinis* that later played a pivotal role in Otto's work.
131 For a basic overview of pre-animism, see e.g. Marett (1909).
132 Widengren (1945: 96).
133 Riesebrodt (1997: 172) rather characterized Marett's work as a 'Markstein im Übergang vom Evolutionismus zum Funktionalismus'.
134 Marett (1914: xxviii).
135 Riesebrodt (1997: 183): 'Seine Fragestellung beruht auf dem unerschütterlichen Glauben, daß der westlich-zivilisierte, protestantische Mensch die Kröne der Schöpfung bzw. den Höhepunkt der Evolution verkörpere.'
136 Schmidt (1930: 14): 'Die älteste naturmythologische Schule befolgte eine im engeren Sinne des Wortes historische Methode [...]. Alle übrigen Theorien dagegen, entstanden nach dem Anbruch des Materialismus und Darwinismus, arbeiteten nur mit der naturwissenschaftlich-evolutionistischen Methode, die alles Niedere und Einfache an den Anfang setzt und alles Höhere und Reiche nur als Produkt mehr oder weniger langen Entwicklung gelten läßt.' English translations by H. J. Rose.

137 Schmidt (1930: 16): 'Was das für die Methode der Religionsgeschichte bedeutete, ist bereits dargelegt. Für den Geist der Forschung bedeutete es eine sich steigernde Unfähigkeit, das tiefere Wesen der Religion zu erfassen, ihre höheren Formen zur Geltung gelangen zu lassen, und die Neigung, die äußeren Teile zu überschätzen, den Geist zu unterschätzen oder ganz zu vernachlässigen. Im Ganzen genommen besagt das eine fast schwerere Schädigung der Religionsgeschichte, als sie in der vorhergehenden Periode eingetreten war.'
138 Waldenfels (1997: 191). Meslin (1973: 52) similarly concluded the following: 'Sa thèse de la croyance en un dieu unique est impossible à prouver autrement que comme la projection d'une Rélévation surnaturelle sur les origines mêmes de l'homme et sa place dans le monde.'
139 As Capps (1995: 88) ironically pointed out, Schmidt attributed to the 'high God' of the primitive religions characteristics that are perhaps all too transparently drawn from Christian theology.

5 Naturalism and protectionism in the study of religions (2): The rise and fall of phenomenology

1 Wach (1958: 12).
2 King (1984: 40): 'The field is characterized by an extreme fragmentation so that one can discern almost as many different phenomenologies as there are phenomenologists.'
3 Sharpe (1997: 160).
4 Schleiermacher, Über die Religion, 63: 'Wer von ihr etwas ausspricht, muß es nothwendig gehabt haben.'
5 Schleiermacher, Über die Religion, 79.
6 Sharpe (1969: 270): 'To Söderblom, the fact of religious experience, and its *sui generis* character, was beyond all discussion. It is there, and its own conviction, in whatever religion it may be found, is that it bears a distinct relation to powers or deities beyond the sphere of human life.'
7 The phrase is that of Ján Komorovský, one of the founding fathers of the study of religions in Slovakia, cf. his preface to Eliade (1995: 13).
8 Söderblom (1914: 731): 'Holiness is the great word in religion; it is even more essential than the notion of God. Real religion may exist without a definite conception of divinity, but there is no real religion without a distinction between holy and profane.' As Lange (2011: 247) pointed out, Söderblom wrote already in 1909 the entry 'the Holy' for a Swedish lexicon *Nordisk familjebok*.
9 Sharpe (1997: 161).
10 Tworushka (2011: 97): 'In zwei religiösen Erlebnissen (1892, 1893) widerfährt Söderblom eine direkte Begegnung mit Jesus Christ und mit der Heiligkeit Gottes.' For a detailed biography of Söderblom, see esp. Jonson (2016); his role in the ecumenical movement is covered well in Lange (2011: 310–414).
11 Söderblom (1942: 1): 'Religion muß vorhanden sein und in der Seele des Menschen aufkeimen, ehe sie in seinen Worten und Taten, Gebräuchen und Institutionen Ausdruck findet. Sie muß, bevor sie Angelegenheit der Gemeinschaft wird, im Einzelmenschen vorhanden sein.'
12 Söderblom (1979: 341): 'Und wenn sie sich bedeutsamer zeigen als Geister und Seelen, so fehlt ihnen andererseits der Wert für die wirkliche Religion [...].'

13 Söderblom (1979: 343): 'Wie aber verhält es sich mit dem einzigen Urmonotheismus auf der Welt, der diesen Namen verdient, mit dem biblischen Offenbarungsglauben in seiner Vollendung?'
14 Söderblom (1942: 373): 'In der Tat entspricht dem Zusammenhang, der alle Religionsformen zu einer einheitlichen Gruppe von Erscheinungen verbindet, der prophetische und christliche Glaube an eine göttliche Selbstmitteilung auch außerhalb des "auserwähltes Volkes" und der Christenheit. An anderer Stelle habe ich, was die verschiedenen Völker und Kulturen betrifft, versucht, den christlichen Glauben an eine göttliche Offenbarung anzuwenden. Worin das Offenbarungsmoment in einer bestimmten Religionsform nach christlichem Glauben besteht, das ist oft schwer zu bestimmen; es wird unmöglich, wenn man eine intellektualistische Betrachtungsweise anwendet. Aber daß ein Maß von Offenbarung, d. h. von göttlichen Selbstmitteilung, vorliegt, wo auch immer wir religiöse Aufrichtigkeit finden, das ist ausdrücklich vom Offenbarungsglauben innerhalb und außerhalb des Christentums ausgesprochen worden.'
15 Söderblom (1979: 345): 'Den weltumfassenden geistigen Prozeß, aus dem die siegreiche Gotteserkenntnis als ein gemeinsamer Besitz der gesamten Menschheit hervorgehen soll, hat die Mission in vollem Ernst ins Leben gerufen und treibt ihn seiner Vollendung entgegen.'
16 Sharpe (1986: 155).
17 Sharpe (1986: 158–59) noted that on his deathbed, Söderblom told his friends and family the following: 'I know that God lives; I can prove it by the history of religion.'
18 Capps (1995: 274). Cf. also Jonson (2016: 65): 'His study of Ritschl had taught Söderblom that the more generously, unreservedly, and honestly one acknowledged that which is good, true, and moral in other religions and the more substantively one endeavored to understand the faith present in those religions, the clearer it became that Christianity was unrivaled and irreplaceable. The study of religion could be the best defense of Christian faith.'
19 Sharpe (1997: 167).
20 Bolle (1984: 301). Cf. also Sharpe (1986: 161): '[*Das Heilige*] now holds a near-canonical status as one of the books which every student of comparative religion imagines himself or herself to have read.' The long shadow of Otto's *opus magnum* in the fields of theology and study of religions in the twentieth century is mapped by Gooch (2000: 1–8).
21 Bolle (1984: 324).
22 For a detailed analysis of this category, see Raphael (1997); Gooch (2000: 104–31); Crowder (2003).
23 Otto (1963: 7): 'Da diese Kategorie [*scil.* das Numinöse] vollkommen *sui generis* ist so ist sie wie jedes ursprüngliche und Grund-datum nicht definibel im strengen Sinne sondern nur erörterbar. Man kann dem Hörer nur dadurch zu ihrem Verständnis helfen daß man versucht, ihn durch Erörterung zu dem Punkte seines eigenen Gemütes zu leiten wo sie ihm dann selber sich regen entspringen und bewußt werden muß.' English translations by J. W. Harvey.
24 Otto (1963: 137): '. . . eine Kategorie rein *a priori* . . .'.
25 Alles (1997: 206). The influence of Kant on Otto's thought has been discussed further by Almond (1984: 34–38) and Gooch (2000: 52–77).
26 Otto (1963: 8): 'Wir fordern auf, sich auf einen Moment starker und möglichst einseitiger religiöser Erregtheit zu besinnen. Wer das nicht kann oder wer solche Momente überhaupt nicht hat, ist gebeten nicht weiter zu lesen.'

27 Otto (1963: 173): 'Das etwaige Vermögen, das Heilige in der Erscheinung echt zu erkennen und anzuerkennen, wollen wir *Divination* nennen.'
28 Otto (1963: 6): 'Aber mit ausgezeichneter Kräftigkeit lebt es in den semitischen Religionen und ganz vorzüglich hier wieder in der biblischen.'
29 Otto (1963: 171): 'Auch nach diesem Maßstabe ist das Christentum die schlechthin überlegene über ihre Schwester-religionen auf der Erde.'
30 Alles (1997: 200): 'Schutz der Religion im allgemeinen vor antireligiöser Kritik.'
31 Otto (1963: 174): 'Das religiöse Gefühl selber empört sich gegen diese Versteifung und Materialismus des Zartesten was es in der Religion gibt: Des Gott-begegnens und -findens selber. Denn wenn irgendwo der Zwang durch Beweise, die Verwechslung mit logischem oder juridischem Verfahren ausgeschlossen ist, wenn irgendwo Freiheit im Anerkennen und inniges Zugestehen aus freiester Regnung inwendigster Tiefe ist ohne Theorie und Begriff, so ist es da wo ein Mensch in eigenem oder fremdem Geschehen, in Natur oder Geschichte, des waltenden Heiligen inne wird. Nicht erst "Naturwissenschaft" oder "Metaphysik" sondern schon das gereifte religiöse Gefühl selber stößt solche Massivitäten von sich, die aus Rationalismus geboren Rationalismus zeugen und echte Divination nicht nur hemmen sondern sie als Schwärmerei Mystizismus oder Romantik verdächtigen. Mit Naturgesetz und Beziehung oder Nichtbeziehung darauf hat echte Divination überhaupt nichts zu tun. Sie fragt garnicht nach dem Zustandekommen eines Vorkommnisses, sei es Ereignis Person oder Sache, sondern nach seiner Bedeutung, nämlich nach der Bedeutung ein 'Zeichen' des Heiligen zu sein. Das Vermögen der Divination verbirgt sich in der erbaulichen und in der dogmatischen Sprache unter dem schönen Namen des *testimonium spiritus sancti internum* (das hier begrenzt wird auf die Anerkennung der Schrift als des Heiligen).' Gooch (2000: 76) showed that in Otto's use of the terms like *spiritus sanctum in corde* or *testimonium spiritus sancti internum* 'Lutheran doctrine is transported onto the history of religion as a whole, and the *testimonium spiritus sanctum [sic] internum* is conceived as a general capacity for recognizing the holy in history (DH 174), *and* for distinguishing the relative validity of individual manifestations of the holy.'
32 Meslin (1973: 73): 'Otto s'était déjà élevé contre toute théorie réductrice du phénomène religieux à de simples mécanismes psychologiques.' Tworuschka (2011: 117) reached more or less the same conclusion: 'Ottos Grundthese: Religion fängt mit sich selber an. Sie ist eine eigenständige Größe, nicht von anderen psychischen oder sozialen Gegebenheiten ableitbar.'
33 Lanczkowski (1978: 39): 'Wesentlich ist das folgende: die Einführung des Begriffes beruht auf der Intention, die Selbstständigkeit der Religion herauszustellen und damit zugleich die Unmöglichkeit, sie aus nichtreligiösen Erscheinungen ableiten und begründen zu wollen.'
34 Sharpe (1986: 166) sarcastically added that Otto's requirement of personal faith on the part of the scholar of religion or his reader is 'surely an odd request to make in a work of comparative religion', but this qualification for working in the field of the study of religions was not at all odd in the context of earlier religious phenomenology and has been advocated, under various guises, by most, if not all of its main protagonists.
35 Cf. James (1995: 199): 'For Kristensen there can be no doubt that the depth of one's interpretation [of religion] depends upon the nature and breadth of one's own religious apperceptions.'
36 Kristensen (1960: 15–18).
37 Kristensen (1960: 10).

38　Kristensen (1960: 6).
39　Kristensen (1960: 14).
40　Kristensen (1960: 13).
41　Strenski (2006: 176). Similar conclusions have been reached Capps (1995: 125), according to whom 'true phenomenological approach should supplant all interpretations that function reductionistically'. For a detailed analysis of Kristensen's critique of reductionism, see James (1995: 175–200).
42　Waardenburg (1978: 244).
43　Waardenburg (1997b: 264).
44　Van der Leeuw (1938: 80): 'eines der merkwürdigsten Bücher, die je geschrieben wurden'; on the next page, *Das Heilige* is hailed as 'geniales Buch' (ibid., 81). Van der Leeuw also accepted Otto's definition of the Sacred as 'ganz Andere', cf. Van der Leeuw (1963: 681).
45　Waardenburg (1997b: 271): 'Was van der Leeuw mit «Macht» andeutet, ist von Söderblom, Rudolf Otto und auch Friedrich Heiler als «Heiliges» gefaßt und von Otto systematisch durchdacht worden.'
46　Van der Leeuw (1938: 82): 'Otto ist nicht müde geworden, immer wieder vor der "Epigenesis" in jeder Form zu warnen, die Selbstständigkeit und Eigengesetzlichkeit des religiösen Erlebnisses gegen jeden Versuch der Ableitung aus anderen Motiven zu schützen.'
47　Cf. Waardenburg (1978: 236). James (1995: 274–75) wondered whether, according to Van der Leeuw, an atheist (or a non-believer) would be able to say anything meaningful about religion and concluded that this question would be a non-starter for Van der Leeuw since in his view every single human being is in his or her deepest nature *homo religiosus* (Eliade will eventually adopt this line of argument as well): 'Van der Leeuw had already stated that nothing concerning religion or faith can be known without existential engagement. Yet he is saved from considering such a person by his claim that in one way or another one's perspective is always religiously determined because the human person is *homo religiosus*. As with the case of Kristensen's appeal to the *sui generis* feature of religion, the difficulty here is the evident origin of the notion of humanity as *homo religiosus* in a theological doctrine of man.'
48　Van der Leeuw (1926: 4): 'Es gilt hier nicht einen Kausalzusammenhang festzustellen (den könnte man ja überhaupt nicht «nacherleben»), sondern in den Zusammenhang des Bewusstseinsstroms hineinzudringen, der sich in quantifizierenden, zählenden oder messenden, von aussen herantretenden Versuchen nicht «erfassen» lässt, sondern nur von innen heraus verstehen. Es gilt hier dieses ungebrochene Ganze in seiner Ganzheit auf sich wirken zu lassen.'
49　Van der Leeuw (1926: 6): 'Er analysiert intuitiv, nicht rationell; er hat es nicht mit den empirisch fassbaren Erlebnissen zu tun, sondern mit den unmittelbar verständlichen Erlebnissen in ihrer Wesensallgemeinheit.'
50　Van der Leeuw (1926: 8).
51　Van der Leeuw (1926: 10); Van der Leeuw (1963: 675).
52　Waardenburg (1978: 200–01).
53　Waardenburg (1978: 201).
54　Van Baaren (1973: 46); Bolle (1984: 318); Capps (1995: 131–32), cf. also Tworuschka (2011: 193–94): 'Trotz des von der Leeuw so hoch gehalten Prinzipes der *epoché* finden sich in seiner Phänomenologie viele ausgesprochene bzw. verdeckte Wert- und Wahrheits-urteile.'
55　Van der Leeuw (1963: 684).

56 Van der Leeuw (1963: 688).
57 Strenski (2006: 191). Capps (1995: 129) identified in Leeuw's writings an 'opposition to reductionistic treatments of religion's essence'.
58 Waardenburg (1997a: 30).
59 Capps (1995: 132): 'The aesthetic quality of *Religion in Essence and Manifestation* is the vehicle through which a phenomenological account became a doxology – a doxology to the God Christians worship.'
60 Scheler (1933: 367): 'Denn eben weil man hier den Wahrheitsanspruch der Religion mehr oder weniger *zurückwies*, wurde die Religion den Positivisten nichts als eine Gruppe psychischer Erscheinungen, die man zu beschreiben, kausal zu erklären und im höchsten Falle als eine bestimmte Stufe im Prozesse der Anpassung des Menschen an seine Umwelt auch teleologisch (im biologischen Sinne) zu begreifen habe.' English translations by B. Noble.
61 Scheler (1933: 373): 'Gewiß gibt es neben der (atheistischen) erklärenden sog. Religionspsychologie [...] noch eine ganz andere Untersuchungsrichtung, die wir am besten bezeichnen als: *Konkrete* Phänomenologie der religiösen Gegenstände und Akte.' For a more detailed analysis of Scheler's phenomenology of religion, see Kelly (1997: 157–75).
62 Scheler (1933: 371): 'Da ein religiöses Objekt seinem *Wesen* nach nur durch und in einem Akte des *Glaubens* seine mögliche Realität aufzuweisen vermag, ist für alle diejenigen, die den je betreffenden Glauben an eine religiöse Wirklichkeit nicht besitzen, die *Voraussetzung* gar nicht erfüllt, unter der eine erlebbare Einwirkung des religiösen Gegenstandes auf die Seele beobachtet und erkannt werden kann. Es ist z. B. klar: Niemand kann die seelischen Erlebnisse, die eine fromme Beiwohnung eines Katholiken bei der hl. Messe auslöst, irgendwie auch nur *beschreiben* wollen, der den *Glauben* an die reale Gegenwart Christi im Abendmahl nicht besitzt.'
63 Frick (1928: 19–26).
64 Frick (1928: 12): 'Die Ehrfurcht aber von dem, was unter uns ist, die auch das Niedrige, das Leid und den Tod als göttlich anerkennt, ja noch Sünde und Verbrechen als Fördernis des Heiligen verehrt, das ist das Letzte und Höchste, das Christentum.'
65 Frick (1928: 134): 'Hält sich also vergleichende Religionswissenschaft innerhalb ihres fest umschränkten Bezirkes, so bedeutet sie nicht nur keine Gefahr für die theologische Selbstbesinnung, sondern stellt sich vielmehr als unentbehrliche Disziplin aktueller Theologie dar.'
66 Under the influence of Söderblom's thinking, Heiler eventually converted to Protestantism, but he upheld much of Catholic dogmatism; thus, his confessional allegiances remain slightly obscure, cf. Tworuschka (2011: 198–99).
67 Pye (1997: 278).
68 Heiler (1921: 22): 'Wer niemals selbst einen religiösen Impuls gespürt hat, wird nie in die an Wundern und Rätseln so reiche Welt der Religion eindringen.'
69 See Mensching (1959) and Goldhammer (1960). Mensching (1959: 18–19) included the Sacred in the *definiens* of religion twice: '... erlebnishafte Begegnung mit dem Heiligen und antwortendes Handeln des vom Heiligen bestimmten Menschen ...'; in Goldhammer (1960: *passim*), the term appeared in the title to every single chapter of the second part of his work, cf. 'Umgang mit dem Heiligen' (Chapter V), 'Heilige Gemeinschaft' (Chapter VI), 'Die Welt vor dem Heiligen' (Chapter VII), 'Das Heilige und der Tod' (Chapter VIII), cf. further Tworuschka (2011: 308).
70 Heiler (1961: 16): 'Die fünfte methodische Forderung ist die phänomenologische Methode: vom φαινόμενον gilt es zum εἶδος, zum Wesen vorzustoßen. Die

Erscheinungen sind nur zu untersuchen um des Wesens willen, das ihnen zugrunde liegt, und im Blick auf dieses.'
71 Heiler (1961: 17): 'Was vor allem nottut, ist *Ehrfurcht* vor aller wirklichen Religion.'
72 Heiler (1961: 17): 'Das nächste Erfordernis ist *persönliche religiöse Erfahrung*. Ohne sittliches Gefühl kann man nicht Ethik treiben, [...] ohne Religiosität im weitesten Sinne des Wortes nicht Religionswissenschaft.'
73 Heiler (1961: 17): 'Das dritte Erfordernis ist das *Ernstnehmen des religiösen Wahrheitsanspruches*: man kann nicht Religion recht verstehen, wenn man sie als Aberglaube, Illusion, als Popanz abtut. [...] Alle Religionswissenschaft ist letztlich Theologie, insofern sie es nicht nur mit psychologischen und geschichtlichen Erscheinungen, sondern mit dem Erlebnis jenseitigen Realitäten zu tun hat.'
74 Pye (1997: 285): 'Sie [sc. Religionswissenschaft] wird zu einer Art liberaler, philosophischer Theologie.'
75 King (1984: 66).
76 Wach was interested mainly in sociology of religion (one of his most famous works bears the very title, namely *The Sociology of Religion*, published in 1944), but, as Cox (2006: 173) pointed out, 'Wach's sociology of religion was phenomenological through and through.'
77 Flasche (1997: 301).
78 Whaling (1984: 231); Smart (1973: 60). Wach (1950: 115) considered the works of Söderblom, Otto and Van der Leeuw as 'neue Phase in der Entwicklung unserer Forschung'.
79 Wach (1944: 13–14).
80 Wach (1950: 119): 'Es gibt nichts Peinlicheres als den hilflosen Versuch, religiöse Texte oder Denkmäler zu interpretieren durch jemand, der nicht weiß, was Ehrfurcht und heilige Schauer sind, oder für den diese Zeugnisse menschlichen Suchens nach der Vereinigung mit der letzten Wahrheit nur äußerliche Zeugnisse des Empfindens "seelisch kranker" oder zurückgebliebener Menschen sind.'
81 Wach (1944: 14).
82 Wach (1968: 130).
83 Wach (1923: 34): 'Wir können und wollen uns also nicht allein auf die empirische Forschung hinweisen lassen, wir halten es für falsch, wenn gelegentlich gesagt wird, alle Versuche *explicite* herauszustellen, was notwendig *implicite* allein lebendig sei, seien nicht nur überflüssig, sondern auch schädlich.'
84 Wach (1951: 35–36): 'We must reject all theories of religion which conceive of it as the fulfilment which imaginative or crafty individuals have supplied for a subjective, that is illusory, need.'
85 Wach (1958: 12).
86 Wach (1968: 137). As Cox (2006: 175) argued, this relationship goes both ways and the participation of the scholar of religions on the 'foreign religious life' strengthens his or her own religious convictions: 'When the scholar describes and penetrates to the meaning of the social expressions of religion, the scholar's own religious impulse is fortified.'
87 Cf. e.g. Preston (2010).
88 Wach (1958: 9).
89 Wach (1958: 9), cf. also Wach (1968: 127–29).
90 Flasche (1997: 300): 'Religionswissenschaft dient nun dem Aufweis der natürlichen Offenbarung einerseits und der Hinführung aller unter dieser stehenden Religionen zu der speziellen Offenbarung in Jesus Christus als der höchsten Form der Selbstoffenbarung Gottes andererseits.'

91 Eliade is arguably one of the more contentious figures in the history of the study of religions, which is reflected also in variegated assessments of his legacy. An essentially positive view of Eliade was presented e.g. by Dudley (1977), who proposed to reform some of Eliade's more controversial methodological theses, but in a wider context considered his programme of the study of religions inspiring; Cave (1993) defended Eliade's concept of 'new humanism'; a more critical assessments are those of McCutcheon (1997, see esp. 74–100), McCutcheon (2001b) or Dubuisson (2005); Ellwood (1999: 79–126) focused on the influence of Eliade's political and ideological views on his scholarly output. In the realm of edited volumes, Idinopoulos – Yonan (1994, esp. 65–197), Rennie (2001) and Wedemeyer – Doniger (2010: 101–323) are among the most useful. The best recent account of 'Eliadology' and its dismantling is that of Ambasciano (2019: 93–144).

92 Strenski (2006: 309): 'one of the most influential comparativists and interpreters of religion in the twentieth century'; Cox (2006: 177): 'no figure has exercised such an extensive influence over the academic study of religions in North America, and arguably elsewhere, as Mircea Eliade.'

93 Eliade (1949); Eliade (1995).

94 Eliade (1959: 88).

95 Berner (1997: 344): 'Eliade kein Historiker sei, sondern ein Vertreter der Religionsphänomenologie'. The same conclusion has been reached by Meslin (1973: 147), Cox (2006: 187) or Pals (2015a: 231). Bianchi (1975: 186), drawing on Pettazzoni, asked with respect to Eliade 'why religion, as such, should be absolutely antipathetic to history'; Strenski (2006: 312) concluded that 'Eliade is flat out opposed to the historical study of religion'.

96 Whaling (1984: 219): 'it is clear that Eliade's way of doing comparative religion is based not so much upon objective empirical criteria but rather upon his own underlying presuppositions.'

97 For a detailed description of this method, see Eliade (1969: 57–64).

98 Strenski (2006: 326): 'Eliade does keep faith with phenomenology's assertion of the autonomy of religion, but he does so in the most extreme way by declaring his methods of studying religion absolutely autonomous.'

99 Olson (1992: 23): 'It is Eliade's conviction that no humanistic discipline should conform to models taken from the natural sciences.'

100 Eliade (1965: 15). Eliade (1969: 23) held in high regard Otto's concept of the study of religions as the last bastion of values on the backdrop of the corrupted and secularized modern West: 'Otto is important also for other reasons: he illustrates in what sense history of religions could play a role in the renewal of the contemporary Western culture.'

101 Eliade (1961: 6). Cf. also Kitagawa (1959: 21): 'To be sure, Eliade is aware that there are no purely religious phenomena, because no phenomenon can be exclusively religious. But we agree with him that this does not mean that religion can be explained in terms of other functions, such as social, linguistic, or economic.' Pals (2015a: 230, 254) considered the rejection of reductionism to be one of the axioms of Eliade's approach.

102 Eliade (1969: *preface*, pages not numbered): 'In the most radically secularized societies and among the most iconoclastic contemporary youth movements (such as a "hippie" movement, for example), there are a number of apparently nonreligious phenomena in which one can decipher new and original recoveries of the sacred – although, admittedly, they are not recognizable as such from a Judeo-Christian

perspective.' Eliade's concept of 'latent religiosity' has been analysed in more detail by Capps (1995: 142), Cox (2006: 186) and Pals (2015a: 252–53).

103 Eliade (1969: 97–99). Cf. also Rennie (1996: 258): 'Eliade's system cannot support the valorization of any exclusive religion, but rather of religion itself, of religiousness, which he perceives to be a human universal. His thought is inherently, almost *a priori*, pluralist. It thus militates against "areligiousness" as a form of self-deception [. . .], but it cannot militate for any specific form of religion.'

104 King (1984: 113).

105 Eliade (1969: 67): 'In brief, the history of religions affirms itself as both a "pedagogy", in the strong sense of that term, for it is susceptible of changing man, and a source of creation of "cultural values", whatever may be the expression of these values, historiographic, philosophic, or artistic.'

106 Van Baaren (1973: 45).

107 Leertouwer (1973: 80).

108 Honko (1979: xxiii).

109 Whaling (1984: 280). Wahling (1985: 16) also considered the use of *epoché* to be a 'mainstream tendency' in the study of religions.

110 Gerardus van der Leeuw was the president of the first congress in 1950 and Geo Widengren assumed the same position in years 1960 and 1965; Jouco Bleeker has been active as a secretary in the years 1950–1965, cf. King (1984: 49) and Sharpe (1986: 267–93).

111 Especially the seventies of the past century announced a renewal of interest in the methodology of the study of religions. Jacques Waardenburg founded the series *Religion & Reason*, publishing monographs dedicated largely to the methodology of religious studies. Waardenburg himself contributed to the series with a classic 1973 compilation *Classical Approaches to the Study of Religion*, reprinted as Waardenburg (1999); Günter Lanczkowski collected one year later a volume of essays dedicated to theory and methodology of the study of religions under the title *Selbstverständnis und Wesen der Religionswissenschaft* in an important German series *Wege der Forschung* (Lanczkowski 1974); and numerous edited volumes dedicated largely to methodology appeared, cf. e.g. Bianchi, Bleeker and Bausani (1972); Van Baaren and Drijvers (1973); Honko (1979).

112 King (1984) mapped this conflict in some detail.

113 Bianchi (1975: 170). Bianchi in this context thematized and criticized especially the so-called 'Marburg school' (i.e. Hauer, Otto, Heiler and Benz; ibid., 170–77).

114 Pettazzoni (1959: 66): 'Religious phenomenology and history are not two sciences but are two complementary aspects of the integral science of religion [. . .]'; see further the editorial to the very first issue of the newly founded journal of IAHR, *Numen*, in Pettazzoni (1954a), reprinted also in Pettazzoni (1954b: 215–19). Similar conclusions were reached by Meslin (1973: 151–52) and, on part of the phenomenologists, by Lanczkowski (1980: 50): 'Die Lösung des Konfliktes dürfte in einer möglichst engen Verbindung der Religionsphänomenologie mit der Religionsgeschichte zu erblicken sein.' See now also Ambasciano (2019: 82–90).

115 Drijvers (1973: 61).

116 Bianchi (1975: 4). Cf. also Bianchi (1961: 78): 'Au contraire, nous sommes convaincus que déjà une recherche historique objective donnera des indications positives que la portée ontologique des faits religieux est inéliminable et irréductible et que – sans elle – les faits seraient *de fait* méconnus.'

117 Radcliffe-Brown (1952: 154).

118 Evans-Pritchard (1965: 101).

119 Jackson (1985: 221).
120 Evans-Pritchard converted to Catholicism in 1944, cf. Schnepel (1997: 306) and Pals (2015a: 265). As Jackson (1985: 205) argued, it would be hard to deny that his conversion directly influenced his approach to religion.
121 Pals (2015a: 286).
122 Larsen (2014: 222): 'E. B. Tylor was the Christian who lost his faith through studying anthropology; the Turners were the agnostics who found their Christian faith through studying anthropology. The Frazer chapter likewise corresponds to the chapter on Douglas. Both Sir James Frazer and Dame Mary Douglas advanced these theses through a bold use of the comparative method. Both wrote in a lively manner that allowed their works to reach a wider audience. Frazer, however, sought to use general anthropological theories to undermine the case for Christianity, while Douglas advanced broader anthropological categories in order to make the claims of the Church more compelling.'
123 Rappaport (1999: 2): 'Nevertheless, the claim that elements of religion may have been indispensable to humanity's evolution may seem to threaten to subordinate the more abstract, rarefied and meaning-laden aspect of human life to so coarse a utilitarian interpretation that its deep meaningfulness is rendered invisible and inaudible. No such reduction is intended, nor will it take place. Neither religion "as a whole" nor its elements will, in the account offered of them, be reduced to functional or adaptive terms. An account of religion framed, *a priori*, in terms of adaptation, function or other utilitarian assumption or theory would, moreover, and paradoxically, defeat any possibility of discovering whatever utilitarian significance it might have by transforming the entire inquiry into a comprehensive tautology. The only way to expose religion's adaptive significance (should such there be) as well as to understand it "in its own right" is to provide an account that is "true to its own nature".'
124 Biezais (1979: 145) described Bleeker as a 'loyal champion of Van der Leeuw's phenomenological method', but he did emphasize also the fact that Bleeker did not accept Van der Leeuw's main methodological premises uncritically, a point that has been also made by Sharpe (1986: 236) and Cox (2006: 126). Lanczkowski (1978: 25) considered Bleeker to be Van der Leeuw's most devoted disciple. Bleeker (1959) is a good summary of his methodological approach.
125 Bleeker and Widengren (1969; 1971). The two-volume work has been subject to significant criticism; see e.g. King (1984: 60): 'If the editors wanted a survey of the history of religions which would at the same time present the unity of religion and reveal its structure, this goal has not been achieved.' Similar critique has been levelled on *Historia Religionum* by Drijvers (1973: 59–60).
126 Bleeker (1979: 175). The same requirement is formulated by Bleeker also in his other texts; see e.g. Bleeker (1971: 646).
127 Bleeker (1979: 176).
128 Bleeker (1979: 177).
129 Bleeker (1975: 32). However, elsewhere – namely in *Historia Religionum* (co-edited with Widengren) – Bleeker (1971: 649) sounded quite sceptical when pondering the prospects of the study of religion to ever fulfil these pragmatic goals: 'Some believe that the purpose of the science of religion and also of the history of religions is to create a form of religion that satisfies the needs of the modern, spiritually-uprooted man. Others expect that the history of religions should be used to promote mutual understanding among the faithful and thus strengthen world peace. Our branch of study cannot satisfy these demands.'

130 Widengren (1969).
131 Leertouwer (1973: 80) criticized the arbitrariness of chosen thematic and typological distributions, but he otherwise regards Widengren's work highly, cf. also Lanczkowski (1980: 49): 'Sie verbindet in einer idealen Weise die philologisch-historische mit der systematischen Forschung.'
132 According to a classification proposed for a pre-War phenomenology by Eva Hirschmann, Husserl's doctoral student and nowadays unfortunately a rather forgotten scholar, Widengren would belong to 'purely descriptive phenomenologists of religion' alongside Chantepie de la Saussaye, cf. Hirschmann (1940: 113).
133 Cf. e.g. Whaling (1984: 264): 'what he [scil. Widengren] actually produced was not phenomenological typology but comparative suggestions and analogies arising out of inductive history.'
134 King (1984: 91).
135 Widengren (1945: 103–05), drawing on Walter Baetke's work *Das Heilige im Germanischen*, cf. Baetke (1942). Baetke (1952: 139), who was otherwise quite critical of Otto, argued strongly against a possibility of a naturalistic explanation of the origins of religion: 'Die Wissenschaft kann über den Ursprung der Religion so viel oder wenig feststellen wie über den Ursprung des Menschen oder der Welt.'
136 Widengren (1968: 259): 'Jedoch scheint es, daß dieses Prinzip der *epochè* auch von Gelehrten, die sich zu ihm bekannten, recht unvollkommen verwirklicht worden ist.'
137 Widengren (1945: 113): 'Der Ursprung der Religion liegt jenseits des wissenschaftlich Erforschbaren; wir können uns lediglich eine ungefähre Vorstellung von den ältesten vorstellbaren Formen der Religion machen. Der Versuch, den Ursprung der Religion zu finden, muß ebenso aufgegeben werden wie die alten evolutionistischen Methoden.' This line of argument has been accepted also by Lanczkowski (1978: 19): 'Evolutionismus, insbesondere seitens der Ethnosoziologie, langanhaltend und hartnäckig der Religionsgeschichte Schemata zu oktroyieren versucht, in denen sich die Tendenz äußerte, die Religion natürlich erklären und damit doch letztlich als Religion überwinden zu wollen'; cf. further Lanczkowski (1980: 88–90).
138 Smart (1973: 20).
139 See esp. Cox (2006: 131–36).
140 Smart (1973: 55–7) criticized esp. Cantwell Smith, as well as Wach and Eliade (ibid., 64–67).
141 Smart (1973: 74–91) rejected the main theses of Berger's *The Sacred Canopy* (Berger 1969), which was primarily focused on reductive explanation (religion was to be explained away as a projection of sorts).
142 Smart (1973: 110–34).
143 Smart (1973: 139–40).
144 Cited in Kitagawa (1959: 3).
145 Frick (1950: 125): 'Angesichts dieser Voraussetzungen erhebt sich in allem Ernst die Frage, ob die eingangs skizzierte "Neutralität" wissenschaftlicher Haltung weiterhin ausreicht, insbesondere auch, ob sie noch in der traditionellen Form sittlich gerechtfertigt ist.'
146 Frick (1950: 132): 'Damit haben wir, wenn nicht alles täuscht, die entscheidende religiöse Frage der Gegenwart vor Augen, und mir scheint, daß unser Kongreß über die bloße neutrale Information und Forschung hinaus daran mitwirken sollte, eine lösende Antwort – und das kann ja nur die richtige Antwort, die sachlich begründete Antwort sein – auf die Frage zu finden.'
147 Benz (1966).

148 Benz (1959: 131): 'the history of religions and the history of the development of the religious consciousness must be seen as coterminous with the history of salvation. If the revelation in Christ is really the fulfilment of time, then it must also be the fulfilment of the history of religions.'
149 Heiler (1959: 139); Mensching (1959: 371–79) also argued for the inner unity of religions in this sense.
150 Heiler (1959: 160).
151 Smith (1959: 42). On the next page (ibid., 43) Cantwell Smith explained in some detail the workings of such a principle put into practice: 'Non-Christians might write an authoritative history of the church but however clever, erudite, or wise they can never refute Christians on what the Christian faith is. The only way that outsiders can ever ascertain what Christianity is, is by inference from Christian work or art or deed; and they can never be better qualified than those Christians to judge whether their inferences are valid. Indeed, some Christians have maintained that in principle no one can understand Christianity who does not accept it. We do not go so far, but we recognize substance in this contention. We recognize also that a similar point applies to all religions. Anything that I say about Islam as a living faith is valid only in so far as Muslims say "amen" to it.'
152 These events are reported by Schimmel (1960). The declaration has been signed – ironically enough – also by Mircea Eliade, of course not because he would not have believed that the ultimate goal of the study of religion is to elevate people above the secular misery of their lives, but because he rejected the specifically Christian flavour of most of these ecumenical invitations.
153 Werblowsky (1959: 180): 'Wenn man die vielen Äußerungen zu diesem Thema liest und hört, gewinnt man oft den Eindrück, daß eine Welt, die von Haß, Zwietracht, gegenseitigem Mißtrauen und häßlichen Leidenschaften aller Art zerrissen ist, nur des sanften Lichts der Religion und der Ausstrahlung ihres Geistes milder Weisheit und Toleranz bedürfe, um wieder sicher auf den Pfad der Vernunft und des echten menschlichen Fortschritts zurückzufinden.' For a direct relation of the events that transpired in Marburg, see Werblowsky (1960), who considered as one of the most dangerous risks for the future of the IAHR congresses (and the future of the study of religions in general) 'the basically theological preoccupation of many participants, wrongly claiming to attend as *Religionswissenschaftler*' (ibid., 218).
154 Van Baaren (1973: 50).
155 Leertouwer (1973: 80): 'Concepts such as "the power" and "the sacred" are in fact mystifications and therefore not suitable for the explanation of empiric data. Moreover they stand in the way of other explanations: when cultural anthropologists and other sociological researchers try to elucidate religious data by establishing what asymmetrical human relationships they reflect, and precisely who or what is inviolable (sacred), i.e. when they attempt to find an empirical foundation for the power and the sacred, they are only too often reproached from the phenomenological side with being reductionists. This reproach is ridiculous: every science reduces reality, and phenomenology does so too.'
156 Drijvers (1973: 73) argued from a behavioural perspective that we can observe only reactions, never thoughts and beliefs of the believers.
157 Bianchi (1975: 18): 'In fact, apart from the fact that it would render futile all historical studies on ancient religions, the fact remains that the followers of a religion, although they may be representative of the average feeling of its adherents today, are not

always good interpreters of their religion as it was in the past, or of the historical interpretative problems closely allied with it.'
158 Werblowsky (1979: 536): 'They want to seize "the faith of the believer". This is surely a laudable programme though I doubt, on theoretical and methodological grounds, that it is capable of realization. But even if it were, the realization would bring us to a first level only. Once this particular job is accomplished, we have to move on to another level of analysis, and here I don't mind a bit if the believer fails to recognize himself, but vigorously object and protest. His protests will not bother me in the least, for my analysis (unlike the initial phenomenological account) is not judged by the believers but only by my professional colleagues. It is they who also have the right to judge whether an allegedly "reductionist" analysis is wrong, or possibly right.'
159 Waardenburg (1978: 127).
160 Waardenburg (1978: 128).
161 Waardenburg (1978: 129).
162 Waardenburg (1973: 58).
163 Waardenburg (1973: 9–21; 91–137). Waardenburg's methodological theses were criticized, e.g. by Drijvers and Leertouwer (1973: 166–68).
164 Van Baaren (1973: 42).
165 Pye (1979: 534).
166 Similar conclusion has been reached recently by Ambasciano (2019: 55–91) in his overview of the same period in the history of the study of religions (the chapter is, quite appropriately, termed 'Goodbye Science').
167 Wulff (1985: 32).
168 Jackson (1985: 179).
169 Cf. especially Wiebe (1980), who argued in favour of the return of the naturalistic explanation into the study of religions and for the necessity to abandon the *sui generis* approach. Wiebe (ibid., 228) admitted on one hand that history and phenomenology of religion had, in its post-classical form, achieved some interesting results, but immediately added that '[t]he "scientific" or "critical" study of religion, however is out for more than simple description: its goal is "explanation". [...] To summarize then, I think it fair to say, first, that the descriptivist approach to the study of religious phenomena is bound to achieve a meager result. And, second, one can [...] draw the modest conclusion that even though "religious truth" is something more than mere propositional truth, [...] it is nevertheless intimately (necessarily) connected with propositional truth thereby making it subject to objective discussion, analysis, and criticism.' On reductionism, see also the edited volume by Idinopulos – Yonan (1994).
170 For a critique of AAR, see e.g. Wiebe (2000: 235–75).
171 Wiebe (2000: 250).
172 Good recent summaries of the achievements of the CSR are e.g. McCauley (2017: 117–50); Lawson (2017); Whitehouse (2017) and Schjødt – Geertz (2017). Slone – McCorkle (2019) is an extremely useful collection of key CSR empirical studies.

6 Cognitive science of religion (1): Methodology

1 Descartes, *Regulae ad directionem ingenii* (AT X, 371): *Necessaria est methodus ad rerum veritatem investigandam*. English translation by E. Anscombe and P. T. Geach.

2 Schleiermacher, *Über die Religion*, 48: 'Mein Endzweck ist gewesen, in dem gegenwärtigen Sturm philosophischer Meinungen die Unabhängigkeit der Religion von jeder Metaphysik recht darzustellen und zu begründen.'
3 Pals (1987: 268).
4 Strenski (2006: 89). The differentiation of 'comparative' and 'theoretical' theology is paralleled in Cantwell Smith's differentiation of 'cumulative tradition' and 'faith'. It is symptomatic that both Müller and Cantwell Smith rejected reductionism and argued in favour of the *sui generis* interpretation of the religious experience.
5 Müller (1893: 16): '... there is in man a third faculty, which I call simply the faculty of apprehending the Infinite, not only in religion, but in all things; a power independent of sense and reason, a power in a certain sense contradicted by sense and reason, but yet a very real power, which has held its own from the beginning of the world, neither nor reason being able to overcome it, while it alone is able to overcome in many cases both reason and sense.'
6 Schleiermacher, *Über die Religion*, 63.
7 Otto (1963: 8).
8 Eliade (1965: 15).
9 Eliade (1961: 6).
10 Caillois (1959: 11); Eliade (1965: 15).
11 Kristensen (1960: 23).
12 McCutcheon (1997: 66).
13 Analytical philosophy and existentialism are often seen as incommensurable entities, but, as Kaufmann (1958: 12) observed, 'this lack of mutual understanding and this downright contempt for each other are due largely to what both camps have in common: both have repudiated most traditional philosophy and thus lost common ground; both have messianic overtones, and rival messiahs can scarcely be expected to be sympathetic toward each other; and both are often all but untranslatable'.
14 It is impossible to discuss all relevant literature here, see further Tweyman (1995: 485–577); Irwin (2008: 614–17); Putnam (2002: 7–27); Botros (2006); Cohon (2008: 25–28); Mackie (1980: 61–63); MacIntyre (2004: 68–80). For the aims and purposes of this work, it is not essential to discuss, and much less to arrive at a conclusion with respect to many facets of the 'is-ought' dichotomy. What is important to highlight is that the differentiation of facts and values as mutually incommensurable categories has been widely accepted in the twentieth-century philosophy, see e.g. Brown (2008: 229).
15 Hume, *A Treatise of Human Nature*, 302.
16 It would be incorrect, however, to simply conflate Hume's thesis and Moore's naturalistic fallacy argument. As Sylvester (1990: 157–84) argued, Moore's thesis on the irreducibility of the good in any natural property is distinct from Hume's 'is-ought' dichotomy. Compare also Baldwin (1990: 86): 'Moore's theory is often taken to involve a "fact/value" gap of the kind Hume is supposed to uphold; indeed it is common to accuse those who think that one can derive "ought" from "is" of committing the naturalistic fallacy. But since Moore holds that obligations are derivable from intrinsic values, and that there are necessary connections between the properties definitive of kinds of states of affairs and their intrinsic value, it follows that he is committed to necessary "is/ought" connections.'
17 Moore (1959: 11).
18 Hutchinson (2001: 39).
19 Thompson (1999: 447).

20 Moore (1959: 48).
21 Compare Christensen (2011: 805): 'The ethical point of the *Tractatus* lies in the realization that philosophy can only show the reality of ethics, not contribute to it, and by insisting on a second, unwritten part of the *Tractatus*, Wittgenstein marks his refusal to add to such contributions.'
22 Wittgenstein (1922: §§ 6.41; 6.42; 6.421): 'Wenn es einen Wert gibt, der Wert hat, so muss er ausserhalb alles Geschehens und So-Seins liegen. [...] Darum kann es auch keine Sätze der Ethik geben. [...] Es ist klar, dass sich die Ethik nicht aussprechen lässt. Die Ethik ist transzendental.'
23 Churchland (2011: 188).
24 Harris (2010) provided some possible paths for bridging facts and values; Churchland (2011: 8) considered 'Hume's law' to be 'unfortunate'; Hauser (2006: 96) argued that 'although we must be cautious not to equate these different levels of analysis, it is also a mistake to reject outright what our intuitive moral psychology brings to the table'.
25 Nietzsche, *Götzen-Dämmerung* (*KSA* VI, 98): 'Man kennt meine Forderung an den Philosophen, sich jenseits von Gut und Böse zu stellen – die Illusion des moralischen Urtheils *unter* sich zu haben. Diese Forderung folgt aus einer Einsicht, die von mir zum ersten Male formulirt worden ist: dass es gar keine moralischen Thatsachen giebt. Das moralische Urtheil hat Das mit dem religiösen gemein, dass es an Realitäten glaubt, die keine sind. Moral ist nur eine Ausdeutung gewisser Phänomene, bestimmter geredet, eine Missdeutung.' English translation by J. Norman.
26 Heidegger (2006: 42): 'Das "Wesen" des Daseins liegt in seiner Existenz'.
27 Sartre (1970: 17).
28 Nietzsche, *Die fröhliche Wissenschaft* (*KSA* III, 481).
29 Sartre (1970: 34–36).
30 Sartre (1943: 674): 'Mais le résultat principal de la psychanalyse existentielle doit être de nous faire renoncer à *l'esprit de sérieux*. L'esprit de sérieux a pour double charactérisitique, en effet, de considérer les valeurs comme des données transcendantes indépendantes de la subjectivité humaine, et de transférer le caractère «désirable», de la structure ontologique des choses à leur simple constitution matérielle.' One could argue that the evolutionary anti-realism came to the same conclusion. That much is true, but the evolutionary anti-realism arrived at this conclusion on a very different train of thought. It does not argue (as Wittgenstein or Sartre do), that objective morality is impossible, because people do not have any human nature, but precisely because they do have one – namely, a collection of largely unconscious predispositions which explain most of our moral emotions.
31 Heidegger (2006: 49): 'Das fehlende ontologische Fundament kann auch nicht dadurch ersetzt werden, daß man Anthropologie und Psychologie in eine allgemeine Biologie einbaut.'
32 Gould (1997); Gould (2002).
33 Gould (2002: 6).
34 Weinberg (1994: 249).
35 Gould (2002: 64).
36 See e.g. Nomamul Haq (1999: 831), in review for *Nature*: 'Gould still comes out as the winner. He has not written this work for specialists; it is aimed rather at the general reader. It operates on a common-sense level and, ultimately, it makes sense. So, whatever issues one may legitimately have with its "details", in its general thrust this small book is heftier than the volumes of inaccessible, jargon-wrapped material produced every year by some academic historians and philosophers.'

37 Harris (2010: 6).
38 Artigas, Glick and Martínez (2006: 21–23).
39 Dawkins (2006: 429–37).
40 For a classical work discussing 'rites de passage', see Gennep (1960), cf. also Favazza (1996: 22–46) and Yu (2012) for Chinese religions. Kelly (2011: 312) concluded that the aspects are not mere marginalities of various religions, but 'significant similarities between considerations of self-harm in various Buddhist and non-Buddhist traditions, including qualified acceptance of certain forms of self-harm, the identification of altruism as a motivation for self-harm or suicide, the use of self-immolation as a form of political protest'.
41 One may mention here the fate of Origenes, see Eusebius Caesariensis, *Historia ecclesiastica* 6.8. Kushner (1967) showed that these cases are reported even in modern times.
42 Schopenhauer died in 1860, one year after the publication of Darwin's *opus magnum*. Magee (1997: 98) noted that one of the last texts that the German philosopher read was the review of the *On the Origin of Species* in *The Times* and with respect to the potential importance of Darwin's theses for Schopenhauer's philosophy 'an active sense of loss is induced by the fact that he was denied the time in which to consider them'. Mill's essay *On Nature* has been published in 1874, but its elaboration may be dated before 1859. Nietzsche's relation to Darwin is a serious doxographic problem. Nietzsche clearly knew Darwin's theory, but he tried very hard to distance himself from 'Darwinists', a tendency that is strongly present especially in his later work *Ecce Homo*, which, in words of Kaufmann (1974: 66), amounts to a 'vitriolic denunciation of any Darwinistic construction of the overman'.
43 Schopenhauer, *Die Welt als Wille und Vorstellung* (ZA IV, 680): 'Tummelplatz gequälter und geängstigter Wesen, welche nur dadurch bestehn, daß eines das andere verzehrt, wo daher jedes reißende Thier das lebendige Grab tausend anderer und seine Selbsterhaltung eine Kette von Martertoden ist.'
44 Nietzsche, *Jenseits von Gut und Böse* (KSA V, 21–22): '"Gemäss der Natur" wollt ihr *leben*? Oh ihr edlen Stoiker, welche Betrügerei der Worte! Denkt euch ein Wesen, wie die Natur ist, verschwenderisch ohne Maass, gleichgültig ohne Maass, ohne Absichten und Rücksichten, ohne Erbarmen und Gerechtigkeit, fruchtbar und öde und ungewiss zugleich, denkt euch die Indifferenz selbst als Macht – wie *könntet* ihr gemäss dieser Indifferenz leben? Leben – ist das nicht gerade ein Anders-sein-wollen, als diese Natur ist?' English translation by J. Norman.
45 Mill, *Essays on Ethics, Religion and Society*, 385.
46 Adams (1992: 441).
47 This idea harks back to Callicles' argumentation in Plato's dialogue Gorgias, where he defends the identification of 'strong' with 'good' on one side and 'weak' with 'evil' on the other; see Plato, *Gorgias*, 483a; 483e–484a.
48 Huxley (1895: 75).
49 Huxley (1895: 81–3).
50 Darwin, *The Descent of Man*, 817–38; 867–81.
51 Singer (2011).
52 Hamilton (1996: 47–48).
53 Trivers (2002: 21–23).
54 An iterative version of Prisoner's Dilemma is defined by Axelrod (2006: 206–07) as a 'two-player game in which each player can either cooperate (C) or defect (D). If both cooperate, both get the reward R. If both defect, both get the punishment P. If one

cooperates and the other defects, the first player get the sucker's payoff, S, and the other gets temptation, T. The payoffs are ordered T > R > P > S, and satisfy R > (T+S)/2. [...] each move is worth less than the move before, by a factor of w, where 0 < w < 1. Therefore in the iterated game, the cumulative payoff to either of two players who always cooperate with each other is $R + wR + w^2R \ldots = R/(1 - w)$'.

55 Axelrod (2006).
56 Ridley (1997: 75–80).
57 Trivers (2002: 53). As Henrich and Henrich (2006: 230) later noted, Tit-for-Tat is not as robust as originally thought.
58 Alexander (1987: 85).
59 Amotz and Zahavi (1997: 229).
60 Nowak (2006).
61 Dawkins (2006a).
62 Hamilton (1996: 14).
63 Williams (1966: 255).
64 Williams (1993).
65 Dawkins (2006a: 139).
66 Dawkins (2006a: 201).
67 Dennett (1995: 18).
68 Dawkins (2006a: ix).
69 Haidt (2006: 235).
70 For a defence of the group selection, see esp. Wilson – Sober (1994) and Nowak (2011: 81–94). Kundt (2015: 35–64) provides a critical assessment of the use of group selection theories to explain sociocultural phenomena (like religion) and concludes, quite rightly so, that these accounts 'fail to meet the fundamental principles of neo-Darwinian theory of natural selection and thus do not reach the criteria of its legitimate extensions'.
71 Alexander (1974: 336).
72 De Waal (1996: 15).
73 Henrich – Henrich (2006: 221).
74 De Waal (2006: 58).
75 Ridley (1997: 20).
76 Wilson (2000).
77 Wilson (1998a: 72).
78 Snow (1993: 2).
79 Dilthey, *Einleitung in die Geisteswissenschaften*, 4–21. See further Talmont-Kaminski (2013: 23–27).
80 Boas (1938: 167).
81 Lowie (1917: 66).
82 Benedict (2005: 14).
83 Durhkeim (1960: 22): 'La société est une réalité *sui generis*; elle a ses caractères propres qu'on ne retrouve pas, ou qu'on ne retrouve pas sous la même forme, dans le reste de l'univers.'
84 Geertz (1973: 49).
85 Chruchland (2011: 17).
86 Lieberman (2011: 530).
87 Tooby and Cosmides (1992: 23).
88 Wilson (1997: 17).

89 Space does not permit to track these later developments in any detail; see Lyotard (1979) for a programmatic rejection of 'grand narratives'; well-argued rebuttals of postmodernist and constructivist attacks on science are found in Koertge (1998); Weinberg (2001); Boghossian (2006) and Sokal (2008).
90 Wright (1995: 345). For a more expansive list of the borderline hysterical *ad hominem* reactions on Wilson and his work, see Pinker (2002: 108–12).
91 Frank (1988: 44).
92 Boyer (1994: 295).
93 Bausell (2007).
94 Haidt (2009: 280): 'I think E. O. Wilson deserves more credit than he gets for seeing into the real nature of morality and for predicting the future of moral psychology so uncannily. He is in my pantheon, along with David Hume and Charles Darwin.' Haidt (2008: 69) even admitted that his social-intuitionist model is 'essentially Wilson's theory of moral judgment but with more elaboration on the social nature of moral judgment'.
95 Wilson (2000: 3).
96 Wilson (2000: 562).
97 Wilson (1998b: 62). Philosophers, of course, protested. Singer (2011: 68) argued that Wilson might be overstating his case here, yet it is undeniable that Singer himself (quite in line with what Wilson suggested) considered the evolutionary viewpoint in Ethics as essential. Frans de Waal on one hand agreed with Singer (De Waal 1996: 10–11); on the other hand, he triumphally concluded at the end of his work *Good Natured* that 'we seem to be reaching a point at which science can wrest morality from the hands of philosophers' (ibid., 218).
98 Wilson (1998b: 64).
99 Wilson (1998a: 281).
100 Churchland (2011: 3).
101 Hauser (2006: 425).
102 Geertz (2008a: 348).
103 Pyysiäinen (2004: 21–27).
104 Lawson and McCauley (1990: 8) argued in one of the founding monographs of the CSR that 'themes in this book are likely to interest scholars from at least five different disciplines, viz., philosophy, religion, anthropology, psychology and linguistics. We owe much to the work of researchers from each of those fields'. Whitehouse (2004: 174) concluded that the cognitive approach to religion is, 'of necessity, a cross-disciplinary project'; Tremlin (2006: 174) emphasized a 'truly interdisciplinary profile' of CSR and the same holds true for evolutionary ethics. Indeed, as Haidt (2001: 80) put it, '[a]ll of the disciplines that study the mind should contribute to the debate'.
105 Boyer (1994: 286).
106 This citation opens Gombrich's famous monograph *Art and Illusion*, cf. Gombrich (2000: 3).
107 Pinker (1999: 210).
108 Tremlin (2006: 146).
109 Pinker (1999: 24): 'the mind is not the brain but what the brain does, and not even everything it does, such as metabolizing fat and giving off heat.'
110 Tooby and Cosmides (1992).
111 Haidt (2001: 826).

112 Wilson (2002: *passim*) understood religions as adaptive units created via group selection; Bering (2006) argued that at least some religious experiences have adaptive character; Sosis (2009) introduced the 'religion-as-adaptation' as an alternative to the 'religion-as-by-product' approach.
113 Gould and Lewontin (1979).
114 Boyer (2003); Pyysiäinen and Hauser (2009: 108) argued that 'although religion did not originally emerge as a biological adaptation, it can play a role in both facilitating and stabilizing cooperation within groups, and as such, could be the target of cultural selection'.
115 Pyysiäinen – Hauser (2009: 108).
116 Wilson (1997: 235): 'Moral and political philosophy must begin with a statement about human nature [...] we cannot escape the fact that we have a nature – that is, a set of traits and predispositions that set limits to what we may do.'
117 Boehm (2012: 98).
118 Lawson and McCauley (1990: 184).
119 Boyer (2001); Atran (2002). On a necessity of integrating CSR and evolutionary theorizing, see Kundt (2018).
120 For this strawman fallacy, see e.g. Lewontin, Rose and Kamin (1984).
121 Sperber (1996).
122 Frank (1988: 64–65).
123 Atran (2002: 11).
124 Boehm (2012: 237).
125 Hauser (2006: 72–74); Chomsky (1995: 25–26).
126 Chomsky (1995: 25–26).
127 De Waal (1996).
128 Guthrie (1993: 52); Harrod (2009).
129 See Barrett (2012) on children and religion and Bloom (2013) on children and morality.
130 McNamara (2009); Farah (2010).
131 Andersen (2001: 275).
132 James (2011: 208).
133 Lawson *in* Tremlin (2006: xi).
134 Cicero, *Tusculanae disputationes*, 5.4.10.

7 Cognitive science of religion (2): Terminology

1 Augustinus, *Confessiones*, 11.14: *Si nemo ex me quaerat, scio; si tamen quaerenti explicare velim, nescio.*
2 McKinnon (2002: 67) argues that the participants of the debate know what religion actually is, they only have difficulties in arriving at a connotative definition; likewise; Pals (1987: 261) notes that there is a pre-theoretical 'Vorverständnis' on what religion is. In contrast, Martin (2009: 167) strictly denies that there is any singular pre-theoretical understanding of the term in question, because its use changes both diachronically and synchronically within the social context. Fitzgerald (1996: 215) concurs by noting that the term 'religion' and its derivatives are used with multifarious meanings, 'often with little to no critical reflection'.
3 Kishimoto (1961: 236) considers the definition of the religion to be 'an indispensable premise for the study of religion'; Horyna (2011: 9, 15) states in a recent major study of

the methodological bases of the study of religion that any attempt to define religion is an instance of methodological failure.
4   Pals (1987: 272); an almost identical expression is used by Harrison (2006: 137); Guthrie (2007: 64), very much in the same spirit, argues that 'the problems of definition are also the problems of the theory'.
5   For a book-length treatment, see Feyerabend (1986); the main theses of methodological anarchism, succinctly summarized by its creator himself, can be found in Feyerabend (1999: 113–18).
6   Few scholars of religion seriously consider the possible social ramifications of their studies. Among those who do are, for instance, Wax (1984: 6); Asad (2001: 220); McKinnon (2002: 67); Harrison (2006: 145–47).
7   McCutcheon (1995: 306). Donald Wiebe has been one of the most prominent critics of what he identifies as the infiltration of confessional (mainly Protestant) theology into religious departments under the disguise of the 'science of religion'; see especially Wiebe (1999: 69–90).
8   Dawkins (2009: 436).
9   To include just one example from the distant past, when one of the most prominent philosophers of the early twentieth century, Bertrand Russell, objected to the war machine of the First World War, he was promptly dismissed from Trinity College (1916) and later even imprisoned (1918), while many Quakers could appeal to the status of conscientious objector on the grounds of their religious commitments.
10 Gunn (2003: 191).
11 This has also been pointed out by Comstock (1984: 500).
12 Guthrie (1993: 197).
13 Barrett (2000: 29).
14 Boyer (2001: 7). Boyer introduces this statement as a 'finding of anthropology', but it resonates well with the concept of minimally counter-intuitive agents, around which his discussion of religion gravitates.
15 Atran (2002: 4).
16 Pyysiäinen (2003: 227).
17 Whitehouse (2004: 2).
18 Slone (2004: 68). A few pages on (ibid., 71), Slone elaborates further: 'A religion involves postulations and presumptions that superhuman agents exist, and any religious system that includes such features counts, in most people's minds, as more like a religion than one that does not (note that definitions follow from theories).'
19 Barrett (2011: 130).
20 Engler and Gardiner (2009: 22).
21 Lawson and McCauley (1990: 124). In a follow-up study, McCauley and Lawson (2002: 20), the so-called 'principle of superhuman agency' is upheld without any serious modifications: 'Religious rituals, while engaging the same representational resources, possess a distinctive feature that marks them off not only from everyday actions but also from the other sorts of routine religious actions we mentioned above (such as standing at various points during a worship service). That distinctive feature is that religious rituals (in our technical sense) always presume an end point to such causal or rational explorations. In religious ritual representations things come to an end. Causal chains terminate; reasons find a final ground. In short, the buck stops with the gods.'
22 Smith (2004: 165). This statement, if applied to the history of the study of religion, is patently false. As we will see presently, Durkheim strongly opposed the definition of religion based on gods or supernatural beings and his approach has generated a strong

following. For instance, Sloan Wilson (2002: 222), states that '[w]ithout wishing to vindicate Durkheim in all respects, I think this definition is on the right track because it acknowledges the functional nature of religion'. Bellah (2011: 1), in a recent landmark study of ancient religions, makes use of what he himself calls a 'simplified Durkheimian definition', which is almost indistinguishable from the original: 'Religion is a system of beliefs and practices relative to the sacred that unite those who adhere to them in a moral community'.

23 There is no space or need to discuss here the perennial problem of Socratic and Platonic scholarship, namely the attribution of the philosophical theses found in Platonic dialogues to either Socrates or Plato. *Euthyphro* is an early elenctic dialogue (cf. Vlastos 1991: 46) and therefore usually associated with historical Socrates. More to the purpose of this article, it is to be noted that Aristotle (*Metaphysica*, 1078b28–29) credits Socrates with the first use of general definitions (τὸ ὁρίζεσθαι καθόλου).

24 Plato, *Euthyphro*, 4e5–6.

25 Plato, *Euthyphro*, 6d10–11.

26 Euthyphro defines piety variously as 'that which is dear to gods' (τὸ μὲν τοῖς θεοῖς προσφιλὲς, Plato, *Euthyphro*, 6e10); 'what all the gods love' (ὃ ἂν πάντες οἱ θεοὶ φιλῶσιν, ibid., 9e1–2); 'what is just' (δίκαιον, ibid., 11e5); and as the 'knowledge of sacrifice and prayer' (ἐπιστήμην τινὰ τοῦ θύειν τε καὶ εὔχεσθαι, ibid., 14c4–5).

27 More technically, as McPherran (1996: 39) notes in a discussion of *Euthyphro*, 'Socrates generally seems to be after (ideally) a definition of the form "F is(=) D," where there is a relation of mutual entailment and extensional identity between the definiendum F and definiens D, and where the definiens gives a complete *explanation* of why any individual action or thing x is F, an explanation that will put one in a position to recognize any F-instance x as being an F-instance.' An essentialist definition of this type, notwithstanding some modifications, has exerted profound influence throughout the history of Western thought. For instance, Spinoza, in his *Tractatus de intellectus emendatione* (XIII, 95) still defends an essentialist approach: 'In order to be called perfect, a definition will have to explain the innermost essence of the thing [that is being defined]' (Definitio *ut dicatur* perfecta, *debebit intimam essentiam rei explicare*).

28 Harrison (2006: 133–34).

29 Goody (1961: 144). According to Wax (1984: 14), patriotism would undoubtedly be classified as a religion, should we adopt Durkheim's definition.

30 Tylor (1871: 383–84).

31 Preus (1987: 132).

32 Durkheim (1960: 41–45).

33 Orrù – Wang (1992: 59), consider Durkheim's portrayal of Buddhism to be 'seriously defective'; in contrast, Southwood (1978: 363), on the basis of his own fieldwork, states the following: 'I found that what Durkheim wrote about Buddhism was substantially true, and impressively perceptive: his case against the applicability of the theistic conception to Buddhism requires little revision.'

34 Southwood (1978: 368). This is not the only problem of Durkheim's argument. Penner (1971: 96–97), drawing on a previous work by one of the most influential philosophers of science in the twentieth century, Carl Hempel, argued against the inherent functionalism of Durkheim's position – very successfully, in my opinion.

35 Durkheim (1960: 65).

36 Orrù – Wang (1992: 49–50). The term 'Sacred' has eventually become (in)famous, especially in its use by Mircea Eliade. Goody (1961: 151), denies that the sacred/profane dichotomy is present in all cultures; McCutcheon (1997: 23) criticizes the

'phantom objectivity' of the term which veils its ideological underpinnings; Horyna (2011: 31) objects to the *a priori* character of the 'Sacred', which makes serious scientific scrutiny impossible.
37 Cf. Soames (2003: 213): 'Wittgenstein's views about metaphysical simples and the way they combine to form atomic facts are among the darkest and most implausible aspects of the *Tractatus*.'
38 Wittgenstein (2001: §§ 66, 68).
39 Smith (1991). Asad (2001: 205) considers Cantwell Smith's work to be the first to take a resolute stand against the essentialist definitions of religion. Yet it has to be noted that Cantwell Smith does so largely in order to pursue his own theological agenda and deconstructs the term 'religion' only to mark a distinction between faith (the core of religion) and what he terms 'cumulative tradition' (the mere outward manifestations of faith). McCutcheon (1995: 286) argues plausibly that, for Cantwell Smith, religion is an '*a priori* mystery' and the sole aim of his intellectual strategy is to eliminate reductionism; Asad (ibid., 220) sees in *The Meaning and End of Religion* a 'pietistic conception of religion as faith that is essentially individual and otherworldly'; for McKinnon (2002: 69), the book represents 'a kind of intellectual Protestant imperialism'; likewise, Fitzgerald (2003: 240), notes that 'much of the book reads as a Protestant manifesto for a world theology'.
40 Smith (1991) characterizes the term as 'confusing', 'unnecessary', 'distorting' (ibid., 50); 'unnecessary', 'much less serviceable and legitimate than they once seemed' (ibid., 121); 'imprecise' and 'liable to distort' (ibid., 125).
41 For the rejection of the essentialist definition of religion see, for instance, Horton (1960: 211); Southwood (1978: 371); Asad (1983: 252); Herbrechtsmeier (1993: 15); McKinnon (2002: 81); Harrison (2006: 148). The family resemblance approach to the definition of religion has been advocated by McDermott (1970: 390); McKinnon (2002: 80); Hick (2004: 4); Harrison (2006: 149); Comstock (1984: 507–15), comes to a similar conclusion via an analysis of literary theory and postmodernism; according to him, the definition of religion should function as an 'open text' which only approximately marks the starting point of the study. Smith (1982: 1–8) provides a seminal introduction to polythetic classification in the field of religious studies.
42 Southwood (1978: 370–71) lists items such as godlike beings, sacred/profane dichotomy, salvation, ritual, faith-based beliefs, ethical code, mythology, oral or scriptural tradition, religious elite; Dow (2007: 8–9), mentions three basic behavioural modules, namely 'a cognizer of unobservable agents', 'a sacred category classifier' and 'public sacrifice'; Martin (2009: 165) uses the list compiled by William Alston, which includes belief in supernatural beings, sacred/profane dichotomy, ritual, moral code, religious feelings, prayer, anthropocentric worldview and the like; Harrod (2011: 344) includes items such as worship, ceremony, numinous feelings, holiness, the sacred and sacrifice.
43 Martin (2009: 165–66) differentiates between three competing approaches to the non-essentialist definition of religion: (1) a list of key properties, which are not necessary and sufficient; (2) the family resemblance approach described above; (3) a random collection of disconnected items, which Martin terms 'grab-bag use' and argues that contemporary use of the term 'religion', within the context of our language game, corresponds to this last interpretation. Harrod (2011: 346–47), on the other hand, thinks that there is a well definable inner structure and complementarity within the different items of the polythetic class, which is 'more than an *ad hoc* list', since 'components appear to be governed by an internal logic of recombinations'.

44 In his *Zarathustra* (KSA IV, 74), the concept of the 'will to power' is already present in full, accounting for what different nations and cultures accept as values: 'Eine Tafel der Güter hängt über jedem Volke. Siehe, es ist sein er Überwindungen Tafel; siehe, es ist die Stimme seines Willens zur Macht.' In later writings, the descriptive concept becomes normative, for instance, in the *Antichrist* (KSA V I, 170), Nietzsche asks: 'Was ist gut? – Alles, was das Gefühl der Macht, den Willen zur Macht, die Macht selbst im Menschen erhöht. Was ist schlecht? – Alles, was aus der Schwäche stammt.'

45 Lock – Strong (2010: 245) note that the work of Nietzsche has proved to be an important influence for Foucault and the 'attraction was to Nietzsche's view of history not as a process that unfolds in a rational, progressive way, developing ever higher forms of reason, but through the exercise of power'.

46 Cf. *El idioma analítico de John Wilkins in* Borges (1974: 708).

47 Foucault (1966: 7–11).

48 Wittgenstein (2001: § 1). It is worth noting that indexes to this work do not even mention the word 'Macht' or 'power'.

49 Foucault (1972: 108).

50 Bourdieu (2001: 64).

51 Fitzgerald (1996: 216); cf. also Fitzgerald (2003: 250). Fitzgerald even argues that the conception of 'language games' is in itself an ideology, as has been the imperialistic Western essentialist concept of religion. Elsewhere in the same paper (ibid., 230), he argues that 'if "religion" can be everything, it is nothing at all' – yet if this is true, does the same thesis not hold for ideology? Because it surely seems that for Fitzgerald, everything is ideologically coloured and there are no such things as 'pure facts', only facts in relation to a theory, which is itself motivated mostly by practical (political, ideological), not epistemological needs.

52 Hick (2004: 4); Comstock (1984: 507) correctly points out that 'ultimate concern' can be 'everything from hedonism to political fanaticism'.

53 McCutcheon (1997: 183).

54 Fitzgerald (2003: 217). This translates directly to the institutional study of religions, where the power structures operate analogically to the religions themselves. For instance, Fitzgerald (2000: 19) notes that 'ecumenical theology in the form of phenomenology has significant and de facto institutional control over the meaning of the category religion'.

55 McCutcheon (1997: 191).

56 Lease (2009: 132).

57 Lease (2009: 130).

58 Geertz (2008: 347).

59 Locke, *An Essay Concerning Human Understanding*, 48–103, spends considerable time and effort (in fact, the whole of Book I of his *Essay Concerning Human Understanding*) to pulverize any glimpse of the existence of innate ideas. The myth of the mind as a 'blank slate' is still going strong in the twenty-first century – see, for instance, an overview of the problem by Pinker (2002).

60 Kant, *Kritik der reinen Vernunft*, B XIX.

61 Kant, *Kritik der reinen Vernunft*, B XVII–XVIII. English translation is that of N. Kemp Smith.

62 Chomsky showed that behaviourist premises about the nature of acquisition of natural languages are untenable, see Chomsky (2002). *Syntactic Structures* were hailed as 'the snowball which began the avalanche of the modern "cognitive revolution"' by David W. Lightfoot in the introduction to the work just cited (ibid., v).

63 Chomsky (1995: 14). The CSR is reluctant to postulate a separate 'religious module'; as Tremlin (2006: 74) notes, 'no special domain for religious thought need be postulated'.
64 Cosmides and Tooby (1992: 91). Both authors apparently recognize the connection to Kant's philosophical views, since they term this approach 'evolutionary Kantian position' (ibid., 70).
65 It must be noted that most of the scholars working in the cognitive tradition do not consider religious ideas to be necessarily adaptive. It is more likely that they are only by-products or 'spandrels'. E.g. Atran (2002: 264) concludes that 'religions are not adaptations and they have no evolutionary functions as such'.
66 Boyer (1994: 111). Given the origin of these representations, one could also speak about 'evolutionary universals', yet the term has been taken by Parsons (1964: 339) to denote 'any organizational development sufficiently important to further evolution that, rather than emerging only once, it is likely to be "hit upon" by various systems operating under different conditions'.
67 Preus (1987: 138) notes that Tylor was 'impressed by the unity of humankind' and that the very 'validity of the comparative method for establishing developmental sequences depended on the essential sameness of the human capacity and the human condition'. In a similar manner, Strenski (2006: 112) argues that for Tylor, '[h]uman nature was something fundamentally universal, constant, and invariant'.
68 Gazzaniga, Ivry and Mangun (2009: 398).
69 Pinker (1995: 436).
70 Jerry Fodor, who popularized the term 'modularity' in his *The Modularity of Mind: An Essay on Faculty Psychology* (1983), concludes that 'there are good reasons to doubt that MM is true: Taken literally, it verges on incoherence. Taken liberally, it lacks empirical plausibility', cf. Fodor (2000: 55). More constructive criticism can be found in Sterelny (2003: 177–210), who argues that although the modular theory of language in particular might be essentially sound, it should not pass as a blueprint for other presupposed mental modules.
71 Mithen (1998: 65–78).
72 LeDoux (2002: 86).
73 Spiro (1966: 96).
74 Horton (1960: 204); yet he is largely in agreement with the definition proposed by Tylor. Southwood (1978: 367), considers any theistic definition to be 'too superficial'; Wax (1984: 10), rejects the dichotomy of 'natural' and 'supernatural' as a Western intellectual construction dependent on the idiosyncratic development of scientific knowledge (and therefore not applicable to cultures with different paths of sociocultural evolution); according to Herbrechtsmeier (1993: 5), 'the category "superhuman" is inherently flawed and should be abandoned'; McKinnon (2002: 65) considers the term 'supernatural' to be 'a very ambiguous concept'.
75 Pyysiäinen (2003: 163). See also a more elaborate discussion of Buddhist supernatural agents in Pyysiäinen (2009: 137–172), which, in addition to buddhas, also draws attention to other counter-intuitive beings, such as spirits (*yakkha*), giants (*asura*) or gods (*devas*).
76 For an illuminating discussion of the term 'universal' and its different meanings see Norenzayan and Heine (2005).
77 Strenski (1998: 358).
78 For instance, Boyer (2001: 276) notes that '[s]ince the services of literate religious groups *are* dispensable, the religious schools that do not yield some measure of

political leverage are very likely to end up as marginal sects, a process that has happened repeatedly in history'.
79 In the description of the two systems, I draw largely on Kahneman (2011: 19–105). For discussion of the dual processing of religious concepts, see Tremlin (2005: 69–83).
80 Tremlin (2006: 144).

8 Cognitive science of religion (3): Practical application

1 Vaňorný was an illustrious Czech translator of both Homeric epics and the epigram introduces his translation of the *Iliad*.
2 Pucci (1977: 1–44) and Arthur (1986) have examined invocations of the Muse in Hesiod (in particular, the enigmatic verses of *Th.* 27–28) by means of Derridean deconstruction, concluding that the poet's aim was to emphasize the inability of natural language to describe reality objectively and without distortion. Ferrari (1988: 68), in a critique of the aforementioned scholars, urges 'caution (at the very least) in the use of their metaphysical presuppositions and of the blunt instrument they provide for the analysis of Greek thought'. A semiotic interpretation of Hesiodean invocations has been offered by Calame (1982), cf. also Calame (1983) for a semiotic analysis of archaic Greek poetry in general. Narratological approaches have been fruitfully explored by De Jong 2004 (45–53), cf. also De Jong (2014) for a general perspective on narratology and classical studies. Elements of a cognitive approach are present in Minchin (2001: 161–80), who focused on the function of memory and shares little more than some important methodological principles with the present study.
3 Lesky (1999: 29). For a recent overview of the 'Homeric question', see e.g. Fowler (2004).
4 The oral origin of Homeric epics has been historically championed by Parry (1971) and Lord (2000); for a recent summary see e.g. Foley (1997).
5 Hom. *Od.* 24.60.
6 Hes. *Th.* 77–79. While it is undoubtedly true that the tradition of nine Muses reached almost canonical status in later Greek and Roman literature, Pausanias (9.29.2–3) and Plutarch (*Mor.* 744c1–2) have preserved a rather marginal strand of tradition that accepted three Muses, see also Van Groningen (1948: 289–96).
7 Otto (1955: 24–25); Barmeyer (1968: 64–5); Murray (2005: 152) & Murray (2008: 201–03); Hardie (2009: 15). For Camilloni (2008: 16), the Muses in Homer 'sono nove, eppure hanno un cuor solo, un'unica volontà'. Pötscher (1986: 18) proposed an interesting yet untestable hypothesis of an evolution from a single Muse to multiple ones. According to this author, every poet originally invoked a single Muse, yet seeing that there were other singers like him (each having his own personal Muse), the number eventually grew. Nisbet and Hubbard (1970: 283) noted that even as late as Horace (*Carm.* 1.24.3), 'the assignment of provinces [of the Muses] was still vague'.
8 Hom. *Il.* 1.604, 2.484, 2.594, 2.598, 2.761, 11.218, 14.508, 16.112; Hom. *Od.* 1.1, 8.63, 8.73, 8.481, 8.488, 24.60, 24.62. The last mention included here (Hom. *Od.* 24.62) is considered by some scholars to be a later interpolation, since it seems that this is the only instance of the term 'Muse' used to refer not to the goddess, but to the song itself, see Barmeyer (1968: 55, 62). This double meaning would be in line with remarks made by Murray (2005: 150), for whom the Muse is 'both a process and a product', yet,

barring this single dubious attestation, the Muse in Homeric epics and in Hesiod is exclusively a 'process'.
9   Hes. *Th.* 1, 25, 36, 52, 75, 93, 94, 96, 100, 114, 916, 966, 1022; *Op.* 1, 658, 662; *Sc.* 206.
10 Hom. *Il.* 1.1–8; Hom. *Od.* 1.1–10.
11 The integrity of the proem to the *Iliad* has been defended by Pagliaro (1955: 379), for whom 'appare chiaro che il proemio deve essere considerato interamente genuino'. See also Redfield (1979), who in some respects expanded on Pagliaro's observations.
12 Bassett (1923: 340) noted the 'striking likeness of the two proems'. For a detailed comparison, see Lenz (1980: 21–26), who argued that 'die Struktur der Einleitung keine Erfindung der Dichter von *Ilias* und *Odysee* ist, sondern auf eine vorhomerische hymnische und kultische Vergangenheit züruckblickt'. Edwards (1980: 4–5) considered the proem to the *Iliad* to be an already formalized 'type-scene'.
13 I am using masculine pronouns relative to the poet simply because I believe that the bards of the earliest Greek epic poetry were all male.
14 See e.g. Falter (1934: 12). Schleiser (1982: 139) somewhat sarcastically noted that '[p]armi les 115 vers de ce texte, il n'y en a pas un seul dont l'authenticité n'ait été contestée, et il y eut un temps où tenir pour «vrai» plus qu'une très mince partie du prologue était considéré comme un affront envers la science philologique'.
15 Friedländer (1914) was one of the first scholars to defend the integrity of the proem to the *Theogony* and one of the first to identify in it elements shared with religious hymns. His analysis was followed by Méautis (1939) and Accame (1963: 404). Clay (1989: 324) concluded that the 'overall unity of *Theogony* and the proem in particular has been established'; for Berlinzani (2002: 190), 'il proemio teogonico costituisca un'unità organica e coerente creata da una sola mano'.
16 An almost 'numerological' analysis of sorts was provided by Schwabl (1963); for a critique, see Lenz (1980: 126). More recently, Johnson (2006: 234) argued that some of the proem's puzzling aspects may be explained by its priamel structure. Verdenius (1972: 259) denied that the proem to Hesiod's *Theogony* could have been built on any elaborate structural patterns, but he did not deny its integrity. For him, the poet simply 'tried to combine the traditional elements of a hymn with the personal conception of the Muses'.
17 See in particular Rijksbaron (2009).
18 Some scholars, such as Marg (1957: 8), Maehler (1963: 36–37) and Kambylis (1965: 35), have argued that the entire introductory sequence (Hes. *Th.* 1–115) is best understood as a hymn. Von Fritz (1956: 35) is of the opinion that hymnic elements are present only in the second part of the proem, while Lenz (1980: 186–92) denied that the proem could be simply equated with a hymn. Minton (1962: 192) considered the entire proem to be an 'invocation in spirit'.
19 Falter (1934: 12); Lenz (1980: 131–81) differentiated the 'inner' (Hes. *Th.* 105–15) and 'outer' (Hes. *Th.* 1–104) proem, with the inner containing an invocation and the outer two separate hymns.
20 Van Groningen (1946: 290).
21 Hes. *Op.* 1–4.
22 Hom. *Il.* 2.484–93.
23 Minton (1962: 206) saw the Catalogue of Ships as 'originating in late Mycenaean'; Edwards (1980a: 82) shared this dating, noting that some toponyms attested in the Catalogue are not identifiable with any known settlements in the early Archaic age, and thus the Catalogue (or at the very least some of its parts) must have originated in an earlier period.

24 This is the opinion of Kirscher (1965: 8–9), who, however, resolutely denied that κλέος would imply a substantial lack of knowledge. His interpretation has been to the most part accepted also by Lenz (1980: 29–30). For Barmeyer (1968: 98), the singer positioned himself 'zwischen der göttlichen Allwissenheit und der menschlichen Unwissenheit'.
25 Scodel (1998: 178); Heiden (2008: 133).
26 Zellner (1994: 312–13), in opposition to the aforementioned interpretations, argued that 'there is nothing in Homer (other than 2.486!) to suggest that a κλέος is inherently unreliable, or requires independent confirmation to count as knowledge'. According to this author, the lines are to be read as an expression of awe towards the goddess, realized in a process where '[a]n ascription (or an implied ascription) of a property F to the gods is coupled with a denial of F to humans'.
27 As part of the 'minor' invocations, we may also add three sections of the *Iliad* (Hom. *Il.* 5.703–704, 8.273, 11.229–300) in which the singer asks a question without mentioning the Muse explicitly. According to Minchin (2001: 172–74), who termed these invocations 'faded', the questions are to be understood as being implicitly addressed to the Muse and the answers are to be taken as their replies.
28 Hom. *Il.* 2.760–62, 11.218–20, 14.508–10, 16.112–13.
29 Hes. *Th.* 965–68, 1021–22.
30 Hom. *Il.* 8.62–75, 477–91.
31 The term is that of Kambylis (1965).
32 Hom. *Od.* 8.63.
33 Hom. *Od.* 8.73.
34 Hom *Od.* 8.480–81; a few lines later, Apollo is included into the fold of possible inspirations as well, see Hom. *Od.* 8.488: ἤ σέ γε Μοῦσ' ἐδίδαξε, Διὸς πάϊς, ἤ σέ γ' Ἀπόλλων.
35 Hom. *Od.* 8.489. It is not entirely clear, however, what exactly the term κατὰ κόσμον means. Accame (1963: 272) translated it as 'secondo verità'; Barmeyer (1968: 125–26) was of the opinion that the term rather denotes congruent arrangement of particular pieces of information. For Svenbro (1976: 21), κατὰ κόσμον means 'dans l'ordre même où la querelle, selon Ulysse, s'est déroulée'. Verdenius (1983: 53) did not understand the term in epistemic categories, but rather as a 'correspondence between subject-matter of literature and its artistic representation', while adding that 'artistic appropriateness is not clearly distinguished from factual correctness'. Adkins (1972: 12–17), in a discussion of all of the attested instances of the word in Homeric epics, concluded that although κατὰ κόσμον in Homer does not necessarily and everywhere signify 'truth', in this particular instance it did.
36 Hom. *Od.* 22.347–48.
37 Katz – Volk (2000: 128).
38 Verdenius (1983: 22).
39 Ritoók (1989: 342).
40 Accame (1963: 387). A similar conclusion was also reached by Setti (1958: 150), for whom 'essere, noi diremmo, poeta originale che compone e «inventa» i suoi canti, ed essere ispirato dal dio, sono la stessa cosa'. See also Pötscher (1968: 12): 'Er [Phemios] bezeichnet sich ja nicht als Autodidakt; er will damit vielmehr sagen, daß seine Sangeskunst eine echte, d.h. eine auf die Gottheit zurückgehende Begabung, nicht bloß eingelerntes Zeug ist.'
41 Hes. *Th.* 22–34.
42 In spite of the oblique description of poetic creativity through literary characters, there is no good reason to doubt that the comments made by Demodokos, Phemios and

Odysseus reflect the views of the author(s) of the Homeric epics. As Verdenius (1983: 21) noted, for instance, 'Odysseus obviously represents the view of Homer himself when he says that the Muse has taught (ἐδίδαξε) singers their songs'.
43 Hes. *Th.* 31–32. All translations of Hesiod are those of Glenn Most.
44 Hes. *Th.* 22.
45 Hes. *Th.* 27–28.
46 This interpretation was proposed by Sikes (1931: 6), who found in these lines a 'rebuke to the Homeric singer, whose imagination is condemned as "lie"'. Similar conclusions have been reached by Maehler (1963: 40–42); Kambylis (1965: 63); and Verdenius (1972: 234). Neitzel (1980: 401) argued that ψεύδεα ἐτύμοισιν ὁμοῖα could not possibly refer to Hesiod's own poetry, and therefore the expression must refer to other poems (possibly the Homeric epics). For Arrighetti (1992: 47), the term 'non può che significare polemica antiomerica'.
47 Setti (1958: 157): '[i]l mondo eroico non è la loro «verità»'.
48 Svenbro (1976: 65, 70–71).
49 Snell (1958: 20). Notopoulos (1938: 472–43) even translated 'Muses' as 'Remainders'.
50 Barmeyer (1968: 106).
51 Stroh (1976: 112); Ritoók (1989: 340). According to Clay (1989: 328–29), Hesiod 'wisely refrains from making an explicit claim for the truthfulness of his theogonic song'; cf. also Belfiore (1985: 57): 'Hesiod says exactly what he means: the Muses, his Muses, are both lying poets and speakers of the truth. These two functions, however, do not produce confusion or ambiguity, but clearly mark off two different kinds of subject matter. On this interpretation, the proem to the *Theogony* does not open with an attack on unnamed rival poets or with vague praise of "fiction", but with a statement reflecting a view of myth very similar to that of Plato'. I find this reading of Hesiod through the lens of Plato to be strangely anachronistic. Stern-Gillet (2014: 40), who also tried to establish links between Hesiod's poetry and Plato, argued that the former 'placed the highest value, not indeed upon the truth of the poetic word, but on its ability to please and comfort'.
52 Heiden (2007: 171).
53 A similar conclusion, albeit one lacking a careful analysis of the term ὁμοῖος, was previously reached by Accame (1963: 407), who argued that the words are addressed to the audience of the shepherds who were insufficiently educated, and so Hesiod's poetry might seem to them to be a lie. The Muse always tells the truth and only to the uneducated might it seem to be a lie.
54 Maehler (1963: 14).
55 It is often claimed, for instance, that in the Homeric epics we do not find any 'ideological' agenda (while we do in Hesiod) and that their purpose is simply to delight their audience. On the contrary, it has been argued that Hesiod introduced a 'strong moral and religious bias', as Tigerstedt (1970: 170) observed. For Sikes (1934: 4), only in Hesiod is it true that 'the singer first becomes an inspired teacher, with a divine message to deliver'. Von Fritz (1956: 36) argued, correctly in my opinion, that these views are largely unfounded and denied that Hesiod was more 'moralizing' than Homer, since Xenophanes (DK 21 B 11) criticized them both to the same measure.
56 Sperduti (1950: 228).
57 For Murray (2005: 147), 'Homer's Muses are different from Hesiod's'; Stern-Gillet (2014: 27) concluded that the invocations in the Homeric epics and in Hesiod are 'markedly different overall'.
58 Maehler (1963: 35) argued with respect to Hesiod for 'durchaus unhomerische Selbstauffassung und das Verhältnis zu seinem eigenen Dichtertum'; Svenbro (1976:

72) saw in Hesiod 'rupture révolutionnaire avec la conception homérique de l'aède'. For Kambylis (1965: 16), 'Homer und die homerischen Sänger sind berufen, Hesiodos (und später Kallimachos und Properz) werden berufen'. As Barmeyer (1968: 93) showed, the verb ἐδίδαξαν, which Kambylis took as referring to a singular event in the past, may also be interpreted as 'ein wiederholtes Erscheinen'.

59 Van Groningen (1946: 289) noted that 'Hesiod's method is practically the same as Homer's way of thinking', but the argument in the present text does not require that this strong statement holds true. It is only necessary to assume, as Calame (1983: 262) does, that the proem to Hesiod's *Theogony* 'relève encore de ce qu'il est convenu d'appeler la poésie homérique'.

60 See e.g. Falter (1934: 3–4): 'nicht der Mensch, der Dichter schafft das Werk, sondern die Gottheit [...] [der Dichter] nur als Instrument in der Hand seines Gottes erscheint'.

61 DK 68 B 18. Democritus explicitly argued for the applicability of his theory to the Homeric epics (DK 68 B 21): Ὅμηρος φύσεως λαχὼν θεαζούσης ἐπέων κόσμον ἐτεκτήνατο παντοίων', ὡς οὐκ ἐνὸν ἄνευ θείας καὶ δαιμονίας φύσεως οὕτως καλὰ καὶ σοφὰ ἔπη ἐργάσασθαι. See also Horace's *ingenium misera quia fortunatius arte | credit et excludit sanos Helicone poetas | Democritus* [...] (*Ars* 295–97).

62 Plato, *Ion* 534e2-5: οὐκ ἀνθρώπινά ἐστιν τὰ καλὰ ταῦτα ποιήματα οὐδὲ ἀνθρώπων, ἀλλὰ θεῖα καὶ θεῶν, οἱ δὲ ποιηταὶ οὐδὲν ἀλλ' ἢ ἑρμηνῆς εἰσιν τῶν θεῶν, κατεχόμενοι ἐξ ὅτου ἂν ἕκαστος κατέχηται.

63 Otto (1955: 31): '[d]ie Sänger und Dichter hängen ganz von der Muse ab.'

64 Lenz (1980: 200): 'das Hervortreten Hesiods im Proöm keine Autonomie im Verhältnis des Dichters zu den Musen bedeutet, sondern nur das Verhältnis zum Publikum betrifft.'

65 Read (1964: 147).

66 See in particular Tigerstedt (1970). Verdenius (1983: 38) argued that 'there is an important difference between the archaic conception of inspiration and Plato's theory'; similarly, Murray (1981: 87) concluded that 'there is no evidence to suggest that the early Greek poets thought of inspiration in this way'; for Wheeler (2002: 34), 'bardship did not involve possession or μανία' and 'Muse-possession is unknown to Homer'. In the context of Presocratic philosophy, Kranz (1967: 7–8) distinguished three different models of the relationship between the Muse and the poet/philosopher: (1) complete dependence (Parmenides-type); (2) partial collaboration (Empedocles-type); and (3) autonomy (Heraclitus-type).

67 Marg (1957: 8) described it as 'bedeutungsvoll offen und schwebend'.

68 Podbielski (1994: 176), with Hesiod in mind, argued for 'ein aktives Zusammenwirken des Dichters und der Gottheit'; Murray (2008: 207) emphasized the 'collaboration entre le poète et la Muse', noting, however, that 'la Muse est le partenaire dominant'.

69 De Jong (2006: 191).

70 Katz and Volk (2000: 128), in a discussion regarding scholars defending a more active role for the poet, concluded that '[t]hese observations, though accurate, are in our opinion unable to prove that the concept of the poet as the Muses' mouthpiece was unknown in the Archaic period'. Satterfield (2011) attempted to show that the Muse is so dominant that she is, in fact, portrayed as actively changing the poet's original poetical aims. Stern-Gillet (2014: 42) argued for a 'close match' between the Socratic theory of poetry in Plato's *Ion* and Hesiod's theory of poetry in his *Theogony*.

71 Murray (1924: 96–97).

72 Calhoun (1938: 159).

73 Quite to the contrary, as De Jong (2006: 192) argued, an invocation of the Muse may function as an 'indirect advertisement of the narrator's extraordinary ability to memorize long stories crammed with names and events'. Notopoulos (1938: 468–73) further differentiated two distinct uses of 'memory', namely the 'use of memory as an end' (consisting of the celebration of κλέα ἀνδρῶν) and the 'use of memory as a means in the process of creation' (paralleling De Jong's 'advertisement of the narrator's ability to memorize long stories').
74 Maehler (1963: 38) wrote in this context about 'konventionelle Musenanruf des Epos'; Wheeler (2002: 37) about the 'force of convention' and 'literary conceit'; and Stern-Gillet (2014: 39) about 'stylistic artifice'.
75 Verg. *A.* 1.8–11: *Musa, mihi causas memora, quo numine laeso, | quidue dolens, regina deum tot uoluere casus | insignem pietate uirum, tot adire labores | impulerit. tantaene animis caelestibus irae?*
76 Dante, *Inf.* 2.7–9: 'O muse, o alto ingegno, or m'aiutate; | o mente che scrivesti ciò ch'io vidi, | qui si parrà la tua nobilitate.'
77 Milton, *Par. Lost* 1.1–8: 'Of Man's First Disobedience, and the Fruit | [...] | Sing Heav'nly Muse, that on the secret top | Of Oreb, or of Sinai, didst inspire | That Shepherd, who first taught the chosen Seed'.
78 Among those scholars who noticed this inconsistency, Kambylis (1965: 53) argued that '[e]ine lange literarische Tradition, die eventuell den Boden für eine solche Fiktion hätte vorbereiten können, fehlte'; Barmeyer (1968: 10) concluded that we can speak of the topicality of invocations of the Muse only from the Hellenistic age onwards. For Notopoulos (1938: 474) and Lenz (1980: 64), the transformation of the Muse into an artificial and topical element is connected with the move from oral to written poetry.
79 For the etymology of the term 'Muse', see Beekes (2010: 972–73); Setti (1958: 129); Barmeyer (1968: 53–54); Pötscher (1986: 15–17); and especially Camilloni (1998: 5–8), who collected both ancient and modern hypotheses.
80 Watkins (1995: 73).
81 For instance, Murray (2008: 203) argued that '[l]e mot Mousa n'a pas en soi de sens. Mousa n'est pas un nom abstrait, et il n'est pas possible de dire que les Muses personnifient un simple concept de la manière dont le fait, par exemple, leur mère Mnémosyne'.
82 As Detienne (1996: 52) observed, the 'truth' of the bard is 'a performative truth, never challenged or demonstrated'.
83 Hom. *Od.* 8.479–81: πᾶσι γὰρ ἀνθρώποισιν ἐπιχθονίοισιν ἀοιδοὶ | τιμῆς ἔμμοροί εἰσι καὶ αἰδοῦς, οὕνεκ' ἄρα σφέας | οἴμας Μοῦσ' ἐδίδαξε, φίλησε δὲ φῦλον ἀοιδῶν.
84 Hes. *Th* 30.
85 Hes. *Th.* 80–103.
86 Solmsen (1954: 5) considered this section of the *Theogony* to be unique in that it is 'the only instance in which Hesiod expanded the sphere of a deity whom he knew from tradition', noting that Hesiod's normal *modus operandi* was to create new deities for those domains of competence not covered by the Homeric pantheon. Barmeyer (1968: 150–51) explained the association of the Muse with rulers or judges by the reliance of the latter on exact information (and truly reliable information is provided only by a goddess). A similar view has been espoused by Roth (1976: 337), for whom the Muse is a patron over unwritten laws, since these, very similarly to epic poetry, are heavily reliant on the capacity of memory storage. For Scodel (1998: 190), Muses are patrons of rulers or judges because 'they are, like bards, neither self-serving in what they say nor servants of any faction, but of the good of all'.

87 Stodddard (2003: 13).
88 Finkelberg (1990: 296). A connection between invocation and epistemic justification has also been highlighted by Sperduti (1950: 230), who took the invocation in Hesiod's *Theogony* to be a 'plea for the infallibility of his disquisition on the genesis and nature of the gods and their universe'. This view is shared by Murray (1981: 91) ('a plea for the infallibility of the poem as a whole'). For Minton (1960: 293), the Muse functions 'to inspire confidence and belief', while for De Jong (2006: 192), she 'adds to the status of his [*sc.* the poet's] own work, more specifically, to its reliability'.
89 This line of thought is defended by Svenbro (1976: 32–35), but only for the Homeric epics, as he argued that Hesiod was already to a great extent autonomous of the audience or local ruler. Camilloni (1998: 12) likewise thought that, for the poet, the figure of the Muse is 'garanzia sociale per la sua figura professionale'.
90 Sperduti (1950: 237).
91 Arist. *Rh.* 1415a11–16: ἐν δὲ προλόγοις καὶ ἔπεσι δεῖγμά ἐστιν τοῦ λόγου, ἵνα προειδῶσι περὶ οὗ ἦ ὁ λόγος καὶ μὴ κρέμηται ἡ διάνοια: τὸ γὰρ ἀόριστον πλανᾷ: ὁ δοὺς οὖν ὥσπερ εἰς τὴν χεῖρα τὴν ἀρχὴν ποιεῖ ἐχόμενον ἀκολουθεῖν τῷ λόγῳ. διὰ τοῦτο "μῆνιν ἄειδε, θεά", "ἄνδρα μοι ἔννεπε, μοῦσα" [. . .].
92 *Schol. Vet. in Hom.* A b (be3) T ad *Il.* 2.484–487: ὑμεῖς γὰρ θεαί ἐστε <—οὐδέ τι ἴδμεν>: ὡς ἐπὶ ἐργώδη καὶ θαυμασίαν περιπέτειαν τὰς Μούσας παρακαλεῖ ὡς τὸν ἀκροατὴν διὰ τὸ μέγεθος ὄρεξιν ἔχειν καὶ συγγινώσκειν τοῖς ἐνδεέστερον λεγομένοις. εὐτελίζων δὲ τὴν ἰδίαν φύσιν τὴν ἀπὸ τῶν ἀκουόντων ἐπεσπάσατο εὔνοιαν.
93 Quint. *Inst.* 10.1.48: *age vero, non utriusque operis sui ingressu in paucissimis versibus legem prooemiorum non dico servavit sed constituit? nam benevolum auditorem invocatione dearum, quas praesidere vatibus creditum est, et intentum proposita rerum magnitudine et docilem summa celeriter comprehensa facit.*
94 Marg (1957: 10); Setti (1958: 146–47).
95 Minchin (2001: 90–91) argued that the poet's address to the Muse serves 'to indicate to his audience that he is about to undertake a more demanding passage'; for Minton (1960: 293), the Muses 'focus their [*sc.* the audience's] attention to what was to follow'; according to Murray (1981: 90), the Muses 'focus the attention of the audience at strategic points'.
96 Calhoun (1938: 162): 'the apostrophe to the Muses seems to mark the appearance of crucial and intensely dramatic moments in the action.'
97 West (2007: 92–93).
98 However, as Calame (1982: 23) rightly surmised, 'le caractère conventionnel du langage poétique n'était nullement exclusif de l'authenticité de l'éxperience dont il permet de rendre compte'.
99 Van Groningen (1946: 279).
100 Minton (1960: 292).
101 Wheeler (2002: 36–37).
102 Cf. Dodds (1951: 2), very well worth quoting in full: 'To some classical scholars the Homeric poems will seem a bad place to look for any sort of religious experience. "The truth is," says Professor Mazon in a recent book, "that there was never a poem less religious than the Iliad." This may be thought a little sweeping; but it reflects an opinion which seems to be widely accepted. Professor Murray thinks that the so-called Homeric religion "was not really religion at all"; for in his view "the real worship of Greece before the fourth century almost never attached itself to those luminous Olympian forms." Similarly Dr. Bowra observes that "this complete

anthropomorphic system has of course no relation to real religion or to morality. These gods are a delightful, gay invention of poets." Of course – if the expression "real religion" means the kind of thing that enlightened Europeans or Americans of to-day recognise as being religion. But if we restrict the meaning of the word in this way, are we not in danger of undervaluing, or even of overlooking altogether, certain types of experience which we no longer interpret in a religious sense, but which may nevertheless in their time have been quite heavily charged with religious significance?'

103 Verdenius (1983: 38). Similarly, Svebro (1976: 22) concluded that '[l]e rapport entre récit et réalité est donc compris de façon réligieuse'. The invocation of the Muse prefacing the Catalogue of Ships is defended as an expression of genuine religious sentiment by both Accame (1963: 263) and Zellner (1994: 314), the latter being of the opinion that the 'religious explanation of these texts is sufficient to explain what they say'.

104 Hesiod's *Dichterweihe* is considered by Falter (1934: 13) to be 'durchaus echt und möglich'; for Méautis (1939: 579) it is 'l'un des produits les plus purs et les plus profonds de la piété hellénique'; and for Otto (1955: 32), 'lebendiger Erfahrung mit die Göttinnen'; Fritz (1956: 32) and Lenz (1980: 148) view the proem to the *Theogony* as depicting 'ein wirkliches Erlebnis', while for Podbielski (1994: 179), it is 'ein Erlebnis vom Religionscharakter'.

105 Murray (1981: 90).

106 Minchin (2001: 70).

107 For a detailed analysis of the SSSM and its juxtaposition with the cognitive and evolutionary approaches, Tooby and Cosmides (1990) remains essential.

108 Sperber (1975: xi–xii). Sperber (1996) provides a general theory of the 'epidemiology of beliefs'.

109 Wilson (2000, first edition 1975).

110 Dawkins (2006, first edition 1976, 189–201).

111 Boyer (1994: 263–96) provides a well-informed, if slightly dated discussion of the three theories of cultural transmission mentioned above.

112 For a general overview, see Pinker (1997).

113 Pinker (1997: 24).

114 Brown (1991); Pinker (2002).

115 The origins of the cognitive approach to religious phenomena may be traced to Guthrie (1980) and especially Lawson and McCauley (1990). For a 'pre-history' of the approach, see Lane (2017). Among the best introductions to the CSR are Boyer (2001); Atran (2002); Pyysiäinen (2003); Barrett (2004); and Tremlin (2006). In the field of classical studies, Burkert (1996) ranks among the first to have highlighted the importance to classics of recent developments in the nature–culture debate, but he does not deal directly with the CSR. Larson (2016) provided a pioneering and well-realized application of the central tenets of the CSR to ancient Greek religion, which also contained a very brief but useful bibliographical essay concerning the CSR; see Larson (2016: 379–84).

116 Hypertrophy of agency detection in human beings has been well-known for decades, see, e.g., the now classical Heider and Simmel (1944). The concept of hyperactive agency detection as a cognitive module was introduced by Barrett (2000: 31–32), who in turn drew from the wealth of material collected in Guthrie (1993). For detailed discussions of this device, cf. Boyer (2001: 144–48); Atran (2002: 59–63); Barrett (2004: 31–44); Pyysiäinen (2004: 5–7); Tremlin (2006: 75–86); Dennett (2006:

108–14); Pyysiäinen (2009: 12–22). Barrett (2012: 15–42) documented that agency detection develops very early in childhood.
117 Guthrie (1993: 45).
118 As in the case of hyperactive agency detection, it is impossible to give a full account of minimal counter-intuitiveness here. See Boyer (2001: 51–91); Atran (2002: 83–113); Barrett (2004: 21–30) and Pyysiäinen (2009: 22–30) for a standard account. An invaluable recent overview of this concept, containing a healthy dose of criticism, may be found in Purzycki and Willard (2016).
119 Boyer (2001: 60–61).
120 Barrett (2004: 23). It is interesting to note that, although she does not use the concept of minimal counter-intuitiveness, Minchin (2001: 18, 208) echoed the idea in the statement that a good narrator tells a story that is (1) understandable and easy to follow for the audience (we could say that it is 'intuitive'), and (2) also contains 'an element of the unexpected' (we could say that it contains a 'counter-intuitive feature'). Compare this with Atran (2002: 107), who argued that a 'small proportion of minimally counterintuitive beliefs gives the story a mnemonic advantage over stories with no counterintuitive beliefs or with far too many counterintuitive beliefs' and 'such beliefs grab attention, activate intuition, and mobilize inferences in ways that greatly facilitate their mnemonic retention, social transmission, cultural selection, and historical survival'.
121 Hom. *Il.* 2.591–600: Οἵ δὲ Πύλον τ' ἐνέμοντο καὶ Ἀρήνην ἐρατεινὴν | καὶ Θρύον Ἀλφειοῖο πόρον καὶ ἐΰκτιτον Αἰπὺ | καὶ Κυπαρισσήεντα καὶ Ἀμφιγένειαν ἔναιον | καὶ Πτελεὸν καὶ Ἕλος καὶ Δώριον, ἔνθά τε Μοῦσαι | ἀντόμεναι Θάμυριν τὸν Θρήϊκα παῦσαν ἀοιδῆς | Οἰχαλίηθεν ἰόντα παρ' Εὐρύτου Οἰχαλιῆος· | στεῦτο γὰρ εὐχόμενος νικησέμεν εἴ περ ἂν αὐταὶ | Μοῦσαι ἀείδοιεν κοῦραι Διὸς αἰγιόχοιο· | αἳ δὲ χολωσάμεναι πηρὸν θέσαν, αὐτὰρ ἀοιδὴν | θεσπεσίην ἀφέλοντο καὶ ἐκλέλαθον κιθαριστύν. On the Thamyris story, see further Otto (1955: 47–49).
122 My discussion is a condensation of Boyer (2001: 150–67).
123 To use terms coined by Barrett (2002), fallible gods (e.g. Demeter eating part of Pelops' shoulder at Tantalus' infamous dinner party) are 'dumb gods', while infallible and omniscient gods with full access to information (such as the Muse) are 'smart gods'. That Olympian gods do not generally have full access to information is clear from the fact that they are often capable of playing tricks on each other – a fact highlighted in Xenophanes' critique of them, see DK 21 B 11: πάντα θεοῖσ' ἀνέθηκαν Ὅμηρός θ' Ἡσίοδός τε, | ὅσσα παρ' ἀνθρώποισιν ὀνείδεα καὶ ψόγος ἐστίν, | κλέπτειν μοιχεύειν τε καὶ ἀλλήλους ἀπατεύειν.
124 See e.g. Hom. *Il.* 2.485 (ὑμεῖς γὰρ θεαί ἐστε πάρεστέ τε ἴστέ τε πάντα) or Hes. *Th.* 38 (εἴρουσαι τά τ' ἐόντα τά τ' ἐσσόμενα πρό τ' ἐόντα).
125 Minton (1962: 190). Murray (1981: 91) focused on the problem of inspiration in the earliest Greek poetry and concluded that 'inspiration might consist largely of information'. For Snell (1959: 19), the Muse offered the singer 'wirklich nichts anderes als Erinnerung'; for Lenz (1980: 34), the goddess supplies 'kein theoretisches Wissen, sondern das dinghaft-konkrete Wissen des Augenzeuges'. The ideal of direct sensory perception was also emphasized by Stoddard (2003: 12), who concluded that '[t]he Muses grant poets the ability to make events seem to happen again before the eyes of the audience'. Accame (1963: 264) argued that the Muse provides 'dati di fatto', while for Minton (1962: 188); Roth (1976: 336); and Redfield (1979: 98), what the Muse transfers to the poet is 'information' plain and simple. Maehler (1963: 18–19) called it 'genaue, sachliche Berichterstattung' and 'genaue und zuverlässige Information'.

According to Minchin (2001: 166), the Muse grants the poet 'factual details' for his song. The only dissenting voice to the 'inspiration-as-information' camp is Pötscher (1986: 15), who, however, failed to present any substantive counterarguments.

126 Cf. Hom. *Il.* 11.219 (ὅς τις δὴ πρῶτος Ἀγαμέμνονος ἀντίον ἦλθεν); Hom. *Il.* 14.509–10 (πρῶτος βροτόεντ' ἀνδράγρι' Ἀχαιῶν | ἦρατ' [...]); Hom. *Il.* 16.113 (ὅππως δὴ πρῶτον πῦρ ἔμπεσε νηυσὶν Ἀχαιῶν).

127 Alcm. frg. 27 Campbell: Μῶσ' ἄγε Καλλιόπα θύγατερ Διὸς | ἄρχ' ἐρατῶν Ϝεπέων, ἐπὶ δ' ἵμερον | ὕμνωι καὶ χαρίεντα τίθη χορόν.

128 Murray (1981: 89). A more cautious formulation may be found in Murray (2005: 155): 'Muses are, amongst other things, personifications of the psychological faculties that constitute inspiration, but this still leaves many questions to be answered'. I hope to have answered at least some of these questions in this chapter.

129 According to Nietzl (1980: 394), the information/inspiration comes to the poet 'plötzlich und unvermittelt, d.h. sie kommt gewissermaßen von "außen", ohne daß der Erkennende (Vernehmende) etwas dazu täte'. For Lenz (1980: 47–48), the inspiration/information is 'Tätigkeit einer Macht in sich selbst [...] [d]iese Macht wurde von dem Dichter sichtlich nicht als Teil seiner Persönlichkeit erlebt, sondern als objektives Gegenüber, als Gottheit'. For Camilloni (1998: 11), the Muse is simply 'una forza externa'.

130 See Otto (1955: 85–87); Barmeyer (1968: 16–37). Murray (1981: 88), following a review of literature pertaining to the nature of poetic inspiration in general, concluded that '[t]he basic feature in all these experiences of inspiration seems to be the feeling of dependence on some source other than the conscious mind'. Reid (1964: 158), described his own experience in the following way: 'I know, from personal experience supported by the evidence of other poets, that in the rare moments when I am writing poetry, I am in a "state of mind" totally distinct from the state of mind in which I composed this lecture, or am now reading this lecture; totally distinct, too, from the state of mind in which I go about my practical activities while awake – that is to say, while conscious.' It is, of course, important to emphasize that this description of poetic creativity does not apply to all poets at all times – one only need consider Poe's meticulously rational process for composing the *Raven*; cf. Poe (2003: 430–42).

131 On 'person' as an ontological category, see (Boyer 2001: 60–61).

132 See especially the theory of relevance by Dan Sperber and Deirdre Wilson, summarized in Boyer (2001: 160–64). Simply put, we often do not care about what is true but rather what is relevant for us. On confirmation bias, see Kahneman (2011: 80–81).

133 Paus. 9.29.1: θῦσαι δὲ ἐν Ἑλικῶνι Μούσαις πρώτους καὶ ἐπονομάσαι τὸ ὄρος ἱερὸν εἶναι Μουσῶν Ἐφιάλτην καὶ Ὦτον λέγουσιν, οἰκίσαι δὲ αὐτοὺς καὶ Ἄσκρην·

134 Kambylis (1965: 36) argued that Pausanias' description of the cult of the Muse at Helicon was influenced by Hesiod and that its establishment postdates him. In contrast, Von der Mühll (1970) argued that the cult is more ancient than Hesiod. Peek (1977) showed that the cult's location was still active in the third century CE.

135 Paus. 2.31.3: οὐ πόρρω δὲ ἱερὸν Μουσῶν ἐστι, ποιῆσαι δὲ ἔλεγον αὐτὸ Ἄρδαλον παῖδα Ἡφαίστου· καὶ αὐλόν τε εὑρεῖν νομίζουσι τὸν Ἄρδαλον τοῦτον καὶ τὰς Μούσας ἀπ' αὐτοῦ καλοῦσιν Ἀρδαλίδας.

136 Plut. *Mor.* 149f8–150a2: ἦν δὲ Τροιζήνιος ὁ Ἄρδαλος, αὐλῳδὸς καὶ ἱερεὺς τῶν Ἀρδαλείων Μουσῶν, ἃς ὁ παλαιὸς Ἄρδαλος ἱδρύσατο ὁ Τροιζήνιος.

137 Plut. *Mor.* 402c5–6. On places of worship of the Muse, see Otto (1955: 62–68).

138 Hes. *Th.* 32.
139 Hom. *Il.* 1.70. Tigerstedt (1970: 196) noted that 'like the mantic gods, the Muses teach the poet the truth about the past and the present', the difference being that the poet does not enter ἔκστασις, while the prophet does.
140 As Katz – Volk (2000: 127) explained, 'we suggest that when the Muses address Hesiod as a "belly", they are referring to the role that he is about to play, his role as a recipient, or, rather, a receptacle of inspiration. Men who are γαστέρες οἶον are vessels for the divine voice that the goddesses of poetry breathe into them; the force of οἶον is that human beings do not become poets through their own doing, but are mere mouthpieces of the divinity, mediums to be possessed, just like the lowlier ἐγγαστρίμυθοι.'
141 Sikes (1931: 3); Falter (1934: 14–15).
142 Barmeyer (1968: 99); Minchin (2001: 166): 'an invocation is normally phrased as a subspecies of prayer.'
143 For instance, Accame (1963: 278) observed that 'in questo primitive pensiero indistinto l'operare profetico e il poetico si identifichino'; for Vicaire (1963: 81), '[l]a poésie, celle qui compte, celle qui est inspirée, est pour les Grecs une incantation'. The only scholar I know of who explicitly denied any connection between poetry and prophecy is Setti (1958: 136), who argued that 'poesia [...] è per il cantore omerico operazione umana, e di effetti umani, oserei dire operazione profana e laica'.
144 See Chadwick (1942: 14): 'Everywhere the gift of poetry is inseparable from divine inspiration. Everywhere this inspiration carries with it knowledge – whether of the past, in the form of history and genealogy; of the hidden present, in the form of commonly scientific information; and of the future, in the form of prophetic utterance in the narrower sense. [...] Invariably we find that the poet and seer attributes his inspiration to contact with supernatural powers, and his mood during prophetic utterance is exalted and remote from that of his normal existence.'
145 See especially Norenzayan (2013: 13–54).

9 Conclusion: A return of the prodigal son?

1 Shakespeare, *Macbeth* 2.3, vv. 108–09.
2 Baetke (1952: 154): 'Aller echten Religionen eigentümlich ist der Glaube an die Realität des religiösen Objekts. Dieses ist dem fest in seiner Religion Stehenden keine bloße Idee oder Vorstellung, sondern lebendige Wirklichkeit. In diesem Glauben liegt das tragende Fundament und zugleich das Geheimnis aller Religion. Man kann sagen: Der Glaube des Menschen ist das Korrelat zur Realität der Gottheit; eines bedingt das andere.'
3 Waardenburg (1999: viii–ix).
4 Whaling (1985: 16): 'It would be futile to suggest that the personal equation has no bearing upon the questions a scholar asks, the theories and methods that he employs to answer them, or the conclusions that he draws. After all, even interpreting a graph requires some personal input from the scholar. One's own religious position, whether it be strong, weak, or negative is not irrelevant; one's own temperament, ability, upbringing, motives, and personal vision have some influence upon one's academic work. The atheism of a Freud or a Marx is clearly a factor within explanatory theories of religion they propounded, and the Christian commitment of an Evans-Pritchard is not irrelevant in the sphere of scholarship.'

5 McCutcheon (2001a).
6 See King (1984: 87): 'Generally speaking, the phenomenological approach has stressed the need for objectivity by insisting on a value-free, detached investigation, as far as possible free from all presuppositions, and it has upheld an ideal of scholarship which is sympathetic towards its data.' The actual *modus operandi* of phenomenologists is, however, quite different; as King herself (ibid., 88) noted, 'it is hard to see how some of these and similar aims can be combined with a non-normative approach to the study of religion'.
7 Hubbeling (1973: 10).
8 Van Baaren (1973: 47).
9 Bianchi (1975: 22).
10 Cf. e.g. Boyer (2001: 328–29); Atran (2002: 274–80); McCauley (2011: 244–52).
11 See esp. Dawkins (2006b: 163–207); Dennett (2006: 97–115); Harris (2010: 147–57); Edis (2008: 183).
12 *Method & Theory in the Study of Religion*, first volume of the year 2008.
13 Geertz (2008b: 9). For a critique of Dennett and Dawkins, see also Geertz (2009). More positive assessments of the duo may be found in Peterson (2007); Wiebe (2008); Martin (2008).
14 Pascal, *Manuscrit Périer*, 1300: '*Dieu d'Abraham, Dieu d'Isaac, Dieu de Jacob*, non des philosophes et des savants.'
15 Barrett (2004: 123): For a more detailed development of this argument, see Barrett (2011). Leech and Visala (2011), Barrett and Church (2013) and Jong, Kavanagh and Visala (2015) likewise denied any interference of CSR with the truth or epistemic values of religion or theism, but it is worth noting that they are interested in the relation of CSR to 'classical theism', not in the relation of CSR and any given religious tradition.
16 Cf. also Freud (1993: 135–36): 'Wenn es sich um Fragen der Religion handelt, machen sich die Menschen aller möglichen Unaufrichtigkeiten und intellektuellen Unarten schuldig. Philosophen überdehnen die Bedeutung von Worten, bis diese kaum etwas von ihrem ursprünglichen Sinn übrigbehalten, sie heißen irgendeine verschwommene Abstraktion, die sie sich geschaffen haben, »Gott« und sind nun auch Deisten, Gottesgläubige vor aller Welt, können sich selbst rühmen, einen höheren, reineren Gottesbegriff erkannt zu haben, obwohl ihr Gott nur mehr ein wesenloser Schatten ist und nicht mehr die machtvolle Persönlichkeit der religiösen Lehre.'
17 Boyer (2001: 281–5).
18 Barrett (1999); Slone (2004).
19 Tillich (1957: 1).
20 Bultmann (1951).
21 Cited *in* Strenski (2006: 41).
22 Murphy (2009: 277).
23 Barrett (2009: 97): 'God could have guided natural selection to develop the sorts of minds humans have. Perhaps the 'random mutations' from which natural selection selected were not random after all. The environmental contingencies that favored one organism over another could have been designed or directed to bring about humans with their particular minds.'
24 Murphy (2009: 274).
25 Russell (1997: 542–48).
26 Henderson (2006).
27 Cf. Aristoteles, *Metaphysica*, 990b1–4; Ockham, *Summa logicae*, 1.12 (*frustra fit per plura quod potest fieri per pauciora*); Newton, *Principia Mathematica* (Koyré et al. II,

550): *causas rerum naturalium non plures admitti debere, quam quae & verae sint & earum phaenomenis explicandis sufficiant.*

28 Lawson – McCauley (1990: 3); Pyysiäinen (2003a: 22); Whitehouse (2004: 1); Tremlin (2006: 9).
29 Lawson – McCauley (1990: 8); Whitehouse (2004: 174); Tremlin (2006: 198).
30 Einstein (1909: 817): 'Als man erkannt hatte, daß das Licht die Erscheinungen der Interferenz und Beugung zeige, da erschien es kaum mehr bezweifelbar, daß das Licht als eine Wellenbewegung aufzufassen sei. Da das Licht sich auch durch das Vakuum fortzupflanzen vermag, so mußte man sich vorstellen, daß auch in diesem eine Art besonderer Materie vorhanden sei, welche die Fortpflanzung der Lichtwellen vermittelt. Für die Auffassung der Gesetze der Ausbreitung des Lichtes in ponderabeln Körpern war es nötig, anzunehmen, daß jene Materie, welche man Lichtäther nannte, auch in diesen vorhanden sei, und daß es auch im Innern der ponerabeln Körper im wesentlichen der Lichtäther sei, welcher die Ausbreitung des Lichtes vermittelt. Die Existenz jenes Lichtäthers schien unbezweifelbar.'
31 Cicero, *De natura deorum*, 1.43–44: *Quae est enim gens aut quod genus hominum, quod non habeat sine doctrina anticipationem quondam deorum? [...] Cum enim non instituto aliquo aut more aut lege sit opinio constituta maneatque ad unum omnium firma consensio, intellegi necesse est esse deos, quoniam insitas eorum vel potius innatas cognitiones habemus; de quo autem omnium natura consentit, id verum esse necesse est; esse igitur deos confitendum est.*
32 Compare Taliaferro (2009: 200–01): 'So, part of my own response to this general question of why some of us experience the divine is the somewhat simple response: because there is a divine beneficent reality to be experienced or, putting the point more formally, the best account of why some of us experience God includes the reality and activity of an omnipresent God.'
33 Einstein (1909: 817): 'Heute aber müssen wir wohl die Ätherhypothese als einen überwundenen Standpunkt ansehen. Es ist sogar unleugbar, daß es eine ausgedehnte Gruppe von die Strahlung betreffenden Tatsachen gibt, welche zeigen, daß dem Lichte gewisse fundamentale Eigenschaften zukommen, die sich weit eher vom Standpunkte der Newtonschen Emissionstheorie des Lichtes als vom Standpunkte der Undulationstheorie begreifen lassen. Deshalb ist es meine Meinung, daß die nächste Phase der Entwicklung der theoretischen Physik uns eine Theorie des Lichtes bringen wird, welche sich als eine Art Verschmelzung von Undulations- und Emissionstheorie des Lichtes auffassen läst.'
34 Quine (1980: 1–19).
35 Boyer (2001: 329–30).
36 Berger (1969: 100) called this position 'methodological atheism': 'Needless to say, it is impossible within the reference of scientific theorizing to make any affirmations, positive *or* negative, about the ultimate ontological status of this alleged reality. Within this frame of reference, the religious projections can be dealt with only as such, as products of human activity and human consciousness, and rigorous brackets have to be placed around the question as to whether these projections may not *also* be something else than that (or, more accurately, *refer to* something else than the human world in which they empirically originate). In other words, every inquiry into religious matters that limits itself to the empirically available must necessarily based on a "*methodological* atheism".'
37 For a relation of science and religion, see esp. Clayton and Simpson (2006).

38 Martin and Wiebe (2012) highlighted how the apologetic elements of the protectionist paradigm intrude into the CSR and came to some rather pessimistic conclusions with respect to the possibilities of a study of religions free from theological bias (ibid., 18): 'We were wrong. We now understand that we were both deluded by our overly-optimistic but cognitively naïve expectations for the development of a truly scientific field for the study of religion in the context of a modern, research university.' See also Martin – Wiebe (2016: 331–36), with explicit references to Barrett.
39 Wiebe (1984: 160).
40 Horatius, *Ars poetica*, 1–5: *Humano capiti cervicem pictor equinam | iungere si vellit et varias inducere plumas | undique collatis membris, ut turpiter atrum | desinat in piscem mulier formosa superne, | spectatum admissi risum teneatis, amici?* English translation by G. Colman.

Editions

Acta Andreae, Acta Joannis
Hechos de los Apóstolos I: Hechos de Andrés, Juan y Pedro (eds Antonio Piñero and Gonzalo Del Cerro). Madrid: Biblioteca de Autores Cristianos 2012 (*BAC* 646).

Acta Pauli
Hechos apócrifos de los Apóstoles II: Hechos de Pablo y Tomás (eds Antonio Piñero and Gonzalo Del Cerro). Madrid: Biblioteca de Autores Cristianos 2005 (*BAC* 656).

Acta Petri
Hechos de los Apóstolos I: Hechos de Andrés, Juan y Pedro (eds Antonio Piñero and Gonzalo Del Cerro). Madrid: Biblioteca de Autores Cristianos (*BAC* 646).

Aristides Atheniensis
Apologia (ed. Carlotta Apligiano). Firenze: Nardini (*BP* 11).

Aristoteles
Aristotelis ars rhetorica (ed. W. David Ross). Oxford: Clarendon Press 1964.
Aristotelis de arte poetica liber (ed. Rudolf Kassel). Oxford: Clarendon Press 1968.
Metaphysica (ed. W. David Ross). Oxford: Clarendon Press 1924.

Aquinas, Thomas
Sancti Thomae de Aquino Summa theologiae (ed. Editiones Paulinae). Torino: Edizioni San Paolo 1999.

Athenagoras
Legatio & De resurrectione (ed. William R. Schoedel). Oxford: Clarendon Press 1972 (*OECT*).

Aurelius Augustinus
Sancti Augustini Confessionum libri XIII (ed. Luc Verheijen). Turnhout: Brepols 1981 (*CCSL* 27).
De doctrina Christiana (ed. Joseph Martin). Turnhout: Brepols 1962 (*CCSL* 32).

Cicero
M. Tulli Ciceronis scripta quae manserunt omnia, fasc. 44: Tusculanae disputationes (ed. M. Pohlenz). Stuttgart: Teubner 1918.
M. Tulli Ciceronis scripta quae manserunt omnia, fasc. 45: De natura deorum (ed. W. Ax). Stuttgart: Teubner 1933.

Clemens Alexandrinus
Le protreptique (ed. C. Mondésert). Paris: Éditions du Cerf 1949 (*SC* 2).
Clemens Alexandrinus, Stromata (eds Otto Stählin, Ludwig Früchtel and Ursula Treu). Berlin: Akademie Verlag 1960–1970 (vols. II–III).

Clemens Romanus
The Apostolic Fathers: Greek Texts and English Translations (ed. Michael W. Holmes). Grand Rapids: Baker Academic 2007.

Critias
Die Fragmente der Vorsokratiker (eds Hermann Diels and Walther Kranz). Zürich: Weidmann 2005.

Dante Alighieri
Inferno, vol. I: Text (ed. Charles S. Singleton). Princeton: Princeton University Press 1970.

Darwin, Charles
From So Simple a Beginning: Darwin's Four Great Books (Voyage of the Beagle, The Origin of Species, The Descent of Man, The Expression of Emotions in Man and Animals) (ed. Edward O. Wilson). New York and London: W. W. Norton & Company 2006.

Democritus
Die Fragmente der Vorsokratiker (eds Hermann Diels and Walther Kranz). Zürich: Weidmann 2005.

Descartes, René
Oeuvres de Descartes, tome X (eds Charles Adam and Paul Tannery). Paris: Léopold Cerf 1908.

Didache
The Apostolic Fathers: Greek Texts and English Translations (ed. Michael W. Holmes). Grand Rapids: Baker Academic 2007.

Dilthey, Wilhelm
Einleitung in die Geisteswissenschaften (ed. Bernard Groethuysen). Leipzig and Berlin: Teubner 1922.

Diogenes Laertius
Vite e dottrine dei più celebri filosofi (eds Giovanni Reale, Giuseppe Grigenti and Ilaria Ramelli). Milano: Bompiani 2005.

Donne, John
The Complete Poetry and Selected Prose of John Donne (ed. Charles M. Coffin). New York: The Modern Library 2001.

Euripides
Euripidis fabulae, vol. III (ed. James Diggle). Oxford: Clarendon Press 1994.

Eusebius Caesariensis
Historia ecclesiastica (ed. Gustave Bardy). Paris: Les éditions du cerf 1955 (*SC* 41).

Evangelium Thomae, Evangelium Pseudo-Matthaei, Evangelium Nicodemi
Los Evangelios Apócrifos (ed. Aurelio de Santos Otero). Madrid: Biblioteca de Autores Cristianos 2006 (*BAC* 148).

Goethe, Johann Wolfgang von
Werke: Hamburger Ausgabe in 14 Bänden (eds Erich Trunz et al.). München: C. H. Beck 1981.

Heraclitus
Die Fragmente der Vorsokratiker (eds Hermann Diels and Walther Kranz). Zürich: Weidmann 2005.

Herodotus
Herodoti Historiae (ed. Carolus Hude). Oxford: Clarendon Press 1927.

Hesiodus
Hesiodi Theogonia, Opera et dies, Scutum & Fragmenta selecta (eds Friedrich Solmsen, Rudolf Merkelbach and Martin L. West). Oxford: Clarendon Press 1990.

Hobbes, Thomas
Leviathan (ed. Richard Tuck). Cambridge: Cambridge University Press 1996.

Homerus
Ilias, Volumen prius: Rhapsodiae I–XII (ed. Martin L. West). Stuttgart and Leipzig: B. G. Teubner 1998.
Ilias, Volumen alterum: Rhapsodiae XIII–XXIV (ed. Martin L. West). München and Leipzig: K. G. Saur 2000.
Homeri Odyssea (ed. Peter Von der Mühll). Stuttgart: B. G. Teubner 1984.
Scholia Graeca in Homeri Iliadem: Scholia vetera (ed. Hartmut Erbse). Berlin: Walter de Gruyter 1969–1988.

Horatius
Opera (ed. David R. Shackleton Bailey). München and Leipzig: K. G. Saur 2001.

Hume, David
A Treatise of Human Nature (eds David F. Norton and Mary J. Norton). Oxford: Oxford University Press 2000.

Ignatius Antiochenus
The Apostolic Fathers: Greek Texts and English Translations (ed. Michael W. Holmes). Grand Rapids: Baker Academic 2007.

Irenaeus
Epideixis – Adversus haereses (eds Norbert Brox et al.). Freiburg im Breisgau: Herder 1993 (*FC* 8, Serie 1).

Justinus Martyr
Iustini Martyris Apologiae pro Christianis (ed. Miroslav Marcovich). Berlin and New York: Walter de Gruyter 1994 (*PTS* 38).
Iustini Martyris Dialogus cum Tryphone (ed. Miroslav Marcovich). Berlin and New York: Walter de Gruyter 1997 (*PTS* 47).

Kant, Immanuel
Kritik der reinen Vernunft (ed. Jens Timmermann). Hamburg: Felix Meiner Verlag 1998.

Kierkegaard, Sören
Entweder – Oder: Teil I und II (eds Hermann Diem and Walter Rest). München: Deutscher Taschenbuch Verlag 2005.

Locke, John
An Essay Concerning Human Understanding (ed. Peter H. Nidditch). Oxford: Clarendon Press 1975.

Lucretius
Lucreti De rerum natura libri sex (ed. Cyril Bailey). Oxford: Clarendon Press 1959.

Martyrium Montani, Martyrium Polycarpi
The Acts of the Christian Martyrs (ed. Herbert Musurillo). Oxford: Clarendon Press 1972.

Marx, Karl and Engels, Friedrich
Werke: Band I (ed. Institut für Marxismus-Leninismus beim ZK der SED). Berlin: Dietz Verlag 1981.

Miguel de Cervantes
Don Quichote de la Mancha (ed. Martín de Riquer). Barcelona: Planeta 2004.

Mill, John Stuart
Essays on Ethics, Religion and Society (ed. John M. Robson). Toronto: University of Toronto Press.

Milton, John
The Complete Poetry and Essential Prose of John Milton (eds William Kerrigan, John Rumrich and Stephen M. Fallon). New York: The Modern Library.

Minucius Felix
M. Minvci Felicis Octavius (ed. Bernhard Kytzler). Leipzig: Teubner 1982.

Newton, Isaac
Philosophiae naturalis principia mathematica (eds Alexandre Koyré, I. Bernard Cohen and Anne Whitman). Cambridge, MA: Harvard University Press 1972.

Nietzsche, Friedrich
Kritische Studienausgabe (eds Giorgio Colli – Mazzino Montinari). München: Walter de Gruyter and Deutscher Taschenbuch Verlag 1999.

Novum Testamentum
Novum Testamentum Graece (eds Erwin Nestle, Barbara Aland and Kurt Aland). Stuttgart: Deutsche Bibelgesellschaft 1993.

Ockham, Guillelmus de
Guillemi de Ockham Opera Philosophica et Theologica. Opera Philosophica, vol. 1: Summa logicae (ed. P. Boehner, G. Gal and S. Brown). St Bonaventure, NY: The Franciscan Institute 1974.

Origenes
Origène. Contre Celse, vol. I (ed. Marcel Borret). Paris: Éditions du Cerf 1967–1968 (*SC* 132).

Pascal, Blaise
Les provinciales, Pensées et opuscules divers (eds Gérard Ferreyrolles and Philippe Sellier). Paris: Classiques Garnier 1999.

Pausanias
Pausaniae Graeciae descriptio (ed. Friedrich Spiro). Leipzig: Teubner 1903.

Petrus Damiani
Die Briefe des Petrus Damiani, Teil 3, Nr. 91–150 (ed. Kurt Reindel). München: Monumenta Germaniae Historica 1989 (*MGH* 4).

Philo Judaeus
Philonis Alexandrini opera quae supersunt, vol. VI (eds Leopold Cohn and Siegfried Reiter). Berlin: Reimer 1915 (repr. De Gruyter, 1962).

Pindarus
Pindarus, pars I: Epinicia (ed. Herwig Maehler). Berlin and New York: Walter de Gruyter 2008.

Plato
Platonis Opera, vol. I (eds Elizabeth A. Duke et al.). Oxford: Clarendon Press 1995.
Platonis Opera, vol. II–V (ed. John Burnet). Oxford: Clarendon Press 1901–1915.

Plutarchus
Septem Sapientium Convivium in *Plutarch's moralia, vol. II.* (ed. Frank C. Babbitt). Cambridge, MA: Harvard University Press 1928 (*LCL* 222).
De Pythiae Oraculis in *Plutarchi moralia, vol. III.* (ed. Walter Sieveking). Leipzig: Teubner, 1929.

Pomponazzi, Pietro
De incantationibus (ed. Vittoria Perrone Compagni). Firenze: Leo S. Olschki 2011.

Prodicus
Die Fragmente der Vorsokratiker (eds Hermann Diels and Walther Kranz). Zürich: Weidmann 2005.

Protevangelium Jacobi
Los Evangelios Apócrifos (ed. Aurelio de Santos Otero). Madrid: Biblioteca de Autores Cristianos 2006 (BAC 148).

Pseudo-Plutarchus
Plutarchi Moralia, vol. 5.2.1. (ed. Jürgen Mau). Leipzig: Teubner 1971 [*Placita philosophorum*].

Quintilianus
M. Fabi Quintiliani Institutionis Oratoriae Libri XII. (eds Ludwig Radermacher and Vinzenz Buchheit). Leipzig: Teubner 1971.

Richardson, Jonathan
The Works of Jonathan Richardson (ed. Jonathan Richardson, Jr). Hildesheim: Olms 1969.

Sappho
Greek Lyric, vol. I: Sappho – Alcaeus (ed. David A. Campbell). Cambridge, MA and London: Harvard University Press 1990 (*LCL* 142).

Schleiermacher, Friedrich
Über die Religion (ed. Günter Meckenstock). Berlin and New York: Walter de Gruyter 2001.

Schopenhauer, Arthur
Zürcher Ausgabe: Werke in zehn Bänden (eds Arthur Hübscher et al.). Zürich: Diogenes Verlag 1977.

Shakespeare, William
The Complete Works (eds Stanley Wells and Gary Taylor). Oxford: Clarendon Press 2005.

Spinoza, Benedictus
Benedicti de Spinoza Opera quae supersunt omnia (ed. Carolus Hermannus Bruder). Leipzig: B. Tauchnitz 1844.

Stoicorum veterum fragmenta
Stoici antichi: Tutti i frammenti raccolti da Hans von Arnim. (ed. Roberto Radice). Milano: Bompiani 2002.

Tatianus
Oratio ad Graecos & Fragments (ed. Molly Whittaker). Oxford: Clarendon Press 1982 (*OECT*).

Terentius
P. Terenti Comoediae (ed. Alfred Fleckeisen). Leipzig: Teubner 1895.

Tertullianus
Opera, vol. I: Opera catholica, Adversus Marcionem (eds Eligius Dekkers et al.). Turnhout: Brepols 1954 (*CCSL* 1).
Opera, vol. II: Opera montanistica (eds Aloïs Gerlo et al.). Turnhout: Brepols 1954 (*CCSL* 2).

Theognis
Greek Elegiac Poetry (ed. Douglas E. Gerber). Cambridge, MA and London: Harvard University Press 1999 (*LCL* 258).

Theophilus Antiochenus
Ad Autolycum (ed. Robert M. Grant). Oxford: Clarendon Press 1970 (*OECT*).

Tragicorum Graecorum Fragmenta
Tragicorum Graecorum fragmenta (ed. A. Nauck). Leipzig: Teubner 1889.
Tragicorum Graecorum fragmenta: Supplementum (ed. B. Snell). Hildesheim: Olms 1964.

Vasari, Giorgio
Le vite de' piú eccellenti pittori, scultori ed architetti (eds Luciano Bellosi and Aldo Rossi). Torino: Einaudi 1986.

Vergilius
P. Vergili Maronis Opera (ed. Roger A. B. Mynors). Oxford: Clarendon Press 1969.

Voltaire
Oeuvres complètes de Voltaire, vol. X: Contes en vers – Satires – Épitres – Poèsies mêlées (ed. Louis Moland). Paris: Garnier 1877.

Xenophanes
Die Fragmente der Vorsokratiker (eds Hermann Diels and Walther Kranz). Zürich: Weidmann 2005.

Xenophon
Opera omnia, vol. II (ed. Edgar C. Marchant). Oxford: Clarendon Press 1921.

References

Accame, Silvio (1963). L'invocazione alla musa e la «verità» in Omero e in Esiodo. *RFIC* 91: 257–81, 385–415.
Ackerman, Robert (1987). *J. G. Frazer: His Life and Work*. Cambridge: Cambridge University Press.
Adams, James E. (1992). Philosophical Forgetfullness: John Stuart Mill's *On Nature*. *JHI* 53 (3): 437–54.
Adkins, Arthur W. H. (1972). Truth, κόσμος, and ἀρετή in the Homeric Poems. *CQ* 22 (1): 5–18.
Adomenas, Mantas (1999). Heraclitus on Religion. *Phronesis* 44 (2): 87–113.
Alexander, Richard D. (1974). The Evolution of Social Behavior. *Annu Rev Ecol Evol Syst* 5: 325–83.
Alexander, Richard D. (1987). *The Biology of Moral Systems*. New York: Aldine de Gruyter.
Alles, Gregory D. (1997). Rudolf Otto. In: Michaels (1997), pp. 198–210.
Almond, Philip C. (1984). *Rudolf Otto: An Introduction to His Philosophical Theology*. Chapel Hill and London: The University of North Carolina Press.
Álvarez Salas, Omar (2011). Sabiduría divina vs. conocimiento humano en Hesíodo y Jenófanes. In: Aquino, Galaz, García et al. (2011), pp. 239–74.
Ambascianbo, Leonardo (2019). *An Unnatural History of Religions: Academia, Post-truth and the Quest for Scientific Knowledge*. London and New York: Bloomsbury Academic.
Andersen, Jensine (ed.) (2001). *Religion in Mind: Cognitive Perspectives on Religious Belief, Ritual, and Experience*. Cambridge: Cambridge University Press.
Antes, Peter, Geertz, Armin W. and Warne, Randi R. (eds) (2008a). *New Approaches to the Study of Religion, Volume 1: Regional, Critical, and Historical Approaches*. Berlin and New York: Walter de Gruyter (R+R 42).
Antes, Peter, Geertz, Armin W. and Warne, Randi R. (eds) (2008b). *New Approaches to the Study of Religion, Volume 2: Textual, Comparative, Sociological and Cognitive Approaches*. Berlin and New York: Walter de Gruyter (R+R 43).
Aquino, Silvia, Galaz, Mariateresa, García, David and Álvarez Salas, Omar (eds) (2011). *La fascinación por la palabra: Homenaje a Paola Vianello*. México: Universidad Autónoma de México.
Arrighetti, Graziano (1992). Esiodo e le Muse: Il dono della verità e la conquista della parola. *Athenaeum* 80: 45–63.
Arthur, Marilyn (1983). The Dream of a World without Women: Poetics and the Circles of Order in the *Theogony* prooemium. *Arethusa* 16 (1/2): 97–116.
Artigas, Mariano, Glick, Thomas F. and Martínez, Rafael A. (2006). *Negotiating Darwin: The Vatican Confronts Evolution 1877–1902*. Baltimore: The Johns Hopkins University Press.
Asad, Talal (1983). Anthropological Conceptions of Religion: Reflections on Geertz. *Man* (n.s.) 18 (2): 237–59.
Asad, Talal (2001). Reading a Modern Classic: W. C. Smith's 'The Meaning and End of Religion'. *HR* 40 (3): 205–20.
Atran, Scott (2002). *In Gods We Trust: The Evolutionary Landscape of Religion*. Oxford: Oxford University Press.

Aune, David E. (1983). *Prophecy in Early Christianity and the Ancient Mediterranean World*. Grand Rapids: Eerdmans.
Axelrod, Robert (2006). *The Evolution of Cooperation*. New York: Basic Books.
Babut, Daniel (1974a). Xénophane critique des poètes. *AC* 43 (1): 83–117.
Baetke, Walter (1942). *Das Heilige im Germanischen*. Tübingen: J. C. B. Mohr (Paul Siebeck).
Baetke, Walter (1952). Aufgabe und Struktur der Religionswissenschaft. In: Lanczkowski (1974), pp. 133–58.
Bakker, Stephanie and Wakker, Gerry (eds) (2009). *Discourse Cohesion in Ancient Greek*. Leiden: Brill.
Baldwin, Thomas (1990). *G. E. Moore*. London and New York: Routledge.
Bańkowski, Andrzej (1962). Prodikos z Keos i jego teoria religii. *Euhemer* 3: 8–22.
Banton, Michael (ed.) (1966). *Anthropological Approaches to the Study of Religion*. New York: Praeger.
Barcala, Andrés (1976a). «Con más razón hay que creer . . .» (Un pasaje olvidado de Tertuliano). *EEcl* 51 (198): 347–67.
Barcala, Andrés (1976b). El antifilosofismo de Tertuliano y la fe como reconocimiento. *RET* 36 (1–2): 233–50.
Barkow, Jerome, Cosmides, Leda and Tooby, John (eds) (1992). *The Adapted Mind: Evolutionary Psychology and the Generation of Culture*. Oxford: Oxford University Press.
Barmeyer, Eike (1968). *Die Musen: Ein Beitrag zur Inspirationstheorie*. München: Wilhelm Fink.
Barnard, Leslie W. (1967). *Justin Martyr: His Life and Thought*. Cambridge: Cambridge University Press.
Barnes, Jonathan (1982). *The Presocratic Philosophers*. London and New York: Routledge.
Barnes, Jonathan (1997). Raison et foi: Critique païenne et réponses chrétiennes. *StudPhil* 56: 183–209.
Barnett, Paul (1997). *The New International Commentary on the New Testament: The Second Epistle to the Corinthians*. Grand Rapids: William B. Eerdmans.
Barrett, Justin L. (1974b). Sur la «théologie» de Xénohpane. *RPhilos* 164 (4): 401–40.
Barrett, Justin L. (1974c). *La religion des philosophes grecs: De Thalès aux Stoïciens*. Paris: Presses Universitaires de France.
Barrett, Justin L. (1999). Theological Correctness: Cognitive Constraint and the Study of Religion. *MTSR* 11 (4): 325–39.
Barrett, Justin L. (2000). Exploring the Natural Foundations of Religion. *Trends Cogn Sci* 4 (1): 29–34.
Barrett, Justin L. (2004). *Why Would Anyone Believe in God?* Lanham: AltaMira Press.
Barrett, Justin L. (2009). Cognitive Science, Religion, and Theology. In: Schloss and Murray (2009), pp. 76–99.
Barrett, Justin L. (2011). *Cognitive Science, Religion, and Theology*. West Conshohocken: Templeton Press.
Barrett, Justin L. (2012). *Born Believers: The Science of Children's Religious Belief*. New York: Free Press.
Barrett, Justin L. and Church, Ian M. (2013). Should CSR Give Atheists Epistemic Assurance? On Beer-Goggles, BFFs, and Skepticism Regarding Religious Beliefs. *The Monist* 96 (3): 311–24.
Barton, Stephen C. (ed.) (2003). *Holiness Past and Present*. London and New York: T&T Clark.

Bartsch, Hans W. (ed.) (1951). *Kerygma und Mythos*. Hamburg: Herbert Reich-Evangelischer Verlag.
Bassett, Samuel E. (1923). The Proems of the Iliad and the Odyssey. *AJPh* 44 (4): 339–48.
Bauer, Johannes B. (1970). Credo, quia absurdum (Tertullian, *De carne Christi* 5). In: Flieder (1970), pp. 9–12.
Bausell, R. Barker (2007). *Snake Oil Science: The Truth about Complementary and Alternative Medicine*. Oxford: Oxford University Press.
Beckaert, André (1961). L'évolution de l'intellectualisme grec vers la pensée religieuse et la relève de la philosophie par la pensée chrétienne. *REByz* 19: 44–62.
Bediako, Gillian M. (1997). *Primal Religion and the Bible: William Robertson Smith and his Heritage*. Sheffield: Sheffield Academic Press (*JSOT* Supplement Series 246).
Beekes, Robert (2010). *Etymological Dictionary of Greek*. Leiden and Boston: Brill.
Belfiore, Elizabeth (1985). 'Lies Unlike the Truth': Plato on Hesiod, *Theogony* 27. *TAPhA* 115: 47–57.
Bellah, Robert N. (2011). *Religion in Human Evolution: From Paleolithic to the Axial Age*. Cambridge, MA and London: The Belknap Press of Harvard University Press.
Benedict, Ruth (2005). *Patterns of Culture*. New York: Mariner Books.
Benjamin, Andrew E. (ed.) (1988). *Post-Structuralist Classics*. London and New York: Routledge.
Benz, Ernst (1959). On Understanding Non-Christian Religions. In: Eliade and Kitagawa (1959), pp. 115–31.
Benz, Ernst (1966). Die Bedeutung der Religionswissenschaft für die Koexistenz der Weltreligionen heute. In: Lanczkowski (1974), pp. 243–56.
Berger, Peter L. (1969). *The Sacred Canopy: Elements of a Sociological Theory of Religion*. New York: Anchor Books.
Bering, Jesse (2006). The Folk Psychology of Souls. *Behav Brain Sci* 29: 453–98.
Berlinzani, Francesca (2002). La voce e il canto nel proemio della *Teogonia*. *Acme* 55 (3): 189–204.
Berner, Ulrich (1997). Mircea Eliade. In: Michaels (1997), pp. 343–53.
Bianchi, Ugo (1961). Après Marbourg (Petit discours sur la méthode). *Numen* 8 (1): 64–78.
Bianchi, Ugo (1975). *The History of Religions*. Leiden: E. J. Brill.
Biezais, Harald (1979). Typology of Religion and the Phenomenological Method. In: Honko (1979), pp. 143–61.
Bleeker, C. Jouco (1971). Epilegomena. In: Bleeker and Widengren (1971), pp. 642–51.
Bleeker, C. Jouco (1975). Looking Backward and Forward. In: Bleeker, Widengren and Sharpe (1975), pp. 23–32.
Bleeker, C. Jouco (1979). Commentary. In: Honko (1979), pp. 173–77.
Bleeker, C. Jouco and Widengren, Geo (eds) (1969). *Historia Religionum: Handbook for the History of Religions, volume 1: Religions of the Past*. Leiden: E. J. Brill.
Bleeker, C. Jouco (1971). *Historia Religionum: Handbook for the History of Religions, volume 2: Religions of the Present*. Leiden: E. J. Brill.
Bleeker, C. Jouco, Widengren, Geo and Sharpe, Eric J. (eds) (1975). *Proceedings of the XIIth International Congress of the International Association for the History of Religions*. Leiden: E. J. Brill.
Bloom, Paul (2013). *Just Babies: The Origins of Good and Evil*. New York: Crown.
Boas, Franz U. (1938). *The Mind of Primitive Man*. New York: The Macmillan Company.

Bochet, Isabelle (2008). Transcendence divine et paradoxe de la foi chrétienne: La polémique de Tertullien contre Marcion. *RecSR* 96 (2): 255–74.

Boehm, Christopher (2012). *Moral Origins: The Evolution of Virtue, Atruism, and Shame*. New York: Basic Books.

Boghossian, Paul (2006). *Fear of Knowledge: Against Relativism and Constructivism*. Oxford: Oxford University Press.

Bolle, Kees (1984). Myths and Other Religious Texts. In: Whaling (1984), pp. 297–363.

Borges, Jorge Luis and Frías, Carlos V. (ed.) (1974). *Obras Completas 1923–1972*. Buenos Aires: Emecé Editores.

Botros, Sophie (2006). *Hume, Reason and Morality: A Legacy of Contradiction*. London and New York: Routledge.

Bourdeau, Michel (2003). Auguste Comte et la religion positiviste: Présentation. *RSPh* 87 (1): 5–21.

Bourdeau, Michel (2006). *Les trois états: Science, théologie et métaphysique chez Auguste Comte*. Paris: Éditions du Cerf.

Bourdieu, Pierre (2001). *Langage et pouvoir symbolique*. Paris: Éditions du Seuil.

Bowie, Fiona (2006). Anthropology of Religion. In: Segal (2006), pp. 3–24.

Boyer, Pascal (1994). *The Naturalness of Religious Ideas: A Cognitive Theory of Religion*. Berkeley: University of California Press.

Boyer, Pascal (2001). *Religion Explained: The Evolutionary Origins of Religious Thought*. New York: Basic Books.

Boyer, Pascal (2003). Religious Thought and Behaviour as By-Products of Brain Function. *Trends Cogn Sci* 7 (3): 119–24.

Boyer, Pascal (2010). *The Fracture of an Illusion: Science and the Dissolution of Religion*. Göttingen: Vandenhoeck & Ruprecht.

Bradner, Leicester (1956). The Rise of Secular Drama in the Renaissance. *Stud Renaissance* 3: 7–22.

Braun, René (1962). *Deus Christianorum: Recherches sur le vocabulaire doctrinal de Tertullien*. Paris: Presses Universitaires de France.

Braun, René (1971). Tertullien et la philosophie païenne: Essai de mise au point. *BAGB* 1 (2): 231–51.

Bremmer, Jan (2007). Atheism in Antiquity. In: Martin (2007), pp. 11–26.

Brent, Allen (2007). *Ignatius of Antioch: A Martyr Bishop and the Origin of Episcopacy*. London and New York: T&T Clark.

Brisson, Luc (2004). *How Philosophers Saved Myths: Allegorical Interpretation and Classical Mythology*. Chicago and London: Chicago University Press.

Brown, Charlotte R. (2008). *Hume on Moral Rationalism, Sentimentalism, and Sympathy*. In: Radcliffe (2008), pp. 219–39.

Bultmann, Rudolf (1951). Neues Testament und Mythologie. Das Problem der Entmythologisierung der neutestamentlichen Verkündigung. In: Bartsch (1951), pp. 15–48.

Burckhardt, Jakob (1855). *Der Cicerone: Eine Anleitung zum Genuss der Kunstwerke Italiens*. Basel: Schweighauser'sche Verlagsbuchhandlung.

Burkert, Walter (1996). *Creation of the Sacred: Tracks of Biology in Early Religions*. Cambridge, MA and London: Harvard University Press.

Burnet, John (1908). *Early Greek Philosophy: Second Edition*. London: Adam & Charles Black.

Burnet, John (1920). *Early Greek Philosophy: Third Edition*. London: Adam & Charles Black.

Caillois, Roger (1959). *L'homme et le sacré*. Paris: Gallimard.

Calame, Claude (1982). Enonciation: véracité ou convention littéraire? L'inspiration des Muses dans la *Théogonie*. *AS* 4 (34): 1–24.

Calame, Claude (1983). Entre oralité et écriture: Énonciation et énoncé dans la poésie grecque archaïque. *Semiotica* 43 (3/4): 245–73.

Calhoun, George M. (1938). The Poet and the Muses in Homer. *CPh* 33 (2): 157–66.

Camilloni, Maria T. (1998). *Le Muse*. Roma: Editori Riuniti.

Campbell, Stephen J. and Cole, Michael W. (2012). *A New History of Italian Renaissance Art*. London: Thames & Hudson.

Capps, Walter H. (1995). *Religious Studies: The Making of a Discipline*. Minneapolis: Fortress Press.

Carrasco Meza, Carlos G. (2010). La tradición en la teología de Jenófanes. *ByzNH* 29: 55–72.

Cave, David (1993). *Mircea Eliade's Vision for a New Humanism*. New York and Oxford: Oxford University Press.

Černušková, Veronika, Kovacs, Judith L. and Plátová, Jana (eds) (2017). *Clement's Biblical Exegesis: Proceedings of the Second Colloquium on Clement of Alexandria (Olomouc, May 29–31, 2014)*. Leiden and Boston: Brill.

Chadwick, Henry (1993). The Gospel a Republication of Natural Religion in Justin Martyr. *ICS* 18: 237–47.

Chadwick, Nora K. (1942). *Poetry and Prophecy*. Cambridge: Cambridge University Press.

Chantepie de la Saussaye, Pierre D. (ed.) (1897). *Lehrbuch der Religionsgeschichte*. Freiburg im Breisgau and Leipzig: J. C. B. Mohr.

Chomsky, Noam (1995). *The Minimalist Program*. Cambridge, MA and London: The MIT Press.

Chomsky, Noam (2002). *Syntactic Structures*. Berlin and New York: Mouton de Gruyter.

Christensen, Anne-Marie S. (2011). Wittgenstein and Ethics. In: Kuusela and McGinn (2011), pp. 796–818.

Churchland, Patricia (2011). *Braintrust: What Neuroscience Tells Us About Morality*. Princeton and Oxford: Princeton University Press.

Clay, Jenny S. (1989). What the Muses Sang: *Theogony* 1–115. *GRBS* 29 (4): 323–33.

Clayton, Philip and Simpson, Zachary (eds) (2006). *The Oxford Handbook of Religion and Science*. Oxford and New York: Oxford University Press.

Cohon, Rachel (2008). *Hume's Morality: Feeling and Fabrication*. Oxford: Oxford University Press.

Comstock, W. Richard (1984). Toward Open Definitions of Religion. *J Am Acad Relig* 52 (3): 499–517.

Cosmides, Leda and Tooby, John (1992). The Psychological Foundations of Culture. In: Barkow, Cosmides and Tooby (1992), pp. 19–136.

Comte, Auguste (1934). *Cours de philosophie positive: Tome premier, contenant les préliminaires généraux et la philosophie mathématique*. Paris: Alfred Costes.

Countryman, L. William (1982). Tertullian and the *Regula Fidei*. *JECS* 2 (4): 208–27.

Cox, James L. (2006). *A Guide to the Phenomenology of Religion: Key Figures, Formative Influences and Subsequent Debates*. London and New York: T&T Clark International.

Cranston, Jodi (2003). Tropes of Revelation in Raphael's "Transfiguration". *RenQ* 56 (1): 1–25.

Crépey, Cyrille (2009). Marc Aurèle et Justin Martyr: Deux discours sur la raison. *RHPhR* 89 (1): 51–77.

Cross, Frank L. (1972). *Studia patristica XI: Papers presented to the 5. International Conference on Patristic studies held in Oxford 1967*. Berlin: Akademie-Verlag.

Crowder, Colin (2003). Rudolf Otto's *The Idea of the Holy* Revisited. In: Barton (2003), pp. 22–47.

Cruciat, Diego (2016). Tertulliano e la filosofia: Una proposta metafilosofica. *Augustinianum* 56 (2): 347–66.
Curd, Martin – Cover, J. A. – Pincock, Christopher (2013). *Philosophy of Science: The Central Issues*. New York and London: W. W. Norton & Company.
D'Alès, Adhémar (1905). *La théologie de Tertullien*. Paris: Beauchesne.
Dal Covolo, Enrico (1998). Conoscenza «razionale» di Dio, contemplazione ed esperienza «mistica»: Ignazio di Antiochia, Clemente e Origene. In: Padovese (1998), pp. 237–51.
Dassmann, Ernst (2009). San Pablo en la primera teología cristiana hasta Ireneo. *AHIg* 18: 239–57.
Davies, Malcolm (1989). Sisyphus and the Invention of Religion ('Critias' *TrGF* 1 (43) F 19 = B 25 *DK*). *BICS* 36: 16–32.
Dawkins, Richard (2006a). *The Selfish Gene*. Oxford: Oxford University Press.
Dawkins, Richard (2006b). *The God Delusion*. Boston and New York: Houghton Mifflin.
Dawkins, Richard (2009). *The Greatest Show on Earth: The Evidence for Evolution*. New York: Free Press.
Defosse, Pol (ed.) (2003). *Hommage a Carl Deroux, tome V: Christianisme et Moyen Âge, Néo-latin et survivance de la latinité*. Brussels: Latomus.
De Jong, Irene J. F. (2004). *Narrators and Focalizers: The Presentation of the Story in the Iliad*. London and New York: Bristol Classical Press.
Deichgräber, Karl (1938). Xenophanes Περὶ φύσεως. *RhM* 87: 1–31.
Delitzsch, Friedrich (1902). *Babel und Bibel: Ein Vortrag*. Leipzig: J. C. Hinrichs'sche Buchhandlung.
Delitzsch, Friedrich (1903). *Zweiter Vortrag über Babel und Bibel*. Stuttgart: Deutsche Verlags-Anstalt.
Dennett, Daniel C. (1995). *Darwin's Dangerous Idea: Evolution and the Meanings of Life*. New York: Simon & Schuster.
Dennett, Daniel C. (2006). *Breaking the Spell: Religion as a Natural Phenomenon*. New York: Viking.
Detienne, Marcel (1996). *The Masters of Truth in Archaic Greece* New York: The MIT Press.
De Vecchi, Pierluigi (2002). *Raphael*. New York and London: Abbeville Press.
De Vogel, Cornelia J. (1978). Problems Concerning Justin Martyr: Did Justin Find a Certain Continuity between Greek Philosophy and Christian Faith? *Mnemosyne* 31 (4): 360–88.
De Waal, Frans (1996). *Good Natured: The Origins of Right and Wrong in Humans and Other Animals*. Cambridge, MA: Harvard University Press.
De Waal, Frans (2006). *Primates and Philosophers: How Morality Evolved*. Princeton and Oxford: Princeton University Press.
DiCenso, James J. (1999). *The Other Freud: Religion, Culture and Psychoanalysis*. London and New York: Routledge.
Diggle, James (1996). Critias, *Sisyphus* (fr. 19 Snell, 1 Nauck). *Prometheus* 22 (2): 103–04.
Dihle, Albrecht (1977). Das Satyrspiel 'Sisyphos'. *Hermes* 105 (1): 28–42.
Dodds, Eric R. (1951). *The Greeks and the Irrational* Berkeley, Los Angeles & London: The University of California Press.
Dow, James W. (2007). A Scientific Definition of Religion. www.anpere.net/2007/2.pdf [28/02/2019].
Drechsler, Wolfgang and Kattel, Rainer (2004). Mensch und Gott bei Xenophanes. In: Witte (2004), pp. 111–29.
Drijvers, Han J. W. (1973). Theory Formation in Science of Religion and the Study of the History of Religions. In: Van Baaren and Drijvers (1973), pp. 57–77.

Drijvers, Han J. W. and Leertouwer, Lammert (1973). Epilogue. In: Van Baaren and Drijvers (1973), pp. 159–68.
Drobner, Hubertus R. (2011). *Patrologie: Úvod do studia starokřesťanské literatury.* Praha: Oikoymenh.
Droge, Arthur J. (1987). Justin Martyr and the Restoration of Philosophy. *ChHist* 56 (3): 303–19.
Dubuisson, Daniel (2005). *Impostures et pseudo-science: L'oeuvre de Mircea Eliade.* Villeneuve d'Ascq: Presses Universitaires du Septentrion.
Dudley, Guilford (1977). *Religion on Trial: Mircea Eliade and His Critics.* Philadelphia: Temple University Press.
Dunn, Geoffrey D. (2002). Rhetorical Structure in Tertullian's *Ad Scapulam. VChr* 56 (1), 47–55.
Dunn, Geoffrey D. (2005). Rhetoric and Tertullian's *De virginibus velandis. VChr* 59 (1), 1–30.
Dunn, Geoffrey D. (2008). *Tertullian's Adversus Iudaeos: A Rhetorical Analysis.* Washington, D. C.: The Catholic University of America Press.
Durkheim, Émile (1960). *Les formes élémentaires de la vie religieuse.* Paris: Presses Universitaires de France.
Edis, Taner (2008). *Science and Nonbelief.* Amherst: Prometheus.
Edwards, Mark J. (1991). Xenophanes Christianus? *GRBS* 32: 219–28.
Edwards, Mark W. (1980). Convention and Individuality in *Iliad* 1. *HSCPh* 84: 1–28.
Edwards, Mark W. (1980a). The Structure of Homeric Catalogues. *TAPhA* 110: 81–105.
Ehrman, Bart D. (2009). *Jesus, Interrupted: Revealing the Hidden Contradictions in the Bible.* New York: HarperOne.
Ehrman, Bart D. (2012). *The New Testament: A Historical Introduction to the Early Christian Writings.* New York and Oxford: Oxford University Press.
Einstein, Albert (1909). Über die Entwicklung unserer Anschauungen über das Wesen und die Konstitution der Strahlung. *Physik Z* 10 (22): 817–25.
Eisenberger, Herbert (1970). Demokrits Vorstellung vom Sein und Wirken der Götter. *RhM* 113: 141–58.
Eisenstadt, Michael (1974). Xenophanes' Proposed Reform of Greek Religion. *Hermes* 102: 142–50.
Eliade, Mircea (1949). *Traité d'histoire des religions.* Paris: Payot.
Eliade, Mircea (1959). Methodological Remarks on the Study of Religious Symbolism. In: Eliade and Kitagawa (1959), pp. 86–107.
Eliade, Mircea (1961). History of Religions and a New Humanism. *HR* 1 (1): 1–8.
Eliade, Mircea (1965). *Le sacré et le profane.* Paris: Gallimard.
Eliade, Mircea (1969). *The Quest: History and Meaning in Religion.* Chicago and London: The University of Chicago Press.
Eliade, Mircea (1995). *Dejiny náboženských predstáv a idejí I: Od doby kamennej po eleusínske mystériá.* Bratislava: Agora (přel. Ľubica Vychovalá).
Eliade, Mircea and Kitagawa, Joseph M. (eds) (1959). *The History of Religions: Essays in Methodology.* Chicago and London: The University of Chicago Press.
Ellwood, Robert (1999). *The Politics of Myth: A Study of C. G. Jung, Mircea Eliade, and Joseph Campbell.* Albany: State University of New York Press.
Engler, Steven and Gardiner, Mark Q. (2009). Religion as Superhuman Agency: On E. Thomas Lawson and Robert McCauley, Rethinking Religion (1990). In: Stausberg (2009), pp. 22–38.
Erbse, Hartmut (ed.) (1956). *Festschrift Bruno Snell zum 60. Geburtstag am 18. Juni 1956 von Freunden und Schülern überreicht.* München: C. H. Beck.

Evans-Pritchard, Edward E. (1965). *Theories of Primitive Religion*. Oxford: Clarendon Press.
Falter, Otto (1934). *Der Dichter und sein Gott bei den Griechen und Römern*. Würzburg: Konrad Triltsch.
Farah, Martha J. (ed.) (2010). *Neuroethics: An Introduction with Readings*. Cambridge, MA and London: The MIT Press.
Farkasfalvy, Denis (1968). Theology of Scripture in St. Irenaeus. *RBen* 78: 319–33.
Farmer, William R. (1984). Galatians and the Second-Century Development of the *Regula Fidei*. *JECS* 4 (3): 143–70.
Favazza, Armando R. (1996). *Bodies under Siege: Self-Mutilation and Body Modification in Culture and Psychiatry*. Baltimore: The Johns Hopkins University Press.
Fee, Gordon D. (1987). *The New International Commentary on the New Testament: The First Epistle to the Corinthians*. Grand Rapids: Eerdmans.
Félix, Viviana L. (2014). Las filosofías en la teología de Justino Mártir. *T&V* 55 (3): 435–48.
Ferrari, Giovanni (1988). Hesiod's Mimetic Muses and the Strategies of Deconstruction. In: Benjamin (1988), pp. 45–78.
Ferguson, Everett (2008). The Appeal to Apostolic Authority in the Early Centuries. *Restor Q* 50 (1): 49–62.
Ferguson, Thomas C. K. (2001). The Rule of Truth and Irenaean Rhetoric in Book 1 of 'Against Heresies'. *VChr* 55 (4): 356–75.
Fernández, P. Samuel (2004). *Regulae fidei et rationis*: Tradición, razón y Escritura en los primeros siglos. *T&V* 45: 103–21.
Feyerabend, Paul (1986a). *Wider der Methodenzwang*. Frankfurt am Main: Suhrkamp.
Feyerabend, Paul (1986b). Eingebildete Vernunft: Die Kritik des Xenophanes an den Homerischen Göttern. In: Lenk (1986), pp. 205–23.
Finkelberg, Aryeh (1990). Studies in Xenophanes. *HSCPh* 93: 103–67.
Finkelberg, Margalit (1990). A Creative Oral Poet and the Muse. *AJPh* 111 (3): 293–303.
Fitzgerald, Timothy (1996). Religion, Philosophy and Family Resemblances. *Religion* 26 (3): 215–36.
Fitzgerald, Timothy (2000). *The Ideology of Religious Studies*. New York and Oxford: Oxford University Press.
Fitzgerald, Timothy (2003). Playing Language Games and Performing Rituals: Religious Studies as Ideological State Apparatus. *MTSR* 15 (3): 209–54.
Fitzmyer, Joseph A. (2008). *The Anchor Yale Bible: First Corinthians*. New Haven and London: Yale University Press.
Flasche, Rainer (1997). Joachim Wach. In: Michaels (1997), pp. 290–302.
Flieder, Viktor (ed.) (1970). *Festschrift Franz Loidl zum 65. Geburtstag, Band I*. Wien: Hollinek.
Fodor, Jerry (1983). *The Modularity of Mind: An Essay on the Faculty Psychology*. Cambridge, MA: The MIT Press.
Fodor, Jerry (2000). *The Mind Doesn't Work That Way: The Scope and Limits of Computational Psychology*. Cambridge, MA: The MIT Press.
Foucault, Michel (1966). *Les mots et les choses: Une archéologie des sciences humaines*. Paris: Gallimard.
Foucault, Michel (1972). *Histoire de la folie à l'âge classique*. Paris: Gallimard.
Fowler, Robert (ed.) (2004). *The Cambridge Companion to Homer*. Cambridge: Cambridge University Press.
Fowler, Robert (ed.) (2004). The Homeric Question. In: Fowler (2004), pp. 220–32.
Fowler, Robert (ed.) (2011). Mythos and Logos. *JHS* 131: 45–66.
France, Richard T. (2007). *The New International Commentary on the New Testament: The Gospel of Matthew*. Grand Rapids: William B. Eerdmans.

Franek, Juraj (2011). Lucretius and the Modern Interdisciplinary Critique of Religion. *GLB* 16 (1): 15–28.
Franek, Juraj (2013). Presocratic Philosophy and the Origins of Religion. *GLB* 18 (1): 57–74.
Franek, Juraj (2014). Has the Cognitive Science of Religion (Re)defined 'Religion'? *Religio* 22 (1): 3–27.
Frank, Robert H. (1988). *Passions within Reason: The Strategic Role of Emotions*. New York and London: W. W. Norton & Company.
Frazer, James G. (1910). *Totemism and Exogamy: A Treatise on Certain Early Forms of Superstition and Society*. London: Macmillan & Co.
Frazer, James G. (1920). *The Golden Bough: A Study in Magic and Religion, Part I: The Magic Art and the Evolution of Kings, volume 1*. London: Macmillan & Co.
Freeman, Charles (2009). *A New History of Early Christianity*. New Haven – London: Yale University Press.
Frend, William H. C. (2008). *Martyrdom and Persecution in the Early Church: A Study of a Conflict from Maccabees to Donatus*. Cambridge: James Clarke & Co (repr.).
Freud, Sigmund (1975). *Der Mann Moses und die monotheistische Religion: Schriften über die Religion*. Frankfurt am Main: Fischer Taschenbuch Verlag.
Freud, Sigmund (1991). *Totem und Tabu: Einige Übereinstimmungen im Seelenleben der Wilden und der Neurotiker*. Frankfurt am Main: Fischer Taschenbuch Verlag.
Freud, Sigmund (1993). *Massenpsychologie und Ich-Analyse. Die Zukunft Einer Illusion*. Frankfurt am Main: Fischer Taschenbuch Verlag.
Freud, Sigmund, Mitscherlich, Alexander (ed.), Richards, Angela (ed.) and Strachey, James (ed.) (1989). *Studienausgabe, Band I: Vorlesungen zur Einführung in die Psychoanalyse und Neue Folge*. Frankfurt am Main: S. Fischer Verlag.
Frick, Heinrich (1928). *Vergleichende Religionswissenschaft*. Berlin and Leipzig: Walter de Gruyter (*SG* 208).
Frick, Heinrich (1950). Die aktuelle Aufgabe der Religionsphänomenologie. In: Lanczkowski (1974), pp. 124–32.
Friedländer, Paul (1914). Das Proömium der *Theogonie*. *Hermes* 49: 1–16.
Fumerton, Richard (2002). Theories of Justification. In: Moser (2002), pp. 204–233.
Fustel de Coulanges, N. Denis (1900). *La cité antique*. Paris: Librairie Hachette.
García López, José (1986). Interpretación y crítica del mito en los primeros filósofos griegos. *Myrtia* 1 (1): 43–64.
Garland, David E. (2003). *Baker Exegetical Commentary on the New Testament: 1 Corinthians*. Grand Rapids: Baker Academic.
Gazzaniga, Michael S., Ivry, Richard B. and Mangum, George R. (2009). *Cognitive Neuroscience: The Biology of the Mind*. New York and London: W. W. Norton.
Geertz, Armin W. (2008a). Cognitive Approaches to the Study of Religion. In: Antes, Geertz and Warne (2008b), pp. 347–99.
Geertz, Armin W. (2008b). How Not to Do the Cognitive Science of Religion Today. *MTSR* 20 (1): 7–21.
Geertz, Armin W. (2009). New Atheistic Approaches in the Cognitive Science of Religion. In: Stausberg (2009), pp. 242–63.
Geertz, Clifford (1973). *The Interpretation of Cultures*. New York: Basic Books.
Gemelli Marciano, M. Laura (2005). Xenophanes, Antike Interpretation und kultureller Kontext: Die Kritik an den Dichtern und der sogennante >Monismus<. In: Rechenauer (2005), pp. 118–33.
Gerson, Lloyd P. (1990). *God and Greek Philosophy: Studies in the Early History of Natural Theology*. London and New York: Routledge.

Gilson, Étienne (1986). *La philosophie au Moyen Âge: Des origines patristiques à la fin du XIVe siècle*. Paris: Éditions Payot.
Godfrey-Smith, Peter (2003). *Theory and Reality: An Introduction to the Philosophy of Science*. Chicago and London: The University of Chicago Press.
Goldenweiser, Alexander A. (1910). Totemism: An Analytical Study. *JAF* 23: 179–293.
Goldhammer, Kurt (1960). *Die Formenwelt des Religiöses: Grundriß der systematischen Religionswissenschaft*. Stuttgart: Kröner.
Gombrich, Ernst H. (1986). *Gombrich on the Renaissance, Volume 4: New Light on Old Masters*. London: Phaidon.
Gombrich, Ernst H. (2000). *Art and Illusion: A Study in the Psychology of Pictorial Representation*. Princeton and Oxford: Princeton University Press.
González, Justo L. (1974). Athens and Jerusalem Revisited: Reason and Authority in Tertullian. *ChHist* 43 (1): 17–25.
Gooch, Todd A. (2000). *The Numinous and Modernity: An Interpretation of Rudolf Otto's Philosophy of Religion*. Berlin and New York: Walter de Gruyter.
Goody, Jack (1961). Religion and Ritual: The Definitional Problem. *Br J Sociol* 12 (2): 142–64.
Görgemanns, Herwig and Schmidt, Ernst A. (eds) (1976). *Studien zum antiken Epos*. Meisenheim am Glan: Hain.
Gould, Cecil (1982). Raphael versus Giulio Romano: The Swing Back. *BM* 124 (953): 479–87.
Gould, Stephen J. (1997). Nonoverlapping Magisteria. *NatHist* 106 (3): 16–22.
Gould, Stephen J. (2002). *Rocks of Ages: Science and Religion in the Fullness of Life*. London: Vintage.
Gould, Stephen J. and Lewontin, Richard C. (1979). The Spandrels of San Marco and the Panglossian Paradigm: A Critique of the Adaptationist Programme. *Proc R Soc B* 205: 581–98.
Granger, Herbert (2007). Prose and Poetry: Xenophanes of Colophon. *TAPhA* 137 (2): 403–33.
Grant, Robert M. (1952). *Miracle & Natural Law in Graeco-Roman and Early Christian Thought*. Amsterdam: North-Holland Publishing Co.
Green, Thomas J. (2016). 'Vedāntist of Vedāntists'? The Problem of Friedrich Max Müller's Religious Identity. *PEGS* 85 (2–3): 180–90.
Greene, Joshua D. (2003). From Neural 'Is' to Moral 'Ought': What Are the Moral Implications of Neuroscientific Moral Psychology? *Nat Rev Neurosci* 4: 847–50.
Greene, Joshua D. and Haidt, Jonathan (2002). How (and Where) Does Moral Judgment Work? *Trends Cogn Sci* 6 (12): 517–23.
Greene, Joshua D., Sommerville, Brian R., Nystrom, Leigh E., Darley, John M. and Cohen, Jonathan D. (2001). An fMRI Investigation of Emotional Engagement in Moral Judgment. *Science* 293: 2105–08.
Guerra, Anthony J. (1991). Polemical Christianity: Tertullian's Search for Certitude. *JECS* 8: 109–23.
Gunn, Jeremy T. (2003). The Complexity of Religion and the Definition of 'Religion' in International Law. *Harv Hum Rts J* 16: 189–215.
Guthrie, William K. C. (1962). *A History of Greek Philosophy, Volume 1: The Earlier Presocratics and the Pythagoreans*. Cambridge: Cambridge University Press.
Guthrie, William K. C. (1965). *A History of Greek Philosophy, Volume 2: The Presocratic Tradition from Parmenides to Democritus*. Cambridge: Cambridge University Press.
Guthrie, William K. C. (1971). *The Sophists*. Cambridge: Cambridge University Press.

Guthrie, Stewart E. (1993). *Faces in the Clouds: A New Theory of Religion.* Oxford: Oxford University Press.

Guthrie, Stewart E. (2007). Opportunity, Challenge and a Definition of Religion. *JSRNC* 1 (1): 58–67.

Hager, Fritz-Peter (1978). Zum Bedeutung der griechischen Philosophie für die christliche Wahrheit und Bildung bei Tertullian und bei Augustin. *A&A* 24: 76–84.

Hägglund, Bengt (1958). Die Bedeutung der »regula fidei« als Grundlage theologischer Aussagen. *STh* 12 (1): 1–44.

Haidt, Jonathan (2001). The Emotional Dog and Its Rationalist Tail: A Social Intuitionist Approach to Moral Judgment. *Psychol Rev* 108 (4): 814–34.

Haidt, Jonathan (2006). *The Happiness Hypothesis.* New York: Basic Books.

Haidt, Jonathan (2008). Morality. *Perspect Psychol Sci* 3 (1): 65–72.

Haidt, Jonathan (2009). Moral Psychology and the Misunderstanding of Religion. In: Schloss and Murray (2009), pp. 278–91.

Halfwassen, Jens (2008). Der Gott des Xenophanes: Überlegungen über Ursprung und Struktur eines philosophischen Monotheismus. *ARG* 10: 275–94.

Hamilton, William D. (1996). *Narrow Roads of Gene Land, volume 1: Evolution of Social Behaviour.* New York: W. H. Freeman.

Hardie, Alex (2009). Etymologising the Muse. *MD* 62 (1): 9–57.

Harris, Horton (1990). *The Tübingen School: A Historical and Theological Investigation of the School of F. C. Baur.* Grand Rapids: Baker.

Harris, Sam (2010). *The Moral Landscape: How Science Can Determine Human Values.* New York: Free Press.

Harrison, Stephen (1990). Lucretius, Euripides and the Philosophers: De Rerum Natura 5.13–21. *CQ* 40 (1): 195–98.

Harrison, Victoria S. (2006). The Pragmatics of Defining Religion in a Multi-Cultural World. *IJPR* 59: 133–52.

Harrod, James B. (2011). A Trans-Species Definition of Religion. *JSRNC* 5 (3): 327–53.

Hastings, James (ed.) (1914). *Encyclopaedia of Religion and Ethics, volume 6: Fiction – Hyksos.* New York: Charles Scribner's Sons.

Hauck, Robert J. (1988). 'They Saw What They Said They Saw': Sense Knowledge in Early Christian Polemic. *HThR* 81 (3): 239–49.

Hauser, Marc D. (2006). *Moral Minds: The Nature of Right and Wrong.* New York: Ecco.

Havrda, Matyáš (2011). Galenus Christianus? The Doctrine of Demonstration in Stromata VIII and the Question of its Source. *VChr* 65 (4): 343–75.

Havrda, Matyáš (2012). Demonstrative Method in Stromateis VII: Context, Principles, and Purpose. In: Havrda, Hušek and Plátová (2012), pp. 261–75.

Havrda, Matyáš, Hušek, Vít and Plátová, Jana (eds) (2012). *The Seventh Book of the Stromateis: Proceedings on the Colloquium on Clement of Alexandria (Olomouc, October 21-23, 2010).* Leiden and Boston: Brill 2012.

Hefner, Philip (1964). Theoretical Methodology and St. Irenaeus. *JR* 44 (4): 294–309.

Heidegger, Martin (2006). *Sein und Zeit.* Tübingen: Max Niemeyer.

Heiden, Bruce (2007). The Muses' Uncanny Lies: Hesiod, *Theogony* 27 and Its Translators. *AJPh* 128: 153–75.

Heiler, Friedrich (1921). *Das Gebet: Eine religionsgeschichtliche und religionspsychologische Untersuchung.* München: Ernst Reinhardt.

Heiler, Friedrich (1959). The History of Religions as a Preparation for the Co-operation of Religions. In: Eliade and Kitagawa (1959), pp. 132–60.

Heiler, Friedrich (1961). *Erscheinungsformen und Wesen der Religion.* Stuttgart: Kohlhammer (*RM* 1).
Heine, Ronald E. (1993). Stoic Logic as Handmaid to Exegesis and Theology in Origen's Commentary on the Gospel of John. *JThS* 44 (1): 90–117.
Henderson, Bobby (2006). *The Gospel of the Flying Spaghetti Monster.* New York: Villard Books.
Henrich, Joseph and Henrich, Natalie (2006). Culture, Evolution and the Puzzle of Human Cooperation. *Cogn Syst Res* 11 (3): 220–45.
Henrichs, Albert (1975). Two Doxographical Notes: Democritus and Prodicus on Religion. *HSCPh* 79: 93–123.
Henrichs, Albert (1976). The Atheism of Prodicus. *BCPE* 6: 15–21.
Henrichs, Albert (1984). The Sophists and Hellenistic Religion: Prodicus as the Spiritual Father of the Isis Aretalogies. *HSCPh* 88: 139–58.
Herbrechtsmeier, William (1993). Buddhism and the Definition of Religion: One More Time. *JSSR* 32 (1): 1–18.
Herschbell, Jackson P. (1983). The Oral-Poetic Religion of Xenophanes. In: Robb (1983), pp. 125–33.
Hick, John (2004). *An Interpretation of Religion: Human Responses to the Transcendent.* New Haven and London: Yale University Press.
Hill, Michael (1985). Sociological Approaches (I). In: Whaling (1985), pp. 89–148.
Hirschmann, Eva (1940). *Phänomenologie der Religion: Eine historisch-systematische Untersuchung von 'Religionsphänomenologie' und 'religionsphänomenologischer Methode' in der Religionswissenschaft.* Groningen: Triltsch.
Hjelde, Sigurd (ed.) (2000). *Man, Meaning, & History: Hundred Years of History of Religions in Norway, The Heritage of W. Brede Kristensen.* Leiden and Boston: Brill.
Holzhausen, Jens (1999). Zu *TrGF* 43 F 19 (= VS 88 B 25). *Hermes* 127 (3): 286–92.
Honko, Lauri (ed.) (1979). *Science of Religion: Studies in Methodology.* The Hague and Paris: Mouton (*R+R* 13).
Horton, Robin (1960). A Definition of Religion, and Its Uses. *JRAI* 90 (2): 201–26.
Horyna, Břetislav (2001). Czech Religious Studies: Past, Present, Future. *MTSR* 13 (1): 254–68.
Horyna, Břetislav (2011). *Kritik der religionswissenschaftlichen Vernunft: Plädoyer für eine empirisch fundierte Theorie und Methodologie.* Stuttgart: Kohlhammer.
Hourcade, Annie (2000). Protagoras et Démocrite: Le feu divin entre mythe et raison. *RphA* 18 (1): 87–113.
Hubbeling, Hubertus G. (1973). Theology, Philosophy and Science of Religion and their Logical and Empirical Presuppositions. In: Van Baaren and Drijvers (1973), pp. 9–33.
Hutschinson, Brian (2001). *G. E. Moore's Ethical Theory: Resistance and Reconciliation.* Cambridge: Cambridge University Press.
Hutton, Patrick H. (1981). The History of Mentalities: The New Map of Cultural History. *H&T* 20 (3): 237–59.
Huxley, Thomas H. (1895). *Ethics and Evolution.* London: Macmillan & Co.
Idinopoulos, Thomas A. and Yonan, Edward A. (eds) (1994). *Religion & Reductionism: Essays on Eliade, Segal, & the Challenge of the Social Sciences for the Study of Religion.* Leiden: E. J. Brill.
Irwin, Terence (2008). *The Development of Ethics: A Historical and Critical Study. Volume II: From Suarez to Rousseau.* Oxford: Oxford University Press.
Jackson, Anthony (1985). Social Anthropological Approaches. In: Whaling (1985), pp. 179–230.
Jaeger, Werner (1947). *The Theology of Early Greek Philosophers: Gifford Lectures 1936.* Oxford: Clarendon Press.

James, George A. (1995). *Interpreting Religion: The Phenomenological Approaches of Pierre Daniël Chantepie de la Saussaye, W. Brede Kristensen, and Gerardus van der Leeuw.* Denton: Aquiline.
James, Scott M. (2011). *An Introduction to Evolutionary Ethics.* Malden and Oxford: Wiley-Blackwell.
James, William (1922). *The Varieties of Religious Experience: A Study in Human Nature.* New York and London: Longmans, Green, & Co.
Johnson, William A. (2006). Hesiod's *Theogony*: Reading the Proem as a Priamel. *GRBS* 46: 231–35.
Jones, Robert A. (2005). *The Secret of the Totem: Religion and Society from McLennan to Freud.* New York: Columbia University Press.
Jong, Jonathan (2015). On (not) defining (non) religion. *SRC* 2 (3): 15–24.
Jong, Jonathan, Kavanagh, Christopher and Visala, Aku (2015). Born Idolaters: The Limits of the Philosophical Implications of the Cognitive Science of Religion. *NZSTh* 57 (2): 244–66.
Jonson, Jonas (2016). *Nathan Söderblom: Called to Serve.* Grand Rapids: William B. Eerdmans.
Jossa, Giorgio (2003). La valutazione Cristiana dei Greci da Giustino a Ippolito. In: Defosse (2003), pp. 170–79.
Jungić, Josephine (1988). Joachimist Prophecies in Sebastiano del Piombo's Borgherini Chapel and Raphael's *Transfiguration. JWI* 51: 66–83.
Kahn, Charles H. (1997). Greek Religion and Philosophy in the Sisyphus Fragment. *Phronesis* 42 (3): 247–62.
Kahneman, Daniel (2011). *Thinking, Fast and Slow.* New York: Farrar, Straus & Giroux.
Kambylis, Athanasios (1965). *Die Dichterweihe und ihre Symbolik: Untersuchungen zu Hesiodos, Kallimachos, Properz und Ennius.* Heidelberg: Carl Winter.
Katz, Joshua and Volk, Katharina (2000). 'Mere Bellies'? A New Look at *Theogony* 26–8. *JHS* 120: 122–31.
Kaufman, Peter I. (1991). Tertullian on Heresy, History, and the Reappropriation of Revelation. *ChHist* 60 (2): 167–79.
Kaufmann, Walter (1958). *Critique of Religion and Philosophy.* Princeton: Princeton University Press.
Kaufmann, Walter (1974). *Nietzsche: Philosopher, Psychologist, Antichrist.* Princeton: Princeton University Press.
Kee, Howard C. (1986). *Medicine, Miracle and Magic in New Testament Times.* Cambridge: Cambridge University Press (*SNTSMS* 55).
Keener, Craig S. (1999). *A Commentary on the Gospel of Matthew.* Grand Rapids: William B. Eerdmans.
Kehrer, Günther (1997). Max Weber. In: Michaels (1997), pp. 121–32.
Kelhoffer, James A. (1999). Ordinary Christians as Miracle Workers in the New Testament and the Second and Third Century Christian Apologists. *BR* 44: 23–34.
Kelhoffer, James A. (2001). The Apostle Paul and Justin Martyr on the Miraculous: A Comparison of Appeals to Authority. *GRBS* 42: 163–84.
Kelly, Brendan D. (2011). Self-Immolation, Suicide and Self-Harm in Buddhist and Western Traditions. *Transcultural Psychiatry* 48 (3): 299–317.
Kelly, Eugene (1997). *Structure and Diversity: Studies in the Phenomenological Philosophy of Max Scheler.* Dordrecht: Springer.
King, Catherine (1982). The Liturgical and Commemorative Allusions in Raphael's *Transfiguration* and Failure to Heal. *JWI* 45: 148–59.

King, Ursula (1984). Historical and Phenomenological Approaches to the Study of Religion: Some Major Developments and Issues under Debate since 1950. In: Whaling (1984), pp. 29–164.
Kippenberg, Hans G. (1997a). William Robertson Smith. In: Michaels (1997), pp. 61–76.
Kippenberg, Hans G. (1997b). Émile Durkheim. In: Michaels (1997), pp. 103–19.
Kirk, Geoffrey S. (ed.) (1985). *The Iliad: A Commentary, Volume 1, Books 1–4*. Cambridge: Cambridge University Press.
Kirk, Geoffrey S., Raven, John E. and Schofield, Malcolm (2004). *Předsókratovští filosofové: Kritické dějiny s vybranými texty*. Praha: Oikoymenh (přel. Filip Karfík, Petr Kolev & Tomáš Vítek).
Kishimoto, Hideo (1961). An Operational Definition of Religion. *Numen* 8 (3): 236–40.
Kitagawa, Joseph M. (1959). The History of Religions in America. In: Eliade and Kitagawa (1959), pp. 1–30.
Kleinbub, Christian K. (2008). Raphael's *Transfiguration* as Visio-Devotional Program. *ABull* 90 (3): 367–93.
Klibengajtis, Tomasz (2004). Die Wahrheitsbezeichnungen des Clemens von Alexandrien in ihrem philosophischen und theologischen Kontext. *VChr* 58 (3): 316–31.
Klimkeit, Hans-Joachim (1997). Friedrich Max Müller. In: Michaels (1997), pp. 29–40.
Koertge, Noretta (ed.) (1998). *A House Built on Sand: Exposing Postmodernist Myths about Science*. Oxford: Oxford University Press.
Kohl, Karl-Heinz (1997). Edward Burnett Tylor. In: Michaels (1997), pp. 41–59.
Kollmann, Bernd (1996). *Jesus und die Christen als Wundertäter: Studien zu Magie, Medizin unch Schamanismus in Antike und Christentum*. Göttingen: Vandenhoeck & Ruprecht (FRLANT 170).
Kollmann, Bernd (2011). *Neutestamentliche Wundergeschichten*. Stuttgart: Kohlhammer.
Kovacs, Judith L. (2017). Reading the "Divinely Inspired" Paul: Clement of Alexandria in Conversation with "Heterodox" Christians, Simple Believers, and Greek Philosophers. In: Černušková, Kovacs and Plátová (2017), pp. 325–43.
Kraemer, Hendrik (1956). *Religion and the Christian Faith*. London: Lutterworth Press.
Kranz, Walter and Vogt, Ernst (eds) (1967). *Studien zur antiken Literatur und ihrem Fortwirken*. Heidelberg: Carl Winter.
Krischer, Tilman (1965). Die Entschuldigung des Sängers (*Ilias* B 484–493). *RhM* 108 (1): 1–11.
Kristensen, W. Brede (1960). *The Meaning of Religion: Lectures in the Phenomenology of Religion*. The Hague: Martinus Nijhoff.
Kühneweg, Uwe (1988). Die griechischen Apologeten und die Ethik. *VChr* 42 (2): 112–20.
Kundt, Radek (2015). *Contemporary Evolutionary Theories of Culture and Religion*. London and Oxford: Bloomsbury.
Kundt, Radek (2019). Making Evolutionary Science of Religion an Integral Part of Cognitive Science of Religion. In: Petersen, Gilhus, Martin, Jensen and Sørensen (2019), pp. 141–58.
Kushner, A. W. (1967). Two Cases of Auto-Castration Due to Religious Delusions. *Brit J Med Psychol* 40 (3): 293–98.
Kuusela, Oskari and McGinn, Marie (eds) (2011). *The Oxford Handbook of Wittgenstein*. Oxford: Oxford University Press.
Labhardt, André (1950). Tertullien et la philosophie ou la recherché d'une «position pure». *MH* 7 (3): 159–80.
Lanczkowski, Günter (ed.) (1974). *Selbstverständnis und Wesen der Religionswissenschaft*. Darmstadt: Wissenschaftliche Buchgesellschaft (*WdF* 263).

Lanczkowski, Günter (ed.) (1978). *Einführung in die Religionsphänomenologie*. Darmstadt: Wissenschaftliche Buchgesellschaft.
Lanczkowski, Günter (ed.) (1980). *Einführung in die Religionswissenschaft*. Darmstadt: Wissenschaftliche Buchgesellschaft.
Lane, Justin E. (2017). Looking Back to Look Forward: From Shannon and Turing to Lawson and McCauley to ...? In: Martin and Wiebe (2017), pp. 169–80.
Lang, Andrew (1898). *The Making of Religion*. London: Longmans, Green, & Co.
Lang, Andrew (1905). *The Secret of the Totem*. London: Longmans, Green, & Co.
Lange, Dietz (2011). *Nathan Söderblom und seine Zeit*. Göttingen: Vandenhoeck & Ruprecht.
Larmer, Robert A. (2011). The Meanings of Miracle. In: Twelftree (2011), pp. 36–53.
Larsen, Timothy (2014). *The Slain God: Anthropologists and the Christian Faith*. Oxford: Oxford University Press.
Larson, Jennifer (2016). *Understanding Greek Religion: A Cognitive Approach*. London and New York: Routledge.
Latacz, Joachim (ed.) (2002). *Homers Ilias: Gesamtkommentar, Band I, Faszikel 2*. München and Leipzig: K. G. Saur.
Latte, Kurt (1958). Methodenprobleme der modernen Religionsgeschichte. In: Lanczkowski (1974), pp. 168–79.
Lawson, E. Thomas (2017). The Cognitive Science of Religion and the Growth of Knowledge. In: Martin and Wiebe (2017), pp. 7–15.
Lawson, E. Thomas and McCauley, Robert N. (1990). *Rethinking Religion: Connecting Cognition and Culture*. Cambridge: Cambridge University Press.
Lease, Gary (2009). The History of 'Religious' Consciousness and the Diffusion of Culture: Strategies for Surviving Dissolution. *MTSR* 21 (2): 113–38.
Lebedev, Andrei (2000). Xenophanes on the Immutability of God: A Neglected Fragment in Philo Alexandrinus. *Hermes* 128 (4): 385–91.
Le Boulluec, Alain (1999). Le rencontre de l'hellénisme et de la «philosophie barbare» selon Clément d'Alexandrie. In: Leclant (1999), pp. 175–88.
Leclant, Jean (ed.) (1999). *Cahiers de la Villa «Kérylos» N°9: «Alexandrie, une mégalopole cosmopolite»*. Paris: Académie des Inscriptions et Belles-Lettres.
LeDoux, Jospeh (2002). *Synaptic Self: How Our Brains Become Who We Are*. New York: Penguin.
Leech, David and Visala, Aku (2011). The Cognitive Science of Religion: Implications for Theism? *Zygon* 46 (1): 47–64.
Leertouwer, Lammert (1973). Inquiry into Religious Behaviour: A Theoretical Reconnaissance. In: Van Baaren and Drijvers (1973), pp. 79–98.
Lefkowitz, Mary R. (1989). 'Impiety' and 'Atheism' in Euripides' Dramas. *CQ* 39 (1): 70–82.
Lenk, Hans (ed.) (1986). *Zur Kritik der wissenschaftlichen Rationalität: Zum 65. Geburtstag von Kurt Hübner*. Freiburg: Verlag Karl Alber.
Lenz, Ansgar (1980). *Das Proöm des frühen griechischen Epos: Ein Beitrag zum poetischen Selbstverständnis*. Bonn: Rudolf Habelt Verlag.
Lesher, James H. (2012). A Systematic Xenophanes? In: McCoy (2012), pp. 77–90.
Lesky, Albin (1999). *Geschichte der griechischen Literatur*. München: K. G. Saur.
Lewontin, Richard C., Rose, Steve and Kamin, Leon J. (1984). *Not in Our Genes: Biology, Ideology and Human Nature*. New York: Pantheon Books.
Lieberman, Daniel E. (2011). *The Evolution of Human Head*. Cambridge, MA and London: The Belknap Press of Harvard University Press.
Lightbown, Ronald (1989). *Botticelli: Life and Work*. New York and London: Abbeville Press.

Lock, Andy and Strong, Tom (2010). *Social Constructionism: Sources and Stirrings in Theory and Practice*. Cambridge: Cambridge University Press.

Löhr, Winrich (2000). The Theft of the Greeks: Christian Self-Definition in the Age of Schools. *RHE* 95 (3): 403–26.

Lord, Albert B., Mitchell, Stephen (ed.) and Nagy, Gregory (ed.) (2000). *The Singer of Tales*. Cambridge, MA and London: Harvard University Press.

Lortz, Joseph – Manns, Peter (ed.) (1987). *Erneuerung und Einheit: Aufsätze zur Theologie- und Kirchengeschichte aus Anlass seines 100. Geburtstages*. Stuttgart: Steiner Verlag.

Lössl, Josef (2002). Der Glaubenbegriff des Klemens von Alexandrien im Kontext der hellenistischen Philosophie. *Th&Ph* 77 (3): 321–37.

Lowie, Robert H. (1917). *Culture and Ethnology*. New York: Douglas McMurtrie.

Lüdemann, Gerd – Schröder, Martin (1987). *Die Religionsgeschichtliche Schule in Göttingen: Eine Dokumentation*. Göttingen: Vandenhoeck & Ruprecht.

Lütgens, Hans (1929). *Rafaels Transfiguration in der Kunstliteratur der letzten vier Jahrhunderte*. Göttingen: Universität Göttingen (diss.).

Lyotard, Jean-François (1979). *La condition postmoderne*. Paris: Les Éditions de Minuit.

MacIntyre, Alasdair (2004). *Ztráta ctnosti: K morální krizi současnosti*. Praha: Oikoymenh (přel. Pavla Sadílková, David Hoffman).

Mackie, John L. (1980). *Hume's Moral Theory*. London and New York: Routledge.

MacLennan, John F. (1865). *Primitive Marriage: An Inquiry into the Origin of the Form of Capture in Marriage Ceremonies*. Edinburgh: Adam & Charles Black.

MacLennan, John F. (1869/70). The Worship of Animals and Plants. *Fortnightly Review* 6: 407–27, 562–82; 7: 194–216.

MacLennan, John F. (1870). The Worship of Animals and Plants, Part II.: Totem-Gods among the Ancients. *Fortnightly Review* 7: 194–216.

Maehler, Herwig (1963). *Die Auffassung des Dichterberufs im frühen Griechentum bis zur Zeit Pindars*. Göttingen: Vandenhoeck & Ruprecht.

Magee, Bryan (1997). *The Philosophy of Schopenhauer*. Oxford: Clarendon Press.

Maier, Bernhard (2009). *William Robertson Smith*. Tübingen: Mohr Siebeck (*FAT* 67).

Malinowski, Bronislaw (1948). *Magic, Science and Religion and Other Essays*. Boston: Beacon Press.

Mallory, James P. and Adams, Douglas Q. (2006). *The Oxford Introduction to Proto-Indo-European and the Proto-Indo-European World*. Oxford: Oxford University Press.

Marett, Robert R. (1909). The Tabu-Mana Formula. In: Waardenburg (1999), pp. 258–63.

Marett, Robert R. (1914). *The Threshold of Religion*. New York: Macmillan Company.

Marg, Walter (1957). *Homer über die Dichtung*. Münster: Aschendorffsche Verlagsbuchhandlung.

Martin, Craig (2009). Delimiting Religion. *MTSR* 21 (2): 157–76.

Martin, Luther H. (2008). Daniel Dennett's *Breaking the Spell*: An Unapologetic Apology. *MTSR* 20 (1): 61–66.

Martin, Luther H. – Wiebe, Donald (2012). Religious Studies as a Scientific Discipline: The Persistence of a Delusion. *Religio* 20 (1): 9–18.

Martin, Luther H. (eds) (2016). *Conversations and Controversies in the Scientific Study of Religion: Collaborative and Co-authored Essays by Luther H. Martin and Donald Wiebe*. Leiden and Boston: Brill.

Martin, Luther H. (eds) (2017). *Religion Explained? The Cognitive Science of Religion after Twenty-Five Years*. London and Oxford: Bloomsbury.

Martin, Michael (ed.) (2007). *The Cambridge Companion to Atheism*. Cambridge: Cambridge University Press.

Mayhew, Robert (2011). *Prodicus the Sophist: Texts, Translations, and Commentary*. Oxford: Oxford University Press.
McCauley, Robert N. (2011). *Why Religion is Natural and Science is not*. Oxford and New York: Oxford University Press.
McCauley, Robert N. and Lawson, E. Thomas (2002). *Bringing Ritual to Mind: Psychological Foundations of Cultural Forms*. Cambridge: Cambridge University Press.
McCauley, Robert N. with Lawson, E. Thomas (2017). *Philosophical Foundations of the Cognitive Science of Religion: A Head Start*. London and Oxford: Bloomsbury.
McCoy, Joe (ed.) (2012). *Studies in Philosophy and the History of Philosophy, volume 57: Early Greek Philosophy*. Washington, DC: Catholic University of America Press.
McCutcheon, Russell T. (1995). The Category 'Religion' in Recent Publications: A Critical Survey. *Numen* 42 (3): 284–309.
McCutcheon, Russell T. (1997). *Manufacturing Religion: The Discourse on Sui Generis Religion and the Politics of Nostalgia*. Oxford: Oxford University Press.
McCutcheon, Russell T. (2001a). *Critics not Caretakers: Redescribing the Public Study of Religion*. Albany: State University of New York Press.
McCutcheon, Russell T. (2001b). Methods, Theories, and Terrors of History: Closing the Eliade Era with Some Dignity. In: Rennie (2001), pp. 11–24.
McDermott, Robert (1970). The Religion Game: Some Family Resemblances. *J Am Acad Relig* 38 (4): 390–400.
McGibbon, Donal (1965). The Religious Thought of Democritus. *Hermes* 93 (4): 385–97.
McKinnon, Andrew M. (2002). Sociological Definitions, Language Games, and the 'Essence' of Religion. *MTSR* 14 (1): 61–83.
McNamara, Patrick (2009). *The Neuroscience of Religious Experience*. Cambridge: Cambridge University Press.
McPherran, Mark (1996). *The Religion of Socrates*. University Park: The Pennsylvania State University.
Méautis, Georges (1939). Le prologue à la *Théogonie* d'Hésiode. *REG* 52 (248): 573–83.
Mensching, Gustav (1959). *Die Religion: Erscheinungsformen, Strukturtypen und Lebensgesetze*. Stuttgart: Curt E. Schwab.
Meslin, Michel (1973). *Pour une science des religions*. Paris: Éditions du Seuil.
Meunier, Bernard (2006). Paul et les Pères grecs. *RecSR* 93 (3): 331–55.
Michaels, Axel (ed.) (1997). *Klassiker der Religionswissenschaft: Von Friedrich Schleiermacher bis Mircea Eliade*. München: C. H. Beck.
Minchin, Elizabeth (1995). The Poet Appeals to His Muse: Homeric Invocations in the Context of Epic Performance. *CJ* 91 (1): 25–33.
Minchin, Elizabeth (2001). *Homer and the Resources of Memory: Some Applications of Cognitive Theory to the* Iliad *and the* Odyssey. Oxford: Oxford University Press.
Minton, William W. (1960). Homer's Invocations of the Muses: Traditional Patterns. *TAPhA* 91: 292–309.
Minchin, Elizabeth (1962). Invocation and Catalogue in Hesiod and Homer. *TAPhA* 93: 188–212.
Minchin, Elizabeth (1970). The Proem-Hymn of Hesiod's *Theogony*. *TAPhA* 101: 357–77.
Mithen, Steven (1998). *The Prehistory of the Mind: A Search for the Origins of Art, Religion and Science*. London: Phoenix.
Moffatt, James (1916). Aristotle and Tertullian. *JThS* 17 (1): 170–71.
Molendijk, Arie L. (2000a). At the Cross-Roads: Early Dutch Science of Religion in International Perspective. In: Hjelde (2000), pp. 19–56.

Molendijk, Arie L. (2000b). The Heritage of Cornelis Petrus Tiele (1830–1902). *DRCH* 80 (2): 78–114.
Molendijk, Arie L. (2016). *Friedrich Max Müller and the Sacred Books of the East.* Oxford: Oxford University Press.
Moo, Douglas J. (1996). *The New International Commentary on the New Testament: The Epistle to the Romans.* Grand Rapids: William B. Eerdmans.
Moore, George E. (1959). *Principia Ethica.* Cambridge: Cambridge University Press.
Moores, John D. (1995). *Wrestling with Rationality in Paul: Romans 1–8 in a New Perspective.* Cambridge: Cambridge University Press.
Morgan-Wynne, John E. (1984). The Holy Spirit and Christian Experience in Justin Martyr. *VChr* 38 (2): 172–7.
Morris, Leon (1985). *The Tyndale New Testament Commentaries: 1 Corinthians.* Grand Rapids: Eerdmans.
Moser, Paul K. (ed.) (2002). *The Oxford Handbook of Epistemology.* Oxford and New York: Oxford University Press.
Moser, Paul K. (2008). *The Elusive God: Reorienting Religious Epistemology.* Cambridge: Cambridge University Press.
Moser, Paul K. and McFall, Michael (eds) (2012). *The Wisdom of Christian Faith.* Cambridge: Cambridge University Press.
Moss, Candida R. (2010). *The Other Christs: Imitating Jesus in Ancient Christian Ideologies of Martyrdom.* Oxford: Oxford University Press.
Moss, Candida R. (2012). *Ancient Christian Martyrdom: Diverse Practices, Theologies, and Traditions.* New Haven and London: Yale University Press.
Moss, Candida R. (2013). *The Myth of Persecution: How Early Christians Invented a Story of Martyrdom.* New York: HarperOne.
Most, Glenn W. (2013). Heraclitus on Religion. *Rhizomata* 1 (2): 153–67.
Motterlini, Matteo (ed.) (1999). *For and Against Method.* Chicago and London: Chicago University Press.
Mounce, Robert H. (1998). *The New International Commentary on the New Testament: The Book of Revelation.* Grand Rapids: William B. Eerdmans.
Müller, Max (1868). *Chips from a German Workshop, Volume 1: Essays on the Science of Religion.* London: Longmans, Green, & Co.
Müller, Max (1893). *Introduction to the Science of Religion.* London: Longmans, Greene, & Co.
Müller, Max (1907). *Natural Religion: The Gifford Lectures Delivered before the University of Glasgow in 1888.* London: Longmans, Green, & Co.
Munier, Charles (1988). La méthode apologétique de Justin Martyr. *RSR* 62 (2–3): 90–100.
Murphy, Nancey (2009). Cognitive Science and the Evolution of Religion: A Philosophical and Theological Appraisal. In: Schloss and Murray (2009), pp. 265–77.
Mürmel, Heinz (1997). Marcel Mauss. In: Michaels (1997), pp. 211–21.
Murray, Gilbert (1924). *The Rise of the Greek Epic.* Oxford: Clarendon Press.
Murray, Penelope (1981). Poetic Inspiration in Early Greece. *JHS* 101: 87–100.
Murray, Penelope (2005). The Muses: Creativity Personified? In: Stafford and Herrin (2005), pp. 147–59.
Murray, Penelope (2008). Qu'est-ce qu'une Muse? *Mètis* 6: 199–219.
Neitzel, Heinz (1980). Hesiod und die lügenden Musen: Zur Interpretation von *Theogonie* 27f. *Hermes* 108 (3): 387–401.
Nestle, Wilhelm (1966). *Vom Mythos zum Logos.* Aalen: Scientia-Verlag.
Nisbet, Robin G. M. and Hubbard, Margaret (1970). *A Commentary on Horace: Odes, Book I.* Clarendon Press: Oxford.

Nitecki, Matthew H. and Nitecki, Doris V. (eds) (1993). *Evolutionary Ethics*. Albany: State University of New York Press.
Nomamul Haq, Syed (1999). Thou Shalt Not Mix Religion and Science. *Nature* 400: 830–31.
Norenzayan, Ara (2013). *Big Gods: How Religion Transformed Cooperation and Conflict*. Princeton and Oxford: Princeton University Press.
Norenzayan, Ara and Heine, Steven J. (2005). Psychological Universals: What Are They and How Can We Know? *Psychol Bull* 131 (5): 763–84.
Norenzayan, Ara, Atran, Scott, Faulkner, Jason and Schaller, Mark (2006). Memory and Mystery: The Cultural Selection of Minimally Counterintuitive Narratives. *Cognitive Sci* (30): 531–53.
Notopoulos, James A. (1938). Mnemosyne in Oral Literature. *TAPhA* 69: 465–93.
Nowak, Martin A. (2006). Five Rules for the Evolution of Cooperation. *Science* 314: p. 1560–61.
Nowak, Martin A. (2011). *SuperCooperators: Altruism, Evolution, and Why We Need Each Other to Succeed*. New York and London: Free Press.
Oberhuber, Konrad (1962). Vorzeichnungen zu Raffaels 'Transfiguration'. *JBerlM* 4: 116–49.
Olson, Carl (1992). *The Theology and Philosophy of Eliade: A Search for the Centre*. London: Macmillan.
O'Neil, Mary K. and Akhtar, Salman (2009). *On Freud's "The Future of an Illusion"*. London: Karnac.
Oosten, Jarich (1985). Cultural Anthropological Approaches. In: Whaling (1985), pp. 231–64.
Orrù, Marco and Wang, Amy (1992). Durkheim, Religion, and Buddhism. *JSSR* 31 (1): 47–61.
Orwell, George (2008). *1984*. London: Penguin.
Osborn, Eric (1994). Arguments for Faith in Clement of Alexandria. *VChr* 48 (1): 1–24.
Osborn, Eric (1997). *Tertullian: First Theologian of the West*. Cambridge: Cambridge University Press.
Osborn, Eric (2001). *Irenaeus of Lyons*. Cambridge: Cambridge University Press.
O'Sullivan, Patrick (2012). Sophistic Ethics, Old Atheism and "Critias" on Religion. *CW* 105 (2): 167–85.
Otto, Rudolf (1963). *Das Heilige: Über das Irrationale in der Idee des Göttlichen und sein Verhältnis zum Rationalen*. München: C. H. Beck.
Otto, Walter F. (1955). *Die Musen und der göttliche Ursprung des Singens und Sagens*. Düsseldorf and Köln: Eugen Diederichs.
Paden, William E. (2002). *Bádání o posvátnu. Náboženství ve spektru interpretací*. Brno: Masarykova univerzita.
Paden, William E. (2016). *New Patterns for Comparative Religion: Passages to an Evolutionary Perspective*. London and Oxford: Bloomsbury.
Padovese, Luigi (ed.) (1998). *Atti del V Simposio di Tarso su S. Paolo Apostolo*. Roma: Istituto Francescano di Spiritualità & Pontificio Ateneo Antoniano.
Pagliaro, Antonino (1955). Il proemio dell'*Iliade*. *RAL* 10 (5–6): 369–96.
Palmer, John A. (1998). Xenophanes' Ouranian God in the Fourth Century. In: Taylor (1998), pp. 1–34.
Palmer, Michael (1997). *Freud and Jung on Religion*. London and New York: Routledge.
Pals, Daniel L. (1987). Is Religion a *Sui Generis* Phenomenon? *J Am Acad Relig* 55 (2): 259–82.
Pals, Daniel L. (2015a). *Nine Theories of Religion*. Oxford: Oxford University Press.
Parry, Milman and Parry, Adam (ed.) (1971). *The Making of Homeric Verse. The Collected Papers of Milman Parry*. New York and Oxford: Oxford University Press.
Parsons, Talcott (1964). Evolutionary Universals in Society. *ASR* 29 (3): 339–57.

Patočka, Jan (1996). *Nejstarší řecká filosofie: Filosofie v předklasickém údobí před sofistikou a Sókratem.* Praha: Vyšehrad.
Peek, Werner (1977). Hesiod und der Helikon. *Philologus* 121 (2): 173–75.
Penner, Hans H. (1971). The Poverty of Functionalism. *HR* 11 (1): 91–7.
Peršić, Vladan (2005). Πίστις: Philosophical-Scientific and Biblical-Patristic Conception of Faith. *Philotheos* 5: 154–64.
Petersen, Anders K., Gilhus, Ingvild S., Martin, Luther H., Jensen, Jeppe S. and Sørensen, J. (eds) (2019). *Evolution, Cognition, and the History of Religion: A New Synthesis. Festschrift in Honour of Armin W. Geertz.* Leiden and Boston: Brill.
Peterson, Gregory R. (2007). Why the New Atheism Shouldn't Be (Completely) Dismissed. *Zygon* 42 (2): 803–06.
Pettazzoni, Raffaele (1954a). Aperçu introductif. *Numen* 1 (1): 1–7.
Pettazzoni, Raffaele (1954b). *Essays on the History of Religions.* Leiden: E. J. Brill.
Pettazzoni, Raffaele (1959). The Supreme Being: Phenomenological Structure and Historical Development. In: Eliade and Kitagawa (1959), pp. 59–66.
Picot, Jean-Claude and Berg, William (2013). Empedocles vs. Xenophanes: Differing Notions of the Divine. *Organon* 45: 5–19.
Pine, Martin L. (1986). *Pietro Pomponazzi: Radical Philosopher of the Renaissance.* Padova: Editrice Antenore.
Pinker, Steven (1995). *The Language Instinct: How the Mind Creates Language.* New York: Harper Perennial.
Pinker, Steven (1999). *How the Mind Works.* London: Penguin.
Pinker, Steven (2002). *The Blank Slate: The Modern Denial of Human Nature.* New York: Penguin.
Piper, Otto A. (1961). The Nature of the Gospel According to Justin Martyr. *JR* 41 (3): 155–68.
Plantiga, Alvin (2000). *Warranted Christian Belief.* Oxford: Oxford University Press.
Podbielski, Henryk (1994). Der Dichter und die Musen im Prooimion der hesiodeischen Theogonie. *Eos* 82 (2): 173–88.
Poe, Edgar A. (2003). *The Fall of the House of Usher and Other Writings: Poems, Tales, Essays and Reviews* (ed. D. Galloway). London: Penguin.
Pötscher, Walter (1986). Das Selbstverständnis des Dichters in der homerischen Poesie. *LwJb* 27: 9–22.
Preimesberger, Rudolf (1987). Tragische Motive in Raffaels "Transfiguration". *ZfK* 50 (1): 88–115.
Preston, Charles S. (2010). Wach, Radhakrishnan, and Relativism. In: Wedemeyer and Doniger (2010), pp. 79–100.
Preus, James S. (1987). *Explaining Religion: Criticism and Theory from Bodin to Freud.* New Haven: Yale University Press.
Price, Richard M. (1988). 'Hellenization' and Logos Doctrine in Justin Martyr. *VChr* 42 (1): 18–23.
Pucci, Pietro (1977). *Hesiod and the Language of Poetry.* Baltimore: The Johns Hopkins University Press.
Purzycki, Benjamin Grant and Willard, Aiyana K. (2016). MCI Theory: A Critical Discussion. *Religion, Brain & Behavior* 6 (3): 207–48.
Putnam, Hilary (2002). *The Collapse of the Fact/Value Dichotomy and Other Essays.* Cambridge, MA and London: Harvard University Press.
Pycke, Nestor (1961). Connaissance rationnelle et connaisance de grâce chez saint Justin. *EthL* 37: 52–85.

Pye, Michael (1979). Commentary. In: Honko (1979), pp. 528–34.
Pye, Michael (1997). Friedrich Heiler. In: Michaels (1997), pp. 277–89.
Pyysiäinen, Ilkka (2003a). *How Religion Works: Towards a New Cognitive Science of Religion*. Leiden and Boston: Brill.
Pyysiäinen, Ilkka (2003b). Buddhism, Religion, and the Concept of 'God'. *Numen* 50 (2): 147–71.
Pyysiäinen, Ilkka (2004). *Magic, Miracles, and Religion: A Scientist's Perspective*. Walnut Creek: AltaMira Press.
Pyysiäinen, Ilkka (2009). *Supernatural Agents: Why We Believe in Souls, Gods, and Buddhas*. Oxford: Oxford University Press.
Quasten, Johannes (1964). *Patrology, vol. II.: The Ante-Nicene Literature after Irenaeus*. Utrecht & Antwerp: Spectrum Publishers.
Quine, Willard van Orman (1980). *From a Logica Point of View: 9 Logico-Philosophica Essays*. Cambridge, MA and London: Harvard University Press.
Radcliffe, Elizabeth S. (ed.) (2008). *A Companion to Hume*. Malden and Oxford: Blackwell.
Radcliffe-Brown, Alfred R. (1952). *Structure and Function in Primitive Society: Essays and Addresses*. Glencoe: The Free Press.
Radin, Paul (1937). *Primitive Religion: Its Nature and Origin*. New York: The Viking Press.
Radin, Paul (1953). *The World of Primitive Man*. New York: Henry Schuman.
Raines, John (ed.) (2002). *Marx on Religion*. Philadelphia: Temple University Press.
Ramnoux, Clémence (1984). Sur un monotheisme grec. *RPhL* 82 (54): 175–98.
Rappaport, Roy A. (1999). *Ritual and Religion in the Making of Humanity*. Cambridge: Cambridge University Press.
Raphael, Melissa (1997). *Rudolf Otto and the Concept of Holiness*. Oxford: Clarendon Press.
Read, Herbert (1964). The Poet and His Muse. *Arts: The Journal of the Sydney University Arts Association* 2 (3): 145–68.
Rechenauer, Georg (ed.) (2005). *Frühgriechisches Denken*. Göttingen: Vandenhoeck & Ruprecht.
Redfield, James (1979). The Proem of the *Iliad*: Homer's Art. *CPh* 74 (2): 95–110.
Refoulé, François (1956). Tertullien et la philosophie. *RSR* 30 (1): 42–45.
Renan, Ernest (1857). *Études d'histoire religieuse*. Paris: Michel Lévy.
Renan, Ernest (1863). *Vie de Jésus*. Paris: Michel Lévy.
Rennie, Brian S. (1996). *Reconstructing Eliade: Making Sense of Religion*. Albany: State University of New York Press.
Rennie, Brian S. (ed.) (2001). *Changing Religious Worlds: The Meaning and End of Mircea Eliade*. Albany: State University of New York Press.
Ridley, Matt (1997). *The Origins of Virtue*. London: Penguin.
Riedweg, Christoph (1990). The 'Atheistic' Fragment from Euripides' Bellerophontes (286 N^2). *ICS* 15 (1): 39–53.
Riesebrodt, Martin (1997). Robert Ranulph Marett. In: Michaels (1997), pp. 171–84.
Rijksbaron, Albert (2009). Discourse Cohesion in the Proem of Hesiod's *Theogony*. In: Bakker and Wakker (2009), pp. 241–62.
Ritoók, Zsigmond (1989). The Views of Early Greek Epic on Poetry and Art. *Mnemosyne* 42 (3/4): 331–48.
Rizzerio, Laura (1998). L'accès à la transcendance divine selon Clément d'Alexandrie: dialectique platonicienne ou expérience de l'union chrétienne'? *REAug* 44: 159–79.
Robb, Kevin (ed.) (1983). *Language and Thought in Early Greek Philosophy*. La Salle: Hegeler Institute.

Robertson Smith, William (1927). *The Lectures on the Religion of the Semites: The Fundamental Institutions*. New York: The Macmillan Company.
Robertson Smith, William and Black, John S. (ed.) – Chrystal, George (ed.) (1912). *Lectures and Essays of William Robertson Smith*. London: Adam & Charles Black.
Rosenberg, Martin (1985/86). Raphael's *Transfiguration* and Napoleon's Cultural Politics. *ECS* 19 (2): 180–205.
Roth, Catharine P. (1976). The Kings and the Muses in Hesiod's *Theogony*. *TAPhA* 106: 331–8.
Roubekas, Nickolas P. (2014). Ancient Greek Atheism? A Note on Terminological Anachronisms in the Study of Ancient Greek 'Religion'. *Ciências da Religião: história e sociedade* 12 (2): 224–41.
Russell, Bertrand and Slater, John G. (ed.) (1997). *The Collected Papers of Bertrand Russell, volume 11: Last Philosophical Testament 1947-68*. London: Routledge.
Sagan, Carl (1996). *The Demon-Haunted World*. New York: Ballantine Books.
Saler, Benson (1999). Biology and Religion: On Establishing a Problematic. *MTSR* 11 (4): 386–94.
Santoro, Maria C. (1994). Sisifo e il presunto ateismo di Crizia. *Orpheus* 15 (2): 419–29.
Sartre, Jean-Paul (1943). *L'être et le néant: Essai d'ontologie phénoménologique*. Paris: Gallimard.
Sartre, Jean-Paul (1970). *L'existentialisme est un humanisme*. Paris: Nagel.
Satterfield, Brian (2011). The Beginning of the *Iliad*: The 'Contradictions' of the Proem and the Burial of Hector. *Mnemosyne* 64 (1): 1–20.
Scaglioni, Carlo (1972). «Sapientia mundi» e «Dei sapientia»: L'esegesi di *I Cor*. 1,18–2,5 in Tertulliano. *Aevum* 46 (3–4): 183–215.
Scheler, Max (1933). *Vom Ewigen im Menschen*. Berlin: Der neue Geist Verlag.
Schjødt, Uffe and Geertz, Armin W. (2017). The Beautiful Butterfly: On the History of and Prospects for the Cognitive Science of Religion. In: Martin and Wiebe (2017), pp. 57–67.
Schimmel, Annemarie (1960). Summary of the Discussion. *Numen* 7 (2): 235–39.
Schlesier, Renate (1982). Les Muses dans le prologue de la «Théogonie» d' Hésiode. *RHR* 199 (2): 131–167.
Schloss, Jeffrey and Murray, Michael (eds) (2009). *The Believing Primate: Scientific, Philosophical and Theological Reflections on the Origin of Religion*. Oxford: Oxford University Press.
Schmidt, Wilhelm P. (1930). *Ursprung und Werden der Religion: Theorien und Tatsachen*. Münster: Aschendorffsche Verlagsbuchhandlung.
Schnelle, Udo (2014). *Paulus: Leben und Denken*. Berlin and Boston: Walter de Gruyter.
Schneider, Friedrich (1896). Theologisches in Raffaels Disputa und Transfiguration. *Katholik* 13 (1): 11–27.
Schnepel, Burkhard (1997). Edward Evan Evans-Pritchard. In: Michaels (1997), pp. 303–23.
Schoedel, William R. (1959). Philosophy and Rhetoric in the *Adversus Haereses* of Irenaeus. *VChr* 13 (1): 22–32.
Schoedel, William R. and Wilken, Robert L. (eds) (1979). *Early Christian Literature and the Classical Intellectual Tradition: In Honorem Robert M. Grant*. Paris: Éditions Beauchesne.
Schwabl, Hans (1963). Aufbau und Struktur des Prooimions der hesiodischen *Theogonie*. *Hermes* 91 (4): 385–415.
Scodel, Ruth (1998). Bardic Performance and Oral Tradition in Homer. *AJPh* 119 (2): 171–94.
Scott, Ian W. (2009). *Paul's Way of Knowing: Story, Experience, and the Spirit*. Grand Rapids: Baker Academic.

Searle, John R. (1992). *The Rediscovery of the Mind*. Cambridge, MA and London: The MIT Press.
Segal, Robert A. (ed.) (2006). *The Blackwell Companion to the Study of Religion*. Malden and Oxford: Blackwell.
Sesboüé, Bernard (1981). La preuve par les Ecritures chez saint Irénée: À propos d'un texte difficile du livre III de *l'Adversus haereses*. *NRTh* 103 (6): 872–87.
Setti, Alessandro (1958). La memoria e il canto: Saggio di poetica arcaica greca. *SIFC* 30 (1): 129–71.
Sharpe, Eric J. (1969). Nathan Söderblom and the Study of Religion. *Relig Stud* 4 (2): 259–74.
Sharpe, Eric J. (1979). Commentary. In: Honko (1979), pp. 204–212.
Sharpe, Eric J. (1986). *Comparative Religion: A History*. London: Duckworth.
Sharpe, Eric J. (1997). Nathan Söderblom. In: Michaels (1997), pp. 157–69.
Sider, Robert D. (1971). *Ancient Rhetoric and the Art of Tertullian*. Oxford: Oxford University Press.
Sider, Robert D. (1980). Credo quia absurdum? *CW* 73 (7): 417–19.
Sikes, Edward E. (1931). *The Greek View of Poetry*. London: Methuen & Co.
Simmel, Georg (1905). A Contribution to the Sociology of Religion. *AJS* 11 (3): 359–76.
Simmel, Georg (1917). *Grundfragen der Soziologie*. Berlin and Leipzig: G. J. Göschen.
Singer, Peter (2011). *The Expanding Circle: Ethics, Evolution, and Moral Progress*. Princeton and Oxford: Princeton University Press.
Skarsaune, Oskar (1987). *The Proof from Prophecy: A Study in Justin Martyr's Proof-Text Tradition*. Leiden: Brill.
Slone, D. Jason (2004). *Theological Incorrectness: Why Religious People Believe What They Shouldn't*. Oxford: Oxford University Press.
Slone, D. Jason and McCorkle Jr., William W. (eds) (2019). *The Cognitive Science of Religion: A Methodological Introduction to Key Empirical Studies*. London and New York: Bloomsbury Academic.
Smart, Ninian (1973). *The Science of Religion & the Sociology of Knowledge: Some Methodological Questions*. Princeton: Princeton University Press.
Smart, Ninian (1984). The Scientific Study of Religion in its Plurality. In: Whaling (1984), pp. 365–78.
Smith, Jonathan Z. (1982). *Imagining Religion: From Babylon to Jonestown*. Chicago and London: The University of Chicago Press.
Smith, Jonathan Z. (2004). *Relating Religion: Essays in the Study of Religion*. Chicago and London: The University of Chicago Press.
Smith, Wilfred Cantwell (1959). Comparative Religion: Whither – and Why? In: Eliade and Kitagawa (1959), pp. 31–58.
Smith, Wilfred Cantwell (2001). *The Meaning and the End of Religion*. Minneapolis: Fortress Press.
Snell, Bruno (1959). Mnemosyne in der frühgriechischen Dichtung. *ABG* 9: 19–22.
Snow, Charles P. (1993). *The Two Cultures*. Cambridge: Cambridge University Press.
Soames, Scott (2003). *The Philosophical Analysis in the Twentieth Century: Volume 1, The Dawn of Analysis*. Princeton and Oxford: Princeton University Press.
Sokal, Alan (2008). *Beyond the Hoax: Science, Philosophy and Culture*. Oxford: Oxford University Press.
Solmsen, Friedrich (1954). The "Gift" of Speech in Homer and Hesiod. *TAPhA* 85: 1–15.
Sosis, Richard (2009). The Adaptationist-Byproduct Debate on the Evolution of Religion: Five Misunderstandings of the Adaptationist Program. *JOCC* 9: 315–32.

Southwood, Martin (1978). Buddhism and the Definition of Religion. *Man* (n.s.) 13 (3): 362–79.
Söderblom, Nathan (1914). Holiness (General and Primitive). In: Hastings (1914), pp. 731–41.
Söderblom, Nathan (1942). *Der lebendige Gott im Zeugnis der Religionsgeschichte.* München: Verlag Ernst Reinhardt.
Söderblom, Nathan (1979). *Das Werden des Gottenglaubes: Untersuchungen über die Anfänge der Religion.* Hildesheim and New York: Georg Olms Verlag.
Spencer, Herbert (1898). *The Principles of Sociology, volume 1.* New York: D. Appleton & Company.
Spencer, Herbert and Hamilton, Gail (ed.) (1885). *The Insuppressible Book: A Controversy between Herbert Spencer and Frederic Harrison.* Boston: S. E. Cassino & Company.
Sperber, Dan (1975). *Rethinking Symbolism.* Cambridge: Cambridge University Press.
Sperber, Dan (1996). *Explaining Culture.* Malden and Oxford: Blackwell.
Sperduti, Alice (1950). The Divine Nature of Poetry in Antiquity. *TAPhA* 81: 209–40.
Spiro, Melford E. (1966). Religion: Problems of Definition and Explanation. In: Banton (1966), pp. 85–126.
Stafford, Emma and Herrin, Justin (eds) (2005). *Personification in the Greek World: From Antiquity to Byzantium.* Aldershot: Ashgate.
Stanton, Greg R. (1973). Quid ergo Athenis et Hierosolymnis? Quid mihi tecum est? and τί ἐμοὶ καὶ σοί; *RhM* 116 (1): 84–90.
Stausberg, Michael (ed.) (2009). *Contemporary Theories of Religion: A Critical Companion.* London and New York: Routledge.
Sterelny, Kim (2003). *Thought in a Hostile World: The Evolution of Human Cognition.* Oxford: Blackwell.
Stern-Gillet, Suzanne (2014). Hesiod's Proem and Plato's *Ion. CQ* 64 (1): 25–42.
Stockmeier, Peter (1972). Zum Verhältnis von Glaube und Religion bei Tertullian. In: Cross (1972), pp. 242–46.
Stoddard, Kathryn B. (2003). Message of the 'Kings and Singers' Passage: Hesiod, 'Theogony' 80–103. *TAPhA* 133 (1): 1–16.
Stolz, Fritz (1997). Bronisław Kaspar Malinowski. In: Michaels (1997), pp. 247–63.
Strauss, David F. (1837). *Das Leben Jesu: Erster Band.* Tübingen: C. F. Osiander.
Strenski, Ivan (1998). Religion, Power, and Final Foucault. *J Am Acad Relig* 66 (2): 345–67.
Strenski, Ivan (2006). *Thinking about Religion: An Historical Introduction to Theories of Religion.* Malden: Blackwell.
Stroh, Wilfred (1976). Hesiods lügende Musen. In: Görgemanns and Schmidt (1976), pp. 85–112.
Sutton, Dana (1981). Critias and Atheism. *CQ* 31 (1): 33–8.
Svenbro, Jesper (1976). *La parole et le marbre: Aux origines de la poétique grecque.* Lund: Akademisk Avhandling.
Swinburne, Richard (2001). *Epistemic Justification.* Oxford: Clarendon Press.
Swinburne, Richard (2005). *Faith and Reason.* Oxford: Clarendon Press.
Sylvester, Robert P. (1990). *The Moral Philosophy of G. E. Moore.* Philadelphia: Temple University Press.
Taliaferro, Charles (2009). Explaining Religious Experience. In: Schloss and Murray (2009), pp. 200–14.
Talmont-Kaminski, Konrad (2013). *Religion as Magical Ideology: How the Supernatural Reflects Rationality.* Durham: Acumen.
Tambiah, Stanley J. (1990). *Magic, Science, Religion, and the Scope of Rationality.* Cambridge: Cambridge University Press.

Taylor, Christopher C. W. (ed.) (1998). *Oxford Studies in Ancient Philosophy, volume XVI.* Oxford: Clarendon Press.
Theissen, Gerd (1983). *The Miracle Stories of the Early Christian Tradition.* Minneapolis: Fortress Press.
Thompson, Paul (1999). Evolutionary Ethics: Its Origins and Contemporary Face. *Zygon* 34 (3): 473–84.
Tiele, Cornelis P. (1897). *Elements of the Science of Religion, Part I.: Morphological.* Edinburgh and London: William Blackwood & Sons.
Tiele, Cornelis P. (1899). *Elements of the Science of Religion, Part II.: Ontological.* Edinburgh and London: William Blackwood & Sons.
Tigerstedt, E. N. (1970). *Furor Poeticus*: Poetic Inspiration in Greek Literature before Democritus and Plato. *JHI* 31 (2): 163–78.
Tillich, Paul (1957). *Dynamics of Faith.* New York: Harper & Row.
Torres-Guerra, José B. (1999). El Homero de Jenófanes. *Emerita* 67 (1): 75–86.
Tremlin, Todd (2005). Divergent Religion: A Dual-Process Model of Religious Thought. In: Whitehouse and McCauley (2005), pp. 69–83.
Tremlin, Todd (2006). *Minds and Gods: The Cognitive Foundations of Religion.* Oxford: Oxford University Press.
Trivers, Robert (2002). *Natural Selection and Social Theory.* Oxford: Oxford University Press.
Tuckett, Jonathan (2016). Clarifying the Phenomenology of Gerardus van der Leeuw. *MTSR* 28 (3): 227–63.
Turner, David L. (2008). *Baker Exegetical Commentary on the New Testament: Matthew.* Grand Rapids: Baker Academic.
Twelftree, Graham H. (ed.) (2011). *The Cambridge Companion to Miracles.* Cambridge: Cambridge University Press.
Tweyman, Stanley (ed.) (1995). *David Hume: Critical Assessments. Volume IV: Ethics, Passions, Sympathy, 'Is' and 'Ought'.* London and New York: Routledge.
Tworuschka, Udo (2011). *Religionswissenschaft: Wegbereiter und Klassiker.* Köln: Böhlau Verlag.
Tylor, Edward B. (1903a). *Primitive Culture: Researches into the Development of Mythology, Philosophy, Religion, Language, Art, and Custom, volume 1.* London: John Murray.
Tylor, Edward B. (1903b). *Primitive Culture: Researches into the Development of Mythology, Philosophy, Religion, Language, Art, and Custom, volume 2.* London: John Murray.
Van Baaren, Theo P. (1973). Science of Religion as a Systematic Discipline: Some Introductory Remarks. In: Van Baaren and Drijvers (1973), pp. 35–56.
Van Baaren, Theo P. and Drijvers, Han J. W. (eds) (1973). *Religion, Culture and Methodology: Papers of the Groningen Working-group for the Study of Fundamental Problems and Methods of Science of Religion.* The Hague and Paris: Mouton.
Van den Bosch, Lourens P. (2002). *Friedrich Max Müller: A Life Devoted to the Humanities.* Leiden and Boston: Brill.
Van der Leeuw, Gerardus (1926). Über einige neuere Ergebnisse der psychologischen Forschung und ihre Anwendung auf die Geschichte, insonderheit die Religionsgeschichte. *SMRS* 2: 1–43.
Van der Leeuw, Gerardus (1938). Rudolf Otto und die Religionsgeschichte. In: Lanczkowski (1974), pp. 76–86.
Van der Leeuw, Gerardus (1963). *Religion in Essence and Manifestation: A Study in Phenomenology.* New York: Harper & Row.
Van der Loos, Hendrik (1965). *The Miracles of Jesus.* Leiden: Brill.

Van Gennep, Arnold (1911). De la méthode à suivre dans l'étude des rites et des mythes. *Rev Univ Brux* 6: 505–23.
Van Gennep (1920). *L'État actuel du probleme totemique: étude critique des théories sur les origines de la religion et de l'organisation sociale*. Paris: Leroux.
Van Gennep (1960). *Rites of Passage*. Chicago: The University of Chicago Press.
Van Groningen, Bernard A. (1946). The Proems of the *Iliad* and the *Odyssey*. *MKNAW* 9 (1–10): 279–93.
Van Groningen (1948). Les trois Muses de l'Hélicon. *AC* 17 (1): 287–96.
Van Winden, Jacob C. M. (1977). Le portrait de la philosophie grecque dans Justin, "Dialogue" I 4–5. *VChr* 31 (3): 181–90.
Verdenius, W. J. (1972). Notes on the Proem of Hesiod's "Theogony". *Mnemosyne* 25 (3): 225–60.
Verdenius, W. J. (1983). The Principles of Greek Literary Criticism. *Mnemosyne* 36 (1/2): 14–59.
Vernant, Jean-Pierre (1957). Du mythe à la raison: La formation de la pensée positive dans la Grèce archaïque. *Annales (ESC)* 12 (2): 183–206.
Vernant, Jean-Pierre (1996). *Mythe et pensée chez les Grecs: Études de psychologie historique*. Paris: Éditions La Découverte.
Veyne, Paul (2000). *Les Grecs ont-ils cru à leur mythes?: Essai sur l'imagination constituante*. Paris: Seuil.
Vicaire, Paul (1963). Les Grecs et le mystère de l'inspiration poétique. *BAGB* 1: 68–85.
Vlastos, Gregory (1945). Ethics and Physics in Democritus. *PhR* 54 (6): 578–92.
Vlastos, Gregory (1952). Theology and Philosophy in Early Greek Thought. *PhilosQ* 2 (7): 97–123.
Vlastos, Gregory (1991). *Socrates: Ironist and Moral Philosopher*. Ithaca and New York: Cornell University Press.
Von der Mühll, Peter (1970). Hesiods helikonische Musen. *MH* 27 (4): 195–97.
Von Fritz, Kurt (1956). Das Prooemium der hesiodischen *Theogonie*. In: Erbse (1956), pp. 29–45.
Waardenburg, Jacques (1973). Research on Meaning in Religion. In: Van Baaren and Drijvers (1973), pp. 109–136.
Waardenburg, Jacques (1974). *Classical Approaches to the Study of Religion, volume 2: Bibliography*. The Hague and Paris: Mouton (R+R 4).
Waardenburg, Jacques (1978). *Reflections on the Study of Religion*. The Hague and Paris: Mouton (R+R 15).
Waardenburg, Jacques (1997a). *Bohové zblízka: Systematický úvod do religionistiky*. Brno: Masarykova Univerzita and Georgetown.
Waardenburg, Jacques (1997b). Gerardus van der Leeuw. In: Michaels (1997), pp. 264–76.
Waardenburg, Jacques (1999). *Classical Approaches to the Study of Religion: Aims, Methods and Theories of Research*. New York and Berlin: Walter de Gruyter (R+R 3) (repr.).
Wach, Joachim (1923). Zur Methodologie der allgemeinen Religionswissenschaft. In: Lanczkowski (1974), pp. 30–56.
Wach, Joachim (1944). *Socioloy of Religion*. Chicago: University of Chicago Press.
Wach, Joachim (1950). Über das Lehren der Religionsgeschichte. In: Lanczkowski (1974), pp. 114–23.
Wach, Joachim (1951). *Types of Religious Experience: Christian and Non-Christian*. London: Routledge & Kegan Paul.
Wach, Joachim and Kitagawa, Joseph M. (ed.) (1958). *The Comparative Study of Religions*. New York and London: Columbia University Press.

Wach, Joachim and Kitagawa, Joseph M. (ed.) (1968). *Understanding and Believing: Essays by Joachim Wach*. New York and Evanston: Harper Torchbooks.
Waldenfels, Hans (1997). Wilhelm Schmidt. In: Michaels (1997), pp. 185–97.
Waszink, Jan H. (1979). Tertullian's Principles and Methods of Exegesis. In: Schoedel and Wilken (1979), pp. 17–31.
Watkins, Calvert (1995). *How to Kill a Dragon: Aspects of Indo-European Poetics*. Oxford: Oxford University Press.
Wax, Murray L. (1984). Religion as Universal: Tribulations of an Anthropological Enterprise. *Zygon* 19 (1): 5–20.
Weber, Max (2006). *Religion und Gesellschaft: Gesammelte Aufsätze zur Religionssoziologie*. Eggolsheim: Dörfler Verlag.
Wedemeyer, Christian K. and Doniger, Wendy (eds) (2010). *Hermeneutics, Politics, and the History of Religions: The Contested Legacies of Joachim Wach and Mircea Eliade*. Oxford: Oxford University Press.
Weinberg, Steven (1994). *Dreams of a Final Theory: The Scientist's Search for the Ultimate Laws of Nature*. London: Vintage.
Weinberg, Steven (2001). *Facing Up: Science and Its Cultural Adversaries*. Cambridge, MA and London: Harvard University Press.
Werblowsky, R. J. Zwi (1959). Die Rolle der Religionswissenschaft bei der Förderung gegenseitigen Verständnisses. In: Lanczkowski (1974), pp. 180–88.
Werblowsky, R. J. Zwi (1960). Marburg: And After? *Numen* 7 (2): 215–20.
Werblowsky, R. J. Zwi (1979). Commentary. In: Honko (1979), pp. 535–38.
Wernick, Andrew (2001). *Auguste Comte and the Religion of Humanity: The Post-Theistic Program of French Social Theory*. Cambridge: Cambridge University Press.
West, Martin L. (2007). *Indo-European Poetry and Myth*. Oxford: Oxford University Press.
Westermarck, Edward (1891). *The History of Human Marriage*. London: Macmillan & Co.
Whaling, Frank (ed.) (1984). *Contemporary Approaches to the Study of Religion, volume 1: The Humanities*. Berlin and New York: Mouton (R+R 27).
Whaling, Frank (ed.) (1985). *Contemporary Approaches to the Study of Religion, volume 2: The Social Sciences*. Berlin and New York: Mouton (R+R 28).
Wheeler, Graham (2002). Sing, Muse . . .: The Introit from Homer to Apollonius. *CQ* 52 (1): 33–49.
Whitehouse, Harvey (2004). *Modes of Religiosity: A Cognitive Theory of Religious Transmission*. Walnut Creek: AltaMira Press.
Whitehouse, Harvey (2017). Twenty-Five Years of CSR: A Personal Retrospective. In: Martin and Wiebe (2017), pp. 43–55.
Whitehouse, Harvey and McCauley, Robert N. (eds) (2005). *Mind and Religion: Psychological and Cognitive Foundations of Religiosity*. Walnut Creek: AltaMira Press.
Whitmarsh, Tim (2014). Atheistic Aesthetics: The Sisyphus Fragment, Poetics and the Creativity of Drama. *PCPhS* 60: 109–26.
Widengren, Geo (1945). Evolutionistische Theorien auf dem Gebiet der vergleichenden Religionswissenschaft. In: Lanczkowski (1974), pp. 87–113.
Widengren, Geo (1968). Einige Bemerkungen über die Methoden der Phänomenologie der Religion. In: Lanczkowski (1974), pp. 257–71.
Widengren, Geo (1969). *Religionsphänomenologie*. Berlin: Walter de Gruyter.
Wiebe, Donald (1980). *Religion and Truth: Towards an Alternative Paradigm for the Study of Religion*. The Hague and Paris: Mouton (R+R 23).
Wiebe, Donald (1984). Beyond the Sceptic and the Devotee: Reductionism in the Scientific Study of Religion. *J Am Acad Relig* 52: 157–65.

Wiebe, Donald (2000). *The Politics of Religious Studies: The Continuing Conflict with Theology in the Academy.* New York: Palgrave.
Wiebe, Donald (2008). Science, Scholarship and the Domestication of Religion: On Dennett's *Breaking the Spell. MTSR* 20 (1): 54–60.
Williams, Bernard (2006). *Philosophy as a Humanistic Discipline.* Princeton: Princeton University Press.
Williams, George C. (1966). *Adaptation and Natural Selection: Critique of Some Current Evolutionary Thought.* Princeton: Princeton University Press.
Williams, George C. (1993). Mother Nature Is a Wicked Old Witch. In: Nitecki and Nitecki (1993), pp. 217–32.
Wilson, David S. (2002). *Darwin's Cathedral: Evolution, Religion and the Nature of Society.* Chicago and London: The University of Chicago Press.
Wilson, David S. and Sober, Elliott (1994). Reintroducing Group Selection to the Human Behavioral Sciences. *Behav Brain Sci* 17 (4): 585–608.
Wilson, Edward O. (1998a). *Consilience: The Unity of Knowledge.* New York: Vintage.
Wilson, Edward O. (1998b). The Biological Basis of Morality. *Atl Mon* 281 (4): 53–70.
Wilson, Edward O. (2000). *Sociobiology: A New Synthesis.* Cambridge, MA: The Belknap Press of Harvard University Press.
Wilson, James Q. (1997). *The Moral Sense.* New York: Free Press.
Winiarczyk, Marek (1984). Wer galt im Alterthum als Atheist? *Philologus* 128 (2): 157–83.
Winiarczyk, Marek (1987). Nochmals das Satyrspiel „Sisyphos". *WS* 100: 35–45.
Winiarczyk, Marek (1992). Antike Bezeichnungen der Gottlosigkeit und des Atheismus. *RhM* 135: 216–25.
Wiśniewski, Bohdan (1994). La conception de dieu chez Xénophane. *Prometheus* 20: 97–103.
Wißmann, Hans (1997). James George Frazer (1854 – 1941). In: Michaels (1997), pp. 77–89.
Witte, Markus (ed.) (2004). *Gott und Mensch im Dialog: Festschrift für Otto Kaiser zum 80. Geburtstag.* Berlin and New York: Walter de Gruyter.
Wittgenstein, Ludwig (1922). *Tractatus Logico-Philosophicus.* London: Routledge & Kegan Paul.
Wittgenstein, Ludwig (2001). *Philosophical Investigations.* Malden: Blackwell.
Wölfflin, Heinrich (1983). *Die klassische Kunst: Eine Einführung in die italienische Renaissance.* Basel and Stuttgart: Schwabe.
Wolfson, Harry A. (1942). The Double Faith Theory in Clement, Saadia, Averroes and St. Thomas, and Its Origin in Aristotle and the Stoics. *Jew Q Rev* 33 (2): 213–64.
Wright, David F. (1982). Christian Faith in the Greek World: Justin Martyr's Testimony. *EQ* 54 (2): 77–87.
Wright, Robert (1995). *The Moral Animal: Evolutionary Psychology and Everyday Life.* New York: Vintage.
Wulff, David M. (1985). Psychological Approaches. In: Whaling (1985), pp. 21–88.
Yamagata, Naoko (1994). *Homeric Morality.* Leiden and New York: Brill.
Yinger, J. Milton (1970). *The Scientific Study of Religion.* New York: Macmillan Publishing.
Yu, Jimmy (2012). *Sanctity and Self-Inflicted Violence in Chinese Religions, 1500–1700.* Oxford: Oxford University Press.
Yunis, Harvey (1988). The Debate on Undetected Crime and an Undetected Fragment from Euripides' Sisyphus. *ZPE* 75: 39–46.
Zahavi, Amotz and Zahavi, Avishag (1997). *The Handicap Principle: A Missing Piece of Darwin's Puzzle.* Oxford: Oxford University Press.

Zellner, H. M. (1994). Scepticism in Homer? *CQ* 44 (2): 308–15.
Zimmermann, Ruben (ed.) (2013). *Kompendium der frühchristlichen Wundererzählungen, Band 1: Die Wunder Jesu*. Gütersloh: Gütersloher Verlagshaus.
Zinser, Hartmut (1997). Sigmund Freud. In: Michaels (1997), pp. 90–102.
Zuiddam, Benno A. (2010). Early Orthodoxy: The Scriptures in Clement of Alexandria. *APB* 21 (2): 307–19.

Index

absolute knowledge, 10
Accame, Silvio, 134
Acts of John, 35
Acts of Peter, 35
Adams, James, 107
agency, 140–1, 144, 215 n.116, 216 n.118
aims, naturalism, 53
Alexander, Richard, 108
allegorical approach, 26–7
Alles, Gregory, 79
altruism, 106–9
American Academy of Religion, 97
ancestor worship, 54
animatism, 73
animism, theory of, 54–5, 176 n.22
ante-Nicene Christianity, 36
anthropologists, 52
anthropomorphism, 13, 14, 154–5 n.44
apocalypses, 40–1
Apocryphal literature, on miracles, 35
Apostolic literature, 31
Aristides of Athens, 38
Aristotle, 2, 138, 158 n.45
Arthur, Marilyn, 208 n.2
Athenagoras, 38–9
Athens, 20
atomistic theory, 17–9, 27
Atran, Scott, 115
Augustine, St, 83, 124
Augustinus, Aurelius, 48
awe, 22
Axelrod, Robert, 108

Babut, Daniel, 157 n.26
Bachhofen, Johann, 9
Baetke, Walter, 145
Barnes, Jonathan, 18–9, 28–9
Barrett, Justin, 148–9, 149
Beckaert, André, 48
behavioural perspective, 195 n.156

behaviourist stimulus-response analysis, 113
Benedict, Ruth, 111
Benz, Ernst, 93–4
Berger, Peter L., 220 n.36
Bianchi, Ugo, 89, 95, 148, 180–1 n.79
biblical studies, 69–72
Big Brother, 23
Bleeker, Jouco, 91–2, 93, 192 n.110, 193 n.124, 193 n.129
Boas, Franz, 110
Bodin, Jean, 9
Boehm, Christopher, 115
Borges, Jorge Luis, 124
Boyer, Pascal, 113, 142, 151, 174 n.4
brain functions, 114
Braun, René, 28
British School of Social Anthropology, 90–1
Buddhism, 121, 122, 128, 204 n.33
Bultmann, Rudolf, 149
Burckhardt, Jakob, 2–3
Burkert, Walter, 155 n.47
Burnet, John, 13, 158 n.49

Cantwell Smith, Wilfred, 94, 123, 124, 195 n.151, 205 n.39
Capps, Walter, 78
Carvajal, Cardinal Bernardino Lopéz de, 3
causal relations, 82
Chantepie de la Saussaye, Pierre, 67–8, 76, 78, 93
Chomsky, Noam, 115, 127–8, 206 n.62
Christian mission, the, 78
Christianity, 79
    Chantepie de la Saussaye and, 68
    Müller and, 67
    triumph of, 5
Churchland, Patricia, 103
Cicero, 18, 25, 25–6, 28, 150, 159 n.60

circularity, 42
class struggle, the, 63
Classical Antiquity, 4
Clement of Alexandria, 10, 12, 18, 31, 39
    and faith, 46–7, 172 n.126
    and Greek philosophy, 46–7
cognitive approach, 139–44
cognitive science of religion, 97, 148–9
    methodology, 99–116, 146, 151
    naturalism, 116
    practical application, 131–44, 147
    terminology, 117–30, 146–7
comparative approach, 66–9
comparative theology, 66, 100
Comte, Auguste, 53–4, 56, 57, 148, 175 n.6, 175 n.7
consilience, 58–9, 110
Corinthians, I, 32, 34–5, 44–5
Corinthians, 2, 40, 165 n.30
Cosmides, Leda, 110–2, 127–8
Coulanges, Fustel de, 64
Council of Cologne, 105
counter-intuitiveness, 141–2, 143, 144, 147, 149, 216 n.120
Cranston, Jodi, 4
creation stories, 105
creative hermeneutics, 87
Critias, 19, 20, 21–2, 160 n.87, 160 n.88
cultural determinism, 110–2
culture, 110–1, 140
cumulative tradition, 123

danger, life-threatening, 62
Darwin, Charles, 57, 105, 106–7, 109, 149, 199 n.43
Davies, Malcolm, 22
Dawkins, Richard, 108, 109, 109–10, 140
deification, 23, 26
Delitzsch, Friedrich, 71
Democritus, 19, 31, 136, 158–9 n.54, 159 n.65
    atomistic theory, 17–9, 27
    commentary, 17–9
    fragments, 15–7
demythologization, 149
Dennett, Daniel, 109, 148, 155 n.47
developmental psychology, 116
Didache, 38
Dihle, Albrecht, 21

Dilthey, Wilhelm, 110
divination, 80
divine inspiration, 39–41, 145
divinity, mental representation of, 18
Dobzhansky, Theodosius, 113
Douglas, Mary, 91, 193 n.122
dream images, 19
Drijvers, Hans, 95, 195 n.156
Durkheim, Émile, 61, 64–5, 77, 96, 111, 146, 155 n.44, 181 n.79, 181 n.80
    definition of religion, 121–2, 126, 130, 203–4 n.22, 204 n.33

Early Christian literature
    epistemological problems, 32
    faith and reason, 32–3
    on miracles, 33–6
    protectionism, 31–49
ecumenical theology, 93–4
Einstein, Albert, 150–1
Eisenstadt, Michael, 156 n.21
Eliade, Mircea, 76, 85, 87–8, 89, 93, 101, 146, 191 n.91, 191 n.92, 191 n.100, 191 n.101, 192 n.103, 195 n.152
empirical observation, 13, 150
empirical verification, 86
epistemic justification, 27–8, 31, 86, 148
    argumentative strategy, 45
    conflict, 44–8
    divine inspiration, 39–41, 145
    impersonal, 33, 44, 48
    and miracles, 33
    by miracles, 36
    moral superiority, 37
    personal, 33–42, 44, 45, 48, 79, 81, 88, 145–6
    and prophecy, 41–2, 145
    protectionism and, 48–9
epoché, 82
essentialism, 120–2, 129
ethics, 77, 99, 101–2, 104, 146
Euripides, 21, 22, 160 n.87, 162 n.106
Evans-Pritchard, E. E., 90–1, 193 n.120
Evolutionary Ethics, 99, 103, 104, 105–10, 112, 113–6, 114, 116, 117, 146
evolutionary psychology, 114
evolutionism, 92, 147
    critics of, 72–4

existentialism, 103–4, 197 n.13
exorcisms, 166 n.39
experimental psychology, 72–3

faith, 4–5, 64, 81, 84, 87, 145, 149, 154 n.26, 187 n.34, 196 n.158
    Clement of Alexandria and, 46–7, 172 n.126
    meanings, 172 n.125
    Pauline formula of, 44–5
    purity, 48
    and reason, 31, 32–3, 49, 171 n.111
    and revelation, 173 n.141
fallible gods, 216 n.123
Farkasfalvy, Denis, 40
fear, 22
feeling, 100
Feyerabend, Paul, 118
Finkelberg, Margalit, 214 n.88
First Letter of Clement, 42–3
Fitzgerald, Timothy, 124–5, 206 n.51, 206 n.54
force, the, 82
Foucault, Michel, 124
Frank, Robert, 115
Frazer, James G., 54, 55–7, 57, 58, 59, 60, 62, 64, 65, 72, 73, 81, 85, 96, 146, 147, 148, 176 n.27, 176 n.32, 193 n.122
freedom of religion, 118
Freud, Sigmund, 57–60, 61, 65, 96, 146, 148, 178 n.50
    The Future of an Illusion, 59–60
    New Introductory Lectures on Psychoanalysis, 58–9
    Totem and/ Taboo, 57–8
Frick, Heinrich, 76, 84, 93
Friedländer, Max, 113
Fumerton, Richard, 27

Garland, David, 45
Geertz, Armin, 148
Geertz, Clifford, 111
Germany, phenomenology in, 83–5
God
    communication with, 77, 149
    omnipotence, 42
god-representations, origin of, 12
gods, Freud on, 59–60

González, Justo, 47–8
Gould, Cecil, 153 n.8
Gould, Stephen Jay, 104–5, 114, 198 n.36
Grant, Robert, 42
great apes, morality in, 115–6
Greece, ancient
    epic poetry, 10
    piety, 4
    transition from myth to *logos*, 10
Greek gods, moral blemishes of, 39, 216 n.123
Greek philosophy, 78
    reception of, 44–8
    and revelation, 48–9
Groningen Group, 95–6, 148
Guerra, Anthony, 33, 164 n.15
Guthrie, Stewart, 141, 154–5 n.44, 159 n.65, 162 n.106, 162 n.109

Hager, Fritz-Peter, 38
Haidt, Jonathan, 109, 112, 114
Hamilton, William, 107
handicap principle, the, 108
Haq, Nomamul, 198 n.36
Harris, Sam, 104–5
Hauser, Marc, 114, 115
Heidegger, Martin, 103–4, 149
Heiden, Bruce, 135
Heiler, Friedrich, 76, 84–5, 93, 94, 189 n.66
Heraclitus, 6–7
Herculaneum papyrus, the, 26–7
Hesiod, 10, 12, 211 n.51, 218 n.140
    cognitive approach, 141, 142–4
    ideological agenda, 211 n.55
    invocation of the Muse, 131–44, 147, 209 n.13, 209 n.14, 213 n.86, 214 n.88
    invocations *sensu stricto*, 132–3
    other mentions of Muse, 133, 134–6
    religious interpretation, 138–9
    rhetorical interpretation, 138
    social interpretation, 137
    topical interpretation, 137
higher knowledge, 66
Hirschmann, Eva, 194 n.132
historical approach, 89
historical correspondence theory, 41–2
historical rationality, 41–2
history, 46, 87, 88

Hobbes, Thomas, 22
Holy, the, 78–80, 82, 84, 85, 86, 87, 92, 95
Homer, 12, 28, 214–5 n.102
    cognitive approach, 141, 142–4
    ideological agenda, 211 n.55
    Iliad, 10, 132, 132–3, 209 n.11, 209 n.12, 210 n.27
    invocation of the Muse, 131–44, 147, 208 n.7, 208 n.8, 209 n.23, 210 n.35, 215 n.103
    invocations *sensu stricto*, 132–3
    librarian interpretation, 136
    Odyssey, 10, 133–4
    other mentions of Muse, 133–4, 135
    religious interpretation, 138–9
    rhetorical interpretation, 138
    social interpretation, 137, 138
    topical interpretation, 137
Honko, Lauri, 88
Horatius, 152
Hubert, Henri, 64
human nature, 114
    rediscovery of, 110–3, 116
humankind, natural state, 22–3
Hume, David, 101–2, 197 n.16
Hume's law, 198 n.24
Huxley, Thomas Henry, 107, 109
hyperactive agency detection, 140–1, 144, 216 n.118

Ignatius of Antioch, 37
illusion, religion as, 19, 52, 59–60, 61, 63, 69, 75, 80, 81, 86, 145, 147, 148, 161 n.95, 174 n.4, 178 n.46
images, 18–9
Indo-European linguistics, 66
Infancy Gospel of Thomas, 35
Infinite, the, 66–7, 68–9, 73, 146
International Association for the History of Religions, 89
intuition, 100
intuitive empathy, 82
intuitive knowledge, 81
invocation of the Muse, 131–44, 147, 208 n.7, 208 n.8, 209 n.23, 213 n.73, 213 n.86, 214 n.88, 214 n.93, 215 n.103
    cognitive approach, 139–44
    Derridean deconstruction, 208 n.2

etymological interpretation, 137
interpretations of, 136–9
librarian interpretation, 136
minor, 133
other mentions, 133–6
primary data, 132–6
religious interpretation, 138–9
rhetorical interpretation, 138, 144
sensu stricto, 132–3
social interpretation, 137–8, 144
topical interpretation, 137
Irenaeus of Lyons, 31, 40
    and Greek philosophy, 46
    and prophecy, 42
    rule of truth, 48
    and tradition, 43

Jaeger, Werner, 13
James, William, 179 n.60
Jesus Christ
    moral superiority, 37
    resurrection, 47, 170 n.104
    transfiguration of, **xi**, 1–4
Jewish law, 32
Joachim de Fiore, 3
John, Gospel of, on miracles, 34
Judaism, 70
judgement, suspension of, 92
Justin Martyr, 31, 32–3, 78
    Dialogue with Trypho, 32
    and divine inspiration, 40
    and Greek philosophy, 44–6
    on miracles, 35
    and prophecy, 41
    spermatic word, the, 44–6

Kahn, Charles, 19, 160 n.87
Kant, Immanuel, 1, 66, 79, 126–7
Kaufman, Peter I., 197 n.13
Kitagawa, Joseph M., 181 n.91
Kleinbub, Christian K., 4, 154 n.36
knowledge
    absolute, 10
    constitution of, 124
    and faith, 5
    intuitive, 81
    scientific, 55, 65
    stages of, 53
    subjective, 10

theories of, 5
transmission of, 60
Kristensen, Brede, 76, 81–2, 86, 91, 93, 101

Lang, Andrew, 72–3, 77, 147
language games, 122–3, 124, 206 n.51
L'Année sociologique (journal), 64, 180–1 n.79
Larsen, Timothy, 91, 193 n.122
Larson, Jennifer, 155 n.47
laws, 118
    origin of, 23
Lawson, E. Thomas, 115, 116, 201 n.104, 203 n.21
Lease, Gary, 124–5
Lebedev, Andrei, 14
Leertouwer, Lammert, 88, 95, 194 n.131
Lesky, Albin, 131
linguistics, 66, 127–8
Locke, John, 206 n.59
Löhr, Winrich, 46
Lowie, Robert, 110
Luther, Martin, 45

McCauley, Robert N., 115, 119, 201 n.104, 203 n.21
McCutcheon, Russell, 101, 124–5, 147
McGibbon, Donal, 158–9 n.54
MacLennan, John F., 176 n.33
Macmillan, George, 57
magic, and science, 56
Malinowski, Bronislaw Kaspar, 60–1, 179 n.59
Marcion, 46
Marcus Aurelius, 46
Marett, Robert R., 73
Mark, Gospel of, 3, 4
Martyrdom of Polycarp, 37–8
martyrs and martyrdom, 2, 37–8
Marx, Karl, 63, 146, 179 n.64
Marxist interpretation, 62–3
materialism, 72, 80
Matthew, Gospel of, on miracles, 34, 35
Mauss, Marcel, 64
medical materialism, 179 n.60
memes, 140
Menezes da Silva, João de, 3
Mensching, Gustav, 76
metaphysical phenomenology, 93

metaphysics, 77, 100, 149
meteorological phenomena, 14
Method & Theory in the Study of Religion, 148
methodological atheism, 220 n.36
methodological consilience, 113–6, 116
methodological isolationism, 99–100, 100–5, 116, 117, 146
Meza, Carrasco, 157 n.26
Michelangelo, 3
Mill, John Stuart, 106
Minchin, Elizabeth, 139
minimal counter-intuitiveness, 141–2, 143, 144, 147, 149, 216 n.120
Minton, W.W., 142
Minucius Felix, 25, 26
miracles, 33–6, 164 n.21, 165 n.25, 165 n.31, 165 n.32, 166 n.39
    competence to work, 35
    epistemic justification by, 36
    function of, 33, 34, 35, 35–6
Mithen, Steven, 128
Molendijk, Arie, 69, 183 n.111
monotheism, 44–6, 157 n.36
Montanism, 41
Moore, George E., 102, 103, 197 n.16
moral emotions, 115
moral superiority, 37
Morales, Ramon E., 149
morality, 11, 12, 77, 99, 117
    evolutionary explanation, 105–10
    in great apes, 115–6
    and human nature, 110–3
    methodological consilience, 113–6
    methodological isolationism, 101–4
morphology, 68
mortality, 61
Moss, Candida, 38
Müller, Max, 66–7, 68, 73, 77, 79, 100, 181 n.91, 182 n.95
Murphy, Nancey, 149
Murray, Elizabeth, 142
Murray, Gilbert, 136, 142, 217 n.128
Muses, the, 10, 28, 216–7 n.125, 217 n.128, 218 n.140
    cult of, 143
    number of, 131, 208 n.6
    primary data, 132–6
    see also invocation of the Muse

mysterium augustum, 79
mysterium fascinans, 79

natural theology, 46
naturalism, 5, 145, 147–8, 151–2
    aims, 53
    approach, 9
    comparison with protectionism, 52–3
    elimination of, 96–7
    Lang's critique of, 72–3
    main characteristics, 27–9
    Presocratic philosophy, 9–29, 31
    psychological theories, 53, 53–62
    return of, 116
    sociological theories, 53, 62–5
    until 1945, 53–65
Nature (magazine), 104–5
neurocognitive research, 128
neuroimaging, 116
neutrality, declaration of, 71
New Atheism, 148, 151
Nietzsche, Friedrich, 3, 6–7, 27, 37, 38, 103, 124, 199 n.43, 206 n.45
nonoverlapping magisteria, theory of, 104
North American Association for the Study of Religion, 97

Occam's razor, 149, 151
Oedipus complex, the, 58
Olympians, Xenophanes critique of, 10–4
omniscient gods, 216 n.123
ontology, 68
Origen, 31
Origenes, on miracles, 35–6
original monotheism, 73
Orphic theology, 52
O'Sullivan, Patrick, 161 n.95
Otto, Rudolf, 62, 76, 77, 78–80, 82, 84, 86, 87, 92, 93, 95, 100, 100–1, 187 n.34, 191 n.100

pagans and paganism, 47, 48, 78
Pals, Daniel, 90, 100
paradigm, definition, 174 n.3
parapsychology, 72–3
Parliament of the World's Religions, 93
Parmenides, 28
Pascal, Blaise, 148
Paul, St, 32, 36, 44, 165 n.25, 165 n.30
    divine inspiration, 40
    formula of faith, 44–5
    on miracles, 34–5
    moral superiority, 37
    status, 168 n.71, 168 n.73
Pausanias, 143
perfect gnosis, the, 47
Persaeus, 25, 26, 27
Peter, St, 3
Petrus Damiani, 49
Pettazzoni, Raffaele, 89, 192 n.114
phenomenological bracketing, 82
phenomenology, 67–8, 75–97, 147–8, 219 n.6
    after 1945, 88–96
    classical, 75, 76–88, 146, 147
    critique of, 95–6
    domination, 88, 96
    ecumenical theology, 93
    in Germany, 83–5
    the Groningen Group, 95–6
    historical approach, 89
    metaphysical, 93
    methodological imperialism, 88
    post-classical, 91–3
    shared assumptions, 76
    social anthropology, 90–1
    suspension of judgement, 92
    systematics, 92
Pherecydes of Syros, 10
Philo Alexandrinus, 14
Philodemus, 18, 26
Philostratus, 19
piety, 60
Pindaros, 10
Pinker, Steven, 113
Plato, 26, 28, 46, 120–1, 126, 136
Polycarp, 37–8
polytheism, 54
post-classical phenomenology, 91–3
power relations, 129
power structures, 125, 206 n.54
pre-animism, 73
Preimesberger, Rudolf, 154 n.26
Presocratic philosophy, 9–29, 31, 155–6 n.2
    Democritus, 14–9, 27, 31
    omission, 9
    Prodicus, 23–7, 31

Sisyphus-fragment, 19–23, 23, 26
Xenophanes of Colophon, 10–4, 23, 26, 27, 31, 38
Preus, James S., 9
Preus, Samuel, 121
primeval revelations, 73–4
principle of full access, 142
principles and parameters approach, 115
Prodicus, 23, 31
    commentary, 25–7
    fragments, 24–5
prophecy, 41–2, 145
protectionism, 5, 75, 145–6, 147–8, 151–2, 221 n.38
    approach, 9
    biblical studies, 69–72
    comparative approach, 66–9
    comparison with naturalism, 52–3
    critics of evolutionism, 72–4
    domination, 96–7, 146
    early Christian literature, 31–49
    and epistemic justification, 48–9
    key thesis, 83
    methodological isolationism, 146
    until 1945, 65–74
Protestantism, liberal, 69
psychological theories, 53–62, 83–4, 85
Pucci, Pietro, 208 n.2
Pycke, Nestor, 171 n.117
Pye, Michael, 95–6
Pythagorean school, 28
Pyysiäinen, Ilkka, 114, 128, 155 n.44

Quintilian, 138

Radcliffe-Brown, Alfred, 90
Radin, Paul, 61–2, 85
Raphael, *Transfiguration*, **xi**, 1–4, 5, 49, 96, 145, 151, 153 n.5, 153 n.8, 154 n.26
Rappaport, Roy, 91, 193 n.123
rational explanation, 15
reason, 31, 32–3, 44–6, 49, 66
    and faith, 31, 32–3, 171 n.111
reasoning, 14
reciprocal altruism, theory of, 107–8
reductionism, 51, 69, 75, 80, 81, 88, 91, 92, 147, 152, 180–1 n.79, 181 n.80
religion
    freedom of, 118
    legal status, 118
religion, definition, 117, 146–7, 202–3 n.3, 203–4 n.22, 204 n.33, 205 n.42, 205 n.43, 207 n.74
    advantage and disadvantage of, 117–8
    cognitive, 125–9
    and CSR, 118–20
    essentialist, 120–2, 129
    issues, 125–6
    Plato, 120–1
    social constructionist, 122–5, 126, 128–9, 130
    Tylor–Durkheim dichotomy, 121–2, 128, 130
religion, origin of, 71–2, 75
    Comte on, 53–4
    Democritus on, 17–8, 19
    Durkheim on, 65
    Freud on, 57–60
    Malinowski on, 61
    Marx on, 63
    primeval revelations, 73–4
    Prodicus on, 23–7
    Radin on, 61–2
    Sisyphus-fragment on, 19–23
    Tylor on, 54
    Widengren on, 92–3
    Xenophanes on, 12–3
religious behaviour, evolutionary currency, 105
religious commitment, 90
religious experience, 5, 86, 92
    classification, 79
religious power, 82
religious traditions, hierarchical scale, 79
Renan, Ernest, 70
revelation, 44, 45, 46, 78, 80
    and faith, 173 n.141
    and Greek philosophy, 48–9
rich psychology, 113
Richardson, Jonathan, 2
Robertson Smith, William, 70–1, 77
Romans, 35

Sack, Friedrich Samuel Gottfried, 100
Sacred, the, 76, 76–80, 80, 85, 88, 91, 101, 146, 195 n.155, 204–5 n.36
sacrifice, 70, 183 n.119
Salas, Álvarez, 157 n.26

Sartre, Jean-Paul, 103–4
satyr plays, 19, 20, 22
Satyros, 22
sceptics, 152
Scheler, Max, 76, 83–4
Schleiermacher, Friedrich, 76–7, 86, 100, 101
Schmidt, Wilhelm, 73–4, 77, 84, 147
Schoedel, William, 46
Schopenhauer, Arthur, 1, 106, 199 n.43
science, and magic, 56
scientific knowledge, 55, 59, 65
scientific method, 86
Sebastiano del Piombo, 3
Segal, Robert, 151–2
selfish genes, 108–9, 109–10
self-understanding, 5
sense making, 15, 17–8
sensory perception, atomistic theory of, 19
Sesboüé, Bernard, 42
Sextus Empiricus, 10, 17–8, 19–20, 21
Simmel, Georg, 63–4
Sisyphus-fragment, 23, 26, 161 n.95
  authorship, 21–2
  commentary, 21–3
  fragments, 20–1
Smart, Ninian, 93
sneezing, 54–5
Snow, C. P., 110
social anthropology, 90–1
social constructionism, 118, 126, 128–9, 130
  naïve, 122–3, 124, 126
  power-based, 123–5, 126, 129
social control, 23
social Darwinism, 102
social facts, 65
social utility, 23
socio-economic relations, 63
sociological theories, naturalism, 62–5
Socrates, 204 n.27
Söderblom, Nathan, 76, 77–8, 79, 80, 84, 86, 91, 100
soul, the, 54
Spencer, Herbert, 55, 102, 176 n.22
Sperber, Dan, 140
spermatic word, the, 44–6
spiritual beings, belief in, 121–2
spiritual revival, 91

spiritual testimony, 39–41, 79
Spiro, Melford, 128
standard social science model, 139–40
Stoddard, Kathryn, 137
strategic information, 142, 144
Strauss, David Friedrich, 69–70
Strenski, Ivan, 83, 100, 129, 176 n.27, 178 n.57, 181 n.80, 183 n.119
structural relations, 82
subjective knowledge, 10
supernatural beings, 130, 142, 203–4 n.22
survivals, theory of, 54–5, 60
Sylvester, Robert P., 197 n.16
symbolical approach, 26–7

Taliaferro, Charles, 220 n.32
Tambiah, Stanley J., 179 n.59
Terence, 5
terminology, 52, 117–30, 146–7
Tertullian, 31, 38, 173 n.141
  on Christian truth, 33
  On the Flesh of Christ, 32
  and Greek philosophy, 47–8
  on miracles, 35
  notion of faith, 32
  and prophecy, 41–2
  and tradition, 42–3, 43
theological incorrectness, 149
Theophilus of Antioch, 35
theoretical theology, 100
Thomas Aquinas, St, 48–9, 83
thought-experiments, 13
Tiele, Cornelis Petrus, 68–9, 77, 79, 81, 93
Tillich, Paul, 149
Tooby, John, 110–2, 127
totemism, 57–8, 70, 176–7 n.33
tradition, 42–3, 60, 87
Tremlin, Todd, 113, 129
Trivers, Robert, 107–8
true religion, 77
trust, 64
truth, 23, 28, 31, 33, 85, 86, 147, 148, 181 n.91
  historical, 70
  rational, 44–6
  rule of, 48
Tübingen School, 69
Turner, Victor and Edith, 91, 193 n.122

Tylor, Edward B., 54–5, 56, 57, 58, 59, 60,
    64, 65, 72, 73, 85, 91, 96, 146, 147,
    148, 176 n.22, 193 n.122, 207 n.67
  definition of religion, 121–2, 126, 130
Tylor-Durkheim dichotomy, the, 118,
    121–2, 128, 130

United States of America, 85

van Baaren, Theo, 88, 95
van der Leeuw, Gerardus, 76, 82–3, 84, 88,
    89, 93, 95, 188 n.47, 192 n.110,
    193 n.124
van der Loos, Hendrik, 33
Vasari, Giorgio, 2

Waardenburg, Jacques, 9, 59, 95, 147,
    188 n.47
Wach, Joachim, 76, 85–7, 88, 190 n.76,
    190 n.86
warrants of faith, 164 n.15
  divine inspiration, 39–41
  miracles, 33–6
  moral superiority, 37–9
  prophecy, 41–2
  tradition, 42–3
Watkins, Calvert, 137

Werblowsky, Zwi, 95
Whaling, Frank, 89, 147, 218 n.4
Widengren, Geo, 55, 92–3, 93, 192 n.110
Wiebe, Donald, 151–2, 196 n.169, 203 n.7
Williams, George C., 108–9
Wilson, E. O., 58–9, 110, 112–3, 113, 140,
    201 n.94, 201 n.97, 202 n.112
Wilson, James, 114
Winiarczyk, Marek, 21–2
Wittgenstein, Ludwig, 28, 102–3, 104,
    122–3, 124, 126
Wundt, Wilhelm, 64

Xenophanes of Colophon, 10–1, 11–2, 23,
    26, 27, 31, 38, 54, 155 n.44,
    156–7 n.21, 156 n.2, 158 n.45,
    158 n.49, 216 n.123
  commentary, 12–4
  fragments, 11–2
Xenophon, 4

Yunis, Harvey, 22

Zahavi, Amotz and Avishag, 108
Zeno of Citium, 25, 28
Zeus, 10, 22
zoomorphism, 14

www.ingramcontent.com/pod-product-compliance
Lightning Source LLC
Chambersburg PA
CBHW070022010526
44117CB00011B/1682